The British End of the British Empire

D1073822

How did decolonization impact on Britain itself? And how did Britain manage its transition from colonial power to postcolonial nation? Sarah Stockwell explores this question principally via the history of the overseas engagements of key institutions that had acquired roles within Britain's imperial system: the Universities of Oxford and Cambridge, the Bank of England, the Royal Mint and the Royal Military Academy Sandhurst. Using a huge range of new archival sources, the author shows how these institutions fashioned new roles at the end of Empire, reconfiguring their activities for a postcolonial world and deploying their expertise to deliver technical assistance essential for the development of institutions in new Commonwealth states. This study not only pioneers an entirely new approach to the history of the British end of the British Empire but also provides an equally novel cross-sectoral analysis of institution-building during decolonization and highlights the colonial roots of British postcolonial aid.

Sarah Stockwell is Professor of Imperial and Commonwealth History at King's College London, and a leading historian of British decolonization. Her publications include *The Business of Decolonization: British Business Strategies in the Gold Coast* (2000) and, as editor, *The British Empire: Themes and Perspectives* (2007).

The British End of the British Empire

Sarah Stockwell

King's College London

CAMBRIDGE
UNIVERSITY PRESS

University Printing House, Cambridge CB2 8BS, United Kingdom

One Liberty Plaza, 20th Floor, New York, NY 10006, USA

477 Williamstown Road, Port Melbourne, VIC 3207, Australia

314-321, 3rd Floor, Plot 3, Splendor Forum, Jasola District Centre, New Delhi - 110025, India

79 Anson Road, #06-04/06, Singapore 079906

Cambridge University Press is part of the University of Cambridge.

It furthers the University's mission by disseminating knowledge in the pursuit of
education, learning and research at the highest international levels of excellence.

www.cambridge.org
Information on this title: www.cambridge.org/9781107680883
DOI: 10.1017/9781107707382

© Sarah Stockwell 2018

First published 2018
First paperback edition 2019

A catalogue record for this publication is available from the British Library

ISBN 978-1-107-07031-8 Hardback
ISBN 978-1-107-68088-3 Paperback

For Arthur, James,
Alasdair and Douglas

Contents

List of Figures	*page* viii	
List of Tables	ix	
Acknowledgements	xi	
List of Abbreviations and Note on the Text	xv	
Introduction	1	
1 The Imperial Roles of British Institutions	23	
2 Technical Assistance and State-building at the End of Empire	59	
3 Teaching What 'the Natives Need to Know': The Universities of Oxford and Cambridge and Training for Overseas Public Administration	93	
4 'Education and Propaganda': The Bank of England and the Development of Central Banking in African States at the End of Empire	142	
5 Making Money: The Royal Mint and British Decolonization	191	
6 'Losing an Empire and Winning Friends': Sandhurst and British Decolonization	234	
Conclusion	286	
Bibliography	299	
Index	323	

Figures

1.1 Group photo, the Colonial Administrative Service
'First Devonshire' Course (Course 'A'), the University of
Cambridge, 1947   *page* 33

1.2 The British West African two shilling coin, 1949   49

3.1 Group photo, the Colonial Administrative Service 'First
Devonshire' Course (Course A), the University of
Cambridge, 1953–4   111

3.2 Group photo, the Colonial Administrative Service Training
Course A, the University of Cambridge, 1961–2   114

3.3 Group photo, the University of Cambridge Course on
Development, 1970   132

5.1 Ghana 10 shilling coin, 1958   197

5.2 Image of Hastings Banda (by Paul Vincze) on the
obverse of the first coins produced for Malawi, 1964   197

5.3 The reverse (a) and obverse (b) of the two pound Ghanaian
coin issued in 1960 to commemorate Republic Day   204

5.4 Plaster model with effigy of the Queen by Humphrey Paget for
Ghanaian two pound coin, 1959, commissioned to celebrate
the Queen's planned visit to Ghana   221

5.5 Images by Paul Vincze on the reverse of the first Malawian
coin, 1964   224

5.6 The reverse (a) and obverse (b) of the Nigerian one shilling coin,
1959, incorporating portrait of the Queen by Cecil Thomas   225

6.1 West African cadet in front of Old College, RMAS, 1954   241

6.2 Intake 25 Normandy Company, RMAS, September
1958, including Ghanaian Officer Cadets Afrifa and Akuffo   253

6.3 Overseas cadets admitted to Sandhurst between 1947 and
the end of 2009 categorized by region or connection to Britain   268

6.4 President Yakubu Gowon taking the Sovereign's Parade,
RMAS, 14 July 1973   273

6.5 View of Old College, RMAS, 1955   274

Tables

2.1 Senior local appointments in public services in Africa
as of 1 January 1959   *page* 71
2.2 Projected spending on Commonwealth Military
Training Assistance Scheme 1970–1   83
3.1 Students admitted at Oxford, Cambridge and London to the
'First Devonshire' training course, 1946–53   96
3.2 Recruitment to the Colonial Administrative Service Training
Course A at Cambridge and Oxford, 1956/7–1963/4   111
3.3 Geographical origin of overseas students attending the
administrative training/development courses at
Oxford and Cambridge in the 1960s and 1970s   139
4.1 Attendance at the Bank of England Central Banking
Course, 1957–89   179
5.1 Total annual Royal Mint coin production for export, 1954–69   206
5.2 Profits on the Royal Mint's Commercial Account, 1963–4
to 1967–8   207
6.1 Overseas entrants to Sandhurst by country and year 1947–60   245
6.2 Entrants to Sandhurst from Anglophone African
colonies/states by country and year, 1951–89   264

Acknowledgements

This is a book about institutions and, in the course of researching and writing it, I have incurred a very considerable debt to many institutions and to individuals associated with them. First and foremost, I am enormously grateful to the Leverhulme Trust for the award of a fellowship that funded research leave and travel and without which I could not have completed this book. I would also like to thank my own institution, King's College London, and, for assistance with arrangements relating to the fellowship, my former head of department, Adam Sutcliffe, as well as Chris Machut and Rob Templing. My King's colleagues, as well as my students, continue to make the Department of History a wonderfully stimulating environment in which to work.

One of the great pleasures of researching this book has been the opportunity it provided to glimpse inside institutions, not just through their archival holdings, but in several cases by working in them and by meeting some of those they employ. I owe a particular debt of thanks to two of 'my' institutions which do not have regular public archival reading rooms (or did not at the time of research) and whose staff kindly accommodated me in their own working space: the Royal Military Academy Sandhurst and the Royal Mint. At the former, I am very grateful to the curator of the Sandhurst Collection, Dr Anthony Morton, the assistant curator, Sebastian Puncher, the Collection Support Officer, Angela Lucas and also to Lise Simpson. Photographs 6.1–2 and 6.4–5 are reproduced with the permission of the Sandhurst Collection. At the Royal Mint Museum, Llantrisant, my thanks go to its director, Kevin Clancy, to the assistant curator, Chris Barker, as well as to Claire Hughes and to Lucy-Ann Pickering. I am particularly grateful to Abigail Kenvyn for help in locating high-resolution images and to the Royal Mint Museum for permission to reproduce images 1.2 and 5.1–6. At the time of writing, material at both institutions was partly labelled by means of descriptions of on-site locations, which may be subject to change. I explain in the bibliography how I have chosen to reference this.

I also very gratefully acknowledge the Bank of England Archive for permission to consult and cite material from its collections, and, for all their help there, Michael Anson, Joe Hewson and Rachel Muir. I had the privilege of being the first academic researcher to use material in the archive of the Bank of

Ghana, and I could not have done this without the assistance of Mary Edwards, Edna Bruce-Cudjoe, Catherine Ashiley, Nelson Anyomi and Ernest Addison, who put themselves out to help me. I am also grateful to the archivists at the International Monetary Fund for reviewing for me and digitizing files relating to the Fund's Central Banking Department's Technical Assistance programme and for permission to cite from these as well as to the Royal Bank of Scotland Archives for their assistance and consent to reproduce excerpts from papers in their collections. My very sincere thanks too to Simon Bailey, the Keeper of Archives at the University of Oxford, and to Lucy McCann and colleagues in Oxford's Bodleian Library, as well as to the librarians and archivists at Cambridge University Library and other subject libraries within Cambridge. Material from the Archives of the University of Cambridge is used with the permission of the Syndics of the University Library, including photographs 1.1 and 3.1–3 reproduced from their collections. I am also indebted to the special collections staff at the Maugham Library, King's College London, as well as those at King's Liddell Hart Collection for Military Archives. Material from the latter is used with the consent of the Archive's trustees. In London I was also assisted by staff at the Archives of the University of London, especially Richard Temple, and at the Archives of the LSE in the LSE Library. I am grateful to both institutions for allowing me to quote material from their records. Finally, this book could not have been written without access to material in the various national archives. My thanks to the British National Archives and to the staff there, as well as to the Public Records and Archives Administration Department of Ghana and the National Archives of Zambia.

This book brings together, and builds on, research that goes back some way and in the course of which I have learned a great deal. My interest in the Colonial Service was first inspired by listening to lectures by Tony Kirk-Greene, and, some years ago I benefited greatly from his advice and encouragement. For assistance with practical arrangements relating to research in Ghana, I very gratefully acknowledge the help of Kofi Adjepong-Boateng, Kofi Baku, John Parker, Richard Rathbone and Naaborko Sackeyfio-Lenoch. Helen Garnett and Robert Sakala very generously helped me obtain material from Zambia. My understanding of the institutions studied in this book was greatly advanced by talking to Tony Clayton, Graham Dyer, Bill Kirkman, Colin Newbury and John Toye, as well as to interviewees who wish to remain anonymous. Andrew Thompson, Philip Murphy and Richard Toye helped in other ways. It is also a pleasure to acknowledge my editors at Cambridge University Press, Lisa Carter, Ian McIver and especially Michael Watson, and also Geetha Williams for ensuring that production ran smoothly.

Earlier versions of my research have been presented at research workshops and conferences. My thanks to the organizers for inviting me to contribute and to the other participants from whose comments I profited a great deal, especially

Gareth Austin, Jordanna Bailkin, Frederick Cooper, Ruth Craggs, Poppy Cullen, Martin Daunton, Andrew Dilley, Véronique Dimier, Richard Drayton, Felix Driver, Richard Farrimond, Joseph Hodge, Simon Jackson, Miguel Bandeira Jerónimo, Heike Jöns, Harshan Kumarasingham, Ichiro Maekawa, Rory Miller, Shoko Mizuno, Duncan Money, Wm Roger Louis, François Pacquement, Susan Pennybacker, Astrid Rasch, Camilla Schofield, Chibuike Uche, Stuart Ward and Claire Wintle, as well as some of those mentioned earlier. An early version of some of the ideas developed in this book was first advanced in an essay included in a volume that resulted from one of these events, a conference in Lisbon in 2011: *The Ends of European Colonial Empires. Cases and Comparisons,* edited by Miguel Bandeira Jerónimo and António Costa Pinto and published in 2015 by Palgrave Macmillan in its Cambridge Imperial and Post-Colonial Studies series. In other contexts I have learned from Peter Brooke, Catherine Eagleton, Bérénice Guyot-Rechard, Ashley Jackson, Chris Jeppesen, David Killingray, Chibundu Onuzo, Paul Readman, Mike Sheard and David Todd. I am also especially grateful to Tony Clayton, Ruth Craggs, Véronique Dimier, Graham Dyer, Tim Livsey, Chibuike Uche and Jon Wilson for generously reading drafts of particular chapters. Any mistakes remain of course entirely my own. Thanks also to many of these people for company along the way.

My greatest debt is to my wonderful husband, Arthur Burns. He has been his customary source of good sense and advice, and nobly read and commented on the whole manuscript, and made it possible for me to travel away from home for research purposes. I could not have done this book without him. Our three sons, James, Alasdair and Douglas, grew more quickly than the book. They have not only been a welcome distraction from it but have entered into my preoccupations, James through his enthusiasm for history and Alasdair and Douglas by developing an interest in coins. In recent months they have put their technical expertise to use to help with the preparation of the final draft, including, in Alasdair's case, by getting the bibliography into decent shape. As ever, my father, Chris, has been a constant source of encouragement. All these men in my life, big and small, support me in so many ways.

Abbreviations and Note on the Text

BDEE   British Documents on the End of Empire [project]
BESS   British Expatriate Supplementation Scheme
BoE   Bank of England
BoG   Bank of Ghana
CAF   Central African Federation
CAS   Colonial Administrative Service
CCTA   Commission for Technical Co-operation in
        Africa South of the Sahara
CIGS   Chief of Imperial General Staff
CO   Colonial Office
CPP   Convention People's Party (Ghana)
CUL   Cambridge University Library
CWMTAS Commonwealth Military Training Assistance Scheme
DFID   Department for International Development
DTC   Department of Technical Co-operation
EACB   East African Currency Board
EALF   East African Land Forces [Organization]
EEC   European Economic Community
FCO   Foreign and Commonwealth Office
FO   Foreign Office
FSP   Foreign Service Programme [at Oxford University]
GSO   General Staff Officer [British Army]
HMOCS   Her Majesty's Oversea [from 1956, Overseas] Civil Service
IBRD   International Bank for Reconstruction and Development
ICS   Institute of Commonwealth Studies, University of Oxford
IMF   International Monetary Fund
IDS   Institute of Development Studies, University of Sussex
IUC   Inter-University Council [for Higher Education in the Colonies]
JSCCST Joint Standing Committee on Colonial Service Training
KAR   King's African Rifles
LSP   Loan Service Personnel [scheme]
MoD   Ministry of Defence

NCO	Non-Commissioned Officer
ODA	Overseas Development Administration [of the FCO]
ODM	Ministry of Overseas Development
OSAS	Overseas Service Aid Scheme
OSC	Overseas Studies Committee, University of Cambridge
LSE	London School of Economics and Political Science
QEH	Queen Elizabeth House, University of Oxford
RCC	Regular Career Commission course [at Sandhurst]
RMA	Royal Military Academy Woolwich
RMAC	Royal Mint Advisory Committee [on the Design of Coins, Medals, Seals and Decorations]
RMC	Royal Military College Sandhurst
RMAS	Royal Military Academy Sandhurst [from 1947]
RWAFF	Royal West African Frontier Force
RMM	Royal Mint Museum
SMC	Standard Military Course [at Sandhurst]
SRCB	Southern Rhodesian Currency Board
UDI	Unilateral Declaration of Independence [Rhodesia]
UGC	University Grants Committee
UKMTAS	United Kingdom Military Training Assistance Scheme
UN	United Nations
WACB	West African Currency Board
WO	War Office

Note on the Text

Throughout this book, countries have been referred to using the names current at the time: for example, 'Gold Coast' denotes Ghana during the colonial period, whereas 'Ghana' is used thereafter.

Introduction

In 1973, Paul Howell, supervisor of the University of Cambridge Course on Development, noted with pride that the content of the course had recently changed. Rather than trying to teach 'what the natives need to know', it was now tailored to the real needs of its students, primarily drawn from developing countries, especially those within the Commonwealth.[1] The fact that in the preceding decade – some years after most British colonies had secured their independence – those teaching this course could still be construed as having been engaged in telling the 'natives' what they needed 'to know' reflects the complex dynamics of the British decolonization process, and the ways these played out in a domestic context. The Cambridge Course on Development was a legacy of British colonialism: a direct descendant of training courses delivered since the 1920s to young British entrants to the Colonial Administrative Service that survived into the postcolonial era to become, with modifications, a flagship element in Britain's contribution to the training of administrators in the public services of new states. In the 1950s small numbers from Britain's colonies and newly independent countries sat alongside expatriates still hoping for a career in the Colonial Service; by the early 1960s they constituted the entire intake.

The figure of the expatriate colonial officer, whether the heroic *Sanders of the River* or the more subversive depictions in the fiction of George Orwell or Somerset Maugham, has particular traction in popular ideas of empire, and few of the continuities from the colonial to the postcolonial era speak to the ambiguities of 'decolonization' as much as the presence at British universities of elites from countries newly freed from the British colonial yoke occupying desks once filled by generations of white British officers. These public servants of new Commonwealth states entering British higher education in the late 1950s and early 1960s were nonetheless only part of a much wider educational migration. Britain had a long tradition of recruiting overseas students, including from the Empire-Commonwealth, but the late colonial period saw an enormous

---

[1] Cambridge University Library [CUL], University Archives [UA], GBR/0265/CDEV/2/23, P. P. Howell to Dr A. F. Robertson, Dr B. Van Arkadie and Dr H. W. West, 19 October 1973.

increase in their numbers. By 1960, the year in which Macmillan's landmark 'wind of change' speech heralded an accelerated retreat from Britain's African Empire, Britain hosted over 31,000 students from British colonies and the independent Commonwealth enrolled on all kinds of training and higher education programmes.[2] Yet more striking, more than 14,000 pensionable officers were still serving in Her Majesty's Overseas Civil Service and a further 6,500 employed on contract terms still working overseas in some fifty countries.[3] In 1965 officials in Britain's new Ministry of Overseas Development, struggling to marshal sufficient resources and manpower to meet the need for technical assistance among emergent states within the Commonwealth, called for the mobilization of personnel across British society. A British 'professional career', they suggested, 'should normally include a period of work overseas in a developing country'.[4] By then the Commonwealth had been transformed from an association comprising a small number of predominantly white countries into a large multiracial community of states of diverse size and geostrategic interests.[5] Although a process of imperial retreat would continue in relation to smaller territories, most of the Empire had gone, and Britain had entered an era that many would consider 'postcolonial'. Yet even at the start of 1965 there still remained over 13,000 publicly funded Britons working in developing countries, including more than 11,000 British officials distributed across forty-one colonies and ex-colonies;[6] a number comparable to those employed in the Colonial Service at the height of Empire.[7] An on-going British involvement in emergent Commonwealth states engaged the resources of diverse British institutions and individuals, and, ensured that the formal 'end' of the British Empire not only left many legacies within Britain itself, but numerous threads and entanglements linking governments, institutions and individuals in Britain and its former colonies.

---

[2] Calculated from *Technical Assistance from the United Kingdom for Overseas Development (March 1961)*, PP 1960–1 (Cmnd. 1308), annex II, pp. 30–1.

[3] Ibid., para. 27.

[4] *Ministry of Overseas Development. Overseas Development: The Work of the New Ministry (August 1965)*, PP 1964–5, XXX (Cmnd. 2736), paras. 121, 123.

[5] These developments can be followed in Ronald Hyam, *Britain's Declining Empire: The Road to Decolonisation, 1918–1968* (Cambridge University Press, Cambridge, 2006); John Darwin, *The Empire Project: The Rise and Fall of the British World System, 1830–1970* (Cambridge University Press, Cambridge, 2009); and, more briefly, in Sarah Stockwell, 'Ends of Empire' in Stockwell ed. *The British Empire: Themes and Perspectives* (Wiley Blackwell, Oxford, 2008), pp. 269–93.

[6] *Overseas Development*, para. 125; table 4, p. 66. They were in countries which had entered into agreements with the British government under the auspices of the British Overseas Service Aid Scheme introduced in 1961.

[7] The Colonial Service comprised 11,000 regular officers in 1947 and 18,000 in 1954: A. H. M. Kirk-Greene, *On Crown Service: A History of H.M. Colonial and Overseas Civil Services, 1837–1997* (I. B. Tauris, London, 1999), p. 51.

This book explores some of these aspects of the *British* end of the British Empire and Britain's transformation from a colonial power to a postcolonial one. It does so in part via a discussion of British governmental overseas civilian and military aid, but principally by means of a history of the overseas engagements of several British institutions: the Universities of Oxford and Cambridge, the Bank of England, the Royal Mint and the Royal Military Academy Sandhurst. These were all primarily domestic institutions, but had to differing extents become stakeholders in Britain's Empire, responsible for delivering or managing services to the colonies.[8] Oxford and Cambridge had many connections to Empire, including that on which this book focuses: their role in training members of the Colonial Administrative Service. This dated back to the 1920s, but after 1946 principally took the form of a year-long course attended by new Service recruits. The Bank of England's imperial role was the consequence of the City's place as the world's leading financial centre and its responsibilities to sterling as an international reserve currency. The Bank was directly involved in the dependent Empire via the management of the sterling area and its representation on some regional colonial currency boards, which, in the absence of national or central banks and independent currencies, issued and managed colonial currencies. In the course of the nineteenth century the third institution, the Royal Mint, had also taken on an increasingly international and imperial dimension when it began producing coins for other countries, including those within the British Empire. It had overseen the establishment of branches in Australia, Canada and South Africa and, although by 1945 some of these overseas branches had thrown off British control, the Mint continued to supply coins for colonial currency authorities in most British dependencies. Sandhurst's 'imperial role' channelled an important aspect of the wider imperial function of the British Army. Generations of British Army officers, trained at Sandhurst, had been deployed somewhere in Britain's Empire, principally as a result of the British Army's peacetime role garrisoning the colonies, but also in active combat in Britain's numerous nineteenth-century colonial small wars and in the global conflicts of the twentieth century. British officers were also seconded to command colonial forces. Since 1861 Sandhurst had had another more direct 'imperial' function, training British, and in the 1920s Indian, entrants to the Indian Army; after the Second World War it began admitting increasing numbers of cadets from Britain's remaining colonies and from new Commonwealth states.

---

[8] Elements of the argument presented in this book were first advanced in an embryonic form in Sarah Stockwell, 'Exporting Britishness: Decolonization in Africa, the British State and its Clients' in Miguel Banderia Jerónimo and António Costa Pinto eds., *The Ends of European Colonial Empires: Cases and Comparisons* (Palgrave Macmillan, Basingstoke, 2015), pp. 148–77.

These and other institutions provided the frames in which many lives were lived out across the Empire,[9] or through which even those who never left British shores might nevertheless be participants in the enterprise of empire. As Tamson Pietsch argues in her discussion of academic networks before the Second World War, institutions created opportunities for global interactions and exchanges, while also regulating and directing them.[10] They helped forge professional linkages that connected the different worlds of the British Empire, and that constituted what Gary Magee and Andrew Thompson describe for an earlier period as the 'software of empire'.[11] In the 1940s, 1950s and 1960s, as the structures of imperial rule were rolled back, such institutional and professional connections beyond the state became more, not less, important. By building these domestic institutions into a history of decolonization, this book contributes to the furthering of discussion of the processes of decolonization below the level of Westminster policymaking and above the level of the individual, the two themes around which many other accounts are constructed.

The decision to approach the history of colonial-political change from the perspective of these particular domestic institutions derives from my long-standing interest in two areas: the history of decolonization as it affected British organizations beyond the state; and secondly, processes of institution-building in new states accompanying the creation of Westminster-style parliamentary systems. These interests led to an earlier book on British business and the end of Empire in Ghana, which, together with others' research, helped illuminate the ways in which decolonization affected British firms operating within the Empire. This work explored the firms' attempts to influence both imperial policymaking and colonial-political outcomes,[12] and my own investigation of the establishment of a Ghanaian central bank sparked an interest in the Bank of England as well as in the Royal Mint.[13] More recently, this engagement with

[9] See, esp., D. Lambert and Alan Lester eds., *Colonial Lives Across the British Empire: Imperial Careering in the Nineteenth Century* (Cambridge University Press, Cambridge, 2006).

[10] Tamson Pietsch, *Empire of Scholars: Universities, Networks and the British Academic World 1850–1939* (Manchester University Press, Manchester, 2013), esp. p. 4.

[11] Gary Magee and Andrew Thompson, *Empire and Globalisation: Networks of People, Goods and Capital in the British World, c. 1850–1914* (Cambridge University Press, Cambridge, 2012), p. 16.

[12] S. E. Stockwell, 'The Political Strategies of British Business during Decolonization: The Case of the Gold Coast/Ghana, 1945–1957', *Journal of Imperial and Commonwealth History*, 23(1995), pp. 277–300; S. E. Stockwell, *The Business of British Business Strategies in the Gold Coast* (Clarendon Press, Oxford, 2000); Nicholas J. White, *Business, Government and the End of Empire: Malaya, 1942–1957* (Clarendon Press, Oxford, 1996); R. L. Tignor, *Capitalism and Nationalism at the End of Empire* (Princeton University Press, Princeton, NJ, 1998); M. Misra, *Business, Race and Politics in British India* (Clarendon Press, Oxford, 1999); L. J. Butler, *Copper Empire: Mining and the Colonial State in Northern Rhodesia, 1930–1964* (Palgrave Macmillan, Basingstoke, 2007).

[13] S. E. Stockwell, 'Instilling the "Sterling Tradition": Decolonization and the Creation of a Central Bank in Ghana', *Journal of Imperial and Commonwealth History* 26 (1998), pp. 100–19.

how the end of Empire reverberated beyond the state has led me to explore its impact on the domestic Church of England.[14]

Like the Established Church, but unlike British businesses, the institutions discussed in what follows lay on the boundaries of the 'state' narrowly defined, which for these purposes we can describe as the Westminster and Whitehall policymaking centre. They were part of the interface between the state and civil society. They had their own lines of dialogue with the state, and were in some cases formally part of it. They could invoke the state more easily than, for example, most British companies were able to do (although some of the latter, especially where their activities bore directly on Britain's strategic interests, naturally had considerable leverage in Whitehall). In our period, the universities had the weakest ties to the state. Even so, they relied on state funding, including support for their role in delivering the Colonial Service training courses, and there was individual career mobility between departments of governments and the universities, with academics appointed to government committees serving as bridgeheads between these interconnected and porous worlds.

The British polity, however, was pluralistic in character and these institutions had acquired or been given a sense of agency, reflecting the distinctive nature of British political culture. They could not operate entirely independently of the state, but, even if subject in principle to ministerial control, still acted with considerable autonomy. As Patrick Joyce argues, the British state, as it developed in the nineteenth and twentieth centuries, was a 'liberal' one, not only because it was based on principles of political liberty, but also because it was one which permitted persons, places or institutions, which Joyce describes as 'designated governed entities', to operate 'ostensibly on their own, without outside interference'.[15] What is more these might be perceived as distinct from the British state, and their separate identities would be important in their ability to negotiate a changing overseas landscape brought about by decolonization. Within the British system institutions beyond the state also contributed to the business of governance, as Oxford and Cambridge did by training Britain's imperial administrators. Further, within British political culture there was a consensus even among public servants (in

---

[14] Sarah Stockwell, ' "Splendidly Leading the Way?" Archbishop Fisher and Decolonisation in British Colonial Africa' in Robert Holland and Sarah Stockwell eds., *Ambiguities of Empire: Essays in Honour of Andrew Porter* (Routledge, London, 2009), pp. 199–218; Sarah Stockwell, ' "Improper and Even Unconstitutional": The Involvement of the Church of England in the Politics of End of Empire in Cyprus' in S. Taylor ed., *From the Reformation to the Permissive Society: A Miscellany in Celebration of the the 400th Anniversary of Lambeth Palace Library* (Boydell, Woodbridge, 2010), pp. 583–655; Sarah Stockwell, 'Anglicanism in an Era of Decolonization' in Jeremy Morris ed. *The Oxford History of the Anglican Church. Volume 4: The Twentieth Century: Global Western Anglicanism, c. 1910 to the Present* (Oxford University Press, Oxford, 2017), pp. 160–85.

[15] Patrick Joyce, *The State of Freedom: A Social History of the British State since 1800* (Cambridge University Press, Cambridge, 2013), pp. 3, 17–24, 188–93.

the British case generally Oxbridge-educated rather than professionally trained) about the desirability of limiting central state power, that reflected the particular cultural capital of institutions such as Britain's oldest universities.

At different times, these institutions had all been more independent of the state and had evolved their own institutional cultures. Established in 1694, the Bank of England became banker and creditor to the government. At its inception those who subscribed to a loan to the state were incorporated as the 'Governor and Company of the Bank of England'. Over time, the Bank assumed responsibility for managing Britain's gold and currency reserves and for holding the reserves of Britain's other banks; acquired monopoly control over the note issue in England and Wales; and helped manage government borrowing, serving as the ultimate source of credit or as lender of last resort. By the end of the nineteenth century it had largely ceased to operate as a commercial bank and become in effect a public institution serving the national interest, acting as advisor to the Treasury. Yet the Bank was also part of the financial service nexus of the City, with most of its governors drawn from City institutions and companies, and it continued to be owned and controlled by private shareholders until nationalization in 1946.[16] Even then, although nationalization transferred responsibility for the appointment of its most senior figures to the government, the Bank continued to operate relatively free from ministerial control. Rather than diminishing its independent culture, nationalization seems initially to have encouraged the Bank as far as possible to maintain its autonomy from the Treasury. For its part, the Treasury generally continued to respect the Bank's position as an independent source of expertise. It was not until the 1960s that the Bank became a more integral part of government policymaking structures, with a corresponding erosion of its standing as a voice articulating City interests.[17]

The Mint occupied a similarly indeterminate position between 'state' and 'society'. By far the oldest of the institutions discussed, its origins go back to c. 650 and the foundation of a London mint. Until Henry VIII's closure of the last remaining ecclesiastical mints concentrated all coin production at the Tower of London, it was just one of many mints in southern England. The Mint operated independently by Royal prerogative, but in 1688 was brought under the control of the Treasury.[18] In 1870 a new constitution made the Chancellor

[16] Alec Cairncross, 'The Bank of England and the British Economy' in Richard Roberts and David Kynaston eds., *The Bank of England: Money Power and Influence, 1694–1994* (Clarendon Press, Oxford, 1995), pp. 56–82.

[17] Elizabeth Hennessy, 'The Governors, Directors, and Management' in Roberts and Kynaston eds., *The Bank of England*, pp. 185–216; David Kynaston, 'The Bank and the Government' in ibid., pp. 19–55.

[18] Sir John Craig, *The Mint: A History of the London Mint from AD 287 to 1948* (Cambridge University Press, Cambridge, 1953), p. xvii.

of the Exchequer titular head, or Master, of the Mint, and overall management of the mint was vested in a Deputy Master and Comptroller, appointed by the Treasury. Staffs were recruited from other government departments or through the Civil Service Commission. The Mint nevertheless had a more distant relationship with the Treasury than the formal arrangements might indicate,[19] and it occupied an anomalous position within the public sector, engaging in commercial sales as well as discharging its primary responsibility to manufacture coin for domestic circulation. Beginning with changes in 1975 this commercial role was rationalized, culminating in 2010 with the Mint's transformation into a limited company, albeit one wholly owned by the government. It is a parastatal commercial organization of a kind that has received relatively little attention from historians.

On a spectrum from 'state' to 'nonstate' the universities of Oxford and Cambridge, while from their medieval foundation intended to serve the twin needs of church and state, were in some respects more obviously at the periphery, although from the mid-nineteenth century they became subject to greater state regulation. Legislation in 1854 and 1856 intervened to make them less religiously exclusive, which together with the Northcote-Trevelyan civil service reforms, aimed at the creation of a public service class. Further legislation in 1877 stipulated that research and teaching should be among the aims of the universities, while governments also had patronage over some key university appointments. The establishment of the University Grants Committee (UGC) in 1919 and introduction of state funding, in 1923 to Oxbridge, but earlier elsewhere, represented a further development in the relationship of universities to the state with the new Committee instituting quinquennial university reviews. The universities nonetheless retained considerable independence from the state, with government funding accounting for only a proportion of university income and the UGC not inclined towards intervention.[20]

In contrast, in our period Sandhurst was more subordinate to Whitehall. The Academy was re-opened by the War Office in 1947, when the Royal Military College Sandhurst, established at the turn of the nineteenth century, merged with the Royal Military Academy Woolwich. The latter's origins lay in 1741, when an academy had been opened on the site of the workshops of the Royal Arsenal to train recruits to the army's technical branches. Historically the RMC had had a fluctuating relationship to the state. It was built during the Napoleonic Wars with government money, but the return to European peace

---

[19] *Fifth Report from the Estimates Committee, 1967–8: The Royal Mint*, PP 1967–8, IX (Cmnd. 364), para. 3; ibid., Minutes of Evidence Taken before Sub-Committee D of the Estimates Committee, paras. 136–9.

[20] Robert Anderson, *British Universities: Past and Present* (Hambledon, London, 2006), pp. 4, 35–6, 45, 116–18, 131.

saw a steep decline in military spending,[21] and for a period the loss of all state support. Government funding was provided again after the Crimean War, and by 1878 all infantry and cavalry officer cadets of the British Army, as well as entrants to the Indian Army, attended either Sandhurst or Woolwich.[22] Sandhurst had its own distinct institutional culture, but it lacked the capacity for independent initiatives that characterized some of the other institutions. In particular, it did not operate independently of the Army, although the latter was itself not unpolitical, and constituted another 'player' within Britain's pluralistic system, competing for resources within Whitehall as a whole and in relation to Britain's other services, the RAF and Navy.[23] Sandhurst was run by officers in the British Army, appointed to the Academy for relatively short periods, and responsible through the Army's executive, the Army Council, to the Chief of the Imperial General Staff and the Secretary of State for War.

Situated on the margins of the state or beyond, each of these institutions had assumed some form of imperial role and constituted part of the apparatus of the British imperial system. Together they reflect how within that system power was dispersed across the 'state' and 'society'. Insufficient attention has perhaps been paid to this – for all that the pluralistic nature of British imperialism is well established,[24] and postcolonial studies and the 'new imperial history' have illuminated the different forms which 'power' assumed within colonial contexts and the variety of sources from which it emanated.[25] The mixed economy of the British imperial system continued into the twentieth century and was even reinforced by the mid-century expansion of the state, not least because of the development in this period of social sciences and increased reliance on the 'expert'. In British colonial administration, as in other spheres of public life, numerous specialists were appointed to advisory bodies and investigatory commissions,[26] continuing and extending the plurality of the British system. As I will argue, while these experts and institutions were

[21] David French, *The British Way in Warfare, 1688–2000* (Unwin Hyman, London, 1990), pp. 226–7, 232.

[22] Hugh Thomas, *The Story of Sandhurst* (Hutchinson, London, 1961), pp. 53, 97, 121–31; Alan Sheppard, *Sandhurst: The Royal Military Academy Sandhurst and Its Predecessors* (Country Life Books, London, 1980), p. 92; Christopher Pugsley and Angela Holdsworth, *Sandhurst: A Tradition of Leadership* (Third Millennium Publishing, London, 2005), p. 35.

[23] Huw Strachan, *The Politics of the British Army* (Clarendon Press, Oxford, 1997).

[24] Best captured in John Darwin's characterization of the ramshackle collection of overseas British interests and dependencies as a 'world system', held together by a powerful British centre, India, the 'hinterland of the City of London', a "commercial republic"', and the white self-governing colonies: Darwin, *The Empire Project*, pp. 9–12.

[25] On the 'new imperial history' see esp., Kathleen Wilson ed., *A New Imperial History: Culture, Identity, and Modernity in Britain and the Empire, 1660–1840* (Cambridge University Press, Cambridge, 2004).

[26] Joseph Hodge, *Triumph of the Expert: Agrarian Doctrines of Development* (Ohio University Press, Athens, OH, 2007).

bound to the state in multifarious ways, their knowledge gave them 'power' of a semi-independent form. Conversely the co-option of experts and institutions within structures of imperial administration provided the context in which they acquired new expertise – 'knowledge' – which was sometimes thereafter the platform from which they might make their own interventions in the decolonization process. In these and other ways the plurality of the British system gave rise to a multiplicity of sites at which power was articulated, and generated distinct institutional cultures and dynamics. As we will see, the priorities of the Bank of England were not simply those of the Treasury, or the objectives of the academics delivering courses at Oxford and Cambridge those of the Colonial Office. Rather these domestic institutions could possess a form of corporate vocation, an ethos or sense of purpose, which could itself require adjustment in adapting to decolonization and the emergence of a postcolonial world.

As repositories of the knowledge useful to building the governmental and institutional structures deemed essential to independent nation-states, these different institutions utilized their expertise at the end of Empire by developing or becoming involved in delivering new programmes of technical education, and through diasporas of British personnel acting in an advisory capacity or seconded to senior roles within the new Commonwealth states. New states had an urgent and compelling need for assistance and had entered independence woefully ill-prepared, a legacy of colonialism and the speed with which they attained independence, unanticipated by many at the time. Postcolonial states were, Robert Jackson contends, 'quasi-states'. Constitutional decolonization created 'territorial jurisdictions' recognized by the international community as sovereign states, but which lacked established institutions and the personnel to staff them.[27] As we shall see, initiatives on the part of domestic institutions that had become stakeholders in Empire became part and parcel of Britain's package of 'technical assistance' to new states.

The exploration of these initiatives will demonstrate an on-going sense of 'imperial mission' – or perhaps more accurately 'Commonwealth mission' – in a variety of different institutions enduring across the era of decolonization. In private, British officials were realistic about the political difficulties inherent in the translation of the 'old' Commonwealth into the 'new', a process that began with the admission of India and Pakistan, and in which India especially became a significant player and source of influence among decolonizing African states.[28] Nevertheless, this sense of mission reflects the purchase that a Commonwealth ideal attained in public discourse and consciousness after

---

[27] Robert Jackson, *Quasi-States: Sovereignty, International Relations and the Third World* (Cambridge University Press, Cambridge, 1990), pp. 5, 22.

[28] See, e.g., Gerard McCann, 'From Diaspora to Third Worldism and the UN: India and the Politics of Decolonising Africa', *Past and Present* 218 (2013), Suppl. 8, pp. 258–80; Mélanie Torrent, 'A "New" Commonwealth for Britain? Negotiating Ghana's Pan-African and Asian

the war, not least because, as Richard Toye argues, Labour and Conservative politicians 'recruited' the Commonwealth concept into political debate for their own purposes and, in this rhetorical process, the Commonwealth idea was created as a 'public phenomenon'.[29] That a common sense of mission can be identified across quite different institutions within and beyond the state also reflects the values common to British elites, a product of their shared academic and social background.

Individuals were highly significant in fashioning these institutional cultures and practices. This was notably the case at the Bank of England, where institutional cultural norms were shaped by one governor of longstanding tenure. The case study of the Mint similarly shows the importance of individual, dynamic leadership at a potentially destabilizing moment, and illustrates, as others observe, not only that institutions are 'remarkably durable', but how for institutions crises can 'create opportunities of breakthrough'.[30] Appointment and promotion policies allowed values to be cascaded down institutional hierarchies and reproduced, ensuring that they continued to shape institutional cultures. Where British officials were seconded or transferred to emergent Commonwealth states, their return saw their experience fed back into the institutions, sometimes helping sustain interest in the Commonwealth. Equally, institutional lobbying, as those within institutions acted to preserve and perpetuate their own activities, also resulted in their values and distinct, institutionally informed, perspectives percolating up within the British system, feeding into wider assessments and shaping broader policy outcomes.

This consideration of the history of a range of important British institutions – some of which were not principally 'imperial' – will hence be revealed as being as eloquent of the prevalence and development of cultures of imperialism (and the supposedly 'post-imperial') as perhaps more obvious conjunctions and sources, such as the press and other media, or debates around immigration. In particular, it will be argued that British institutions exercised their own 'imperialism' at the end of Empire as they sought to substitute new roles for their established ones within the imperial system.

Whether to advance commercial interests or from a more disinterested sense of responsibility and service, British actors and institutions aimed to embed specifically *British* practices and customs rather than advance less specific

Connections at the End of Empire (1951–8)', *International History Review*, 38 (2016), pp. 573–613.

[29] Richard Toye, 'Words of Change: The Rhetoric of Commonwealth, Common Market and Cold War, 1961–3' in L. J. Butler and Sarah Stockwell eds., *The Wind of Change: Harold Macmillan and British Decolonization* (Palgrave Macmillan, Basingstoke, 2013), pp. 140–58, esp. 154.

[30] A. Born and T. Christensen, 'The Development of Public Institutions: Reconsidering the Role of Leadership', *Administration and Society*, 40 (2008), pp. 271–97, quotation 289. I owe this reference to Véronique Dimier.

'Anglo-American' western values, in ways that correspond to Harshan Kumarasingham's conclusions about a British commitment to exporting the Westminster parliamentary model and to Simon Potter's account of the BBC's role in the development of overseas broadcasting services and its efforts to disseminate a British model of public-service broadcasting.[31] Individuals within British institutions attempted to instil what they perceived as best practice, reflecting their own ideas of good governance. In particular, as they engaged in a process of institution-building, individuals within these institutions acted in ways that, rather than being simply a pragmatic strategy to secure economic interests or institutional advantage, were partly determined by British ideas of the state, and in particular of state power. Ideas of the distinctively liberal identity of the British state and its relations with civil society helped shape the policies and responses of a range of British institutions to the decolonization process. That is, Britons focused on the political neutrality of parastatal institutions and the independence from the state of institutions and organizations within civil society, in several cases by actively seeking to nurture an emergent African, professional, middle class.

In reality there were considerable gulfs between both British perceptions of a liberal and benevolent imperial mission and the often brutal nature of colonialism on the ground, *and* the power the British imagined they possessed to shape developments overseas and their actual ability to do so. They often struggled to exercise the control they wished, and their plans were frequently frustrated. Even so, in the twilight years of Empire individuals within institutions were able to exploit the last elements of Britain's imperial power structures as they sought to inscribe their practices and to advance their interests in a world in which there were influences in all directions, but where the power and force of currents was distinctly unequal. Domestic institutions beyond or on the margins of the state such as the Bank of England used their established connections to the Colonial Office, Commonwealth Relations Office (CRO), or representation on advisory bodies to exercise as much oversight over new Commonwealth institutions as possible. Equally the presence of British officials overseas both in colonial administrations and the CRO, the British Crown

---

[31] Harshan Kumarasingham, *A Political Legacy of the British Empire: Power and the Parliamentary System in Post-Colonial India and Sri Lanka* (I. B. Tauris, London, 2013); Simon Potter, *Broadcasting Empire: The BBC and the British World, 1922–1970* (Oxford University Press, Oxford, 2012), ch. 5. See also Georgina Sinclair, *At the End of the Line: Colonial Policing and the Imperial Endgame, 1945–1980* (Manchester University Press, Manchester, 2006), esp. ch. 3. In contrast British officials were 'cautious about the feasibility or indeed the desirability of exporting their culture, or their political institutions', with British officials worried that the adoption of the Queen as head of state in new Commonwealth states might drag her into murky local political disputes: Philip Murphy, *Monarchy and the End of Empire: The House of Windsor, the British Government and the Postwar Commonwealth* (Oxford University Press, Oxford, 2013), p. 14.

Agents – who had a key role in appointing personnel and in procurement – and, after independence, networks of legacy personnel who remained in post, gave a strategic advantage to British institutions. Emergent states could, and did, however, exercise their new sovereignty. They sourced aid multilaterally, including from other powers and institutions equally convinced of the value of their own expertise and models for postcolonial modernizing projects. In the 1950s and 1960s these alternative sources included other countries in the 'South' as well as the West, while transnational communities of experts and development agencies also played a key part.[32] The two superpowers, the United States and the Soviet Union, were in particular potentially valuable sources of material assistance, as well as of alternative and competing models of development.[33] Nor did local elites in emergent states simply accept uncritically British or other external models; rather they reimagined western ideas and developmental models, appropriating and deploying them in different ways and to their own ends within their own societies.[34] Inevitably the British focus of this book precludes full analysis of these dynamics. Our primary purpose is an investigation of *British* initiatives and of their legacies in Britain itself. Nonetheless, to gain some insight into African responses to the activities and technical assistance programmes developed by the British state and British institutions, I draw on Ghanaian and Zambian sources, as well as those of some international organizations that became alternative, and sometimes competing, sources of expertise to the British.

To focus discussion, the following chapters principally explore the institutions in relation to political change in former British Africa from the 1950s. However, of necessity they ground the discussion of African decolonization within a broader geographical framework, since the institutions themselves did not necessarily differentiate between Africa and other areas of the remaining

[32] See, e.g., McCann, 'From Diaspora to Third Worldism'; Corinna Unger, 'Industrialization vs. Agrarian Reform: West German Modernization Policies in India in the 1950s and 1960s', Abou B. Bamba, 'Triangulating a Modernization Experiment: The United States, France, and the Making of the Kossou Project in Central Ivory Coast', Constantin Katsakioris, 'Soviet Lessons for Arab Modernization. Soviet Educational Aid towards Arab Countries after 1956' all in Andreas Eckert, Stephen Malinowski, and Corinna Unger eds., *Modernizing Missions: Approaches to 'Developing' the Non-Western World after 1945*, special issue of *Journal of Modern European History*, 8 (2010).
[33] There is a large literature on American modernization theory especially, as discussed on p. 74. Additionally there are numerous case studies both old and new that explore the relations between new states and the United States and Soviet Union: see, as an excellent example of an older historiography, W. Scott Thompson, *Ghana's Foreign Policy, 1957–1966* (Princeton University Press, Princeton, NJ, 1969), and more recently the introduction and essays in Leslie James and Elizabeth Leake, *Decolonization and the Cold War: Negotiating Independence* (Bloomsbury Academic, London, 2015).
[34] See some of the contributions to C. A. Bayly, Vijayendra Rao, Simon Szreter, Michael Woodcock eds, *History, Historians and Development Policy: A Necessary Dialogue* (Manchester University Press, Manchester, 2011).

Empire, or even the remnants of an 'informal' Empire in the Middle East. Moreover, to understand the different experiences and perspectives of some of the institutions in the 1950s, we need also to take account of their earlier involvement in the 'old' Commonwealth and India, since this informed their approaches to African decolonization. Many of those who occupied senior posts within the institutions after the war had risen through the ranks in the interwar era, their mindsets shaped by their experience in dealing with the former white settlement colonies of Canada, New Zealand, Australia and South Africa, or with India. In particular, the Bank of England's involvement with the new Commonwealth in the 1950s and 1960s can only be fully understood with reference to its previous engagement in the older Commonwealth states. Despite a historiographical shift to include the dominions in post-war histories of decolonization,[35] they remain relatively marginal to accounts organized around the theme of 'Empire's end'. Once we broaden our focus away from the state, narrowly defined, to incorporate other institutions that had assumed imperial roles in the pluralistic British system, the extent to which (for all the real differences in forms of rule and sovereignty across different locations within the British formal and informal empires) some contemporaries perceived developments in the dependent Empire in the 1950s within the same frame as those of an earlier era comes more firmly into view in a fashion that may be obscured by ways of 'seeing' the Empire derived from Britain's own Whitehall administrative division into 'colonial', 'Indian', 'dominion' and 'foreign'.

The account that follows traces developments relating to the four institutions through to the 1980s. British decolonization was protracted, continuing in the late 1960s in relation to the southern African high-commission territories, and during the 1970s in relation to smaller island dependencies. It is impossible to understand either the 'British end' of the British Empire or the ways in which the British state and British institutions reconfigured their activities for a 'postcolonial' era without taking account of this drawn-out nature of British decolonization. It will be suggested that this is because the British state was 'Janus-faced': one part of it was focused on the still-functioning Empire, and the other half was adapting to a new post-imperial phase. What is more, the structures and legacies within these British institutions left by centuries of involvement with Britain's Empire at some point evolved to become distinctively different from those of the imperial era, ceasing to be simply 'imperial hangovers'. The changes were nevertheless incremental rather than revolutionary, and to understand the full effects of empire and of British decolonization we need to adopt a long perspective.

---

[35] On which, see esp. A. G. Hopkins. 'Rethinking Decolonization', *Past and Present*, 200 (2008), pp. 211–47.

Recent years have seen an enormous, and fruitful, expansion in the historiography of decolonization. We are now accustomed to thinking of it as something that involves much more than simply constitutional change and instead that affected and engaged a wide set of organizations and individuals within the former colonial empires, and had an impact 'at home' as well as overseas. Indeed whereas once historians treated decolonization as something of little bearing on British domestic history, and the domain of historians of empire, a wealth of new studies, building on several decades of scholarship concerning the ways in which imperialism shaped metropolitan society and culture in earlier periods,[36] has exposed the limitations of what historian Stuart Ward dubs a 'minimal impact' interpretation of the British experience of the end of Empire.[37] They range from considerations of imperial issues in post-war party politics to studies of British race relations and immigration, and analyses of culture and media.[38] Alongside significant contributions by Wendy Webster and Stephen Howe,[39] Ward himself opened up study of the cultural

[36] Associated esp. with the pioneering work of John Mackenzie and the Manchester University Press 'Studies in Imperialism' series that for many years he also edited, as well as with scholars such as Catherine Hall, Kathleen Wilson and Antoinette Burton: see, e.g., among many, John Mackenzie ed., *Imperialism and Popular Culture* (Manchester University Press, Manchester, 1986), Catherine Hall and Sonya Rose eds., *At Home with the Empire: Metropolitan Culture and the Imperial World* (Cambridge University Press, Cambridge, 2006), *The Sense of the People: Politics, Culture and Imperialism in England, 1715–1785* (Cambridge University Press, Cambridge, 1998), Antoinette Burton, *Burdens of History: British Feminists, Indian Women, and Imperial Culture, 1865–1915* (University of North Carolina Press, Chapel Hill, NC, 1994). For a more critical view that questions the depth and breadth of imperial impact, see: Bernard Porter, *The Absent-Minded Imperialists: Empire, Society and Culture in Britain* (Oxford University Press, Oxford, 2004); Bernard Porter, 'Further thoughts on Imperial Absent-Mindedness', *Journal of Imperial and Commonwealth History* 36 (2008), pp. 101–17.

[37] Stuart Ward, 'Introduction' in Stuart Ward ed., *British Culture and the End of Empire* (Manchester University Press, Manchester, 2001), p. 4.

[38] On politics, among many, see, Stephen Howe, *Anti-colonialism in British Politics: The Left and the End of Empire 1918–1964* (Clarendon Press, Oxford, 1993); Philip Murphy, *Party Politics and Decolonization: The Conservative Party and British Colonial Policy in Tropical Africa, 1951–1964* (Clarendon Press, Oxford, 1995); Nicholas J. Owen, *The British Left and India: Metropolitan Anti-imperialism, 1885–1947* (Clarendon Press, Oxford, 2007). On ideas of race and immigration, see esp., Camilla Schofield, *Enoch Powell and the Making of Postcolonial Britain* (Cambridge University Press, Cambridge, 2013), and Peter Brooke, 'Duncan Sandys and the Informal Politics of Decolonisation' (PhD thesis, King's College London, 2016); on culture and society, see further references below and also e.g. Lee Grieveson and C. MacCabe eds., *Film and the End of Empire* (Palgrave Macmillan with the British Film Institute, London, 2011). The essays in Andrew Thompson ed., *Britain's Experience of Empire in the Twentieth Century* (Oxford University Press, Oxford, 2011) offer an excellent starting point for exploring these different themes.

[39] Ward ed., *British Culture;* Wendy Webster, ' "There'll Always Be an England": Representations of Colonial Wars and Immigration, 1948–68', *Journal of British Studies* 40 (2001), pp. 557–84; Wendy Webster, *Englishness and Empire 1939–1965* (Oxford University Press, Oxford, 2005); Stephen Howe, 'Internal Decolonization? British Politics since Thatcher as Post-Colonial Trauma', *Twentieth Century British History* 14 (2003), pp. 286–304; Stephen Howe, 'When If Ever Did Empire End? Internal Decolonization in British Culture

dimensions of decolonization in Britain in a pioneering edited collection of essays. Such work was richly suggestive of a post-war 'culture of Empire', but showed that this might take many forms: an enduring popular imperial culture, albeit one in which a 'shift' was occurring as a more unreconstructed imperial culture absorbed and reflected the post-war rhetorics of development and the Commonwealth; the cultural resonance of 'decline' itself; the 'Empire coming home', especially in the form of post-war Commonwealth immigration; and nostalgia for an Empire lost, as well as the struggle for 'post-imperial' national identity and purpose. Through analysis of cultures of Britishness at the Empire's end, including of how imperial retreat has stimulated devolution within the British union, Ward has subsequently explored other dimensions of the metropolitan effects of decolonization.[40] Jordanna Bailkin's discussion of the post-war domestic welfare state has also shown the complex and varied ways in which imperialism and its afterlives shaped Britain itself, and Bill Schwarz how imperial constructions of race were of lasting significance in shaping white British identities.[41] Race and immigration are similarly prominent in Elizabeth Buettner's richly textured and highly engaging account of Britain and other former European colonial powers 'after Empire'. With a view to showing how Europe was '*recreated* once its territorial expanse receded', she focuses especially on movements of people in the form of both returning settlers and Asian, African and Caribbean immigrants to Europe, as well as on multiculturalism and memories of Empire in former European imperial metropoles.[42] A similarly comparative European approach also underpins Ruth Craggs and Claire Wintle's edited collection exploring transnational cultures of decolonization. Among other things, they turn a spotlight on institutions of a cultural kind, such as museums, architectural practices and artists' groups, and showcase research demonstrating how these provided a platform for 'new artworks, displays and styles that promoted decolonization'.[43]

since the 1950s' in Martin Lynn ed., *The British Empire in the 1950s: Retreat or Revival?* (Palgrave Macmillan, Basingstoke, 2006).

[40] As part of his *Embers of Empire* project. See, e.g., Jimmi Nielsen and Stuart Ward, ' "Cramped and restricted at home?" Scottish separatism at empire's end', *Transactions of the Royal Historical Society*, 25 (2015), pp. 159–85; see also an impressive debut by another member of this project: Ezequiel Mercau, 'Empire Redux. The Falklands and the End of Greater Britain' (University of Copenhagen PhD, 2016).

[41] Jordanna Bailkin, *The Afterlife of Empire* (University of California Press, Berkeley, CA, 2012); and Bill Schwarz, *The White Man's World* (Oxford University Press, Oxford, 2011).

[42] Elizabeth Buettner, *Europe after Empire: Decolonization, Society and Culture* (Cambridge University Press, Cambridge, 2016), quotation, p. 9; see also, Elizabeth Buettner, *Empire Families: Britons and Late Imperial India* (Oxford University Press, Oxford, 2004).

[43] Ruth Craggs and Claire Wintle eds. *Cultures of Decolonisation* (Manchester University Press, Manchester, 2015), p. 11.

The history of domestic British institutions more generally at the end of Empire has, however, attracted little attention.[44] Yet, as I have suggested, domestic institutions like the Bank of England can be as revealing of cultures of imperialism as other more obvious sources. Moreover, by focusing on the four institutional case studies we can obtain a new perspective offering a clearer picture of the richly textured, complex and sometimes even contradictory cultures shaped by Britain's involvement in empire in all its different manifestations. These include ideas of race and class and also of imperial power, but were far from exclusively constituted by them, and these were imbricated with many others derived from far different sources or aspects of the imperial project in determining the imperial and 'post-imperial' cultures with which we are concerned.

In this respect, this book thus plugs a significant gap in our understanding both of decolonization and of the history of the institutions covered. The Mint and Sandhurst, the subject of Chapters 5 and 6, respectively, figure rarely, if at all, in existing accounts of the end of Empire, save for Catherine Eagleton's account of the design of coinage for Africa.[45] Indeed, neither institution has hitherto attracted much attention from modern historians more generally excepting those commissioned to produce institutional histories or in-house historians. Of the two, the Mint is the better served;[46] accounts of Sandhurst were either published some time ago and concentrate on its more distant past,[47] or have been produced for a general rather than an academic audience.[48] There are several excellent histories of the British Army, in particular for our period by David French, but these offer only limited discussion of training and of Sandhurst specifically.[49] Nor, despite literatures on colonial armed forces, on British counter-insurgency at the end of Empire, and British defence policy and decolonization,[50] has much been written about British military assistance to new African states, and the training of overseas cadets at British military train-

---

[44] Simon Potter's excellent history of the BBC is one notable exception; however, his principal focus is on the period before the Second World War, and he concentrates on the old Commonwealth rather than the new. Potter, *Broadcasting Empire*.

[45] Catherine Eagleton, 'Designing Change: Coins and the Creation of New National Identities' in Craggs and Wintle eds., *Cultures of Decolonisation*, pp. 222–44.

[46] C. E. Challis ed., *A New History of the Royal Mint* (Cambridge University Press, Cambridge, 1992).

[47] The best is Sheppard, *Sandhurst*.

[48] Holdsworth and Pugsley, *Sandhurst*.

[49] David French, *Army, Empire and Cold War: The British Army and Military Policy, 1945–71* (Oxford University Press, Oxford, 2012); see, also, Strachan, *Politics*.

[50] In relation to Africa, the best are: Timothy Parsons, *The African Rank and File: Social Implications of Colonial Military Service in the King's African Rifles, 1902–1964* (I. B. Tauris, Westport, CT & London, 1999); David Killingray, *Fighting for Britain: African Soldiers and the Second World War* (James Currey, Woodbridge, 2010); David Percox, *Britain, Kenya and the Cold War: Imperial Defence, Colonial Security and Decolonisation* (I. B. Tauris, London, 2004).

ing establishments, a key focus in the discussion of Sandhurst in Chapter 6, although the rise of the military in politics in new Commonwealth states, especially in Africa, did lead to some investigation in the 1960s and 1970s of the 'Sandhurst effect'.[51]

There is similarly little that directly engages with the theme of Oxford and Cambridge and Britain's late colonial Empire,[52] discussed in Chapter 3, although there are extensive and growing literatures on the ways in which academic disciplines, notably the social sciences, were shaped by and shaped Britain's involvement in Empire, on academic networks across the British world, and on overseas students studying in Britain.[53] Because this book addresses Oxford and Cambridge's involvement in Colonial Service training, Chapter 3 is as much about the Colonial Service as it is about the universities. The Service

---

[51] On the latter see, e.g., William Gutteridge, 'A Commonwealth Military Culture? Soldiers in the British Mould', *Round Table*, 60 (1970), pp. 327–37; William Gutteridge, *Military Institutions and Power in the New States* (Pall Mall Press, London and Dunmow, 1964); William Gutteridge, *The Military in African Politics* (Methuen and Co Ltd., London, 1969); and Robin Luckham, *The Nigerian Military: A Sociological Analysis of Authority and Revolt 1960–1967* (Cambridge University Press, Cambridge, 1971). See also Anthony Clayton, 'The Military Relations between Great Britain and Commonwealth Countries, with particular reference to the African Commonwealth Nations' in W. H. Morris-Jones and Georges Fischer eds., *Decolonisation and After: The British and French Experience* (Routledge, London, 1980), pp. 193–223. For more recent, regionally specific examples, see Timothy Parsons, *The 1964 Army Mutinies and the Making of Modern East Africa* (Praeger, Westport, CT, 2003); Tim Stapleton, *African Police and Soldiers in Colonial Zimbabwe, 1923–1980* (Rochester, NY, 2011); Marco Myss, 'A Post-Imperial Cold War Paradox: The Anglo-Nigerian Defence Agreement 1958–1962', *Journal of Imperial and Commonwealth History*, 44 (2016), pp. 976–1000; Poppy Cullen, '"Kenya is No Doubt a Special Place": British Policy towards Kenya, 1960–1980' (University of Durham, PhD, 2015). On long-term British–African defence links see also A. Jackson, 'British-African defence and security connections', *Defence Studies*, 6 (2006), pp. 351–76; Ashley Jackson, 'Empire and Beyond: The Pursuit of Overseas National Interests in the Late Twentieth Century', *English Historical Review*, 122 (2007), pp. 1350–66.
[52] The main exception is the relevant section of Richard Symonds, *Oxford and Empire: The Long Lost Cause?* (Oxford University Press, Oxford, 1986); see also F. Madden and D. K. Fieldhouse eds., *Oxford and the Idea of Commonwealth: Essays Presented to Sir Edgar Williams* (Croon Helm, London, 1982), and the essays by Ronald Hyam on imperial history at Oxford and Cambridge in Ronald Hyam, *Understanding the British Empire* (Cambridge University Press, Cambridge, 2010). There are useful chapters in the standard histories of the Universities: J. G. Darwin, 'A World University' in Brian Harrison ed., *The History of the University of Oxford: Volume VIII. The Twentieth Century* (Clarendon Press, Oxford, 1994), pp. 607–38; Christopher Brooke, *A History of the University of Cambridge: Volume IV 1870–1990* (Cambridge University Press, Cambridge, 1993).
[53] Esp., Pietsch, *Empire of Scholars*; Brett M. Bennett and Joseph Hodge eds., *Science and Empire: Knowledge and Networks of Science Across the British Empire, 1800–1970* (Palgrave Macmillan, Basingstoke, 2011); Helen Tilley and Robert J. Gordon eds., *Ordering Africa: Anthropology, European Imperialism, and the Politics of Knowledge* (Manchester University Press, Manchester, 2007); Hilary Perraton, *A History of Foreign Students in Britain* (Palgrave Macmillan, Basingstoke, 2014); A. J. Stockwell, 'Leaders, Dissidents and the Disappointed: Colonial Students in Britain as Empire Ended', *Journal of Imperial and Commonwealth History*, 36 (2008), pp. 487–507.

of course has its own historiography,[54] but one that focuses more on the inter-war and immediate post-war years than on the last years of African decolonization and that does not take up the issues addressed below.[55]

Of all the institutions represented in this book, the Bank, the subject of Chapter 4, has attracted most attention, not only in histories of the Bank and the City,[56] but more specifically from historians of empire, most prominently P. J. Cain and A. G. Hopkins in their sweeping analysis of 'gentlemanly capitalism' and British imperialism, as well as in Catherine Schenk and Gerold Krozewski's important and more focused accounts of the Empire and the post-war sterling area.[57] Chibuike Uche and Catherine Schenk have joined me in examining the development of central banking in Commonwealth states.[58]

[54] Kirk-Greene, *On Crown Service*; Christopher Prior, *Exporting Empire: Africa, Colonial Officials and the Construction of the Imperial State, 1900–39* (Manchester University Press, Manchester, 2013); Véronique Dimier, *Le gouvernement des colonies, regards croisés franco-britannique* (Presses Universitaire de Bruxelles, Brussels, 2004); Véronique Dimier, 'Three Universities and the British Elite: A Science of Colonial Administration in the UK', *Public Administration*, 84 (2006), pp. 337–66; Robert Heussler, *Yesterday's Rulers: The Making of the British Colonial Service* (Oxford University Press for Syracuse University Press, London, 1963). Nile Gardiner, '"Sentinels of Empire". The British Colonial Administrative Service, 1919–1954' (University of Yale, PhD, 1998).

[55] Kirk-Greene, *On Crown Service*, Sabine Clarke, 'A Technocratic Imperial State? The Colonial Office and Scientific Research, 1940–60', *Twentieth Century British History* 18 (2007), pp. 453–80; Richard Rathbone, 'The Colonial Service and the Transfer of Power in Ghana' in John Smith ed., *Administering Empire: The British Colonial Service in Retrospect* (University of London Press, London, 1999), pp. 149–66; Martin Lynn, 'Nigerian Complications: The Colonial Office, the Colonial Service and the 1953 Crisis in Nigeria' in John Smith ed., *Administering Empire*, pp. 181–205; Chris Jeppesen, 'Sanders of the River. Still the Best Job for a British Boy': Recruitment to the Colonial Administrative Service at the End of Empire', *Historical Journal*, 59 (2016), pp. 469–508. Of very many published memoirs, see, e.g., David Le Breton ed., *I Remember It Well: Fifty Years of Colonial Service Personnel Reminiscences* (published for the Overseas Service Pensioners' Association, Kinloss, 2010).

[56] Esp., Forrest Capie, *The Bank of England 1950s to 1979* (Cambridge University Press, Cambridge, 2010); Roberts and Kynaston eds., *The Bank of England*: David Kynaston, *Till Time's Last Sand. A History of the Bank of England 1694–2013* (Bloomsbury Publishing, London, 2017) was published too late to take proper account of it in this book. Although Kynaston acknowledges the perceived importance of the Empire-Commonwealth within the Bank, he devotes little space to it.

[57] P. J. Cain and A. G. Hopkins, *British Imperialism, 1688–2016* (Harlow, 1st pub., 1993; 3rd edn., 2016); Catherine Schenk, *Britain and the Sterling Area: From Devaluation to Convertibility in the 1950s* (Routledge, London, 1994); *The Decline of Sterling: Managing the Retreat of an International Currency 1945–1992* (Cambridge University Press, Cambridge, 2010); Gerold Krozewski, *Money and the End of Empire: British International Economic Policy and the Colonies, 1947–1958* (Palgrave Macmillan, Basingstoke, 2001).

[58] Catherine Schenk, 'The Origins of a Central Bank in Malaya and the Transition to Independence, 1954–1959', *Journal of Imperial and Commonwealth History*, 21 (1993), pp. 409–31; C. U. Uche, 'From Currency Board to Central Banking: The Politics of Change in Sierra Leone', *African Economic History* 24 (1996), pp. 147–58; C. U. Uche, 'Bank of England vs the IBRD: Did the Nigerian Colony Deserve a Central Bank?', *Explorations in Economic History* 34 (1997), pp. 220–41; C. U. Uche, 'From Currency Board to Central Banking: The Gold Coast Experience', *South African Journal of Economic History*, 10 (1995), pp. 80–94.

But Chapter 4 highlights aspects of the Bank's involvement in post-war decol-onization and in the development of Commonwealth central banking, which have not been explored before, and which can underpin a new interpretation of the Bank of England's role. Elsewhere in the historiography there has been significant discussion of postcolonial African states that were, as Patrick Chabal and Jean-Pascal Daloz, put it, not 'properly institutionalized' – lacking independent bureaucracies free from the control of those who hold political power, staffed by civil servants who regarded 'public employment as a private resource'.[59] Yet institutional development – the second theme of this book, alongside the exploration of the domestic workings out of decolonization – has attracted little attention in broad histories of decolonization, and generated only limited scholarship more generally, and this mostly in relation to defence, policing and intelligence.[60] As we broaden our understanding of decolonization, to incorporate much more than the high politics of imperial policymaking and constitutional independence, this neglect of accompanying and secondary processes of decolonization is all the more striking. The theme featured in some of the scholarship of the late 1960s and early 1970s, when focused studies of the fashioning of new institutions appeared for different regions and sectors, most numerous in relation to African armed forces,[61] and was addressed most directly in Richard Symonds, *The British and their Successors*.[62] But while perceptive and informative, these accounts were mostly written without access to the relevant primary sources, instead analysing near-contemporaneous developments the authors saw unfolding around them. Indeed, many of those writing on the theme of institutional development and transfer were themselves involved in the very processes they sought to analyse, including some on the academic staff at Sandhurst or

[59] Patrick Chabal and Jean-Pascal Daloz, *Africa Works: Disorder as Political Instrument* (James Currey, Oxford, 1999), esp. pp. 4–7.
[60] Parsons, *The 1964 Army*; Stapleton, *African Police and Soldiers*; David Killingray, *The British Military Presence in West Africa* (Oxford Development Records Project, Report 3, 1983); Sinclair, *At the End of the Line*. See also the University of the West of England's major archival project on the Rhodesian army: 'Wars of Liberation, Wars of Decolonisation. The Rhodesian Army Archive Project': http://gtr.ukri.org/projects?ref=AH%2FD002001%2F1, accessed 4 April 2018. On intelligence see, esp. Philip Murphy, 'Creating a Commonwealth Intelligence Culture: The View from Central Africa, 1945–1965', *Intelligence and National Security*, 17 (2002), pp. 131–62; Calder Walton, *Empire of Secrets: British Intelligence, the Cold War and the Twilight of Empire* (William Collins, London, 2012).
[61] See, in addition to the works by Gutteridge and Luckham cited above, also Michael Lee, *African Armies and Civil Order* (Chatto and Windus, London, 1969); Chester Arthur Crocker, 'The Military Transfer of Power in Africa: A Comparative Study of Change in the British and French Systems of Order' (Johns Hopkins University, PhD, 1969); Norman J. Miners, *The Nigerian Army, 1956–1966* (Methuen, London, 1971). Lee was granted access to the primary sources but was not permitted to reference them.
[62] Richard Symonds, *The British and their Successors: A Study of the Government Services in the New States* (Faber, London, 1966).

Oxford.[63] This flowering of contemporaneous studies of different aspects of state-building was itself a product of some of the same dynamics that underpinned the initiatives discussed in this book: another manifestation of a British liberalism that revolved around particular ideas of the nature of the state.

The process of 'decolonizing' colonial institutions and of developing institutions in new states is now beginning to attract renewed scholarly attention.[64] But there remain many gaps in our appreciation of the historical development of institutions in new states at the end of Empire. Moreover, most existing studies of institutional transfer and development have been written about specific regions or sectors, most often the preserve of specialists in military or financial history, or of political scientists. This book therefore attempts for the first time since there has been access to the relevant primary sources for British decolonization to bring together empirical analysis across *different* sectors – administration, finance and defence.[65] By assembling in one volume analysis of institutions normally discussed in quite separate historiographies this book brings into sharper focus the similarities across sectors and institutions. Poppy Cullen has recently shown in her impressive study of British relations with postcolonial Kenya that, although there was no 'single dominant British interest' in the country, a 'combination of different aims and opportunities' nevertheless made Kenya 'particularly significant' to Britain.[66] In comparable ways this book hopes to show that the 'whole' is more than the sum of the parts, demonstrating just how comprehensively, and in mutually reinforcing ways, British officials and institutions, within and outside the British state, engaged in state- and institution-building processes in emergent Commonwealth nations.

In order to contextualize the later considerations of British civil and military technical assistance, Chapter 2, which focuses principally on the British state, explains why little consideration was given to, and little progress made with, institutional transfer, development and Africanization before the 1950s. It also identifies the dynamics and character of policies of technical assistance as an aspect of British international aid, including military assistance, essential for understanding the discussion of Sandhurst in Chapter 6.

Through this discussion – and that in subsequent chapters of the ways in which institutions discussed here delivered forms of technical assistance to new states – this book contributes to growing conversations about Britain's

---

[63] Including William Gutteridge and Richard Symonds.
[64] See, esp. Ellen Feingold, 'Decolonising Justice: A History of the High Court of Tanganyika, c. 1920–71' (University of Oxford, D.Phil., 2011); for an innovative approach to the development of African universities, see, Tim Livsey, 'Suitable Lodgings for Students: Modern Space, Colonial Development and Decolonization in Nigeria', *Urban History*, 41 (2014), pp. 1–22.
[65] But see, Stockwell, 'Exporting Britishness'.
[66] Cullen, 'Kenya is No Doubt a Special Place', p. 26.

relations with postcolonial African states,[67] international educational and technical aid,[68] and of the colonial roots of the postcolonial development industry. Scholars were once slow to acknowledge the colonial lineage of modern development – perhaps as Uma Kothari suggests, because there was a 'political imperative to distance the international aid industry from the colonial encounter'[69] – but we now have more evidence of their interconnection. As Marc Frey and Sönke Kunkel argue, 'at the moment the much heralded "development era" crystallized, there was already in place a European knowledge-power complex which consisted of hundreds, or thousands, of experts, administrators, scientists, bureaucracies and financial resources that, due to the ending of colonial wars and control, could now be disbursed as grants and loans to the "underdeveloped world"'.[70] Joseph Hodge and Véronique Dimier show that in the 1960s and 1970s people formerly associated with European colonial development went on to work in new roles in development bodies. Hodge shows how the postcolonial re-employment of former British personnel in such organizations contributed to a globalization of colonial development practice.[71] Dimier similarly demonstrates that former French colonial officials 'recycled their imperial expertise' through their re-employment in the European Commission's Directorate General for Development and Cooperation. Their interaction with an African elite corresponded, she suggests, to that of the colonial era, for example in systems of indirect rule.[72] My own book reveals other important colonial roots of postcolonial development practice and studies, as well as striking continuities between the colonial and the postcolonial eras. It also shows just how much the nature of British technical assistance reflected institutional priorities and agendas.

Before this we should begin, however, with a discussion of the 'imperial' roles of the domestic British institutions under consideration. This shows how the Mint and the universities had developed a vested interest in the perpetuation of their 'imperial' roles into the post-imperial era, and how the Bank of England – which had overseen the development of central banking

---

[67] Ibid.; see also, e.g., Brooke, 'Duncan Sandys'.

[68] For example, Corinna Unger, 'The United States, Decolonization, and the Education of Third World Elites' in Jost Dülffer and Marc Frey eds., *Elites and Decolonization in the Twentieth Century* (Palgrave Macmillan, Basingstoke, 2011), pp. 241–61.

[69] Uma Kothari, 'From Colonial Administration to Development Studies: A Postcolonial Critique of the History of Development Studies' in Uma Kothari, *A Radical History of Development Studies: Individuals, Institutions, and Ideologies* (Zed Books, London, 2005), pp. 46–66, quotation at 51.

[70] Marc Frey and Sönke Kunkel, 'Writing the History of Development: A Review of the Recent Literature', *Contemporary European History*, 20 (2011), pp. 215–32 [quote from 223].

[71] On which see, e.g., Joseph Hodge, 'British Colonial Expertise, Post-Colonial Careering and the Early History of International Development', in Eckert, Malinowski, and Unger eds., *Modernizing Missions*, pp. 24–44.

[72] Véronique Dimier, *The Invention of a European Development Aid Bureaucracy. Recycling Empire* (Palgrave Macmillan, Basingstoke, 2014), p. 2.

in the dominions and India in the interwar period – developed a distinctive culture that equated Britishness with 'good practice', premised on a sense of British entitlement, as well as responsibility, to shape developments in the new Commonwealth. In this way it offers a point of departure for my wider project by showing that the decolonization process commenced at a point at which these British institutions were in varying degrees and ways more closely engaged in the Empire than ever before.

1   The Imperial Roles of British Institutions

The institutions discussed in this book came into existence to serve essentially domestic purposes. In the mid-twentieth century, their core functions remained domestic, whether in relation to the education or training of young Britons (in the case of the universities and Sandhurst) or the British economy (for the Bank of England and the Royal Mint, whose primary function was the manufacture of coin for domestic use). Nevertheless, centuries of involvement in Britain's Empire had influenced their activities and cultures. Imperial expansion, and especially the acquisition of Britain's 'second' Empire, had transformed previously domestic institutions into 'imperial' ones. If some of this 'imperial' character reflected Britain's broader international engagements, these institutions had nonetheless also acquired more specifically imperial roles, becoming stakeholders in Empire and part of the apparatus of Britain's imperial system.

This chapter traces the historical evolution of these roles over more than two centuries, and their most important manifestations in relation to the Universities of Oxford and Cambridge, the Bank of England, the Royal Mint and the Royal Military Academy Sandhurst (RMAS). Its chief contention is that the middle decades of the twentieth century saw the extension of these imperial roles, and consequently – and paradoxically – a deepening of British institutional engagement with much of the colonial Empire on the eve of its demise.

Within each institution this process was not necessarily linear or even. There were centrifugal as much as centripetal forces at work. In particular, the British withdrawal from, and accompanying partition of, India, saw a transformation and even cessation of that part of the institutions' activities that was directed towards the British Empire in South Asia. This was most obviously the case at Sandhurst, which, upon Indian independence, relinquished its near-century-long role of training British officers for the Indian Army. Again, even as the world wars in some ways constituted an impressive show of imperial might and of unity between Britain and the dominions (the 'old' Commonwealth states of Canada, Australia, New Zealand and South Africa), these were increasingly flexing their muscles and asserting their independence from Britain in ways that shaped the texture and nature of British institutional involvement with them.

Yet other developments in the middle decades of the twentieth century reinforced and, in some respects, intensified, the institutions' engagement with both the residual colonial Empire and the independent Commonwealth – although these developments were not all of equal significance to institutions operating in very different sectors. One was the twentieth-century consolidation of colonial rule in Britain's newer colonies in Africa. Among other things this led in 1926 to the inauguration of Colonial Service training at Oxford and Cambridge and saw the Royal Mint engage in the production of new coins introduced throughout British Africa by colonial currency boards created in the early decades of the twentieth century. A second was a wider renewal of British imperial purpose that began in the late 1930s, as colonial unrest across wide areas of the dependent Empire prompted a more interventionist, and reformist, approach towards the colonies. The Second World War reinforced this dynamic. War necessitated intervention to organize the colonies for conflict, which, inter alia, led through the introduction of exchange control to the creation of the sterling area, thus shaping the Bank of England's involvement in Empire. Concurrently, as the British government sought to present an acceptable face of British imperialism to its American allies and colonial critics, Britain's imperial mission was refashioned with a new emphasis on 'partnership' and 'development'. For Britain, as for other European colonial powers, development became a new rationale for continuing colonialism in an international environment that was increasingly inhospitable to empires. The Colonial Development and Welfare Act, passed in 1940 and renewed and extended periodically thereafter, was the most obvious demonstration of Britain's newfound commitment to developing its colonies, providing for increased expenditure on economic and social welfare projects; this 'turn' to development was also, as we shall see, significant for British universities. Imperial revival was maintained into the post-war era, even as the Empire was in retreat in South Asia and Palestine, and Britain itself was greatly weakened. Indeed, Clement Attlee's post-war Labour government, which had overseen Indian independence, proved rather imperially minded in relation to the residual Empire, identifying in Britain's remaining colonies potential for assisting its own post-war economic recovery. Africa was now the core of Britain's imperial system: the development of its reserves of manpower and resources being briefly perceived as a means of sustaining Britain's world role.

One central argument of this book is that both the long-term evolution of these institutional imperial roles and, more specifically, in some institutions, the deepening of connections in the mid-twentieth century, generated vested interests in the Empire. With the exception of Sandhurst, these domestic institutions had acquired material interests from their imperial involvement that, as we shall see, would shape their response to African decolonization. This was perhaps particularly the case at Oxford and Cambridge (to which this chapter correspondingly devotes more attention than to the other institutions). At the universities, the Bank and the Mint these deepening interests were not simply the result of new 'imperial' functions being handed to the institutions by Whitehall. Rather, all proactively sought an expansion in their imperial roles. For example, a small coterie of academics and senior figures at the universities seized opportunities created by new wartime initiatives to secure an expanded role in training entrants for the British Colonial Service and maximize the resulting material advantages. Before and during the Second World War the Bank of England pursued a form of financial imperialism in promoting the interests of sterling. The wartime transformation of the sterling bloc, a loose association of countries that based their currencies on sterling, into the more tightly regulated 'sterling area' brought new responsibilities to the Bank and increased the importance of British control of colonial currencies and reserves. The Mint's situation was somewhat different. It exploited the commercial opportunities provided by an earlier decolonizing phase in Ireland and elsewhere and gained other new business from the introduction of regional currencies by colonial currency boards.

The ways in which these institutions negotiated and expanded their changing imperial roles consequently also reflected differences in their imperial cultures. Although these cultures do not lend themselves to any simple, or single, characterization, they were manifest in the manner in which individuals associated with different institutions sought to maximize opportunities within the Empire to their own or their institutions' benefit, within the context of a perception that, as it was expressed at the University of Oxford in 1942, 'on the whole the British Empire has been a beneficent Institution'.[1] Such cultures of imperialism were revealed when institutional personnel exhibited a sense of entitlement to shape developments overseas. To understand these institutional 'imperial cultures', we need to see the late 1940s and the early 1950s as contemporaries did: not, initially, as an 'era of decolonization' and associated national decline, but rather, especially in relation to Africa, as a period of on-going colonialism, albeit one increasingly viewed through the prism of development. The generation then occupying senior posts within institutions had advanced through the ranks during the interwar era, and, even once the political direction in postwar Africa became apparent, they sought to shape developments in the new Commonwealth as they had in the old.

---

[1] Bodleian Library, Oxford University Archives (hereafter OUA), UR 6/Col/6, Sir Douglas Veale to Sir Ralph Furse, 11 September 1942.

The Universities of Oxford and Cambridge and the Colonial Administrative Service

There is no better illustration of the revival of British imperial purpose in 1940s than the history of the Colonial Service; and it is this that enables us to understand the universities' role in the delivery of Service training. The post-1945 period might reasonably be considered the 'heyday' of the Service, historically less prestigious than the Indian Civil or Sudan Political Services.[2] Although its origins date back to 1837, the 'modern' Colonial Service had only developed between the world wars, beginning with the creation in 1930 of one unified Service from the amalgamation of a series of territorial services. This was followed by the formation of specialist or professional divisions within the Colonial Service, of which the Colonial Administrative Service was the first. The return of peace in 1945 saw rapid expansion as well as new initiatives to address problems with morale among officers in all branches of the Service, many of whom had endured difficult wartime conditions.[3] Thousands of new officers were recruited to fill posts left vacant during the war and to deliver new development plans. By the mid-1950s more than 18,000 regular officers were employed in over forty different territories, and there were in addition several thousand contract officers recruited by the Colonial Office and the Crown Agents for the Colonies. Most were still male, although the number of female recruits, especially to posts in education and nursing, also rose significantly.[4] The expansion in the technical and specialist branches was particularly striking, but the Administrative branch became an elite cadre.

Central to this reinvigoration of the Colonial Service was the introduction in 1946 of a new, enhanced training regime for the Administrative Service, taught at the Universities of Oxford, Cambridge and London. These 'Devonshire' courses replaced the existing probationers course based since 1926 at Oxford and Cambridge. The content of the interwar course reflected the diverse roles colonial officials then had to play, from those of the archetypal rural district officer or commissioner who maintained the peace and assessed and collected taxes, to those of functionaries posted to secretariats within colonial capitals. Accordingly, training included everything from introductions to English law, accountancy, surveying, Oriental and African languages, and tropical

---

[2] The Indian Civil Service supplied officials to Britain's dependencies in South Asia, and the Sudan Political Service to the Sudan. There was also a separate Malayan Civil Service.

[3] The National Archives (hereafter TNA), CO 847/25/47234, Memorandum on Native Administration Policy, by G. Cartland. See also, R. D. Pearce, 'Morale in the Colonial Service during the Second World War', *Journal of Imperial and Commonwealth History*, 11 (1983), pp. 175–96.

[4] Kirk-Greene, *On Crown Service*, table 2.4, p. 25, and pp. 29–31, ch. 3 esp. 50–1; D. A. Low and John Lonsdale, 'Towards the New Order, 1945–1963' in D. A. Low and A. Smith eds., *History of East Africa. Volume 3* (Oxford University Press, Oxford, 1976), pp. 1–63.

hygiene and medicine, to imperial history, anthropology and systems of 'native administration' and 'indirect rule' in British Africa.[5] Initially aimed at the tropical African colonies, this probationers course had been adapted to provide more systematic training for recruits in the new Administrative Service, in line with the introduction of other training courses for many of the other divisions.[6] The inauguration after the Second World War of the reformed Devonshire course built on this earlier training, but in addition prompted a variety of developments within the universities that deepened their investment in the Empire.

In focusing on this aspect of the Universities of Oxford and Cambridge's 'imperial role', we should not forget that this was inextricably bound up with a multiplicity of other imperial connections, which we should first consider. Of the two institutions, Oxford's associations with the Empire and Commonwealth were more pronounced, not least because in the second half of the nineteenth century Benjamin Jowett, Master of Balliol College, had helped develop a close association with the Indian Civil Service. Indeed, Oxford supplied more graduates to the imperial services than any other university. Many had studied Classical Greats, Oriental languages or history.[7] At both institutions British imperialism generated new scholarly interests and associations. Both had long-established expertise in Oriental languages, later the basis for Oriental Studies, which in turn helped foster new centres for South Asian and Middle Eastern Studies. An Indian Institute opened in Oxford in 1884, rapidly becoming the base for a university course for Indian Civil Service probationers,[8] while also an important focus for the University's South Asian students, contributing to what has been called Oxford's 'special place as a zone of Indian-British encounter' in the late Victorian and early Edwardian eras.[9]

Both universities accumulated particular expertise in a developing subfield of imperial and Commonwealth history, facilitated by the creation of academic posts funded by generous bequests. Distinct traditions emerged at each institution: although Oxford had its share of colonial critics, the holders of new posts in colonial studies became associated with the promotion of a 'Commonwealth Ideal', which the historian Ronald Robinson later identified as the distinguishing feature of the Oxford 'school' of Commonwealth history, as opposed to

[5] Prior, *Exporting Empire*, pp. 35–49.
[6] CO 877/22/13, 'An Inquiry into the system of training the Colonial Service with suggestions for its reform to meet post-war conditions', memo by Sir R. Furse reproduced in S. R. Ashton and S. E. Stockwell eds., *Imperial Policy and Colonial Practice, 1925–1945* (BDEE, Series A, Vol. 1, HMSO, 1996), Part 1, no. 5; Kirk-Greene, *On Crown Service*, p. 27.
[7] Reba Soffer, *Discipline and Power: The University, History and the Making of an English Elite, 1870–1930* (Stanford University Press, Stanford, CA, 1994), pp. 7–8.
[8] Richard Symonds, 'Oxford and India' in Madden and Fieldhouse eds., *Oxford and the Idea of Commonwealth*, pp. 49–72.
[9] Elleke Boehmer, *Indian Arrivals, 1870–1915. Networks of British Empire* (Oxford University Press, Oxford, 2015), pp. 101–9.

that at Cambridge, whose leading scholars were, he thought, more concerned with the processes of 'expansion'.[10]

The twentieth century also saw the emergence of the social sciences, in the British context deeply influenced by Empire.[11] In the interwar years anthropology was the discipline most intimately associated with imperialism, and became the pre-eminent social science in the analysis, classification and description of African societies. While the relationship between anthropologists and colonialism was a complex one,[12] its success at Oxford and Cambridge owed much to its appeal to aspirant members of Britain's imperial services.[13] In the 1930s some of the social sciences, especially economics and anthropology, secured a place in what came to be accepted as the 'science of colonial administration'. The latter was associated especially with the only two academics to hold posts directly in colonial administration: Lucy Mair, an anthropologist at the London School of Economics and Political Science (LSE) in London, and Oxford's Margery Perham. Perham was also a founder-fellow of the new graduate college, Nuffield College, which emerged as a base within Oxford for colonial and Commonwealth studies.[14] That it was the LSE that became the single most important academic centre for the new social sciences, with many of the most notable anthropologists of the day training there and contributing to its expertise within colonial studies,[15] however, fuelled growing resentment at London's exclusion from the probationers course during the interwar years.[16]

---

[10] Ronald Hyam, 'Imperial and Commonwealth History at Cambridge, 1881–1981: Founding Fathers and Pioneer Research Students', *Journal of Imperial and Commonwealth History*, 29 (2001), pp. 296–307; Ronald Robinson, 'Oxford in Imperial Historiography' in Madden and Fieldhouse eds., *Oxford and the Idea of Commonwealth*, pp. 30–48, esp. 38–46; Frederick Madden, 'The Commonwealth, Commonwealth History and Oxford, 1905–1971' in ibid., pp. 7–29, esp. 21.

[11] Demography was one, leading to the emergence of a subfield of 'colonial demography'. Karl Ittmann, *A Problem of Great Importance. Population, Race, and Power in the British Empire, 1918–1973* (University of California Press, Berkeley and Los Angeles, CA, 2013).

[12] These themes are explored in Tilley and Gordon eds. *Ordering Africa*, the introduction of which also provides an authoritative and thoughtful guide to the vast literature on the subject.

[13] Adam Kuper, *Anthropology and Anthropologists: The British School in the Twentieth Century* (Routledge, London, 4th edn., 2015; first published 1973), pp. 66–7; Brooke, *History of the University of Cambridge*, pp. 204–5.

[14] Dimier, 'Three Universities', esp. p. 351; Alison Smith and Mary Bull, 'Introduction' in Alison Smith and Mary Bull eds., *Margery Perham and British Rule in Africa* (Frank Cass, London, 1991), pp. 1–20. Perham's interest in colonial Africa had been sparked by visiting her sister and brother-in-law, the latter a district commissioner in British Somaliland in the 1920s.

[15] Kuper, *Anthropology and Anthropologists*, pp. 71, 73, 76.

[16] Academics there had already formed a committee on colonial studies and, during the war, at the Colonial Office's request the School began offering a colonial social sciences course. See [Archives of the] London School of Economics and Political Science [LSE], Central Filing Registry, Box 326, 288/3/C, Standing Committee on Colonial Studies, 1941–7, minutes 15 November 1946, item 4.

The development of the scientific and professional arms of the imperial services generated further institutional centres of expertise within Oxford and Cambridge. The Imperial Forestry Institute, funded by the Colonial Office, opened in Oxford, receiving the first forestry service probationers in 1924.[17] In contrast, Cambridge became more extensively involved in training those recruited to colonial agricultural posts. In 1925 scholarships were inaugurated for agriculturalists joining the Colonial Service, funding a year at the University's School of Agriculture, which after the war evolved into the Department of Land Economy, and a second at the Imperial College of Tropical Agriculture in Trinidad.[18] A Colonial Agricultural Service was formally established in 1935, and, after the war, the colonial agricultural probationers' course continued to be taught alongside the administrative probationers training course.

Above and beyond the association of different academic fields with entry to the imperial services, British academics were part of an extensive network – dubbed by Tamson Pietsch an 'empire of scholars' – that emerged from the 1870s, encouraged by improving communications, appointment processes and leave, and formalized with the creation of a Congress of Universities of the British Empire, which met for the first time in London in 1912. This circulation of academics and ideas intersected with other transnational academic networks, shaping academic practice and knowledge.[19] These flows of people were replicated at undergraduate and postgraduate levels and included growing numbers of South Asians at both universities in the later nineteenth century.[20] At Oxford, the inauguration in the early twentieth century of Rhodes scholarships to fund students from America and the Empire–Commonwealth[21] brought larger and more consistent numbers of overseas students and accounted for perhaps a third of all overseas students in Oxford in the 1930s.

Alongside the inauguration of the probationers course in 1926, these developments resulted in colonial studies emerging as 'perhaps the most important influence for enlarging and diversifying the University's research interests in the arts and social sciences'.[22] In John Darwin's assessment, the 'imperial connection' was not only 'more pervasive than the European', but

---

[17] Symonds, *Oxford and Empire*, pp. 132–7; Kirk-Greene, *On Crown Service*, p. 28.
[18] G. B. Masefield, *A History of the Colonial Agricultural Service* (Oxford University Press, Oxford, 1972), pp. 34–5, 42; Brooke, *History of the University of Cambridge*, p. 472.
[19] Pietsch, *Empire of Scholars*, pp. 4–5, 8, 199, appendix B. See also, Bennett and Hodge, *Science and Empire*; Helen Tilley, 'Introduction; African, Imperialism and Anthropology' in Tilley and Gordon eds., *Ordering Africa*, pp. 1–45, esp. 26. Pietsch notes that from 1888 universities within the Empire as well as others within Britain and foreign states were given affiliated status at Oxford.
[20] Boehmer, *Indian Arrivals*, p. 101.
[21] And until 1916 also from Germany.
[22] Paul R. Deslandes, '"The Foreign Element": Newcomers and the Rhetoric of Race, Nation and Empire in "Oxbridge" Undergraduate Culture, 1850–1920', *Journal of British Studies*, 37 (1998), pp. 54–90, esp. 60.

probably contributed more to Oxford's transformation over the twentieth century from an institution of 'global reputation' to 'a world university'.[23]

In line with the advance of social sciences and growing reliance on the 'expert', by the late 1930s scholars from Oxford, Cambridge and London were being appointed in greater numbers to the colonial advisory committees that proliferated from the 1920s. The appointees included several later involved both in delivering Colonial Service training and in post-war discussions about it, such as the historian Ronald Robinson, employed as a temporary principal in the Colonial Office. Another key figure was Sir Frank Engledow, Drapers' Professor of Agriculture at Cambridge, appointed to the Committee for Colonial Agricultural, Animal Health and Forestry Research created in 1945. Among the Colonial Office's principal scientific advisors, Engledow was one of a number of scientists whose Empire-focused research contributed to the strength of the imperial connection at Cambridge.[24] In the mid-twentieth century increased funding deepened these links between academics and the Colonial Office. From 1940 the Colonial Development and Welfare Act provided for £500,000 per annum to be spent on colonial research; in 1945 this sum was increased to £1 million and a new Colonial Social Science Research Council was created to administer it. Five years later the imperial government's interest in research was formalized with the inauguration of a separate Research Service as an umbrella organization for the employment of scientists within the Empire outside the professional branches of the service such as the veterinary or agricultural services.[25]

These developments made academics influential across a range of colonial policy, of which colonial higher education was one. Until the 1940s there were few higher education institutions in the colonial Empire outside India. During the war, however, steps were taken to change this, and the Asquith Commission on Higher Education in the Colonies appointed in 1943 recommended that British universities second staff to new colonial university colleges to drive their research and transition to full university status, extending British academic engagement with the Empire and Commonwealth.[26] The Inter-University

---

[23] Darwin, 'A World University', pp. 609–11, 615–17, 635–6.

[24] Heike Jöns, 'The University of Cambridge Academic Expertise and the British Empire, 1885–1962', *Environment and Planning,* 48 (2016), no. 1, pp. 94–114, esp. 103.

[25] Sabine Clarke argues this was to improve the status, and with it the recruitment, of scientific researchers attached to colonial governments: Sabine Clarke, ' "The Chance to Send Their First Class Men Out to the Colonies": The Making of the Colonial Research Service' in Brett M. Bennett and Joseph Hodge, eds., *Science and Empire: Knowledge and Networks of Science across the British Empire, 1800–1970* (Palgrave Macmillan, Basingstoke, 2011), pp. 187–208.

[26] 'Introduction' in Ashton and Stockwell eds., *Imperial Policy,* I, pp. lxxviii–lxxxi; See e.g. correspondence about filling posts at Makerere in: CUL, UA, Papers of the University General Board, GB 760/939, file 1944–1958. Smith and Bull, 'Introduction', p. 16; A. D. Roberts, 'The British Empire in Tropical Africa' in J. M. Brown and W. R. Louis eds., *Oxford History of the British Empire. Volume 4. Historiography* (Oxford History of the British Empire. Volume 4. Historiography), pp. 463–85, esp. 474–5; Toyin Falola, 'West Africa' in ibid., pp. 486–511, esp. 489.

Council for Higher Education in the Colonies (IUC) met for the first time in 1946, with Oxford's Margery Perham one of its key members.[27]

Such connections undoubtedly helped secure Oxford, Cambridge and London's post-war role in the delivery of the enhanced Colonial Service training regime, which in turn generated new vested interest in Empire within the universities. As we shall see, academics and senior figures at Oxford and Cambridge were instrumental in ensuring both the introduction of a new training course and their own place within it. They had a key role in wartime deliberations about future training. These were led by Sir Ralph Furse, Director of Service Recruitment at the Colonial Office 1930–48. Furse is widely seen as 'the father of the modern Colonial Service';[28] Oxford's registrar, Sir Douglas Veale, flattered him by even calling him 'the mastermind of the Colonial Empire'.[29] He had been instrumental in inaugurating the Service training at Oxford and Cambridge in 1926. Véronique Dimier argues that Furse did this not because he believed that probationers would acquire any specific knowledge, but because he hoped to attract the 'cream' of British elites, enhancing the standing of the Service relative to the home, Indian and foreign services.[30] He sought 'qualities of leadership' that he saw as 'essential to the proper handling of natives',[31] consistent with an emphasis on 'character', which in earlier periods especially had been seen as crucial to the construction of difference between ruler and ruled.[32] Furse was himself a Balliol man, strongly attached to Oxford. In 1942 he initiated consideration of future Service training and of the relative merits of continuing training within the universities when compared to the adoption of a dedicated staff college on the French or Belgian model, this alternative approach having been recently advocated in the House of Lords by Lord Trenchard, former Chief of the Air Staff.[33]

At Oxford, Perham and Veale more than any other individuals were central to the wartime discussions of Colonial Service training that Furse had

[27] A. H. M. Kirk-Greene, 'Forging a Relationship with the Colonial Administrative Service, 1921–1939' in A. Smith and M. Bull eds., *Margery Perham* (Frank Cass, London, 1991), pp. 62–82, esp. 63; C. Brad Faught, *Into Africa: The Imperial Life of Margery Perham* (I.B. Tauris, London, 2012), pp. 96–7.

[28] A. H. M. Kirk-Greene, 'Sir Ralph Furse', *Oxford Dictionary of National Biography*, www.oxforddnb.com, accessed 6 October 2015.

[29] Bodleian Library, Mss Brit. Emp. 415 (Furse papers), Box 10/1, folio 66, Veale to Furse, 9 June 1958.

[30] Dimier, 'Three Universities', p. 346.

[31] Cited Heussler, *Yesterday's Rulers*, pp. 36, 41.

[32] See esp., Kathryn Tidrick, *Empire and the English Character* (I.B. Tauris, London, 1990), p. 47; Steven Patterson, *The Cult of Imperial Honor in British India* (Palgrave Macmillan, New York, 2009), pp. 39, 46. E. M. Collingham, *Imperial Bodies: The Physical Experience of the Raj* (Cambridge University Press, Cambridge, 2001), p. 117.

[33] Kirk-Greene, *On Crown Service*, p. 43; CO 877/22/13, 'An Inquiry into the system of training the Colonial Service with suggestions for its reform to meet post-war conditions', memo by Furse, reproduced in Ashton and Stockwell eds., *Imperial Policy*, I, no. 5, note 2.

initiated. Like Furse, Veale's career straddled the universities and the state. He was a former high-flying civil servant; in this earlier career he had coined the term 'British Commonwealth of Nations' during discussions over the 1921 Anglo-Irish treaty.[34] Now University Registrar, Veale was its senior administrative figure, credited as the 'principal architect of the modern Oxford University' through a position he retained until his retirement in 1958.[35] Before the war he had also been involved in delivery of the Oxford probationers course.[36] Together with colleagues from Cambridge, Veale and Perham argued from the outset against the staff college model. Colonial academic subjects, they argued, were 'more likely to flourish when they are not isolated but are specialized branches growing from some main tree of knowledge'.[37] In February 1943 Perham and Veale helped Furse draft a memorandum for a committee to consider further training chaired by the Duke of Devonshire and including representatives of the Colonial Office, Oxford and Cambridge.[38] Furse's memorandum proposed a three-part system. The first element would essentially comprise the continuation of the existing pre-Service training. This would be followed a few years later by a second course of study in Britain that would, he hoped, offer an opportunity to 'check, criticize, and clarify' the experiences cadets had gained, and to counteract the '"bolshevist" tendencies' which were most 'common about the fifth and seventh year of service'. Finally, Furse suggested an opportunity for advanced study for selected high-flying officers.[39] The University of London, whose exclusion from the administrative probationers course in the interwar years had become a source of resentment, was also brought into the discussion.[40]

When published in 1946 the Devonshire Report departed little from Furse's proposals, concluding in favour of the continuation of Colonial Administrative Service training at Oxford and Cambridge. It recommended London participate in the scheme.[41] The proposed new training comprised a year-long

---

[34] E. T. Williams, rev. by H. G. Judge, 'Sir Douglas Veale', *Oxford Dictionary of National Biography*, www.oxforddnb.com, accessed 6 October 2015.

[35] Bodleian, OUA, UR 6/Col/16. file 1, Brief for the Vice-Chancellor, 1 August 1953.

[36] Nile Gardiner, 'Sentinels of Empire', p. 49.

[37] Circular memo by Perham and Veale, 28 November 1942, cited in Heussler, *Yesterday's Rulers*, p. 140.

[38] CO 877/22/13, 'An Inquiry into the system of training the Colonial Service with suggestions for its reform to meet post-war conditions', memo by Furse, reproduced in Ashton and Stockwell eds., *Imperial Policy*, I, no. 5.

[39] Ibid.

[40] Dimier, 'Three Universities', pp. 349–56.

[41] *Post-War Training for the Colonial Service: Report of a Committee Appointed by the Secretary of State for the Colonies*, Col. No. 198 (HMSO, London, 1946); Heussler, *Yesterday's Rulers*, p. 162.

Figure 1.1. Group photo, the Colonial Administrative Service 'First Devonshire' Course (Course 'A'), the University of Cambridge, 1947

course, the 'First Devonshire' (later course 'A'), and a 'Second Devonshire Course' (later 'B'), intended for those who had already served a few years overseas. Furse suggested that the first course might be taught principally at Oxford and Cambridge, with probationers moving to the LSE or the School of Oriental and African Studies (SOAS) in London at the end of the Oxbridge academic year for a further three months' intensive language and further training.[42] The First Devonshire Course (see Figure 1.1) was taught for the first time at the three universities the same year, financed by the 1945 Colonial Development and Welfare Act.[43] A joint standing committee of the three universities and the Colonial Office was established to oversee the management of the courses.[44]

[42] Kirk-Greene, *On Crown Service*, p. 43.
[43] *Post-War Training*.
[44] See papers on CUL, UA, GB 760/939, files 1942–4 and 1944–58.

The expansion of Colonial Studies more generally at the three universities was an explicit aim of the Devonshire recommendations, corresponding to concern within the Colonial Office about widespread public ignorance of, and apathy towards, British colonialism.[45] Furse's vision of post-war training was distinctly ideological, designed to disseminate 'a truer appreciation of colonial conditions and problems' across British society by means of more 'effective contact' between serving officers and 'opinion and home'. New entrants to the Service needed to be given a 'just sense of the importance and value of the work' on which they were engaged. Writing in the wake of the defeats in the Far East, Furse feared that 'One of our great dangers at the moment is the loss of confidence in ourselves as a colonial power. We should do well to fortify our young officers against this danger and against ill-informed and defeatist criticism'.[46] That Oxford was well placed to help in such an objective was one argument used by Veale when making the case for the continued location of training at the University as opposed to its removal to a specialist staff college. At Oxford, cadets would be exposed to what he described as 'objective' scholarly assessments of Britain's imperial record, but would still believe in 'the value of what they are doing ... that on the whole the British Empire has been a beneficent Institution'.[47]

Such comments bear testimony to the pervasive nature of imperial ideologies in the period, including at the universities (although the academics engaged with these discussions were commonly associated with a more developmental colonialism).[48] In addition, the commencement of the new training regime generated more material connections. Strikingly, even before the inauguration of the Devonshire training programme, those with interests in the area at the three institutions were already exploiting the opportunities it presented, alongside those resulting from the research element of the Colonial Development and Welfare Act.

Perham and Veale were particularly well placed to exploit these openings. Perham proposed a number of lectureships in colonial subjects, and drew the University's attention to the potential for securing new funds for colonial research. As early as 1942 Veale put in an application to the Colonial Development Fund to finance a colonial studies programme.[49] A new high-powered Committee for Colonial Studies was formed at Oxford the following

[45] CO 859/5/13, Minutes by J. W. Gittens, H. Vischer, C. G. Eastwood and G. L. M. Clauson on education in the United Kingdom about the colonial Empire, 17 July–1 August 1939, reproduced in Ashton and Stockwell eds., *Imperial Policy*, I, no. 1.
[46] CO 877/22/13, 'An Inquiry into the system of training the Colonial Service with suggestions for its reform to meet post-war conditions', memo by Furse, reproduced in ibid., no. 5.
[47] Bodleian, OUA, UR 6/Col/6, Veale to Furse, 11 September 1942.
[48] This was the case with, for example, Perham.
[49] Heussler, *Yesterday's Rulers*, pp. 136–7, 143.

year; members included the University's Vice-Chancellor. Two years later an Institute of Colonial Studies was established in anticipation of the University's future role in the Devonshire Courses. Perham was appointed first director.[50]

At Cambridge a coalition of individuals with academic interests within the Empire and Commonwealth and senior university figures (including some who were both) was similarly quick to appreciate the potential opportunities. Among those with immediately relevant academic interests were Engledow and J. H. Hutton, an ex-Indian Civil Servant and Professor of Anthropology, as well as the historians Ernest Benians, until 1941 the University's vice-chancellor and the key figure in the development of imperial history at Cambridge in the first half of the twentieth century, and Eric Walker, Vere Harmsworth Professor of Imperial and Naval History.[51] In 1942 the two historians urged that new administrative cadets must be educated in the history, values and opportunities of the Empire so as to properly understand the 'significance of their career'.[52] Among the senior University officers were the agriculturalist and historian, John Venn, president of Queens' College and Benian's successor as vice chancellor, as well as an advisor to the Ministry of Agriculture; J. T. Saunders, University Registrar; and Thomas Knox-Shaw, Treasurer of the University, who was also a trustee of the Cambridge Mission to Delhi and a very active committee member of the Universities' Mission to Central Africa.[53] In December 1943 these men urged the University authorities to establish a committee to consider the future provision of colonial studies. 'The administration and development of the Colonial Empire', they wrote, was

one of the greatest of British problems to-day. Apart from our responsibility towards Colonial Peoples, in the discharge of which we shall be judged by the rest of the world, the power and influence of the British people throughout the world, depends to a considerable extent, upon the development of the large dispersed dependent empire. In the tasks which it involves, the Home Universities will be called upon to play an important part.[54]

---

[50] When in 1948 Perham and F. B. H. Drummond, Administrative Secretary to the Institute, both resigned (Perham to concentrate on her study of Lugard) a Committee of Management (comprising the Beit Professor of the History of the British Empire, the Registrar and the Reader in Colonial Administration) assumed responsibility for the Institute until the appointment in 1951 of a new Director, Sir Reader Bullard: Smith and Bull, 'Introduction' p. 14.

[51] Hyam, 'Imperial and Commonwealth History at Cambridge', pp. 498; https://en.wikipedia.org/wiki/Eric_A._Walker_(historian), accessed 6 October 2015.

[52] CUL, UA, GB 760/939, file 1942–5, 'Training for the Colonial Service', note of a meeting, 17 June 1942.

[53] John D. Pickles, 'John Archibald Venn (1883–1958)', *Oxford Dictionary of National Biography*. Venn was son of mathematician John Venn, and, with his father, compiled a prosopography of Cambridge alumni. After the war he was appointed first honorary keeper of the University archives. Saunders was later principal of the University College at Ibadan 1954–60.

[54] CUL, UA, GB 760/939, file 1942–5, 'The University and the Colonial Empire', December 1943.

A new Colonial Studies Committee was duly fashioned from the existing Colonial Service Probationers Committee.

There were similar moves in the University of London. Here the LSE, SOAS and Institute of Education (where in 1927 the Colonial Office had established a department of education in tropical areas to train those appointed to colonial educational posts) hoped to share in the spoils.[55] The University created a new Institute of Empire Studies, which opened as the Institute of Commonwealth Studies (ICS) in 1949.[56] Concurrent developments contributed to the expansion within London of the related field of area studies. Following the recommendations of the 1947 Scarborough Report on Oriental, Eastern European, Slavonic and African Studies in Britain, steps were taken to broaden tuition on language courses by adding lectures on area politics, economies and sociology and Islamic and African customary law, thus transforming the fortunes of the School of Oriental and African Studies.[57]

The inauguration of the new training programme brought small but significant new funding streams to the universities that enabled them to support new research and teaching. In all, in 1947–8 Oxford received just under £8,000, Cambridge nearly £5,500, and London over £18,000. By 1950–1 Oxford received more than £14,000, Cambridge over £10,500 and London in excess of £11,000.[58] The arrangements were not without costs, not least those entailed by delivering tailor-made arrangements for a very small student cohort, resident for a shorter period of time than other students. Reliance on external funds tied to recruitment to particular courses also presented difficulties. Even so, for the academic staff at each institution, access to new funds targeted at specific disciplines was potentially transformative.

[55] 'Introduction' in Ashton and Stockwell eds., *Imperial Policy*, I, pp. lxxxiii and ci, note 157; Archives of the University of London [UoL], Senate House Library, London, ICS 85/D/36, memo submitted by the Institute of Education to the Bridges Committee, paper TPA (62) 69. A five-month course for Colonial Service medical officers was provided at the London School of Hygiene and Tropical Medicine, established in 1924: Kirk-Greene, *On Crown Service*, p. 28.

[56] UoL, AC 1/1/45, minutes 27 September 1948, no. 29; AC 1/1/46, minutes 27 March 1950, nos. 862–3; ICS 85/D/33, memo submitted by the Institute of Commonwealth Studies to the Bridges Committee, paper TPA (62) 53.

[57] UoL, ICS 85/D/34, memo submitted by SOAS to the Bridges Committee, paper TPA (62) 54. See also, *Bulletin* of SOAS, obituary: I owe this reference to Felix Driver. Scarborough was chairman of SOAS from 1951–59.

[58] Bodleian, OUA, UR6, COL/4/1, 'Estimates of Payments Required by the University of Oxford from the CD&W Vote, 1947–8', Table: 'Payment to Universities. Distribution of Expenditure by Academic Years'. Provision for posts to support language tuition for the Devonshire courses at SOAS was subsumed within the additional resource that SOAS won following the Scarborough recommendations, and is excluded from this calculation. Oxford's own estimates for 1947–8 had been for £9,838, and it is not clear whether the Colonial Office refused to meet this sum in full or whether the estimates were later revised.

There was therefore competition between the three universities.[59] At Cambridge in January 1945 Engledow was taken aback to see Oxford propose not just a new post, but a full readership in Colonial Native Agriculture, an area he perceived as falling very much within his own institution's expertise.[60] However, it was between Oxbridge and London that the greater tensions arose, with the latter sometimes seen as an unwelcome interloper. In 1949 the establishment of London's new ICS provoked irritation, perhaps because it was perceived as potential competition for Oxford's own new institute. London's vice chancellor was moved to write 'frankly' to Oxford's after the LSE's director, Sir Alexander Carr-Saunders, complained to her that Oxford was 'showing an intention to interfere in the affairs of the University of London'.[61]

The same year saw the issue of London's role again highlighted as the Colonial Office reviewed the training regime. It had become apparent that the existing arrangement for the first course imposed particular burdens on London. With students from Oxford and Cambridge transferring to the capital for a fourth and final term, academic staff at the LSE and SOAS found that they were responsible for teaching students in the long vacation; this had adverse consequences for their research.[62] Both Oxford and Cambridge agreed to the Colonial Office's proposal that the fourth 'London' term be eliminated and instead that students should be taught a full course at each of the three universities, but only on the condition that, as the Oxford delegate put it, the 'financial side was safeguarded'.[63] The Colonial Office was thus required to guarantee a minimum of thirty students for Oxford and Cambridge, respectively, for each of the next three years, a promise from which the Colonial Office had subsequently and swiftly to retreat. Following the rearrangements, the distribution of students between institutions was to be determined by the match between their individual requirements and what else the universities offered, especially in relation to languages.[64] This ensured that, despite the Colonial Office's pledge, from 1949 London attracted the lion's share. This led to new protests from the other universities, and despite London's particular expertise in African

---

[59] As Dimier also argues in the best existing account of the early history of the courses: Dimier, *Le Gouvernement des Colonies*.

[60] CUL, UA, GB 760/939, file 1942–5, Professor Sir Frank Engledow to J. T. Saunders, Registry, University of Cambridge, 8 January 1945.

[61] The precise nature of the conflict is unclear from the extant correspondence. LSE, Central Filing Registry, Box 327, 288/3/C, the Colonial Studies Committee, letters from Carr-Saunders to Dame Lillian Penson (VC), 18 January 1949, 19 January 1949, and Penson to Carr-Saunders, 21 January 1949.

[62] CUL, UA, GBR/0265/CDEV 11/1, 5th Minutes of the Standing Joint Committee of the Universities on Colonial Service Training, 30 July 1948.

[63] Ibid., Minutes of special meeting, 29 January 1949.

[64] Ibid.; see also Sir Charles Jeffries (CO) to Mr. J. T. Saunders (Secretary General to the Faculties, Cambridge University), 7 February 1949.

languages, to further modifications under which the Colonial Office agreed to send students to Oxford and Cambridge, in some cases regardless of the students' specific language needs, and to the development of additional language tuition at both institutions. The sudden withdrawal of students previously allocated to London forced the cancellation of courses at the LSE only three weeks before the start of term. It was 'intolerable', Carr-Saunders complained to the Colonial Office, that this change had been made following consultation with Oxford and Cambridge only, while the director of SOAS, Ralph Turner, wondered why officials had managed to consult with colleagues at distant Oxford and Cambridge, but not found time to speak to those in London.[65]

In the first half of the twentieth century, at a point when they were not yet competing with newer higher educational institutions, Britain's oldest universities had thus gained resources and interest in colonial studies, and had come to see the area as a source of opportunity as well as prestige. But by 1952 there was growing concern in different quarters about features of the Devonshire training system. Oxbridge's lurking fears about the erosion of its role coincided with anxieties among colonial administrations about the suitability of what was on offer. At this juncture, colonial political change in British Africa introduced a further set of complications. These issues would lead to a major review of the training system in 1953 during which several senior figures at Cambridge, and especially Oxford, would fight to maintain the financial rewards gained from the Devonshire courses.[66]

The Bank of England

At the beginning of the twentieth century the Bank of England was already at 'the Heart of the Empire', the title of artist Neil Lund's 1904 painting of the Bank of England, the City of London's Mansion House and the Royal Exchange.[67] The Bank's role in Britain's imperial and international financial system reflected the City's position as the world's leading financial and trading centre and sterling's rise as an international currency. During the nineteenth century the majority of Britain's self-governing colonies, as well as many foreign states, reliant on raising capital in the City and on conducting their external trade with Britain or via British markets, had adopted sterling

---

[65] LSE, Central Filing Registry, Box 327, 288/3/C, Standing Committee on Colonial Studies, 1947–9, memo on the effects of changes to the courses sent by Turner to Sir A. Carr-Saunders, 8 December 1949; 288/3/D, review of changes to course and their impact on LSE, Appendix 1, to agenda for meeting, 16 January 1950. As also quoted in Dimier, *Le gouvernement des colonies*, p. 58.

[66] See below pp. 98–105.

[67] Iain Black, 'Imperial Visions. Rebuilding the Bank of England, 1919–1939' in Felix Driver and David Gilbert eds., *Imperial Cities* (Manchester University Press, Manchester, 1999), pp. 96–113.

or linked their own currencies to it,[68] and in the late nineteenth century many followed the British practice of making their currencies convertible into gold. After the First World War sterling's role was reinforced when the international gold standard gave way to one in which London and New York became centres for a gold-exchange standard and central banks other than the Bank of England and the New York Federal Reserve Bank held their reserves in either sterling or dollar-denominated assets.

Yet developments in the mid-twentieth century, and specifically the emergence first of an informal sterling 'bloc' and later of a sterling area, would reinforce the importance to the Bank of the Empire and Commonwealth, even as these developments also reflected Britain's growing economic weakness. The emergence of the sterling bloc followed Britain's departure from the gold-exchange standard in 1931. Sterling became a floating currency, and many countries that held their reserves in sterling, or which had strong financial connections to Britain, opted to retain a fixed exchange rate with sterling so that their currencies followed sterling on foreign-exchange markets. The Empire and Commonwealth was at the heart of this informal bloc even though the latter extended beyond it; of British dominions, only Canada and Newfoundland chose to link their currencies to the dollar rather than sterling.[69] The outbreak of the Second World War prompted a further transformation: the development of the 'sterling area'. Acting as agent for the Treasury, the Bank oversaw a system of exchange control that fashioned the loose association of states basing their currencies on sterling into the closely managed sterling area. Since at this point most foreign states detached their currencies from sterling, the sterling area now focused squarely on the Empire and Commonwealth, although it still included a few other countries such as Egypt and Iraq.[70] Members accumulated 'sterling balances' as a result of import and foreign-exchange restrictions, as well as a form of credit for British purchases for wartime supplies and services. The apparatus of the sterling area became in effect a system of financing some of the costs of war.

In the interwar years the promotion of sterling's international role provided the context for a second, related, dimension of the Bank's involvement in empire: its promotion of central banking in the dominions, India and elsewhere. In the nineteenth century the Bank had been the first in Europe to serve as banker to government and, with principal note-issuing rights, to assume the

---

[68] P. L. Cottrell, 'The Bank in Its International Setting' in Richard Roberts and David Kynaston eds., *The Bank of England: Money, Power and Influence, 1694-1994* (Clarendon Press, Oxford, 1995), pp. 83–139, esp. p. 86; M. H. De Kock, *Central Banking* (London, 3rd edn., 1954); John Singleton, *Central Banking in the Twentieth Century* (Cambridge University Press, Cambridge, 2011), p. 47. The following is based principally upon these accounts.

[69] Schenk, *Britain and the Sterling Area*, p. 8.

[70] Paul Bareau, 'The Sterling Area' in R. Sayers ed., *Banking in the British Commonwealth* (Clarendon Press, Oxford, 1952), pp. 460–85, esp. 464.

functions that became associated with central banks. By the twentieth century these functions included the stewardship of the reserves of commercial banks and the role of lender of last resort.[71] Still a relatively new phenomenon, it was not until the 1920s that the term 'central banking' became commonly used to describe this role. More central banks were established following a recommendation by the 1920 League of Nations financial conference, which hoped that they would serve as instruments of internal economic stabilization and development, as well as advancing international financial co-operation.

Under its long-serving (1920–44) governor, Sir Montagu Norman, the Bank of England played a part in the creation of many of these new central banks. Within the Bank this evolving international role led to the creation of new departments to manage relations with other central banks[72] and to an accumulation of expertise on overseas affairs among the senior personnel.[73] In what, as others have argued, was effectively a form of financial imperialism,[74] Norman hoped through the development of central banking to cement the Bank of England's position and to promote sterling as a hard currency, encouraging other central banks to use it as a reserve currency by offering interest on their accounts. He also hoped that the Bank's position would help advance liberal capitalism and champion the English model of a privately owned central bank independent of government control.[75] Norman aimed through the Bank to foster a transnational professional community of central bankers that might co-operate to act independently of their own national governments, an ambition informed by his own experience of the gradual subordination of the Bank's control over monetary policy to the Treasury. The more that central banks formed on an English model were allowed to operate with relative autonomy, the more likely they were, as P. J. Cain and A. G. Hopkins have observed, to rely on Bank of England advice.[76]

Britain's departure from the gold standard and the formation of the sterling bloc increased the importance of British and dominion financial co-operation through central banks during the 1930s. The Bank's encouragement of the

---

[71] Cairncross, 'The Bank of England', pp. 56–82.
[72] Hennessy, 'The Governors, Directors and Management'; Kynaston, 'The Bank and the Government'; Cottrell, 'Bank in Its International Setting'. The discussion which follows of the interwar and war years draws on Cottrell's account.
[73] John Fforde, *Bank of England and Public Policy, 1941–1958* (Cambridge University Press, Cambridge, 1992), pp. 1–3.
[74] A. F. W. Plumptre, *Central Banking in British Dominions* (University of Toronto Press, Toronto, 1940), pp. 192–3; P. J. Cain, 'Gentlemanly Imperialism at Work: The Bank of England, Canada, and the Sterling Area, 1932–1936', *The Economic History Review*, New Series, 49 (1996), pp. 336–57; Cain and Hopkins, *British Imperialism*.
[75] R. S. Sayers, 'Introduction' in R. S. Sayers ed., *Banking in the British Commonwealth* (Clarendon Press, Oxford, 1952), pp. vii–xviii; C. G. F. Simkin, 'Banking in New Zealand' in ibid., pp. 320–49, esp. 332.
[76] Cain and Hopkins, *British Imperialism*, pp. 476–8.

development of central banking hence became increasingly focused on the Empire and Commonwealth and states in South America, part of a residual British 'informal' empire.[77] Central-banking collaboration took a distinct form within the Commonwealth, evidence of the continuation of the kind of networks identified as underpinning a 'British World' economy in earlier periods.[78] Already in the 1920s Norman had appointed a director expressly to promote central banking in the Dominions and India and had provided advisors to assist with the formation of the new banks in Australia, Canada and New Zealand, as well as Argentina and El Salvador. From November 1928 the Bank began producing regular fortnightly letters to central banks in the Empire, and in 1937 the occasion of George VI's coronation provided the opportunity to convene a London conference of their governors.[79] Staff at the Bank of England were seconded to fill many of the senior posts within these central banks, including the first governorships of the new South African and New Zealand reserve banks.[80] The traffic did not run all in one direction, however, as Commonwealth bankers were appointed as advisers to the Bank of England, ranking below executive directors, its most senior executive layer.[81]

The Bank's interwar commitment to Commonwealth central-banking networks is vital for understanding its approach to the development of central banking in emergent states after the war. The Bank's files reveal that in the 1950s its personnel acted in ways that reflected their own confident, almost self-aggrandizing, understanding of the Bank's earlier role, perhaps refracted through some of the early scholarship of the time that bought into the idea of the Bank's suzerainty over Commonwealth banking.[82] In reality there had been tensions between Threadneedle Street and the new dominion central banks, evidence of disintegrative currents that ran counter to what appear otherwise to be integrative trends represented by the evolution of the sterling bloc. While Anglo–Dominion relations were embedded in a shared British culture, and the dominions' financial dependence on London certainly gave the Bank some leverage, the dominions had not always welcomed London's efforts to guide Commonwealth banking, and the Bank's manner towards them tended to be high-handed.[83] Nor was the British model necessarily seen as appropriate to the dominions' own very different economic conditions. New Commonwealth

---

[77] Ibid.

[78] Magee and Thompson, *Empire and Globalisation*, p. 17; Andrew Dilley, *Finance, Politics and Imperialism: Australia, Canada and the City of London, 1896–1914* (Palgrave Macmillan, Basingstoke, 2012).

[79] Cottrell, 'Bank in Its International Setting', p. 107; BoE, OV 21/25, no. 8, note from G. E. H. (Overseas Office) to Mr. Parker, 18 May 1961.

[80] Ibid., Singleton, *Central Banking*, p. 64.

[81] Bareau, 'The Sterling Area', p. 473.

[82] Plumptre, *Central Banking*; Singleton, *Central Banking*, pp. 61–2.

[83] Cain, 'Gentlemanly Imperialism', p. 337.

central-banking systems were not structures on which the British could straight-forwardly inscribe their own practices, but had been shaped by local political and economic dynamics.[84] Other developments had also weakened the Bank of England's ability to exercise influence, with the Bank's private-shareholding model of central banking increasingly questioned. The failure of estab-lished central banks to manage the problems of the Great Depression years – including in Britain, where Norman's efforts to stick to the gold standard were perceived as contributing to domestic unemployment – had seen opin-ion incline towards more ministerial control over central banking. Keynsian economics with their emphasis on the state's role in managing economies and ensuring full employment added to the growing conviction that monetary man-agement was too important to be left to independent central banks. Banks on the British shareholding model were consequently sometimes short-lived: in both Canada and New Zealand private ownership persisted for only a couple of years before the central banks were nationalized.[85]

During the war the Bank of England assumed a new role in relation to Britain's colonial dependencies through its involvement on colonial cur-rency boards. Until the 1950s there were no central banks or other national monetary authorities in the colonial Empire other than in India, and instead money was issued by regional colonial currency boards. In Africa these were the West African Currency Board (WACB) and the East African Currency Board (EACB), formed in 1912 and 1919, respectively, and the Southern Rhodesian Currency Board (SRCB) created in 1938, which also supplied currency to its colonial neighbours Nyasaland and Northern Rhodesia.[86] Little more than local variations of sterling, their currencies were generally fully backed by sterling assets in London and exchangeable with sterling.[87] This could lead to the accumulation of substantial reserves.

---

[84] As Angela Redish cautions, where new banks were established along a British model this should not necessarily be interpreted as evidence of the Bank's success. Rather, she suggests that 'a greater role' was played by 'decision-makers at the "periphery"': Angela Redish, 'British Financial Imperialism after the First World War' in R. E. Dumett ed., *Gentlemanly Capitalism and British Imperialism: The New Debate on Empire* (Longman, London, 1999), pp. 127–40.

[85] G. S. Dorrance, 'The Bank of Canada' in R. S. Sayers ed., *Banking in the British Commonwealth* (Clarendon Press, Oxford, 1952), pp. 121–49, esp. 135–6; Simkin, 'Banking in New Zealand', p. 333.

[86] J. B. Loynes, *The West African Currency Board, 1912–1962* (Eyre and Spottiswoode, London, 1962), p. 2.

[87] W. T. Newlyn, *Money and Banking in British Colonial Africa. A Study of the Monetary and Banking Systems of Eight African Territories* (Clarendon Press, Oxford, 1954) p. 50, table 1; pp. 57–9, table VII; R. A. Sowelem, *Towards Financial Independence in a Developing Economy: An Analysis of the Monetary Experience of the Federation of Rhodesia and Nyasaland, 1952–1963* (George Allen and Unwin, London, 1967), pp. 24–5. From 1947 the SRCB, which, unlike the London-run WACB and EACB, was locally domiciled and led, was uniquely permitted to invest in local government stock.

By 1951 the sterling assets of the WACB surpassed £90 million, and the Board was generating a gross annual income of £2.5 million.[88]

Initially the boards had comprised representatives of the Crown Agents, the Colonial Office, the Treasury and the commercial banks. However, the retirement of the commercial banking member from the WACB in 1942 provided an opportunity for the inclusion of a representative of the Bank of England.[89] When another vacancy arose the following year, in this case on the Palestine Currency Board, the Colonial Office proposed the inclusion of Bank representatives as standard on all the colonial currency authorities alongside the Colonial Office and Crown Agent representatives. The Colonial Office now sought the removal of commercial bank representatives, whose involvement it believed raised too many political difficulties, especially in West Africa, where it might be obliged to select a 'native'.[90] Perhaps because of the Bank's own view of appropriate relations between the state and financial institutions, Norman regarded the proposal to exclude the only representatives with local business or financial knowledge as 'undemocratic – worthy of Nazi' even though, as he commented, the Colonial Office was 'waving the flag of democracy in most countries'. But he was happy to agree to the Bank's participation,[91] and, as the importance of the colonial role in the sterling area increased after the war, the Bank appeared to attach greater importance to its role on the boards, and indeed came to shoulder responsibility for them.[92]

By the end of the war the British and international financial landscapes had been transformed. Britain's reserves had been depleted and enormous debts accumulated in the form of sterling balances. In 1945 an American loan was agreed to ease Britain through its acute financial difficulties. International financial power had now shifted decisively away from Britain and towards America. At Bretton Woods in 1944, the Treasury had signed up to an American vision of a multilateral global financial order involving the construction of new international monetary authorities under the auspices of the nascent United Nations: the International Monetary Fund (IMF) and the International Bank for Reconstruction and Development (IBRD), more commonly known as the 'World Bank'. Both organizations were intended among other things to facilitate international monetary co-operation and collaboration

---

[88] BoE, OV67/1, memo prepared by R. N. Kershaw for the Governor or the Bank, 19 December 1951.

[89] Loynes, *West African Currency Board*, pp. 12–18, 29.

[90] BoE, G1/202, nos. 60L, 61, 63, 65: George Gater to Norman, 28 May 1943; Norman to Gater, 4 June 1963; Gater to Norman, 18 June 1943; note 'London Currency Boards', addressed to Norman, 11 June 1943; Oliver Stanley to Norman, 23 August 1943;

[91] Ibid., nos. 73, 76: Oliver Stanley to Norman, 23 August 1943; 'Colonial Currency Boards', confidential note, 19 July 1943; Norman's annotation, 27 June 1943, on 'Colonial Currency Boards', 25 June 1943.

[92] BoE, OV 7/81, 'Aide Memoire' prepared by Loynes, 15 October 1959.

between governments, corresponding to a growing desire, especially in the United States Treasury, to see control of international finance pass from central bankers to governments, entailing a shift in power from the City of London and Wall Street to the United States Treasury.

One of the first acts of Attlee's Labour government was to nationalize the Bank, but despite nationalization, or perhaps because of it, continuity was the order of the day at the Bank amongst a generation of senior personnel whose outlook remained shaped by the long 'Norman era'. Norman himself had accepted that ultimate authority over monetary and exchange rate policy lay with governments. Nonetheless, Norman's successors, Lord Catto (governor, 1944–9) and Cameron Cobbold (1949–61), were resolved to avoid subordination to the state and to preserve the Bank's traditional role as the exclusive representative of the City to government. All told, the Bank's culture remained insular, and it was not until after Cobbold's departure that this began to change, and the Bank became more subject to government policy-making.[93]

As it sought to negotiate this hostile post-war financial and international environment, the Bank came to have 'a new-found confidence in the peacetime potentialities of the wartime sterling area':[94] in Britain's reduced economic circumstances the Empire and sterling area were of continued, and indeed, enhanced importance to the Bank. From summer 1947, after an abortive attempt to reintroduce sterling convertibility in line with the terms of the American loan, Britain retreated into the closed economic order of the sterling area. Alongside Malaya, the African colonies – where Britain could still exert control – were crucial to this sterling system. By pooling colonial dollar earnings in London and tightly restricting colonial dollar spending, Britain profited from the dollar-trading activities of the colonies, offsetting its own foreign trade deficit and acute dollar famine. The 'Bank of England, the custodian of the gold and dollar pool', sat, as John Singleton observes, 'like a spider at the centre of this web'.[95] Despite some short-term relief from Marshall Aid in 1948 and sterling devaluation the following year, the problems posed by the dollar gap continued to bedevil the British economy into the early 1950s, and ensured the ongoing importance of the Empire-sterling area. Controls were gradually liberalized in the 1950s, but it was not until 1958 that full convertibility was finally achieved.

Until then, upholding London's control over colonial and ex-colonial sterling balances remained important, and, as we shall see, led the Bank first to oppose, and then to try and exercise control over, the creation of national and central banks and currencies within the colonial Empire. 'Preaching the

---

[93] Kynaston, 'The Bank and the Government', p. 51; Singleton, *Central Banking,* pp. 117–19; Capie, *Bank of England.*

[94] Fforde, *The Bank of England,* p. 40.

[95] Singleton, *Central Banking,* p. 155.

sterling area gospel' would become a key consideration shaping the Bank's response to African colonial political change, leading to striking and significant interventions in British colonies and former colonies, and to initiatives that have left lasting legacies within the Bank itself.

The Mint

The Royal Mint has attracted little attention from historians of imperialism. Yet it has been judged to have been by 1914 'one of the great institutions of the British Empire'.[96] Although, as we shall see, a decline in its direct involvement in some parts of the Empire, specifically the old Commonwealth, would occur in the middle decades of the twentieth century, these years would nevertheless see the colonial Empire, including Britain's African colonies, assume an enhanced commercial importance to the Mint.

Before the early nineteenth century the Royal Mint's role was largely domestic.[97] Britain's North American colonies had gained the right to issue their own coinage, which they sourced from a variety of places, while in South Asia the East India Company had been allowed since the late seventeenth century to 'purchase' permission from local Indian rulers to reproduce coins that followed Indian as opposed to English conventions. For the Mint itself the eighteenth century was a period of relative stagnation: British silver and copper coinage was in a poor condition and was in short supply. By the turn of the century a failure to keep up with new technology meant that the Mint trailed behind Matthew Boulton's new plant in Soho, Birmingham, a private mint that opened in the late eighteenth century to manufacture small-value copper coins, which the Royal Mint declined to produce.[98] The end of the Napoleonic wars, however, was followed by currency reform and in 1816–17 recoinage in Britain. In 1818 private coins were made illegal.[99] The Mint, which was still based within the Tower of London, moved to new premises a stone's throw away on Tower Hill. The installation of Boulton's steam-powered machinery, coupled with a French invention, the 'reducing machine', which reproduced original coin designs by machine rather than by hand engraving, enabled for the first time the mass production of high-quality and homogeneous copper

[96] G. P. Dyer and P. P. Gaspar, 'Reform, the New Technology and Tower Hill 1700–1966' in C. E. Challis ed., *A New History of the Royal Mint* (Cambridge University Press, Cambridge, 1992), pp. 398–606, esp. 544.

[97] The account that follows draws on: Craig, *The Mint*, esp. ch. XXII 'Other External Coinages', pp. 374–94; www.royalmintmuseum.org.uk/history/timeline/index.html, accessed 22 November 2012.

[98] Dyer and Gaspar, 'Reform', esp. 398; George Selgin, *Good Money: Birmingham Button Makers, the Royal Mint, and the Beginnings of Modern Coinage, 1775–1821* (University of Michigan Press, Ann Arbor, MI, 2008), pp. 36, 64–5, 79–94; 117, 126, 190, 234–66.

[99] Selgin, *Good Money*, p. xii.

coins and transformed the Mint itself into an 'industrial concern'.[100] These changes coincided with the growth of a 'second' British Empire, and the Mint began producing more coins for overseas dependencies. When in 1806 the Mint's deputy master expressed a hope that the manufacture of coinages for India and the colonies would help to keep the Mint's new Tower Hill facility constantly employed, he was articulating a vision linking its fortunes to the Empire that would persist deep into the twentieth century and in many ways reach its apogee in the early 1950s.[101]

The Mint's production for British colonies took two forms. The first was the manufacture of British coin for use overseas as domestic British coin became increasingly an 'imperial currency', circulating throughout much of the Empire. British gold coin in particular was of increasing international prestige,[102] with the sovereign popular because of a reputation for fineness and accuracy. In addition, a growing variety of different denominations of other British coin was minted for use in specific colonies, not all of which was accepted as legal tender in Britain itself.[103] By 1900 about 50 per cent of all British or 'imperial' coin minted went overseas. Secondly, in the course of the nineteenth century, the Mint began producing a variety of dedicated colonial as well as other foreign coinages, designated 'private' by the Mint, and paid for by the overseas customers.[104] From 1883 the Treasury encouraged all colonies to obtain their local currencies from the Mint. Although the Mint never succeeded in obtaining a monopoly position, by 1914 the manufacture of distinct colonial coinages constituted around 25 per cent of the Mint's output.[105] India did not go down this route; nevertheless when a standard single coinage was introduced in the Indian territories controlled by the East India Company, the Mint supplied the latter with the tools for making the dies in order that the King's image could be reproduced on the new coins.

The second half of the nineteenth century saw a further development in the Mint's imperial role, with the creation of a network of overseas branches following gold discoveries in the Australian colonies and Canada. The first branch opened in Sydney in 1855 (prompted by the emergence of illegal production

[100] Dyer and Gaspar, 'Reform', pp. 467, 544; Eric Helleiner, *The Making of National Money: Territorial Currencies in Historical Perspective* (Cornell University Press, New York, 2003), pp. 19–37.
[101] 14 January 1806, cited in Dyer and Gaspar, 'Reform', p. 472.
[102] Ibid., p. 532.
[103] John Sharples, 'Sovereigns of the Overseas Branches' in G. P. Dyer ed., *Royal Sovereign 1489–1989* (Royal Mint, Llantrisant, 1989), pp. 59–77.
[104] Craig, *Mint*, p. 382. This was not without consequences for the Mint, since the production of a wide variety of coins often for relatively small orders generated costs over and above those charged.
[105] *81st Annual Report of the Comptroller and Deputy Master of the Royal Mint, 1950* (HMSO, 1953) [hereafter *Annual Report*], p. 1; Gaspar and Dyer, 'Reform', p. 546.

of sovereigns in South Australia), a second in Melbourne in 1872, a third in Perth in 1899, and a Canadian branch in Ottawa in 1908.[106] From 1866 Australian sovereigns became legal tender throughout most of the British Empire; by 1900 they accounted for up to 40 per cent of all gold circulating in Britain itself.[107] Another branch was established in South Africa, opening for business in Pretoria in 1923. Authorized independent mints were also established in 1862 in British Columbia and in 1866 in Hong Kong, but neither of these lasted long. The failure of the Hong Kong Mint saw the London Mint assume a new role, until 1875 overseeing the establishment of a Mint in Japan, to which the machinery from Hong Kong was sold. Although the Australian, Canadian and South African mints were financed by their own governments, they nonetheless operated under the management of the Royal Mint. The Mint provided master dies, tested sample coins, and seconded staff. With the establishment of a network of overseas branches the circulation and transfer of personnel between them became common.[108]

Concurrently another development contributed to the Mint's expanding overseas role: the emergence of uniform, national currencies. Whereas previously most monetary systems had been heterogeneous, often with a two-tiered system in which low denomination tokens or copper or bronze coins were used by the poor, industrial production enabled the manufacture for the first time of large quantities of low-value coin, and its integration into a standardized official monetary order. Coupled with technological innovation in note production, and a broader process of nation-state formation, by 1914 this had led to the establishment of territorially homogeneous national currencies in much of western Europe, Japan and the United States.[109] Under the leadership of Colonel (later Sir) Robert Johnson, deputy master 1922 to 1938, the Mint capitalized on the continuation of this trend by actively soliciting commissions from overseas governments. He successfully exploited the opportunities created by the creation of new states in Egypt and Ireland, and took orders to produce new coins for Poland, Latvia, Lithuania, Albania, Romania and Yugoslavia, as well as from the Soviet Union, and countries in the Middle East and Latin America.[110] Within the Empire, new coinages were introduced for the Commonwealth of Australia in 1910, the Union of South Africa in

---

[106] Craig, *Mint*, p. 389; Sharples, 'Sovereigns of the Overseas Branches', pp. 70–4.

[107] Dyer and Gaspar, 'Reform', pp. 530–1.

[108] Sharples, 'Sovereigns of the Overseas Branches', pp. 74–5.

[109] Helleiner, *Making of National Money*, esp. pp. 19–37, 46–51, ch. 8; Emily Gilbert and Eric Helleiner eds., *Nation States and Money: The Past, Present and Future of National Currencies* (Routledge, London, 1999), 'Introduction', pp. 1–22, esp. 3–9.

[110] Dyer and Gaspar, 'Reform', pp. 561–4.

1923, and New Zealand in 1933, as well as for the British dependencies of Mauritius in 1911 and Fiji in 1934.[111]

In British Africa, the creation of colonial currency boards was another source of new business.[112] Here the issue of new colonial coinages in part reflected the wider movement towards territorially specific currencies intended to reduce domestic transaction costs, facilitate economic development, and to serve an additional political function, in this case symbolizing British imperial authority. But in British Africa it was also intended to serve other, more precise, purposes. In West Africa the Colonial Office hoped to secure for colonial administrations some of the seignorage profits that currently accrued to the Treasury from the import of British silver coin, and, through the introduction of a colonial currency also to address other concerns about the use of British coin in the region.[113] In East Africa the authorities aimed at the elimination of the Indian rupee as the principal circulating currency.[114] For the Mint itself colonial currency boards were (in contrast to foreign governments) in effect 'tied' clients, a secure source of commercial business. During the early twentieth century, however, the transition towards the use of single colonial currencies in British Africa was far from complete. In West Africa, where once historians argued that traditional currencies such as manilas and cowries had by the 1920s more or less disappeared from all the main trading centres, eclipsed by what was hailed as a 'currency revolution', more recent scholarship has revealed the degree to which precolonial currencies continued to be used deep into the colonial period. Changes in the monetary order were greatly disruptive to local communities who received no compensation for the colonial state's attempts to de-monetize traditional currencies. British or colonial coins were also sometimes too high in value to be used as a unit of exchange in African markets, and

---

[111] *81st Annual Report, 1950*, p. 1.

[112] Ibid.

[113] In the event these profits largely bypassed colonial governments since the reserves of the new boards were maintained and invested in Britain yielding only low rates of interest. The Treasury was also worried about the potentially destabilizing impact on the British economy should the large volume of British silver coin entering the West African colonies suddenly be repatriated to Britain. The use of sterling was also problematic since the Colonial Office did not want to permit a fiduciary issue of the kind permitted at home, and because in some locations its use was resented by local populations: A. G. Hopkins, 'The Creation of a Colonial Monetary System: The Origins of the West African Currency Board', *International Journal of African Historical Studies* 3 (1970), pp. 101–32, esp. 125–6; J. S. Hogendorn and H. A. Gemery, 'Continuity in West African Monetary History? An Outline of Monetary Development', *African Economic History* 17 (1988), pp. 127–46, esp. 138–42.

[114] This came in the context of a post-war 'East African rupee crisis' following a significant post-war appreciation in its value relative to sterling, which had the effect of eroding the capital assets of the settler population. Wambui Mwangi, 'Of Coins and Conquest: the East African Currency Board, the Rupee Crisis, and the Problem of Colonialism in the East African Protectorate', *Comparative Studies in Society and History* 43 (2001), pp. 763–87.

(a)   (b)

Figure 1.2. The British West African two shilling coin, 1949

might be regarded with distrust, a reflection of wider suspicion of the colonial presence, but also because they proved easily counterfeited and tarnished.[115]

Coins alongside bank notes became important symbols of British authority, their iconography at once both a reflection of imperial ideologies and a means of promoting them. Colonial coins carried on their reverse images reflecting British ideas of their colonies (see, for example, Figure 1.2a) while also serving as a medium for projecting ideas about the colonial project.[116] On their obverse, like all coins circulating in the United Kingdom, they bore an image of the British monarch (Figure 1.2b). During the reign of Edward VII on home coinage and some Indian coins this had taken the form of an uncrowned effigy, but after a negative reaction in India, it became common practice to use a crowned image on all colonial and dominion coinages. The division served a practical purpose, since while sterling still circulated in some parts of the Empire, it offered an easy means of distinguishing between homeland and overseas currency, should the former be withdrawn from circulation or demonetised. These arrangements were modified in the 1930s when it was determined that the dominions would also be able to use the uncrowned effigy, a visual demonstration of their status as independent members of the Commonwealth given legal expression in the 1931 Statute of Westminster.[117]

The Mint played a key role in the design process. When new territorial and colonial currencies were introduced, the Mint was generally responsible for

[115] A. G. Hopkins, 'The Currency Revolution in South-West Nigeria in the late Nineteenth Century', *Journal of the Historical Society of Nigeria* 3 (1966) pp. 471–83, esp. 483; Walter Ibekwe Ofonagoro, 'From Traditional to British Currency in Southern Nigeria. Analysis of a Currency Revolution 1880–1948', *Journal of Economic History* 39 (1979), pp. 623–54. Jane F. Guyer ed., *Money Matters: Instability, Values and Social Payments in the Modern History of West African Communities* (James Currey, London, 1985), esp. Felicia Ekejiuba, 'Currency Instability and Social Payments among the Igbo of Eastern Nigeria, 1890–1990', pp. 133–61; see also Mwangi, 'Of Coins and Conquest'.

[116] See on notes, Virginia Hewitt, 'A Distant View. Imagery and Imagination in the Paper Currency of the British Empire 1800–1960' in Emily Gilbert and Eric Helleiner eds., *Nation States and Money: The Past, Present and Future of National Currencies* (Routledge, London, 1999), pp. 97–116.

[117] Philip McLoughlin, 'Crowned and Uncrowned Effigies: Developing a System of Portraits', *Coin News*, 51 (October 2014), pp. 47–9. I am grateful to Chris Barker for drawing my attention to this article.

commissioning and design, acting on the advice of the Standing Committee on Coins, Medals and Decorations formed in 1922, later known as the Royal Mint Advisory Committee on the Design of Coins, Medals, Seals and Decorations.[118] The Committee would eventually advise on the design of most currencies within the Empire–Commonwealth. It was not always, however, able to shape the process as fully as it wished. For example, the government of New Zealand appointed a local committee to choose designs for its new coinage after it decided not to take up those commissioned by the Mint's Advisory Committee. When the Committee in London saw the New Zealand designs, which showed the signing of the 1840 Treaty of Waitangi, it unanimously judged them too 'pictorial in character'. Fresh designs were commissioned in London to be produced in the 'spirit' of the New Zealand ones.[119]

The Second World War inevitably saw some disruption to the Mint's activity. The production of coins for East Africa and Mauritius switched temporarily to the mint in Pretoria and to one in Bombay, while the US Mint supplied coins to Australia and Fiji. By this point the Mint's relationship with the dominion branches was changing too. The Ottawa branch became independent of the Mint in 1931 and the Pretorian one in 1941.[120] In Australia, the Sydney branch closed in 1926 although the two more modern branches, where production was now concentrated, remained under the Mint's jurisdiction. As national or colonial currencies were more comprehensively and consistently employed, the use of British imperial coin in the dominions and colonies declined. By 1949 only around 1 per cent of imperial coins produced in London were issued to the Empire or Commonwealth, and it was consequently decided that the term 'imperial coin' would be discarded and the coinage henceforth known as United Kingdom coinage.[121]

However, even as these developments reduced the Mint's direct involvement in some areas of the Empire, different trends were simultaneously deepening its engagement with others. Africa was now of growing importance. The parallel currency systems that had persisted through the interwar years finally ended and colonial currencies were adopted more widely, encouraged by payments in British money to veterans returning from the war, and by the greater numbers of Africans now employed within both British administration and companies.[122]

---

[118] Christopher Frayling, 'Continuity through Change: The Royal Mint Advisory Committee' in Kevin Clancy ed., *Designing Change: The Art of Coin Design* (Royal Mint, Llantrisant, 2008), pp. 38–65, esp. 41.

[119] Royal Mint Museum [RMM], 'Standing Committee on Coins, Medals, and Decorations' ['Royal Mint Advisory Committee'], minutes, 79th meeting, 28 June 1933; 80th meeting, 13 December 1933; 84th meeting, 13 June 1934.

[120] Dyer and Gaspar, 'Reform', pp. 577–81.

[121] *80th Annual Report 1949* (HMSO, 1951), p. 1.

[122] Ekejiuba, 'Currency Instability and Social Payments among the Igbo of Eastern Nigeria, 1890–1990', p. 144.

The sea change in African use of colonial coin coincided with other circumstances to stimulate demand for new coin. There are several reasons why such demand can arise. New coins may be issued to replace worn-out coin, which is more easily counterfeited. It may also reflect changes in economic conditions or fiscal policy, or political changes. From the late 1940s most of these factors were present in British Africa. As world trade conditions turned in favour of primary producers, colonial exports commanded higher prices on world markets and more coin was needed to pay African producers. This demand was amplified by the tendency among African producers to hoard rather than to release coins back into the economy.[123] By the late 1940s large orders for African colonial coins were flooding into the Mint in London, and the Mint was producing ever-growing volumes of coins for the dependent Empire. What is more the return of peace, and a wave of international political change including the first phase of post-war decolonization, brought new commercial business to the Mint's door. Orders were received from Burma for its new coinage, as well as from Jordan where an independent state was established in 1946, and from Libya in 1951.[124]

As discussed in Chapter 5, this all made 1952 a bumper year for the Mint in which overseas work accounted for as much as 90 per cent of the Mint's production. Of all overseas business, that relating to the colonial Empire was acknowledged by the Mint as 'by far the most important'.[125] Maintaining and indeed increasing this business was crucial to a planned re-development of the Mint itself and, as we shall see, provided the context for the Mint's ambition in seeking the contracts to produce the new currencies of emergent states.

Sandhurst

At first glance it may seem as if the history of the RMAS does not conform to this pattern of a deepening, rather than dwindling, colonial engagement in the mid-twentieth century. Indeed, when the new RMAS formed from the merger of the old Royal Military Academy Woolwich and the Royal Military College Sandhurst opened in 1947, it was the history of European warfare that served as its obvious cultural point of reference. The companies to which cadets arriving at Sandhurst were admitted from 1947 were mostly named after major European engagements: Blenheim, Dettingen, Waterloo and Inkerman (the companies of Old College); Marne; Ypres, the Somme (New College,

---

[123] *69th Annual Report, 1938* (HMSO), p. 12; *77th Annual Report, 1946* (HMSO, 1950), p. 4.

[124] Dyer and Gaspar, 'Reform', pp. 581–2; *80th Annual Report*; *82nd Annual Report, 1951* (HMSO, 1953).

[125] TNA, MINT 20/2563, letters from Sir Lionel Thompson to A. N. Galsworthy (CO) and Sir Herbert Brittain (T), 11 July 1955; Thompson to Galsworthy, 27 July 1955, enclosing note on the services of the Royal Mint.

with Gaza the sole non-European-named company); and Normandy and Rhine (Victory College, where they were balanced by Alamein and Burma). Culturally the post-war Academy was conservative and inward looking. Yet, of all the institutions discussed in this book, the Academy had the most directly outward-facing role, producing generations of cadets who would see service somewhere overseas. What is more although the opening of the new Academy coincided with Indian independence, bringing to an end one significant phase in the institution's imperial history, as discussed below it quickly acquired a new imperial role.

Military training at Sandhurst had commenced at the turn of the nineteenth century,[126] although the RMA Woolwich, which trained recruits in technical areas, dated back to 1741. Until the opening of Sandhurst there had been no British military training school, and British regiments were instead led largely by sons of landed aristocracy and gentry who had secured their commissions from the King through the purchase system. The French Revolutionary and Napoleonic Wars, which led to a six-fold increase in the size of the Army, had provided a spur to reform, and the new facility formally opened in 1812 with the completion of what became known as 'Old College'.[127] The first half-century was a story of decline, however, reflecting the steep fall in military spending that accompanied the return of European peace, and it was not until the Cardwell Army reforms that the system of purchase was finally abolished.[128] By 1878 all infantry and cavalry officers of the British Army attended either Sandhurst or Woolwich. The South African War led to further reforms, and in 1912 the College was enlarged through the building of 'New College'.[129]

Many of those trained at Sandhurst were destined for deployment somewhere in Britain's Empire. In the nineteenth century, while Britain engaged in only one European war after 1815, the British Army was almost continuously deployed somewhere within the British Empire and in the later part of the century frequently in combat in the many colonial 'small wars'. It was the garrison requirements of Britain's expanding Empire that sustained the size of the Army, providing opportunities for career advancement for generations of officers. Empire was a crucial engine of professionalization within the British Army, as well as in the persistence within the Army of the British regimental tradition, mimicked at Sandhurst in the company system. With their small size,

---

[126] French, *The British Way*, pp. 92, 226, 228.
[127] Thomas, *Story of Sandhurst*, pp. 15–16, 22, 28–32, 41; Sheppard, *Sandhurst*, pp. 19–28; Pugsley and Holdsworth, *Sandhurst*, ch. 4.
[128] Sir John Smyth, *Sandhurst: the History of the Royal Military Academy, Woolwich, the Royal Military College, Sandhurst, and the Royal Military Academy Sandhurst, 1741–1961* (Weidenfeld and Nicolson, London, 1961), p. 18.
[129] Thomas, *Story of Sandhurst*, pp. 53, 97, 105–10, 123–31; Sheppard, *Sandhurst*, pp. 92, 123; Pugsley and Holdsworth, *Sandhurst*, p. 35.

the regiments, or battalions within regiments, were ideally suited to transportation and deployment within the colonial Empire and to colonial campaigns.[130]

Sandhurst's own most direct association to Empire was in relation to training for the Indian Army, by 1914 as large as the British Army. Both the RMC and RMA had briefly trained cadets for India before the East India Company had opened its own academy in 1810. They resumed this role when the British government assumed control of India and the Indian Army from the East India Company after the Indian revolt in 1857 and the closure of the Company's academy. From 1903 direct appointments to the Indian Army were made only after cadets had completed their training. India became a popular destination among those passing out from Sandhurst as the Indian Army paid more and it was easier to live well in India on a smaller salary.[131]

Other colonial forces were formed in the wake of Britain's expanding imperial frontier, and, although there was no separate entry route into these, newly commissioned officers leaving Sandhurst might well end up commanding one of them. The two most important were the Royal West African Frontier Force (RWAFF), created in 1887, and, in East and Central Africa, the King's African Rifles (KAR), formed in 1902.[132] Each comprised a number of different colony battalions or regiments. Both regular career and national service British officers and non-commissioned officers (NCOs) were seconded to them for extended periods of service, amounting to around 3 per cent of the British Army's total officer class in the 1930s and 5 per cent in the mid-1950s.[133] Before the war most served a tour of between four to six years; after the war they were generally seconded for a three-year term.

As well as British cadets, between the wars Sandhurst admitted 254 from overseas.[134] While a few of these came from foreign states, including those within the British informal empire, such as Egypt, the end of the First World War also saw the arrival of the first South Asian cadets at Sandhurst. Since 1857 the commissioned ranks for the Indian Army had been reserved for British officers, although a small number of Indians, promoted to serve in effect as liaison officers between the British and the Indian rank and

---

[130] Strachan, *Politics of the Army*, p. 74, 206–23.

[131] Smyth, *Sandhurst*, pp. 49, 62–3, 74, 135–8; Sheppard, *Sandhurst*, p. 61.

[132] These colonial forces were separate from additional units such as the Kenya Regiment established in 1937 or the Nyasaland Volunteer Reserve Force whose officers were drawn from the local white communities. On the KAR see esp., H. Moyse-Bartlett, *The King's African Rifles: A Study in the Military History of East and Central Africa, 1870–1945* (Gale and Polden Ltd, Aldershot, 1956); Killingray, *British Military Presence in West Africa*; Anthony Clayton and David Killingray, *Khaki and Blue. Military and Police in British Colonial Africa* (Ohio University Center for International Studies, Athens, Ohio, 1989).

[133] TNA, CAB 129/76, CP (55) 89, 'Cabinet. Security in the Colonies', July 1955, incorporating 'Report on Colonial Security' by General Sir Gerald Templer, 23 April 1955, para. 272.

[134] Perraton, *A History of Foreign Students in Britain*, pp. 65–6.

file, had been designated 'Viceroy's Commissioned Officers'. During the First World War some of these VCOs were made eligible for a King's Commission, and from 1917 ten places were reserved at Sandhurst for 'suitable Indians', defined as those who came from families which had served during the 1914–18 war. This token gesture was intended only to conciliate India's moderates, with nationalist efforts to promote Indianization of the Indian Army largely foundering in the face of resistance from the British military authorities and Conservative die-hards.[135] In Britain the authorities were concerned that admitting too many Indian cadets could adversely impact on the Academy's character and tradition;[136] as we shall see, such concerns also framed the Academy's policies towards overseas cadets after the Second World War.

As well as a high preponderance of those from 'military families', most Indians deemed eligible for admission to Sandhurst – and able to meet the costs – tended to be from aristocratic and wealthy backgrounds: sons of princes, zamindars and planters.[137] While they were willing to acculturate to British traditions, they reportedly struggled at Sandhurst when required to engage in unfamiliar tasks which appeared menial to these high-born Indians, to submit to disciplinary measures for petty offences, or indeed simply when berated by staff sergeants. The attrition rate was significant. Between 1918 and 1926 the drop-out rate among Indians was as high as 30 per cent, ten times that for British entrants. The establishment in 1922 of a feeder college at Dehra Dun (the location later also of the Indian Military Academy) established on the model of a British public school, helped, however, and its graduates tended to do statistically better than those who had not been through its doors.[138] If the cadets were generally ill-prepared for life at Sandhurst, most experienced little collegiality there, with Indian cadets tending to stick together rather than mixing with their British counterparts.[139] When in 1931 the British government finally yielded to nationalist pressure in agreeing to establish an Indian military academy which opened the following year, Indian cadets ceased to train

---

[135] Stephen Cohen, *The Indian Army, Its Contribution to the Development of a Nation* (2nd edn., Oxford University Press, Oxford, 1990), p. 74; David Omissi, *The Sepoy and the Raj. The Indian Army 1860–1940* (Palgrave Macmillan, Basingstoke, 1994), p. 240; P. S. Gupta, 'The Debate on Indianization, 1918–1939', in P. S. Gupta and A. Deshpande eds., *The British Raj and Its Indian Armed Forces, 1857–1939* (Oxford University Press, Oxford, 2002), pp. 228–69, esp. 228. For an alternative view, which stresses that Indianization was never meant to be a 'half-hearted measure to mollify Indian nationalist politicians', see Pradeep P. Barua, *Gentleman of the Raj: The Indian Army Officer Corps, 1817–1949* (Praeger, Wesport, CO, 2003), p. 45.

[136] Gutteridge, *Military Institutions*, p. 127.

[137] Cohen, *Indian Army*, pp. 119–21.

[138] Bryon Farwell, *Armies of the Raj. From the Mutiny to Independence, 1858–1947* (Viking, London, 1989), pp. 293–4; Cohen, *Indian Army*, pp. 76, 119; Omissi, *Sepoy and the Raj*, p. 162.

[139] See e.g., General J. N. Chaudhuri, quoted in Pugsley and Holdsworth, *Sandhurst*, p. 76.

in Britain, although British officers in the Indian Army continued to be trained at either Sandhurst or Woolwich. The British Army had resisted the establishment of an Indian Military Academy, but, like the other institutions discussed in this book, now began to collaborate in localization initiatives – as it would also do in post-war British Africa. When the new Indian institution opened, it was modelled on Sandhurst.[140] British officers provided the instruction. While something of Sandhurst was exported to the sub-continent, from the late nineteenth century increasing numbers of retired Indian Army officers and officials chose to settle near Sandhurst, bringing with them their Indian servants who became a 'regular sight' in Camberley High Street.[141]

For Sandhurst the Second World War was a period of upheaval. It was transformed to become one of several Officer Cadet Training Units and the course shortened to an average of six months. Already by the end of the 1930s the proposal to amalgamate the RMC and RMA, previously resisted on the grounds that standards at Sandhurst were lower than at Woolwich, was revived and set in motion amidst some criticisms of Sandhurst, an institution where, one critic alleged, '"snobbishness" and "graft" are rampant ... Crass ignorance is widespread and most cadets are unsuited to think for themselves'.[142] When the College was reconstituted by the War Office in 1947 the two were finally merged.

For the Army, the Second World War saw a deepening importance of imperial manpower for Britain, not just in relation to the Indian Army, but in respect of the other colonial forces. Relatively small in peacetime, when the battalions principally supported the police in internal security operations, they expanded greatly during the two world wars when additional line battalions and field regiments were raised from each colony. In East Africa between 1939 and 1945 they increased from 11,000 to 238,000 men, and in West Africa from 8,000 to 146,000.[143] African forces served against the Italians in North Africa and against the Japanese in Burma. By the end of the war the total strength of military forces in the colonial Empire was over 473,000.[144] In all, over half of all divisions or their equivalents raised by Britain, the Empire and Commonwealth during the war were from the colonies, India or the dominions, and of all the

---

[140] Gupta, 'Debate', p. 246; Alan Jeffreys, 'Training the Indian Army, 1939–1945' in Alan Jeffreys and Patrick Rose eds., *The Indian Army 1939–1947. Experience and Development* (Ashgate, Farnham, 2012), pp. 69–86.

[141] Pugsley and Holdsworth, *Sandhurst*, pp. 49–51, 54.

[142] Liddell Hart Military Archive, King's College London, KCLMA, Liddell Hart papers, LH 15/3/58, no. 2, p. 3, unsigned paper, 'the RMC' [undated, but probably c. 1937].

[143] Ashley Jackson, 'The Evolution and Use of British Imperial Military Formations', in Alan Jeffreys and Patrick Rose eds., *The Indian Army 1939–1947. Experience and Development* (Ashgate, Farnham, 2012), pp. 9–29.

[144] *Report on the Colonial Empire (1939–1947)*, PP 1946–7, X (Cmnd. 7167), pp. 17–18.

major British Army units it was only in Montgomery's 21st Army Group that British forces predominated.[145]

After the war the British government explored the possibility of continuing to use colonial military manpower for more than colonial internal security and defence. For the most part the War Office was unenthusiastic, loathe to spend any of its decreasing defence allocation on colonial manpower, although when the onset of the Korean War made manpower a greater constraint than finance the question received renewed attention. However, having assumed direct control of both the KAR and RWAFF during the war, the War Office retained the wartime command structure in order to keep its options open.[146] In the case of the KAR there had been no reversion to local command and administration by the time the emergency was declared in Kenya. In 1953, with the creation of the Central African Federation (CAF), the Nyasaland and Northern Rhodesian battalions of the KAR were transferred to become part of the armed forces of the new federal government. Despite reservations within the Colonial Office that the use of African troops outside their own regions might cause 'political and many other difficulties', in the early 1950s KAR battalions were deployed in Malaya, as were the Rhodesian African Rifles in 1956–8; they were also used in the Suez Canal Zone between late 1951 and December 1952.[147]

As the new joint RMA Sandhurst opened, the British flag came down in India. The Indian Army was divided between the two successor nations, India and Pakistan, and all remaining British officers moved from active command to staff posts. The British withdrawal from the Indian Army closed one chapter in Sandhurst's history of association with empire, consigned to the past with the creation of an Indian Memorial Room in the old chapel to accommodate objects relating to the old Indian Army regiments.[148] Independence for Britain's South Asian colonies marked not an end of Sandhurst's imperial role, however, but the beginnings of a new one.

Recent wartime experience of imperial military strength and collaboration led the War Office to propose that, from the outset, a significant number of places at the new Academy should be set aside for overseas cadets, principally from the Empire–Commonwealth – even though, as discussed in Chapter 6, the new Academy was foremost conceived with a view to the creation of a high-calibre British officer class.[149] While the allocation of a significant number of vacancies was not intended to facilitate the replacement in colonial regiments

---

[145] French, *The British Way*, pp. 205–6.
[146] Crocker, 'The Military Transfer of Power in Africa', p. 186.
[147] TNA, CO 537/5323, minutes by Andrew Cohen and S. E. V. Luke, 2 and 14 August 1950; extracts from *Colonial Reports*, Nyasaland (1953–4), Kenya (1953–4); Stapleton, *African Police*, p. 9.
[148] Sheppard, *Sandhurst*, pp. 158, 170–4.
[149] See pp. 237, 240.

of British with local officers, the impact of the British withdrawal from South Asia was nevertheless quickly felt in the arrival of cadets from Burma, Ceylon (Sri Lanka) and Pakistan, as well as from Malaya and Jordan. In the next few years these overseas cadets would be joined by many more from Britain's African colonies, and, by 1955, greatly increasing overseas demand for vacancies at the Academy was prompting significant concern at Sandhurst and in the War Office. Sandhurst, like the Universities of Oxford and Cambridge and the Bank of England, would thus become involved in the extension of technical assistance to emergent states within the Commonwealth, but unlike the other institutions, it was not master in its own house. It instead became a tool of colonial, Commonwealth and foreign policy, a role which successive officers in charge of the Academy sought to keep within distinct limits.

Conclusion

For each of the institutions discussed in this book several centuries of British imperialism had led to the acquisition of distinct 'imperial roles'. These had not necessarily resulted in the creation of new institutional structures or brought about fundamental reform. Even where they had led to institutional change, as for example at the Universities of Oxford and Cambridge, where involvement in the delivery of Colonial Service training resulted in the development of new institutions and academic studies, these might be distinctly marginal to the institution as a whole. Nonetheless, each institution had become to some degree part of the apparatus of the British imperial system. While this chapter has focused on charting these 'imperial roles', these also reflected – or in some cases generated – identifiably imperial cultures. For example, the Bank sought to replicate an English central-banking model overseas as well as to protect and develop the position of sterling. The Bank's part in the history of Commonwealth central banking would inform its own understanding of the role it should play in the development of central banking within the new Commonwealth. At the universities, there was a similar conviction of the value of their own expertise, illustrated in this chapter in relation to providing administrative training. All our institutions sought to export their values and practices, and, in Sandhurst's case, to guard against impacts in the other direction. Propagating Britishness was itself one manifestation of 'imperial culture'. Senior figures also acted to advance both their institutions' own material interests and British 'imperial interests' more generally, whether financial, strategic or political.

As this chapter has shown, the 1940s mostly saw growth rather than a decline in these imperial roles. Both pre-war and wartime developments – including the emergence of a more interventionist approach to colonial development, the interwar development of colonial administration, and the evolution of the sterling area – extended existing, and sometimes produced new institutional linkages. In the case of Sandhurst, even as Indian independence ended one phase in the institution's imperial history, the arrival of growing numbers of cadets from South Asia and elsewhere training to take up roles in new national forces opened up another. The core argument of this book is that, for all these institutions, the mid-1950s constituted a significant turning point: the moment at which colonial political change, led by developments in Britain's West African colonies of the Gold Coast (Ghana) and Nigeria, forced a reassessment of their strategies and activities. Among other things the institutions became involved in the delivery of a variety of forms of technical assistance concerned with institutional development in Britain's former colonies. These developments are discussed in Chapters 3–6. Before we continue our discussion of these institutions, however, Chapter 2 turns to consider, first, why Britain had done so little by way of institutional development and transfer before the 1950s; and second, the various different forms that British state civil and military technical assistance could assume.

2 Technical Assistance and State-building at the End of Empire

In March 1957 the Gold Coast, which now adopted the name Ghana, became the first European colony in sub-Saharan Africa to overthrow colonial rule, led to independence by Kwame Nkrumah. In the months immediately preceding and following independence, Nkrumah's Cabinet debated the development or creation of institutions including a central bank; public service; a national army, navy, and airforce; a national archive; national broadcasting services; currencies; and – probably influenced by Britain's own Britannia – even the purchase of a national yacht.[1] Ministers sought both the symbols of independent-nation statehood and the instruments – educational, financial, administrative and military – that might enable them to make their *de jure* independence from Britain a reality. Although Ghana entered independence as a member of the Commonwealth, the government sought to throw off the British colonial yoke, in line with the country's trail-blazing status within the continent and Nkrumah's own ambitions to pan-African leadership. Ghana could and did source aid internationally. But like the other African states that would follow, Ghana nonetheless began independence with British personnel still in senior positions in major institutions and reliant on British assistance. As will be discussed in the first section of this chapter, this was a direct consequence of Britain's critical failure to initiate adequate policies of Africanization and institutional transfer and development. In Ghana and elsewhere constitutional decolonization was consequently accompanied, and – more typically – followed by, a secondary process as new states urgently sought to build the institutions normally associated with independent nation states and to train the staff to run them. 'Independence' was a beginning, and not an end, point in a process of state-building.

In this situation 'technical assistance' became one of the defining features of postcolonial development aid. Technical assistance entered the lexicon of development in the 1940s, popularized by the United Nations, which in 1950 launched its Expanded Programme of Technical Assistance, and the USA, which in the same year established its own Technical Cooperation Administration to

---

[1] PRAAD, Public Records and Archives Administration Department of Ghana, Accra, ADM 13/1/26-28, Cabinet minutes 1957–9.

administer an American foreign aid programme. Britain formed its Department for Technical Co-operation in 1961 as it began reconfiguring state apparatus in the transition from a colonial to a postcolonial era. British institutions that had assumed 'imperial roles' would play a part in this process of varying degrees of scale and importance. First prompted by political change in Ghana and Nigeria, they adapted their imperial roles to a new postcolonial context to provide their own technical assistance to the new states, or offered facilities that became part of Britain's package of technical assistance. In Chapter 1 we saw how British institutional involvement with Empire increased on the eve of its demise; the critical need of new states for technical assistance would be the context in which this involvement would continue long after the British flag had come down in former colonies.

These initiatives are considered in subsequent chapters of this book, but before we turn to these, the second section of *this* chapter surveys British state-led technical assistance programmes, including in relation to the military, to provide context for understanding the contribution of our institutions, especially Sandhurst. While Britain's postcolonial commitment to Africa was smaller and less overt than that of France,[2] British governments and officials used technical and military assistance to advance British interests: strategic, political and commercial.[3] But British postcolonial assistance cannot be reduced to merely a manifestation of a 'neocolonial' project. It was also constituted by different motivations which deliberately sought to reduce dependence rather than maintain it. I would suggest that one way of conceptualizing these motivations is to see British technical assistance as an extension of the process of decolonization beyond the constitutional.

Decolonization and State-building

The rise of technical assistance constituted a response to the unfolding decolonization of colonial empires and to challenges facing the new states. Nowhere were these problems more acute than in colonial Africa, where newly independent states were seriously underprepared, trailing behind those in South and South-East Asia where there had been more gradual processes of 'localization': the appointment of local people to senior posts and institutional transfer and development. Until very late in the colonial era Africans were almost entirely excluded from the higher echelons of both public services and the armed forces, even though both relied overwhelmingly on African labour. Such services were instead stratified on racial lines

---

[2] On which see, recently, E. Schmidt, *Foreign Intervention in Africa: From the Cold War to the War on Terror* (Cambridge University Press, Cambridge, 2013), esp. ch. 7.
[3] As I have argued in Stockwell, 'Exporting Britishness'.

and controlled by a 'thin white line' of expatriates, the hierarchies reinforced by effective social segregation.[4]

This was not what liberally minded Britons had once envisaged. In 1833, in a speech in the House of Commons, Thomas Macaulay set out an ambition that would remain central to British perceptions of their 'civilizing' mission. 'By good government', he argued, 'we may educate our subjects into a capacity for better government; that, having become instructed in European knowledge, they may, in some future age, demand European institutions'. Macaulay spoke before the acquisition of most of Britain's African colonies in the late nineteenth-century 'scramble for Africa'.[5] Nonetheless, for most of the nineteenth century, the appointment of Africans and men of African descent to senior administrative and other posts in the British colony of Sierra Leone, and later the Gold Coast Settlements and Lagos, had been a fairly common practice. In 1865 a Parliamentary Select Committee discussing British settlements in West Africa had proposed that 'the object of our policy should be to encourage in the native the exercise of those qualities which may render it possible for us more and more to transfer to them the administration of all the Governments, with a view of our ultimate withdrawal from all, except, probably Sierra Leone'.[6] Yet this expectation was overtaken by new expansionary dynamics that resulted in the great extension of British African commitments rather than their reduction. Changing ideas of race, coupled with advances in tropical medicine that made the West African colonies less dangerous for expatriates, led to a sharp fall in the number of senior posts filled by Africans. In interwar Africa the division along racial lines was reinforced by the ascendancy within Britain of ideas associated not with those like Macaulay, whom Richard Symonds, in his study of the development of government services in new states, termed 'Anglicizers', but with 'conservationists', who aimed to preserve what they identified as traditional structures in African societies. African organizations demanded the development of African universities and Africanization of senior posts within public services. But the British resisted this as undesirable because it threatened to create a second set of African elites potentially in tension with the 'native authorities' – the chiefs and their advisors – central to the development and widespread implementation of the policy of 'indirect rule'.[7]

By the late 1930s, however, widespread colonial unrest, economic hardship and growing criticism of Britain's colonial record, had led to a reappraisal

---

[4] A. H. M. Kirk-Greene, 'The Thin White Line: The Size of the British Colonial Service in Africa', *African Affairs*, 79 (1980), no. 314, pp. 25–44.

[5] *House of Commons Debates*, Vol. 19, 10 July 1833, col. 536. Macaulay was speaking with reference to India.

[6] Cited in Symonds, *British and their Successors*, pp. 119–21.

[7] Ibid., pp. 17, 123, 128–9.

of British policy. This new approach was reinforced during the Second World War as Britain sought to present its imperial mission in terms more acceptable to international opinion.[8] In 1943 the then Secretary of State for the Colonies, Oliver Stanley, declared the gradual advancement of British colonies 'along the road to self-government within the framework of the British Empire' to be the long-term objective of British policy but stressed that this must be preceded by colonial social and economic development.[9] Paradoxically, one of the first ways in which a reinvigorated British colonialism aimed explicitly at social and economic advancement in preparation for self-government was manifest was in a commitment to expanding and reforming the *expatriate* element of the Colonial Service, as reflected in the wartime discussions of the reform of Service training we have already considered in Chapter 1.

The early 1940s nonetheless saw a surge of activity related to colonial institution building and African advancement. As we also saw in Chapter 1, colonial higher education was among the areas that now received more attention. The urgent need to develop colonial universities as 'soon as their creation can be justified' to produce an educated class equipping colonial peoples to 'stand on their own feet' was pressed on the Colonial Office by H. J. Channon, professor of biochemistry at Liverpool University, one of the most active members of the Colonial Office's educational advisory committee. The enquiries that followed Channon's intervention led to the appointment of the Elliot Commission on higher education in West Africa and the Asquith Commission on the development of higher education throughout the colonial Empire. Concerned that some colonial students studying at British institutions were returning home 'embittered' by their experience of racial prejudice in Britain, and that others might travel to universities in foreign countries if more was not done to expand their access to higher education, the commissions recommended the creation of university colleges in East and West Africa, the West Indies and Malaya. The Asquith recommendations also resulted in the formation in London of the Inter-University Council for Higher Education in the Colonies as well as a University Advisory Grants Committee to manage money provided for colonial higher education under the 1945 Colonial Development and Welfare Act.[10] There were some among the Colonial Office's community of liberally minded academic experts, and a wider network of organizations and individuals interested in colonial affairs, who now enthusiastically embraced a redefined British

---

[8] See p. 24.

[9] Secretary of State for the Colonies Oliver Stanley: *House of Commons Debates*, Vol. 391, 13 July 1943, col. 48.

[10] 'Introduction', Ashton and Stockwell eds., *Imperial Policy*, part I, lxxix–lxxxi; part II, doc. 148, 'Some observations on the development of higher education in the colonies, memo'. By Professor H. J. Channon, January 1941, CO 859/45/2, no. 1. See also, Pietsch, *Empire of Scholars*, p. 182.

imperial mission.[11] Margery Perham argued that British universities now had a 'more important task' in relation to the colonies than 'any handled by the Colonial Office itself' in 'training ... their leaders and experts so that they may take back from us the control of their own affairs'.[12] That war depleted the ranks of British personnel and increased strains on the Colonial Service provided another incentive for change. It was hence in 1942 that the first two Africans, K. A. Busia and A. L. Adu, both from the Gold Coast, were appointed to the Administrative Service.[13] The first West African officer in the RWAFF was also appointed in 1942,[14] although at this stage the British expected that most African officers would be appointed as NCOs.[15]

Yet despite these initiatives, ultimately little real progress with either Africanization or institutional development and transfer was achieved before the mid-1950s in West Africa, and even later elsewhere in the continent. Following Busia and Adu's appointments, there were moves to facilitate Africanization of the public services in West Africa and in 1949 the Gold Coast ceased expatriate recruitment altogether. Even so, by 1950 only one other Ghanaian had been appointed to the Administrative Service. In Nigeria by late 1953, of more than 5,000 'senior' positions, approximately 3,300 were filled by expatriate officials, and only 800 by Nigerians, the remainder being vacant.[16] In East Africa measures to encourage Africanization were only adopted in the 1950s, when committees on the recruitment, training and promotion of Africans to higher posts were formed in Uganda (1952) and in Kenya and Tanganyika (1957), and it was the end of the decade before localization was more energetically pursued.[17] Before 1960 there were no comparable initiatives in Central Africa;

---

[11] On these see especially J. M. Lee, *Colonial Development and Good Government: A Study of the Ideas Expressed by the British Official Classes in Planning Decolonization 1939–1964* (Clarendon Press, Oxford, 1967); Symonds, *British and their Successors*, pp. 151–2. Heike Jöns dubs these 'post-Victorian imperialists' who took Empire for granted but whose reformist stance and activities ultimately help contribute to post-war decolonization: Jöns, 'The University of Cambridge, Academic Expertise and the British Empire', p. 111.

[12] Cited in Roland Oliver, 'Prologue: The two Miss Perhams' in Smith and Bull eds., *Margery Perham*, pp. 21–7, note 24.

[13] Kirk-Greene, *On Crown Service*, p. 111.

[14] Killingray, *Fighting for Britain*, pp. 85–7.

[15] See, e.g., discussion about the establishment of a possible military school in the Gold Coast: PRAAD, RG 3/1/653, nos. 1 and 2, draft note by Maj. G. L. H. Huddlestone with letter, 8 January 1946, addressed to T. Barton, Deputy Director of Education. Huddlestone hoped the school might be a 'first class source of ANCOs'.

[16] World Bank, *The Economic Development of Nigeria* (The Johns Hopkins Press, Baltimore, MD, 1955). http://documents.worldbank.org/curated/en/1955/01/1561193/economic-development-nigeria, p. 23.

[17] *Report of the Public Services Conference Held in the Colonial Office, London, 1–10 March 1960*, Col. No. 347 (HMSO, London, 1960), appendix, pp. 21–5.

the first local African appointments were only made in Nyasaland four years before the country's independence as Malawi in 1964.[18]

Africanization of the officer class in the colonial armed forces lagged even further behind. In 1956, however, Queen's Commissions were opened to suitable candidates who had completed a course at Sandhurst, and serving NCOs and warrant officers became eligible for short-service commissions once they had successfully completed a short course at the British officer cadet schools at Mons or Eaton Hall.[19] In East Africa a new senior warrant officer appointment was also created, the 'Effendi', a governor's commission, inferior to the Queen's Commission but equivalent to the Viceroy's commissioned officer in India, an intermediate rank between warrant officer and officer. Places were reserved at Sandhurst specifically for African students who had satisfied local selection panels, and local officer training facilities were established at Teshie in the Gold Coast in 1953, in East Africa in 1958, and in Zambia in 1964.[20]

For all the energy that had characterized wartime discussions of African development – 'Now is the time, and the time is already late', noted the Elliot Commission – this energy was diminished by what with hindsight we can see were conservative assumptions about the speed with which political change might occur. 'Somewhere within a century, within half a century', the Elliot Commission continued, 'a new African state will be born'.[21] These unrealistic expectations were maintained into the early post-war era in relation to West Africa and until much later in the case of East and Central Africa. Indeed, in 1947 colonial officials still anticipated that it would not be much less than 'a generation' before even the Gold Coast, seen as the most politically advanced of Britain's African colonies, achieved internal self-government, and they advised that this would occur significantly later elsewhere.[22] Moreover, in the 1940s there was agreement across Westminster and Whitehall that social and economic development should precede constitutional advancement. British elites hence anticipated that the pace of political progress would be determined *by*, rather than itself *determine,* the pace of institutional, social and economic development.

British officials and others therefore proceeded as if they had time to build institutions on an optimal model, adhering to established criteria for

---

[18] Adu, *Civil Service*, p. 21; Kirk-Greene, *On Crown Service,* p. 111.

[19] The initiatives followed recommendations made by General Sir Gerald Templer: TNA, CAB 129/76, CP (55) 89, 'Cabinet. Security in the Colonies', July 1955, incorporating 'Report on Colonial Security' by General Sir Gerald Templer, 23 April 1955, paras. 291–4.

[20] Lee, *African Armies*, pp. 38–42; Killingray, *British Military Presence*, pp. 39, 63; Miners, *Nigerian Army*, pp. 33–9, 48–50.

[21] Cited Ashton and Stockwell, 'Introduction', *Imperial Policy*, part I, lxxx.

[22] TNA, CO 847/36/1, no. 9, A.G.C. No. 2, 'Report of the Committee on the Conference of African Governors', 22 May 1947, appendix III, para. 2.

appointments and standards. Channon's 1941 memorandum makes this clear: the development of universities was 'a process which cannot be unduly accelerated' and entailed 'enlightened encouragement' and 'far sighted planning'.[23] In relation to appointments to, and promotion within, the public services, British officials, determined to maintain standards, insisted that local entrants to the Colonial Service meet the same educational criteria as home recruits.[24] In the Gold Coast a working party of civil servants, chaired by Adu, recommended that experience might substitute for the standard academic entry criteria and that a relaxation of standards might be necessary to achieve rapid conversion to a locally based service. But the working party's principal recommendations proved unacceptable to the Gold Coast government. As Kenneth Younger reflected in his contemporaneous study of African public administration, 'something more imaginative than a conscientious striving after British standards' was required.[25]

The shortage of candidates who met standard entry criteria or British expectations was a consequence of long-term failings in the provision of colonial education. While it was a universal problem, it was more acute in some locations than in others. In colonial Nigeria, where by the mid-1950s there were four public services – Western, Eastern, Northern and Federal, as well as a separate service for the mandated territory of Southern Cameroons – poor educational provision in the Northern Region and the Southern Cameroons weakened the prospects for localization. As late as 1958 – two years before Nigeria became independent – only 425 pupils graduated from secondary school across the vast Northern Region. At this date it was estimated that it would be some seven to eight years before the region would produce sufficient Nigerian candidates to fill technical places within public administration, and fourteen to sixteen years for all administrative and professional posts.[26] In Zambia, described in a UN report in 1964 as 'one of the least educated countries in a most undereducated continent', only 1 per cent of the population had completed primary school at independence, and there were only 1,200 secondary school leavers.[27]

Illiteracy was an especially acute problem in the armed forces whose recruitment had hitherto focused on so-called martial races, often drawn from areas where educational provision was the poorest. Military schools were created

---

[23] Ashton and Stockwell eds., *Imperial Policy and Colonial Practice*, part II, doc. 148, 'Some observations on the development of higher education in the colonies, memo'. By Professor H. J. Channon, January 1941, CO 859/45/2, no. 1. para. 9.

[24] Symonds, *British and their Successors*, p. 152.

[25] Kenneth Younger, *The Public Service in New States: A Study in Some Trained Manpower Problems* (Oxford University Press, London, 1960), pp. 77–8.

[26] Ibid., p. 27.

[27] Quoted in Jean Nellie Sindab, 'The Impact of Expatriates on the Zambian Development Process' (University of Yale, PhD, 1984), pp. 97, 199.

which might serve as feeders for Sandhurst and to produce officer material.[28] The first was established in West Africa.[29] Other educational initiatives in relation to the military followed: in East Africa in the form of a KAR Junior Leaders Company to educate local African boys to the General Certificate of Education standard,[30] and, later, in Central Africa with the creation of a Junior Leaders Unit.[31] In the south of Nigeria, where there were more Africans who met the educational criteria, African recruitment to the officer class was nevertheless also impeded because the financial incentives offered were too small to offset the poor image of the army.[32]

With few available candidates for posts there was competition for the best-educated between different services and institutions. When shortly after the war the idea of establishing the military school in West Africa had first been proposed, local British administrators objected on the grounds that this would take away those *they* most needed to fill posts in the public services.[33] In addition, given the acute shortage of educated local personnel, even when a more realistic or imaginative approach was adopted entailing accelerated promotion through the ranks, it had the unfortunate effect of depleting the lower levels of the most able officers, as well as of giving rise to unrealistic expectations of rapid promotion among later public-service entrants. Relaxing entry criteria was also inherently difficult in the case of professions and specialisms such as medicine, where there were internationally accepted standards.[34]

Evaluating what constituted 'British standards', however, was subjective. The determination to adhere rigidly to established criteria reflected local political issues, as well as racial and cultural prejudices, especially in the settler colonies. One British colonial official employed in the Secretariat in Nigeria doubted that the Administrative Service would ever be Nigerianized, as 'an African seems to find a D. O's position and responsibilities exceptionally difficult to assume'. In 1955 Arthur Benson, Governor of Northern Rhodesia, was reluctant to appoint

---

[28] See, e.g., in Sierra Leone: Bodleian, Mss Afr. s. 1734, box 10, file 354, folio 33 (Lt. Col. Robinson).

[29] Although originally conceived as for 'the benefit of the army in West Africa' rather than primarily as a means of encouraging Africanization of the officer corps: PRAAD, RG 3/1/653, ff. 15–16, E. H. M. Counsell, West African Council, to Directors of Education Nigeria and Gold Coast, May 1947; f. 21, 'General Military School for Boys', memo by Maj. Gen. N. M. S. Irwin, GOC W. A. Command, November 1946; ff. 85–90, minutes of committee meeting formed to discuss proposal, 26 July 1947; RG 3/1/348, memo by J. E. Crouch, Director Army Education, War Office, 22 May 1947.

[30] *Daily Telegraph,* 30 March 1961: [Archives of the] RMAS, room D56, Box 1, Cuttings Book 1961–4.

[31] *Evening News,* 17 March 1962: RMAS, room D56, Box 1, Cuttings Book 1961–4; Stapleton, *African Police and Soldiers,* pp. 174–5.

[32] Miners, *Nigerian Army,* p. 57.

[33] PRAAD, RG3/1/653, ff. 85–90, minutes of the committee to consider a military school, 26 July 1947.

[34] Adu, *Civil Service,* pp. 133–5.

Arthur Wina, an African from the colony in whom Margery Perham and others in Britain had taken an interest (and who would later become Zambia's first finance minister) to a post in provincial administration, since he feared his advancement ahead of Europeans in the colony whom he regarded as better qualified would cause political difficulties.[35] Like their counterparts in the Colonial Service, British Army officers who had responsibility for the initial selection of cadets for Sandhurst and Mons were equally reluctant to nominate Africans whom they deemed insufficiently qualified.[36] In Central Africa, even when the British officers' reservations had been overcome, a process of Africanization was held back by resistance from the federal authorities who argued that there were no suitable Africans to fill places reserved for the Federation at Sandhurst.[37] At the Bank of England officials doubted the capacity of Africans to manage central banks and worried that they might prove vulnerable to political pressures.[38]

Some corners of the British establishment were more resistant to African development than others. British authorities saw risks in delegating control over both finance and the armed forces while colonies remained under British rule – even while they also commonly recognized the advantages of initiating action that might allow them to manage a devolutionary process. Together with complacency, innate conservatism and self-interest, this led British authorities to oppose or delay moves to craft new institutions from established colonial ones. For example, both British officials and senior figures at the Bank of England resisted growing demand in Nigeria and the Gold Coast for the creation of new banking institutions.[39] Although they were eventually forced to agree to the creation of a national bank in the Gold Coast, they were unwilling to permit the creation of central banks and the new Bank of the Gold Coast had no currency-issuing functions.[40] The Colonial Office determined that the Secretary of State's control over currency matters could not be surrendered until after British territories had attained full independence, while the Bank was reluctant to dismantle a system that ensured colonial price stability and parity with sterling. When J. L. Fisher, advisor to the Governor of the Bank of England, visited Nigeria in 1952 to advise on banking, he consequently concluded against the establishment of a central bank; Chibuike Uche argues that this outcome was

---

[35] Bodleian, Mss. Brit. Emp. s 415 (Furse Papers), 10/1, ff. 3–6, Tom Scrivener, Nigerian Secretariat, to Furse, 3 August 1951; ff. 42–3, Arthur Benson to Furse, 5 April 1955.

[36] See, e.g., Bodleian, Mss Afr. s. 1715, box 5, file 118, f. 16.

[37] Stapleton, *African Police and Soldiers*, pp. 174–5.

[38] Criticisms embodied in Fisher's 1952 report on Nigeria: see Uche, 'Bank of England vs the IBRD', pp. 228–31.

[39] Ibid., pp. 223–5.

[40] BoE, OV 67/2, E. Melville (CO) to A. K. Potter (Treasury), 8 August 1952; no. 29 g, 'West Africa', memo for Mr Fisher prepared by W. J. Jackson, 18 May 1953; see also Stockwell, 'Instilling'.

predetermined within the Bank.[41] One British objection concerned the absence of other financial infrastructure: without developed commercial banking sectors and local money markets, central banks in developing countries would be unable to fulfil many of the standard central banking functions. But this became a catch-22 situation: as long as the currency boards had limited functions, the colonies lacked the authority to oversee and nurture precisely the kind of institutions that the Bank claimed were necessary for proper central banking, such as local markets in government securities.[42]

Senior officers in the British Army were similarly ambivalent about relinquishing control, in this case, of colonial forces. In West Africa, colonial officials accepted that Britain should now begin the transformation of the Gold Coast Regiment of the Royal West African Frontier Force into a new national army after this movement was proposed at two conferences convened in 1949 and 1953 to discuss the future of the RWAFF.[43] They hoped that this would enable them to exercise oversight over the process and ensure a strong basis for future military cooperation between the colony and the rest of Anglophone West Africa as well as with Britain and the Commonwealth.[44] Among senior British Army officers there was some residual resistance to this change. In West Africa the Vice-Chief Imperial General Staff accepted that there were good reasons for initiating a transfer of control while Britain could exercise oversight, but on balance concluded that since current arrangements worked, it was best to do nothing.[45] In 1955 a Cabinet ministerial committee on security in the colonies, chaired by General Sir Gerald Templer, nevertheless endorsed the Colonial Office view. Templer not only hoped to transfer financial responsibility to local governments, but argued that, since the pace had already been 'set' in the Gold Coast, all they could do 'was make what sense of it we can' and 'the only way to do this, paradoxically enough' was 'to make the ... first stage of the hand-over quicker still', even though he feared the colony would be 'getting an "army" which it will not be fit to have for 20 years'.[46]

Templer's committee laid down no specific policy on Africanization in relation to the KAR, but in line with his prescription that financial responsibility should be assumed locally, the War Office transferred control of the KAR to the East African governments in 1957, establishing an East African Land

---

[41] Uche, 'Bank of England vs. the IBRD', p. 222.
[42] Newlyn and Rowan, *Money and Banking*, pp. 190, 251.
[43] *Report of the West African Forces Conference, Lagos 20–24 April 1953*, Col. No. 304 (HMSO, London, 1954), paras. 9–14.
[44] Although publication of the 1953 conference conclusions had been delayed by negotiations over officers' pay: TNA, CO 968/475, minute by J. Bennett (CO), 7 July 1954; Carstairs to Lt. Gen. Harold Redman, 4 March 1955.
[45] Ibid., no. 5, Lt. Gen. Harold Redman to W. Gorrell Barnes (CO), 1 September 1954.
[46] TNA, CAB 129/76, CP (55) 89, 'Cabinet. Security in the Colonies', July 1955, incorporating 'Report on Colonial Security' by General Sir Gerald Templer, 23 April 1955, paras. 16 and 23.

Forces Organization, which would include the ministers of defence for the three territories. However, the arrangement not only created an unfortunate duplication of services, with separate arrangements such as those relating to supply for British troops in East Africa and for the EALF, but also generated tensions between the three governments who struggled to manage the financial commitment. In 1960 responsibility was returned to the War Office.[47]

From the mid-1950s in West Africa, and the early 1960s elsewhere, the drawn-out timetables officials had imagined for African constitutional change were discarded and the colonies hurtled towards independence. As political change accelerated, new institutions in each of three key sectors – the public services, finance and the armed forces – had to be hastily assembled or transferred to local control. Each colony already had its own public service, with even the expatriates technically employed by the colonial government rather than the British. Nonetheless, all senior appointments were still handled by the Colonial Office or, where delegated to them, the Crown Agents, and appointees to the 'senior service' were required to attend a selection process in London. As independence approached, arrangements consequently had to be made for the transfer to local governments of responsibility for appointments to, and promotion within, the senior service, and to this end public or civil service commissions were created in new constitutions establishing full internal self-government.

Officials at the Bank of England had already begun to revise their earlier opposition to the development of national banks and currencies. By late November 1954, after a visiting IBRD economic mission to Nigeria recommended the creation of a bank with currency-issuing functions,[48] one of the Bank's most senior figures concluded it was not 'good policy any longer' to resist suggestions for central banks in the Gold Coast and Nigeria.[49] These experiences were to prove the context in which the Bank would seek henceforth to assert its own leadership over the development of central banking within the dependent Empire, as we will see in Chapter 4. This did not mean that the Bank abandoned its earlier concerns about the relevance of central banking in developing countries, but, like Templer had done in relation to the armed forces, it had concluded that – if inevitable – it was better to control the process than not. Nevertheless, although in Central Africa a Bank of Rhodesia and Nyasaland was established in 1956 in place of the old currency board, in East Africa the only significant concession within the financial sector pre-African independence was the relocation of the East African Currency Board

[47] David Percox, 'Internal Security and Decolonization in Kenya, 1956–1963', *Journal of Imperial and Commonwealth History* 29 (2001), pp. 92–116; Parsons, *The 1964 Army Mutinies*, pp. 42–6.
[48] Uche, 'Bank of England vs the IBRD', pp. 232–3.
[49] BoE, OV 69/3, 39A, memo by Fisher, 23 November 1954.

from London to East Africa. The Bank's earlier resistance, coupled with that of Whitehall, and on-going opposition to significant deviation from the colonial arrangements in East Africa, ensured that the development of national financial institutions was a process that would occur principally after new states had attained independence.

From 1956 the separate colonial regiments of the RWAFF were transformed into national forces, whose governments assumed financial responsibility for them over the next couple of years.[50] The West African Command was closed, and instead British officers were appointed as military advisers to the West African governments. Within each country steps were taken to create the machinery to administer the new armed forces. Newly independent Ghana led the way, introducing legislation to establish an Armed Forces Council modelled on the British Army Council.[51] In East Africa, where there had been less consideration given to the future of the KAR, the British Army was almost wholly unprepared for the step-change in British policy in 1960.[52] As a result, from 1960 constitutional progress far outpaced institutional development and transfer and ensured that, as in the finance sector, the latter largely occurred after independence. The regional military arrangements remained in place until Tanganyika became the first of the three East African colonies to become independent, and the transfer of the 6th and 2/6 KAR battalions from the GOC East African Command to Tanganyika (where they became the 1st and 2nd Battalions Tanganyikan Rifles) began the breakup of the KAR into national forces. In the Central African colonies, control of the Nyasaland battalion of the KAR and the Northern Rhodesian Regiment had been passed to a Central African Command in 1954 following the creation of the Central African Federation. After the dissolution of the Federation, these units were converted into two new, territorially based, forces, the Malawi Rifles and the national Army of Zambia.[53]

The failure of earlier initiatives in relation to Africanization was now abundantly apparent. In 1960 the first comprehensive review into the development of local public services in Britain's African colonies revealed the full scale of the problem, as Table 2.1 shows; however, establishing the extent – or lack of Africanization – is complicated by a striking failure to differentiate between

---

[50] In the Gambia, however, it was subsequently decided that the colony could not afford a separate military establishment and the government opted instead to rely on the police to fulfill the country's security needs. Killingray, *The British Military Presence in West Africa*, p. 39.

[51] PRAAD, ADM 13/2/35, CM 41(57), 'A Bill to Establish the Gold Coast Armed Forces Council', Cabinet memo by the Prime Minister (January 1957).

[52] Parsons, *The 1964 Army Mutinies*, pp. 60–90.

[53] Ibid., pp. 46, 52–63; Parsons, *African Rank and File*, pp. 40–6. The UK government also re-assumed operational control of the East African forces, at some cost to the British Treasury in late 1959.

Table 2.1. *Senior local appointments in public services in Africa as of 1 January 1959*[a]

Colony	Total senior posts	Local[b]
Nigeria	8,008	4,080
Sierra Leone	800	369
Gambia	172	56
Kenya	6,616	3,001
Uganda	2,434	557
Tanganyika	439	350
Northern Rhodesia	3,553	2,150
Nyasaland	957	80

[a]From *Report of the Public Services Conference*, appendix, p. 21.
[b]No distinction made between locally domiciled white, Asian and African appointees.

Africans and locally domiciled Europeans and Asians.[54] Inevitably the situation was worse in some areas, and in some sections, of the public services than others. In 1962, for example, there were only five Malawians in the entire Nyasaland Administrative Service.[55]

At this juncture the absence of an African administrative class was exacerbated by the failure of attempts to encourage sufficient numbers of British colonial officials working in the public services of states entering independence to 'stay on'. Extensive discussions through the 1950s as to how Britain might best ensure continuity of personnel led in 1954 to the creation of Her Majesty's Oversea (from 1956, Overseas) Civil Service from the old Colonial Service and to the introduction of safeguards to protect expatriate careers. In Nigeria, in an attempt to persuade British officials to remain in the country, the British Government experimented with the introduction of a 'Special List A', and, two years later, a 'Special List B', of officials who would be in the service of the British government but seconded to the Nigerian. The British government originally intended to extend the Nigerian arrangements to other colonies. But the schemes were largely failures, and here and elsewhere arrangements to compensate British officers for career loss led many to return home rather than stay on in uncertain and potentially difficult circumstances.[56] In newly independent Ghana, Nkrumah's Cabinet was aware that the compensation scheme was acting as a 'decisive incentive' to quit for those who had initially remained

[54] *Report of the Public Services Conference*, appendix, pp. 21–5.
[55] Kathryn Morton, *Aid and Dependence. British Aid to Malawi* (Overseas Development Institute, London, 1975), p. 32.
[56] Kirk-Greene, *On Crown Service*, pp. 62–73; Rathbone, 'Colonial Service'; pp. 155–6; Lynn, 'Nigerian Complications'.

in post, potentially leading to a critical manpower problem.[57] Ministers felt understandably let down by the British government when they learned that some British officials who had already left (and to whom Ghana had paid compensation for career loss) had been appointed to new posts in other British colonies.[58] To A. L. Adu, Britain's inability to devise arrangements to persuade expatriate officers to stay on in former colonies was its greatest failure.[59]

There was a comparably acute shortage of senior African army personnel within new states. Their armed forces remained largely under the command of seconded British officers and, in East and Central Africa, overwhelmingly, British Warrant Officers and NCOs as well. Even in West Africa, where there had been a little more progress, there were only 40 Nigerians out of 290 officers in 1959. Major General Norman Foster, arriving to take command of the Nigerian Military forces, later recalled 'the astonishing shortage of Nigerian officers'.[60] Retrospectively many individual members of this last generation of a British officer class in colonial forces were sharply critical of the British failure to embark upon Africanization at an earlier date. The consequences were seen as especially disastrous in East Africa, where the first African cadet, a Tanganyikan, became a commissioned officer in the East African forces only in late 1960.[61] Of the three British East African territories, Kenya was best served, but when Tanganyika attained independence only six of fifty-eight officers were African,[62] and in Uganda there were only nine Ugandan officers in the Ugandan battalion of the KAR at independence.[63] The latter had all been commissioned in the previous year, and except for one, directly from the ranks. When Africanization was sharply accelerated, Idi Amin – recalled by British officers as the 'British idea of a good African warrant officer' being 'smart, athletic, a good shot, a jolly person, played rugger and boxed' – became one of the first two Effendi promoted to receive the Queen's Commission. When a further eight were commissioned, the Effendi rank was abolished.[64] In Central Africa the position was yet worse: here the first Zambian was only commissioned in 1964.[65] Africanization of the officer corps in these forces was so severely out of step with political change, and the composition of the officers mess so

[57] PRAAD, ADM 13/2/46, Cabinet Memo. by the Minister of Finance. 261 (58), 'Overseas Entitled Officers' discussed in Cabinet 1 July 1958.
[58] PRAAD, ADM 13/1/26, Cabinet minutes 3 December 1957, item 25.
[59] A. L. Adu, *The Civil Service in Commonwealth Africa: Development and Transition* (George Allen and Unwin, London, 1969), biographical note, and pp. 92, 141.
[60] Bodleian, Mss. Afr. s. 1734, Box 3, file 142, folio 99.
[61] *East African Standard*, 16 December 1960. RMAS, room D56, Box 1, Cuttings Book 1961–4.
[62] Parsons, *The 1964 Mutinies*, 2003, pp. 67–8.
[63] Gutteridge, *Military in African Politics*, pp. 26–35.
[64] Bodleian, Mss Afr. s 1715, Box 3, file 42, ff. 56–7, 65–6. Lt. Col. H. K. P. Chavasse (Uganda, 1960–2); file 55, folio 27–9, Major Henry Crawford; box 5, file 109, f. 17, Brigadier Ernest Goode.
[65] Lee, *African Armies*, pp. 39–42.

'white', that one British officer recalls how, when the African Chief Minister of Uganda soon after the country became internally self-governing was invited to a guest night in the officers' mess, the first African ever to receive such an invitation, he was detained at the Guard Room. 'We've got a man here in the Guard Room, Sir', reported the African duty warrant officer. 'He says he's the Chief Minister and that he has been invited to dinner with the officers. Could that be right?'[66]

Britain and Postcolonial Africa: The Rise of Technical Assistance

Britain's failure to develop local institutions or to promote Africans to senior positions within them meant that Britain's African colonies were ill-prepared for independence and ensured that the transfers of power would be followed by a secondary decolonizing process that would continue deep into the postcolonial era. Technical assistance, defined by the British government in 1961 as 'the provision of training, experts (including advisory and specialist services) and equipment' would become a crucial feature of Britain's postcolonial relations with new states.[67]

Of course, Britain was far from the only source of technical assistance for Commonwealth countries. Rather, their need for external aid, coupled with their new, and numerically significant, presence within the United Nations and other organizations, ensured that technical assistance became an important political as well as a moral issue for the wider international community.[68] By 1965 Africa attracted the largest share of money provided under the UN's technical assistance schemes after funding for these was increased in 1961 and a supplementary 'Expanded Programme' was introduced in the same year specifically for African countries.[69] The World Bank had already begun undertaking economic surveys of colonies and new states as a basis for deciding on credit allocation, and had established an Economic Development Institute in Washington with the aim of training staff from developing countries to undertake economic and monetary planning. In 1961 it created a Development Advisory Service, staffed by its own experts, to advise governments on development issues,

---

[66] As recalled nearly twenty years later: Bodleian, Mss Afr. s 1715, Box 3, file 42, ff. 74-88, Lt. Col. H. K. P. Chavasse (Uganda, 1960–2).

[67] *Technical Assistance from the United Kingdom for Overseas Development* (March 1961), PP 1960–1, XXVII (Cmnd. 1308), paras. 13 and 82.

[68] For critical accounts of technical assistance see P. T. Bauer, *Dissent on Development* (Weidenfeld and Nicolson, London, 1971) and Tibor Mende, *From Aid to Recolonization: Lessons of a Failure* (Pantheon Books, New York, 1973). For more positive contemporaneous assessments, see Morton, *Aid and Dependence* and Gerald Holtham and Arthur Hazlewood, *Aid and Inequality in Kenya. British Development Assistance to Kenya* (Croom Helm, London, 1976).

[69] F. J. Tickner, *Technical Cooperation* (Hutchinson and Co., London, 1965), pp. 70–1.

while the IMF similarly responded to African decolonization through a series of initiatives to assist new states.[70]

Although the US government, focused on other regions, has been judged as content to play a 'secondary role' to European powers in Africa,[71] the intensifying Cold War, the emergence of so many new African states, and the election of Kennedy as President in 1961, ensured that the Americans too temporarily took a greater interest in the continent. The new President invested significantly in personal relations with African leaders, entertaining a total of twenty-eight heads of state at the White House during his brief administration.[72] Some see the change as one of style rather than substance,[73] but under President Kennedy a distinct American epistemology of development emerged that differentiated American approaches from those of communist states. Walt Rostow's theory of *The Stages of Economic Growth*, published in 1960 as political change swept through sub-Saharan Africa, laid down a model for American policy on overseas development in which a diffusion of American capital and American technology and knowledge would enable new states to advance towards modernity. Although alternative and critical narratives were later produced that argued western intervention led to 'underdevelopment' in a world system in which the fortunes of wealthier states depended on the exploitation of the poorer, Rostow's 'modernization theory' quickly became influential within American policymaking. The year after its publication Kennedy created the 'Alliance for Progress', 'Food for Peace' and the 'Peace Corps', passed the Foreign Assistance Act expanding America's foreign aid programme, and shortly after created the US Agency for International Development.[74]

Since the late 1930s development had been a prominent element of British colonial policy, reflected in the 1940 Colonial Development and Welfare Act. In an international environment increasingly hostile to empires, development had served as a new rationale for continuing colonialism. For a few years after

---

[70] See Chapter 4.

[71] James P. Hubbard, *The United States and the End of British Colonial Rule in Africa, 1941–68* (McFarland and Co., Jefferson, NC, 2011), pp. 165–6, 286–301, 350–63 and Ebere Nwaubani, *The United States and Decolonization in West Africa, 1950–1960* (Rochester, New York, 2001), pp. 243–4. Before c. 1960 Eisenhower's willingness to invest in Ghana's flagship project, the construction of a dam and hydroelectric plant on the Volta River, which Britain itself was unable to fund, represents an exception: Nwaubani, *The United States*, pp. 124–5.

[72] Philip E. Muehlenbeck, *Betting on the Africans: John F. Kennedy's Courting of African Nationalist Leaders* (Oxford University Press, Oxford, 2012), pp. xv, 17–20.

[73] Hubbard, *The United States*, pp. 350–63.

[74] Michael Adas, *Dominance by Design: Technological Imperatives and America's Civilizing Mission* (Harvard University Press, Cambridge, MA, 2006); Mark H. Haefele, 'Walt Rostow's Stages of Economic Growth: Ideas and Actions' in David C. Engerman, Nils Gilman, Mark Haefele and Michael E. Latham eds., *Staging Growth: Modenization, Development and the Global Cold War* (University of Massachusetts Press, Amherst, MA, 2003), pp. 81–103; also Nils Gilman, 'Modernization Theory. The Highest Stage of American Intellectual History' in ibid. pp. 47–80.

the war this turn to development was reinforced by hopes that the expansion of colonial exports might assist Britain's own economic recovery. In 1948 the Colonial Development and the Overseas Food Corporations were formed to manage various projects in the colonies, although interest quickly waned in the wake of a series of expensive flops and a fall in world commodity prices. After the war Britain also became involved in the provision of technical assistance through a variety of multilateral aid programmes, including those of the United Nations and under the Colombo Plan, a Commonwealth initiative to deliver international assistance to developing countries in South-East Asia.[75]

Nevertheless, Britain was initially slow to reconfigure 'colonial development' as aid for a postcolonial age and long into the post-war era the British state understood development as mainly a colonial issue. In July 1957, three months after Ghanaian independence, the British government still held that 'the special responsibility which HMG has for colonial dependencies ceases when they achieve independence', and Ghana's independence bill prevented the British Colonial Development Corporation from undertaking new activity in the country.[76] However, amidst criticism of what was perceived as its parsimonious approach to Ghana, Britain agreed at the Montreal Commonwealth Trade and Economic Conference of 1958 that newly independent Commonwealth countries were entitled to help in the form of Commonwealth Assistance Loans. Britain also accepted that former colonies entering independence should receive technical assistance and be allowed to keep any unspent allowance under the Colonial Development and Welfare legislation. This legislation was renewed and extended for a fifth time in 1959, when the fund was increased by £95 million and an additional £100 million was provided in the form of Exchequer loans. Further revisions led to the introduction of the Commonwealth Development Act in 1963, and in 1965 to the Overseas Development and Service Act, which brought together colonial development and welfare with overseas aid, and extended provision for another five years. From 1963, the Colonial Development Corporation, now restyled as the Commonwealth Development Corporation, was also permitted to commence new projects in independent Commonwealth countries.[77] British multilateral aid to Africa was channelled via the Special Commonwealth African Assistance Plan, agreed upon in 1960 by Commonwealth Finance ministers; and to other, non-Commonwealth, states, under the auspices of the Foundation for Mutual

---

[75] Tickner, *Technical Cooperation*, p. 45.
[76] R. Hyam and R. Louis eds., *The Conservative Government and the End of Empire 1957–1964* (British Documents on the End of Empire, Series A, Vol. 4, 2000), part 1, 'Introduction', p. lxiv.
[77] Ibid., pp. lxii–lxvii; S. R. Ashton and W. R. Louis eds., 'Introduction', *East of Suez and the Commonwealth, 1964–1971* (British Documents on the End of Empire, Series A, Vol. 5, London, 2004), Part I, p. cxv.

Assistance in Africa South of the Sahara formed in 1958 by members of the Commission for Technical Cooperation in Africa South of the Sahara.[78]

Within Whitehall a significant step from the 'colonial' to the 'postcolonial' came in 1961 with the creation of a new institutional home for technical assistance: the establishment of the Department of Technical Co-operation (DTC).[79] This was prompted by the American reorganization of its overseas technical assistance, with the British Secretary of State for the Colonies, Iain Macleod, worried that Britain would otherwise lose ground to the United States in its relationships with the new states.[80] The new department brought together the technical assistance functions of the Colonial, Commonwealth Relations and Foreign Offices. Staffed largely by officials transferred from these departments, the DTC also assumed responsibility for the Overseas Civil Service. Responsibility for capital aid, however, remained with the three departments, and since the new department was not a full ministry led by a cabinet minister, it fell short of what many, particularly in the Labour party, had hoped for. After its success in the general election in 1964, the new Labour government replaced the DTC with the Ministry of Overseas Development (ODM). Initially under Barbara Castle, the new Ministry also took over the remaining overseas aid functions of the Foreign, Commonwealth Relations, and Colonial Offices, although the last retained control over capital aid in Britain's remaining dependencies.[81] When the Conservatives were returned to office in 1970 they absorbed the ODM within the FCO. Labour restored it to full ministry status in 1974, but in 1979 the Conservatives again collapsed it into the FCO. Another development occurred in 1997 when Tony Blair's Labour government created the new Department for International Development (DFID). DFID's historian, Barry Ireton, argues that the shifting departmental arrangements did not result in significant policy differences but concluded that the Ministry tended to enjoy more influence under sympathetic Labour ministers.[82]

Technical assistance came to account for a relatively high and increasing proportion of the total value of British governmental aid spending.[83] This was in line with the needs of new states. But technical assistance was also an inherently attractive form of aid for British governments. As the Cabinet Defence and Oversea Policy Committee noted in 1964, technical assistance was 'pound

---

[78] *Technical Assistance from the United Kingdom for Overseas Development,* paras. 15 and 52–6.
[79] Ibid., para. 6.
[80] See Hyam and Louis eds., *Conservative Government*, part 1, docs. 92 and 93, and editorial note on these.
[81] See H. A. Marquand, *House of Commons Debates*, vol. 639, 25 April, 1961, cols. 256–66; *Overseas Development and Services Bill*, PP 1964–5, XXX (Cmnd. 2736), paras. 69–74.
[82] Barry Ireton, *Britain's International Development Policies: A History of DFID and Overseas Aid* (Palgrave Macmillan, Basingstoke, 2013), pp. 29–33, 65.
[83] *H. M. Treasury: Aid to Developing Countries (September 1963)*, PP 1962–3, XXXI (Cmnd. 2147), p. 30.

for pound the most effective form' of aid and 'relatively inexpensive'. Perhaps most importantly, technical assistance not only showed the 'recipients how to help themselves', helping avoid 'creating in them feelings of inferiority or resentment', but, crucially, helped foster 'a sense of personal association between donor and recipient', creating links binding the recipients towards the West.[84] It presented opportunities for the British state and institutions to exercise leverage over the affairs and institutions of new states, whether for strategic, economic or other purposes, and to disseminate British models. In line with its increased importance, technical assistance constituted nearly 25 per cent of all forms of British state bilateral aid by 1970, and almost 50 per cent once loans were removed from the equation.[85] Thereafter, it remained consistently important in British bilateral aid to Africa.[86]

British military assistance, the context in which Sandhurst came to assume a key role in the decolonization era, was administered and funded in quite different ways. It was delivered by British military personnel and by establishments run by the War Office, and, after 1964 the new, unified, Ministry of Defence formed from the merger of the War Office, Admiralty and ministries of air and aviation with the existing Defence ministry. However, the War Office, and subsequently the Ministry of Defence (MoD), acted in effect, as customers of the Commonwealth Relations and Foreign Offices, which had financial and policy responsibility for the supply of military aid. The Cabinet Defence and Oversea Policy Committee provided further oversight. When the Commonwealth Relations Office (which had merged with the Colonial Office in 1966) was folded within the Foreign Office in 1968, the new Foreign and Commonwealth Office assumed control of British military aid.

In some cases, a package of aid was a result of formal defence agreements, but these were only agreed with a minority of new states when there were particular interests Britain sought to protect.[87] For example, an agreement was signed at independence with Nigeria, where British chiefs of staff wanted over-flying and air-staging rights to compensate for the loss of access to facilities in the Middle East after the Suez crisis and 1958 Iraqi Revolution. But defence agreements were not seen as appropriate in all cases. John Bennett, who had recently been given charge of the Colonial Office's Defence and General Department following a period of secondment

---

[84] TNA, CAB 148/6, DO (O) 64 (36), 10 June 1964, report by the Future Planning Working Group, para. 129.

[85] Calculated from: *Overseas Development*, table 1; ODM/ODA, *British Aid Statistics 1963–1972* (HMSO, 1972).

[86] Tony Killick, 'Policy Autonomy and the History of British Aid to Africa', *Development Policy Review*, 23 (2005), pp. 665–81, see esp. 667.

[87] Clayton, 'Foreign Intervention', pp. 203–58, esp. 222. For Britain's extensive military connections to Africa in recent decades, see Jackson, 'British-African Defence and Security Connections'.

to the Imperial Defence College, argued that time showed 'that cooperation within the Commonwealth depends more on political realities', forti-
fied 'by a strong professional link' than on formal agreements.[88] Military
aid slipped more easily below a public as well as international radar than
formal defence agreements, as events in Nigeria proved when popular opposition to the agreement led to its abrogation in 1962, threatening
Britain's wider political objectives. Instead, the two governments adopted
the more informal mechanism of agreeing that substantial British aid would
continue in return for continued British staging and over-flying rights,
although this agreement proved insufficient to prevent a weakening of
Anglo-Nigerian defence co-operation over the next few years.[89]

British technical assistance became the context for an on-going and significant British presence within institutions in new states and role in training
new elites at different British higher education and other institutions. Far
into the postcolonial era, many Britons were employed in former colonies,
principally via the Overseas Service Aid Scheme (OSAS) established in the
Overseas Aid Act (1961). The introduction of this scheme reflected concerns
in London that a potential exodus of British overseas (colonial) civil servants, fearful for their career prospects, might lead to administrative collapse,
especially in East Africa.[90] Under the terms of the scheme Britain met the
additional costs of employing expatriate staff over local appointees in countries with which Britain signed bilateral Overseas Service aid agreements.
Initially there had been calls within sections of the British political establishment for the creation of a full-blown Commonwealth advisory and technical
service, as much as a solution to the problem of premature career loss for
former colonial civil servants as for reasons of overseas development;[91] an
option finally rejected by the British government in 1962. Nonetheless, the
OSAS constituted a compromise catch-all solution, providing a framework
for managing the supply of British personnel to *both* British dependencies
and independent countries. This was a reflection of the protracted nature of
British decolonization and the tensions produced for the Janus-faced British
state between discharging on-going colonial responsibilities and simultaneously adjusting to a postcolonial order. The scheme agreed on new terms

---

[88] TNA, CO 968/475, memo by John Bennett on the defence implications of the Gold Coast's
transition to independence, 5 July 1954, see esp. section c, para. 4 and section D, para. 7.

[89] Myss, 'A Post-Imperial Cold War Paradox'; on the informal agreement see, TNA, T 296/261,
see telegram from Nigerian prime minister, Abubakar Balewa, to the UK High Commissioner
in Nigeria, 20 January 1962, enclosed with C R Price (CRO) to Russell Edmonds (T), 19 June
1962.

[90] See CAB 128/34, CC 44(60)7, Cabinet conclusions, 21 July 1960, reproduced in Hyam and
Louis eds., *Conservative Government,* part I, doc. 85.

[91] See *Colonial Office: Service with Overseas Governments* (October 1960), PP 1959–60, XXVII
(Cmnd. 1193); *House of Commons Debates*, vol. 633, 24 January 1961, cols. 36–107.

of reference for existing British officials in HMOCS *and* those who might be appointed in future on short-term contract terms, either to posts in remaining British overseas territories or in independent states.

By early 1965 forty-one independent states and colonial administrations had entered into the bilateral agreements with Britain, and there were 11,000 officers employed overseas under the scheme.[92] Additionally, agreements governing the supply of public service officers to Ghana, Nigeria and Sierra Leone, which had by then attained independence, had already been concluded.[93] Initially estimated to cost approximately £12–16 million per annum over ten years, by 1967–8 actual expenditure on OSAS constituted £16.3 million. Overseas governments were required to pay pension costs that could increase with British inflation, a feature that attracted significant criticism and led to some subsequent modification.[94] With so many new states launched on the international stage in the early 1960s it nevertheless quickly became apparent that still more was required if Britain was to provide the assistance it wished, and a corps of continuously employed experts within the ODM was created who would be available to overseas governments on a short-term basis either through OSAS or as employees of the ministry or international agencies. OSAS was further extended in 1966 to include expatriates previously employed by the Central African Federation and also, under the British Expatriate Supplementation Scheme (BESS), British personnel employed in overseas education not covered by the original scheme.[95]

OSAS became the umbrella under which a great number of Britons such as agriculturalists and planners worked overseas in new states struggling to develop their own classes of professionals. As already mentioned, British universities were one potentially valuable source of expertise. The British Council was also a key player in recruiting Britons for overseas work. In 1957 new state funding enabled the Council to increase its recruitment and financial subsidy of British teachers for service overseas, and by summer 1961 it had staff in seventy-five countries within the Commonwealth and beyond; many were involved in teaching English, but their role also extended far beyond this.[96] In all, from its inauguration until the mid-1960s, OSAS accounted for about

[92] Barbara Castle, *House of Commons Debates,* vol. 707, 24 February 1965, cols. 409–18.

[93] Special schemes, with more limited benefits than available under OSAS, were subsequently agreed with the governments of Nigeria and Sierra Leone in 1965 and with Ghana in 1967: *Ministry of Overseas Development. Public Service Overseas: The Future of the Overseas Service Aid Scheme and Other Supplementation Arrangements (April 1969),* PP 1968–9, LIII (Cmnd. 3994). *Public Service Overseas,* para. 12.

[94] For example, in Zambia, where expatriate remittances amounted to £80 million in 1979, straining the country's foreign exchange resources: Sindab, 'The Impact of Expatriates', pp. 158, 177.

[95] *Ministry of Overseas Development: Public Service Overseas.*

[96] Lord Bridges, *House of Lords Debates,* vol. 231, 1 June 1961, cols. 899–901.

half of British bilateral technical assistance spending,[97] and through the 1960s and early 1970s Britons employed under its auspices were numerically more significant than any other foreign nationals in many emergent states, especially the anglophone.[98]

The military equivalent of OSAS was the Loan Service Personnel (LSP) scheme, under which Britain supplied military manpower, often at a sub-sidized rate. Within the War Office, it was considered crucial that British Army officers and NCOs play a key role in building up local forces.[99] As noted earlier in this chapter, new armies in former British African colonies were initially commanded by British officers seconded from the British Army, although within a short period most loaned British military personnel ceased to be in active operational roles and were instead engaged wholly or principally in training local forces.[100] Rhodesia was one exception. Here it was 'cautious' but growing military and other assistance from South Africa that was of 'critical importance' in enabling Ian Smith's white minority Rhodesian Front to make its unilateral declaration of independence (UDI) in November 1965.[101] In the 1960s, although access to British LSP was over-whelmingly concentrated on Commonwealth states, a handful of foreign countries, notably Nepal, Libya (where there was a British base until a mil-itary coup there in 1969) and the Sudan also received subsidized personnel. In 1967/8 Britain spent £3.6 million on loaned personnel, although by 1970 this sum had fallen to £1.75 million as a result of Treasury cuts to the military technical assistance budget.[102]

Alongside these initiatives to facilitate the secondment of Britons for work in new Commonwealth states, the transfers of power in Africa also saw a great increase in the number of colonial and Commonwealth students studying in

---

[97] Calculated from *Overseas Development*, tables 1 and 10.

[98] For example, Kenya and Zambia: Holtham and Hazlewood, *Aid and Inequality in Kenya*, p. 51, table 4; Sindab, 'The Impact of Expatriates', pp. 14, 125.

[99] TNA, WO 216/913, 'Draft. Top Secret. Retention of British influence in Colonial and New Commonwealth Forces' (1958); see also earlier documents, such as CO 968/475, memo by John Bennett on the defence implications of the Gold Coast's transition to independence, 5 July 1954. For the importance attached to this in East Africa, see Parsons, *The 1964 Mutinies*, pp. 63–4.

[100] Details in the case of the armed forces derived from the country entries in John Keegan, *World Armies* (Macmillan Press, London, 1979); Clayton, 'Foreign Intervention'; see also Alain Rou-vez, with Michael Coco, Jean-Paul Paddack, *Disconsolate Empires. French, British and Bel-gian Military Involvement in Post-Colonial Sub-Saharan Africa* (University Press of America Incorp., Maryland, MD, 1994), pp. 236–9.

[101] Sue Onslow, 'Resistance to "Winds of Change": The Emergence of the "Unholy Alliance" between Southern Rhodesia, Portugal and South Africa, 1964–5', in L. J. Butler and Sarah Stockwell eds., *The Wind of Change: Harold Macmillan and British Decolonization* (Palgrave Macmillan, Basingstoke, 2013), pp. 215–34, esp. 222–3.

[102] TNA, FCO 46/490, 'UK Military Technical Assistance' by A. T. Smith (Defence Dept, FCO) addressed to R. Tesh (Defence Dept, FCO), 7 May 1970.

Britain.[103] By 1960 there were some 47,500 overseas students in the UK studying at a range of institutions from universities to teacher training colleges and technical institutions as well as in programmes offered by private organizations and local and central government departments. Together these accounted for about 10 per cent of *all* full-time students in British universities and technical colleges and a significant proportion of those at teacher-training colleges. Over 18,000 came from Britain's dependencies, managed by the Colonial Office in conjunction with the British Council. In 1959–60, the year before Nigerian independence, these included almost 6,000 from Nigeria alone.[104] By the 1960s over half of all overseas students studying at UK institutions were from either British colonies or independent Commonwealth states, and although the proportion fell thereafter, the Commonwealth still accounted for about 40 per cent of the total in the 1970s.[105] Some were funded by British aid, especially following the introduction in 1959 of a British Commonwealth Scholarship and Fellowship Plan. Overseas civil servants enrolled on the Oxbridge Devonshire colonial administrative service training courses (and descendants of these courses) were among the colonial and Commonwealth students studying in Britain.

Commonwealth students travelling to Britain also included those accepted at British military training establishments. Although Britain already hosted cadets from Commonwealth states, from 1959 the CRO inaugurated a new scheme, initially budgeted at £80,000, to help with training for the five Commonwealth countries, India, Pakistan, Ceylon, Malaya and Ghana, which had then achieved independence, in line with efforts to ensure that military assistance was deployed as a means of extending the UK's influence among emergent Asian and African states.[106] Under what became known as the Commonwealth (Relations Office) Military Training Assistance Scheme (CWMTAS), India and Pakistan were allotted the lion's share – 37 per cent and 39 per cent, respectively – Malaya some 11 per cent, Ghana 7 per cent and Ceylon 6 per cent. The stated aim was to 'increase the efficiency of Commonwealth Armed Forces' and to 'confirm and strengthen the links between them and the Armed Forces of the United Kingdom'. The CWMTAS paid for training at a range of British establishments, as well as for British-led training overseas. For example, in the first year the CRO expected Ghana's allotted sum to pay for eight students to attend the RMAS, one to enrol at the Staff College, Camberley, and for two African officers to be attached to British Army units.[107] As we shall see in Chapter 6, in

---

[103] Perraton, *A History of Foreign Students in Britain*.
[104] *Technical Assistance from the United Kingdom for Overseas Development*, para. 10, pp. 66–78.
[105] Perraton, *A History of Foreign Students*, pp. 85, 99, 106.
[106] Following the recommendation of the Brook Committee into the 'Position of the UK in World Affairs'.
[107] TNA, DO 35/9260, draft letter to A. D. Peck (T) from CRO, undated but May 1959.

the late 1950s the increase in overseas cadets arriving at Sandhurst generated acute strains. Within three years the CWMTAS budget had more than tripled to £254,000, from which the United Kingdom continued to support the five original states as well as other emergent Commonwealth nations.[108] Furthermore, although other nations, such as the United States, became a source of military technical assistance – and in some cases superseded the British,[109] including by providing help with the creation of air and naval forces as well as armies – Britain initially at least was often the most important. As Table 2.2 shows, by 1970–1 Britain allocated £700,000 to provide military training assistance to twenty-two Commonwealth countries. At this point, soon after the end of the Nigeria Civil War (1967–70) in which Britain had not only supported but supplied arms to the Nigerian federal government against the breakaway state of Biafra, Nigeria was allotted more than any other state, closely followed by India and Pakistan. Kenya and Ghana were the next two most significant African recipients.[110]

Funding to foreign states developed as a separate stream operating under the banner of the United Kingdom Military Training Scheme (UKMTS), administered by the Foreign Office's Defence Department rather than in the CRO. Although it was not as well supported financially as the CWMTAS, by 1970–1 UKMTS was reaching twenty-seven states, including the Congo, Nepal, Turkey and Finland, and others in the Middle East and North Africa, the Far East and Latin America.[111] In 1968 the merger of the FO and CRO to become the new FCO brought the two schemes under one departmental roof. Although the FCO initially maintained separate identities for the two schemes (since it was seen as useful to have one with 'a Commonwealth' label), they were subsequently combined as the United Kingdom Military Training Assistance Scheme (UKMTAS).[112]

Military assistance raised particular sensitivities, especially for the non-aligned states such as Ghana, which determined initially to reduce its reliance on Britain.[113] Even in more West-oriented Nigeria, British military technical assistance proved sensitive politically, as the popular reaction to the Anglo-Nigerian defence agreement reveals. In turn, Britain's continued supply of arms to the Nigerian federal government attracted strong criticism during the Nigerian Civil War and adversely affected Britain's relations with some Commonwealth and foreign states when images were broadcast around the

---

[108] TNA, T 296/261, G. P. Hampshire, CRO, to A. W. Taylor (T), 15 December 1961.
[109] See, e.g., Miners, *The Nigerian Army*, pp. 102–3.
[110] TNA, FCO 46/491, 'CW Military Training Assistance Scheme. Allocations, 1970/71'.
[111] TNA, FCO 46/492, 'Training in the UK, 1970/71'.
[112] TNA, FCO 46/391, no. 68, Circ. to asst heads of all FCO geographical depts. by J. A. Davidson, 3 June 1969.
[113] PRAAD, ADM 13/1/27, Cabinet minutes, 27 May 1958, item 7.

Table 2.2. *Projected spending on Commonwealth Military Training Assistance Scheme 1970–1*[a]

Country	Allocation in £
Nigeria	120,000
India	110,000
Pakistan	110,000
Malaysia	87,000
Kenya	70,000
Ghana	52,000
Guyana	20,000
Sierra Leone	16,000
Zambia	15,000
Uganda	15,000
Singapore	12,000
Jamaica	12,000
Sri Lanka	12,000
Tanzania	10,000
Malawi	10,000
Trinidad	6,000
Malta	6,000
Gambia	5,000
Mauritius	4,000
Bahamas	3,000
British Honduras	2,500
Fiji	2,500
Total	**700,000**

[a]TNA, FCO 46/491, 'CW Military Training Assistance Scheme. Allocations, 1970/71'.
These were revised allocations following MoD increases in fees at UK military training
establishments. Initially somewhat smaller sums had been allocated, and it had been proposed
to spend most on India and Pakistan, but this was changed in view of a perceived need to assist
Nigeria with the task of post-war reconstruction.

world of Biafran suffering as a result of the federal government's blockade of
aid to the breakaway region.[114]

Zambia offers a particularly good example of the tensions that could arise,
especially over loaned personnel. The country was heavily reliant on British
personnel, and by 1967 found itself 'in the red' as it faced claims from Britain

[114] John W. Young, *The Labour Governments, 1964–1970. Volume 2, International Policy* (Manchester University Press, Manchester, 2003), pp. 199–211.

for reimbursement of their salaries and allowances. These costs amounted to £328,000 a year; on top of which the Zambian government also provided assistance with the employment of domestic labour, accommodation, travel allowances and healthcare.[115] The disparity between the allowances and pay given to loaned British servicemen and those earned by Zambians was a source of controversy in the Defence Force; while the Zambian government did not feel that the British government had kept its bit of the bargain in terms of the costs it had conceded in principle it would meet.[116] However, the political differences between the two governments over Britain's refusal to intervene militarily over Rhodesia following the white minority government's unilateral declaration of independence proved to be the most difficult. At the time of UDI Zambia was the only independent black African state bordering Rhodesia, and was reliant on Rhodesia for supplies of oil and coal as well as to transport its principal export, copper. Unsurprisingly Zambia became the leading advocate in the Commonwealth and the United Nations of the use of military force against Rhodesia. In contrast, Harold Wilson's Labour government was reluctant to engage in action it regarded as politically and militarily risky, preferring to rely on the imposition of sanctions against the white minority Rhodesian regime – a development that risked Rhodesian retaliatory action affecting Zambia. Kenneth Kaunda's government flirted with securing other external aid,[117] but viewed British action as the key to the resolution of the issue. The differences between Kaunda and Wilson became increasingly personal and, while Wilson had offered to position British forces in Zambia, his refusal to allow them to take part in offensive action led Kaunda to decline the proposal.[118] This was the context in which in 1967 the Zambian government rejected British terms for the loan of Army personnel after Wilson refused to see them engage in direct action in any conflict with Rhodesia. Kaunda feared the British terms would leave the Zambian government with no 'effective juris-

---

[115] Zambia National Archives [ZNA], CO 17/1/7, UK Technical Assistance and Aid, 1965–67, nos. 22 and 23, notes on costs associated with loaned army personnel, by A/S. Masiye, Permanent Secretary, Office of the President, 13 and 29 March 1967. Income tax by the loaned personnel was paid in Britain.

[116] Ibid., 'UK Technical Assistance and Aid', 1965–67, paras. 8 and 9; conclusions.

[117] A. J. DeRoche, 'You Can't Fight Guns with Knives': National Security and Zambian Responses to UDI, 1965–1973' in Jan–Bart Gewald, Marja Hinfelaar, and Giacoma Macola eds., *One Zambia, Many Histories* (Brill, Leiden, 2008), pp. 77–97. For recent discussion of British considerations, see Philip Murphy, '"An Intricate and Distasteful Subject": British Planning for the Use of Force against the European Settlers of Central Africa, 1952–65', *English Historical Review*, 121 (2006), pp. 746–77, and Carl Watts, '"Killing Kith and Kin": The Viability of British Military Intervention in Rhodesia, 1964–5', *Twentieth Century British History*, XVI (2005), pp. 382–415. Murphy points to long-standing British reservations about the viability of British military action and Watts to the domestic economic and political constraints facing Wilson's government.

[118] Douglas G. Anglin and Timothy M. Shaw, *Zambia's Foreign Policy: Studies in Diplomacy and Dependence* (Westview Press, Colorado, 1979), pp. 113–68.

diction' over the loaned personnel, representing a derogation of Zambian sovereignty incompatible with the country's 'status as an independent state'.[119] He also worried that it might potentially lead to a situation in which the British would renege on arrangements and recall officers at short notice, although privately the President's Office's concluded that the Labour government was unlikely to engage in a 'sudden vindictive withdrawal of all its servicemen'.[120]

For the individuals 'loaned' to overseas governments secondment to African forces was rewarding in material terms, as they received local living allowances.[121] But as African officers began to outnumber British, their situation could feel less comfortable. Major Kent-Payne, posted to Nigeria 1959–62, reacted against what he perceived as the introduction of 'native table manners and customs' like 'eating with fingers and spitting out things one did not like' as more Africans joined the officers' mess.[122] Another officer found the food in his Nigerian mess had become 'distinctly African in nature and not easy on the European palate'.[123] Experience varied from country to country, but some believed themselves increasingly unwelcome in the mess and found themselves at odds with their new political masters.[124] In Nigeria Major General Norman Foster, from 1959 the officer commanding the Nigerian armed forces, found that his Minister of Defence, Muhammadu Ribadu, a Northern Nigerian appointed to the position in October 1960, would often simply refuse to see him. Ribadu sought every opportunity to advance the position of the North and of Northern Nigerians in the Nigerian Army, and British officers found that it became impossible to fail Northern Nigerian officer cadets whatever their standard.[125] For senior British officers commanding Ghanaian and Nigerian units in the UN force during the Congo crisis, maintaining operational standards while managing rapid Africanization and frequently fraught relations to new African authorities proved difficult.[126] As a result, in West Africa British officers were increasingly convinced that they should cease to serve in operational roles, and by 1964 they were employed exclusively in local training.

---

[119] Clayton, 'Foreign Intervention in Africa', p. 234.

[120] ZNA, CO 17/1/7, 'UK Technical Assistance and Aid', 1965–7, with no. 22 'Loan Personnel Agreement', British High Commission, Lusaka, 3 March 1967; no. 24, Minutes of a meeting to discuss British Loaned Personnel Agreement, 30 March 1967, para. 6.

[121] Bodleian, Mss Afr. S. 1734, box 8, file 301, p. 2, Lt. Col. John Meyrick (Nigeria 1959–62).

[122] Ibid., box 6, file 240, f. 8.

[123] Ibid., box 8, file 301, p. 2, Lt Col. John Meyrick (Nigeria 1959–62).

[124] Bodleian, Mss Afr. s. 1715, box 5, file 108, f. 18, Brigadier George Goode (Kenya 1958–61, Zambia 1967).

[125] Bodleian, Mss Afr. s. 1734, box 3, file 142, Major General Norman Foster, ff. 103–4l see also box 8, file 301, memoir p. 3, Lt. Col. John Meyrick (Chief Instructor, Nigerian Military Training College, Kaduna, 1959–62). In 1961 the Nigerian ministry of defence introduced regional quotas for officer training with a minimum of 50 per cent to be drawn from the North: Miners, *Nigerian Army*, p. 116.

[126] Bodleian, Mss Afr. s. 1734, box 10, Major L. R. Raymond, file 341, f. 100.

In East Africa the equanimity of loaned British personnel was shattered by the experience of mutinies that broke out in 1964, occurring first in Zanzibar but spreading to Tanganyika and then to Uganda and Kenya, with British officers accused by the rebel African soldiers of obstructing African pay and promotion. British officers and NCOs serving with African forces were rounded up and detained before being evacuated from the countries with their wives and children, although, with British intervention, the mutinies were quickly suppressed. Few, however, faced such a delicate situation as Captain Charles Ivey, the officer commanding the Training Company at the Military Training School in East Africa, who was asked to train thirty-one former Mau Mau insurgents who had designated ranks within Mau Mau and now sought commissions in the Kenyan Army. After six months Kenyatta came personally to inspect the Mau Mau cohort; he accepted Ivey's recommendation that only two of the thirty-one met the standards for commission and determined that all should repeat the course. Afterwards, Kenyatta returned and commissioned all thirty-one, and on the same day retired twenty-nine of them affording them immediate pension rights. 'Honour appeared to have been reached all way round'. Ivey, however, had found the whole experience of taking those he perceived as 'very nasty terrorists (and in some cases monsters) out of the forest' to train as officers difficult; his request that he be allowed to return to England was turned down on the grounds of political sensitivity.[127]

For Britain, such was the demand for seconded Army personnel, that by mid-1963 the LSP scheme threatened to tax Britain's own military manpower; in the event the sudden withdrawal of many British personnel following the East African mutinies relieved the pressure.[128] Even so, by 1970 there were still 1,044 servicemen on loan to twenty-six governments. Some of these host governments paid the full costs of the LSP working with their forces, but a majority of those on loan were subsidized by the FCO, and in Libya's case, the MoD.[129]

The dispersal of British technical and military assistance unquestionably needs to be seen as instrumental, designed to serve British interests in a Cold War context, as well as to maintain political and economic stability within the Commonwealth-sterling area.[130] The development of sound institutions was of crucial importance both to the success of the wider British project to transfer power to democracies based on the Westminster system and to stability within

---

[127] Bodleian, Mss Afr. s. 1715, box 6, file 146, ff. 17–18.
[128] TNA, WO 163/679, Minutes of the 732nd meeting of the Exec. Committee of the Army Council 5 July 1963; WO 163/681, ECAB/P (64) 18, 'Demands for Seconded Army Personnel', 14 July 1964.
[129] TNA, FCO 46/490, Leonard Curzon (MoD) to P. Nicholls (Treasury), 29 April 1970.
[130] As evident in parliamentary discussion of the legislation establishing the new DTC: *House of Commons Debates*, vol. 639, cols., pp. 247–350.

the Commonwealth. Through its military training especially, Britain hoped to reach those likely to be of influence. While this included some who were scions of important families, or protégés of them, Britain aimed especially at those who 'may one day attain high rank', positions of 'power and influence' in governments or the armed forces.[131] The advent of military regimes in much of postcolonial Africa reinforced this perspective as connections to military personnel were seen as especially beneficial where the military was in, or might gain, power.[132] What is more, British personnel embedded in the institutions of new states during the early transitional years could serve a useful intelligence function. In Ghana, the first British Army officer to command the force of an independent African state, Major General A. G. V. Paley, wrote frequently and secretly to Templer, the Chief of the Imperial General Staff, and to Templer's successor, Field Marshal Sir Francis Festing.[133]

British military assistance also supported British commercial interests. It was a means of promoting arms sales at a time when the British government was contending with growing competition from other weapon-exporting countries, such as France. This commercial factor became a more prominent consideration from 1964 in line with the Labour government's efforts to extend arms sales, partly to recoup some of the costs associated with the manufacture of arms for Britain's own use.[134] Officials hoped that those who had studied in the United Kingdom using British equipment might acquire a 'taste' for it, and British military training was sometimes even dangled as a carrot where there was a prospect of arms sales.[135] Because Britain's military assistance budget was relatively small, and lower than that of its main competitors in the arms sector, the United States, France and Germany, officials involved in the administration of training aid were urged particularly to push those courses of a technical nature where British hardware would be most on show.[136]

Nevertheless, British technical assistance to emergent African states should not be understood simply or even principally as a form of neocolonialism. Independence liberated new states to pursue their own foreign policies and to seek aid where they could. The Ghanaian government, for instance, determined

---

[131] TNA, FCO 46/932, 'UKMTAS. Note on the administration of the scheme', produced for discussion FCO and MoD, January 1972; see also FCO 46/1862, 'British military assistance', paper produced in FCO, January 1979.

[132] FCO 46/2124, no. 86, 'UKMTA. Note by Officials', draft FCO paper, August 1979.

[133] See, e.g., TNA, WO 216/913, no. 40A, Maj. Gen. V. Paley to General Sir F. Festing, 7 March 1959.

[134] M. Phythian, *The Politics of British Arms Sales since 1964* (Manchester University Press, Manchester, 2000), pp. 1, 10.

[135] For example, when the Philippines converted its entire PAL fleet to British aircraft officials concluded that it was worth increasing the country's share of Britain's training budget with a view to possibly securing more sales: TNA, FCO 46/391, 'Military Training Assistance', note by I. W. Mackley, 5 June 1969.

[136] TNA, FCO 46/932, 'The UKMTAS. Note on the Administration of the Scheme', January 1972.

in April 1961 that the country should take 'maximum advantage' of technical assistance available from all sources.[137] But an established association, common language and similarities in institutions already modelled along British lines inclined African politicians to exploit connections to the old colonial power to access resources needed for their own state-building projects, a 'vertical' axis that, as Frederick Cooper argues in relation to French West Africa, was – for all the inequalities of the relationship between ex-colonies and former metropoles – 'still a relationship'.[138] In some instances a reliance on Britain was reinforced by complications encountered in taking advantage of technical assistance and training provided by other sources.[139] Britain's importance as a source of technical assistance to new states was hence not simply symptomatic of the asymmetries of power between the former colonial power and the former colonized; rather, it also reflected local agency, as elites in new states sought to mobilize whatever resources they could to advance their own development projects. In some cases the employment of expatriates also served specific political ends in new states where political elites were wary of appointing individuals from competing regions, ethnicities or classes.[140] Nor was Britain able to dictate the terms under which assistance was provided; as we have seen, these were subject to accommodation and negotiation.[141]

From the British perspective too, technical assistance, while undoubtedly intended to serve as a form of soft power, was also a means of continuing a policy of *decolonization* beyond the constitutional. In line with this, British policymakers saw aid in part as a fixed-term commitment to assist states through the difficult years following independence. The bilateral agreements governing the remuneration arrangements for the supply of civilian personnel had been arranged for periods of up to ten years, with the majority signed between May and June 1961 following the introduction of the OSAS scheme. Where others were negotiated later (e.g., as was the case with Malaysia in 1965), they were still set a terminal date of 1971; especially striking in view of the considerable differences between states and their varying aid requirements.[142]

Alongside the fixed-term basis on which British technical assistance had originally been offered, British economic weakness, which led to

---

[137] PRAAD, RG 3/1/662, 'United Kingdom Technical Assistance', 12 April 1961, with reference to Cabinet decision, 7 February 1961.

[138] Frederick Cooper, *Citizenship between Empire and Nation: Remaking France and French Africa, 1945–1960* (Princeton University Press, Princeton, NJ, 2014), pp. 187–8.

[139] See, e.g., p. 247; see also in relation to Ghana and India: Torrent, 'A "New" Commonwealth for Britain?', p. 598.

[140] Sindab, 'The Impact of Expatriates', pp. 68–76; Myles Osborne, *Ethnicity and Empire in Kenya: Loyalty and Martial Race among the Kamba c. 1800 to the Present* (Cambridge University Press, Cambridge, 2014), pp. 236–7.

[141] As Cullen shows in the case of Kenya, 'Kenya is No Doubt a Special Place', pp. 134–8.

[142] KCL, Special Collections, FCO collection, FCO 4/520, copies of agreements.

the devaluation of sterling in 1967, and reappraisals of the importance of Africa to Britain, led the British government to try to reduce aid to Africa.[143] As a working group of the Cabinet Defence and Overseas Policy Committee complained in 1964, British aid policy was fashioned by Britain's 'imperial past'. The group judged the proportion of aid directed at Africa unwarranted in terms of either 'western or our national interests'.[144] The following year the British government asked the Americans to increase their aid to Africa.[145] The decision to withdraw British forces from east of Suez further reduced Africa's strategic significance to Britain.[146] From the 1970s the British government cut back on the supply of expatriates to some destinations under the OSAS scheme and became more stringent in its policing of requests for assistance.[147]

In 1970 the Treasury, perceived by the FCO as unsympathetic to military assistance, also sought more vigorously to cap Britain's overall spending on all forms of military aid, and within the FCO itself officials anticipated that the more substantial of Britain's Commonwealth military commitments would eventually 'wither away'.[148]

In the early 1970s this British determination to cut back led some to allege that Britain was 'giving up' on Africa. As Nigeria's head of state, General Gowon, complained to Edward Heath, following British accession to the European Economic Community (EEC), Britain appeared to have 'lost interest in Africa'.[149] From 1974 the new Labour governments, initially under Wilson, and from 1976, his successor as prime minister, James Callaghan, took what Anne Lane characterizes as a 'bigger view of the world and Britain's potential in it' than Heath's Conservative government had done, seeking a re-engagement with the Commonwealth,[150] but Britain's financial situation was weak, necessitating further defence cuts.[151] By summer 1978 British spending on

---

[143] Ichiro Maekawa, 'Neo-colonialism Reconsidered: A Case Study of East Africa in the 1960s and 70s', *Journal of Imperial and Commonwealth History*, 43 (2015), pp. 317–41.

[144] TNA, CAB 148/6, DO (O) 64 (36), 10 June 1964, report by the Future Planning Working Group, para. 24.

[145] S. R. Ashton and W. R. Louis eds., 'Introduction', *East of Suez*, I, p. cv.

[146] See discussion in Rouvez, *Disconsolate Empires*, ch. 6; Saki Dockrill, *Britain's Retreat from East of Suez: The Choice between Europe and the World, 1945–1968* (Palgrave Macmillan, Basingstoke, 2002).

[147] As they did in the case of Kenya, Holtham and Arthur Hazlewood, *Aid and Inequality in Kenya*, pp. 80–1.

[148] TNA, FCO 46/490, 'Military Assistance', note by J. R. W. Parker, Defence Dept, FCO 13 April 1970.

[149] TNA, DEFE 11/8527, record of conversation between Gowon and Edward Heath, 13 June 1973.

[150] Anne Lane, 'Foreign and Defence Policy' in A. Seldon and K. Hickson eds., *New Labour, Old Labour: The Wilson and Callaghan Governments, 1974–79* (Routledge, London and New York, 2004), pp. 154–69, esp. 156.

[151] Ritchie Ovendale ed., *British Defence Policy since 1945* (Manchester University Press, Manchester, 1994), p. 14.

military assistance amounted to a paltry £1.915 million per annum, a sum tiny compared to the £42 million allocated by France and on a par with Australian expenditure; at this juncture the Cabinet decided Britain should once again step up its military assistance to African states to help them guard against internal and external threats.[152]

Yet if the economic crises of the 1970s prevented Britain from playing as large a role as some international and foreign donors of technical and military assistance, it also proved difficult to reduce Britain's commitments. In 1969, in view of the continuing needs of some African states, supplementary arrangements under OSAS and new bilateral agreements were made to cover the period until March 1976.[153] Ten years after Kenyan independence, of 2,791 foreigners in operational, advisory and voluntary posts in Kenya and also the East African Community, 1,565 were British, including 1,134 there as a result of OSAS and 160 through BESS; in contrast, there were 212 Americans and 208 Danes. Fifteen years after Zambia attained independence there were still 944 expatriates employed under the OSAS scheme.[154] As Tony Killick argues, imperialism acted as 'an inertial force', with Commonwealth African states continuing to receive a high percentage of British bilateral aid.[155]

The same was true in the case of military assistance. Kenya was among the states in which the FCO had continued to envisage that the work of the British Army team would be phased out, but where Britain continued to provide military assistance long into the postcolonial period.[156] Ghana was another country where in 1970 it was thought the British commitment would decline, but only a couple of years later, when Ghana reduced the number of places at UK training establishments it paid for because of its own financial difficulties, Britain significantly increased its aid allocation.[157] Over the next decade it continued to attract a sizeable slice of British spending. In Swaziland, more than a decade after independence, the Director of the British Military Assistance Office in the MoD feared that if the British withdrew assistance 'the Army would almost certainly collapse'.[158] In other cases, military assistance served – the British hoped – as a prophylactic

---

[152] TNA, FCO 46/1862, draft letter Secretary of State for FCO to PM, Secretary of State for Defence, and Chancellor undated, but following Cabinet decision 29 June 1978; 'British Military Assistance. Confidential', paper produced in FCO, para. 2, c. January 1979.

[153] *Public Service Overseas*, para. 5.

[154] Figures from Holtham and Hazlewood, *Aid and Inequality in Kenya*. p. 51, table 4; Sindab, 'The Impact of Expatriates', p. 125.

[155] Killick, 'Policy Autonomy', p. 673.

[156] Where a new RAF team was providing training in association with the sale of British aircraft: TNA, FCO 46/490, 'UK Military Technical Assistance' by A. T. Smith (Defence Department, FCO) addressed to R. Tesh (Defence Department, FCO), 7 May 1970. For Anglo-Kenyan relations during the 1970s see, esp., Cullen, 'Kenya is No Doubt a Special Place', ch. 6.

[157] TNA, FCO 46/932, R. Tesh to John Wilson (West African Department, FCO), February 1972.

[158] TNA, FCO 46/2878, no. 13, Maj.-General K. Perkins, Director MAO, to P. J. Weston, head FCO Defence Department, 3 August 1981.

minimizing the risk of former colonies turning to Britain for help in the 'event of crises'.[159] From 1979 under Margaret Thatcher, more focus was also put on military support to the southern African front-line states as an alternative to economic sanctions against South Africa. With the advent of African majority rule in Zimbabwe, Britain became involved once more in delivering military assistance to a new African state.[160] British imperialism continued to shape Britain's postcolonial aid policies, and, as we shall see in Chapter 6, on-going military technical assistance contributed to sustained, long-term foreign and Commonwealth recruitment to Sandhurst.

Conclusion

This chapter has shown the degree to which British colonies entered independence woefully ill-prepared. For a variety of reasons too little was done too late to establish local institutions and to advance an African professional class. Remedying this situation was the most urgent task facing emergent states as well as the wider international community. Technical assistance became a prominent part of Britain's postcolonial aid budget; conversely for many former British colonies, Britain, especially initially, was the most important source of such aid. British technical assistance was designed to deliver influence and serve other British goals, but it was also a way of continuing a policy of decolonization. As such, it should not be seen as constituting a distinct phase in postcolonial British–African relations but a constituent part of the decolonization process.

While this chapter has focused on the British state, British technical assistance was not just a state activity. The new Overseas Development Ministry specifically emphasized the role that organizations beyond the state might play in making Britons available for overseas work. 'A technical assistance programme, to be successful', the ODM stated, 'must make the fullest use of available resources not only inside the Government, but also in universities, technical colleges, research institutes, statutory corporations, employers' associations, trade unions, the co-operative movement, local government bodies and voluntary associations. To be effective technical assistance must be a transfer of know-how from country to country, not simply from government to government'.[161] In Chapter 3, I turn to consider the universities' role in adaptation of the established Colonial Service training regime to cater to African entrants to public administration.[162] Chapter 4 will discuss the Bank of England's part

[159] TNA, FCO 46/2124, no. 86, 'UKMTA. Note by Officials', draft FCO paper, August 1979.
[160] Stapleton, *African Police and Soldiers*, pp. 174–82.
[161] *Ministry of Overseas Development,* para. 115.
[162] *Technical Assistance from the United Kingdom for Overseas Development*, paras. 92–4.

in the development of central banking, an example of technical assistance that fell outside the purview of the British state. Although the Bank's initiatives were devised to serve its own interests, they nonetheless also constituted a form of aid and serve as an example of 'know-how from country to country, not simply from government to government' assistance; an illustration also of how significant forms of British assistance might be effectively invisible in official records. Even the Mint became involved in some forms of technical assistance to new states, as discussed in Chapter 5. Chapter 6 returns to the theme of military assistance and explores the ways in which Sandhurst became an instrument of British soft power in the post-war era. Thus, as the remainder of this book will show, to properly understand the patterns and characteristics of British overseas technical assistance, we need to pay due attention to the role and priorities of a series of institutions of very varied histories and interests as they navigated the consequences of constitutional change.

3 Teaching What 'the Natives Need to Know': The Universities of Oxford and Cambridge and Training for Overseas Public Administration

In summer 1956, Colonial Administrative Service probationers sitting the final exam for Margery Perham's Oxford course on 'Government' would have found it hard to challenge the statement they were being asked to discuss: that 'The British have had more success in creating politicians than in training civil servants in their overseas territories'.[1] There were a handful of colonial cadets among them, but that in this twilight era of colonialism most students were expatriates shortly to take up positions overseas as district officers was evidence of Britain's on-going failure to produce a class of local administrators. Nowhere was the issue more pressing than in Britain's African colonies, where, as we saw in the last chapter, Britain's record of appointing locals to senior administrative positions was lamentably poor. Developing the sound public services crucial to the Westminster parliamentary project and training their staff were perhaps the most urgent issues raised by constitutional change. The late colonial and early postcolonial eras hence saw a variety of initiatives – local, British and international – intended to assist with this task. New institutes of public administration were established in Britain's African colonies, often under the management of British officers, but increasingly funded by American and other international aid; a variety of other schemes were inaugurated in Britain and elsewhere. But when it came to inculcating the values associated with the British civil service 'nowhere', claimed one Oxford source, could this 'be done better than in the older universities such as Oxford'.[2]

Since 1946 the Universities of Oxford and Cambridge, together with the University of London, had delivered the enhanced training regime for entrants to the Colonial Administrative Service recommended by the wartime Devonshire Committee, thus extending their association with the Empire on the eve of its collapse. While this programme must be understood in the context of revitalized post-war British imperialism, developmentalism, and the 'second colonial

[1] Bodleian, Mss Perham, 244/4, f. 14, 'Oversea Course A Examination, 1956. Government'.
[2] Bodleian, OUA, UR 6/Col 4/ file 13, COL/CP/789, 'The Future of Overseas Services Courses A and B at Oxford University' [undated, but 1961].

occupation', as we saw in Chapter 1 the universities themselves had played a key role in its introduction. Academics and administrators had helped frame discussions about the future of the Service and training, advancing the claims of their own disciplines for representation on the reformed training courses.

As the numbers of local recruits entering the Colonial Administrative Service (CAS) slowly increased, the Colonial Office inducted them into this training regime, a decision that eventually resulted in the extraordinary situation whereby courses created for British CAS probationers developed into training programmes aimed wholly at overseas civil servants in independent countries, principally within the Commonwealth, and financed initially by the Colonial Office, and then by the Department of Technical Co-operation and its replacement, the Ministry of Overseas Development. They became a striking feature of Britain's provision of technical cooperation to developing nations.[3] In 1962, although the overall number of overseas students on them was small relative to the scale of appointments needed to Africanize public services, the DTC nonetheless saw the courses as 'key' because they were aimed at high fliers likely to become department heads. In an assessment that reflects the DTC's distinctively British understanding of the central role played by an elite administrative cadre, officials anticipated such individuals would 'probably have a greater influence than any other officials in advising their Governments on policy and in seeing that the decisions of their Governments are effectively carried out'.[4]

The survival of courses originally devised for the district officers who, through their fictional representative, *Sanders of the River*, had become emblematic of British imperialism constitutes a striking continuity between the colonial and postcolonial eras. However, at a point at which the wider direction of events remained unclear and British officials still needed to cater to an on-going colonialism, while also assisting with training their African successors in decolonizing states, adapting the existing structures and architecture of colonialism was a logical step. Furthermore, experience in South Asia may have helped reinforce British expectations that colonial recruits would be inducted into Britain's existing training programme. Although the post-war era saw the inauguration of international schemes to assist with the development and modernization of bureaucracies in emergent states, notably under the United Nations Technical Assistance programme, the American Agency for International Development, and the American Ford Foundation, newly independent South Asian countries had continued to adhere to British practices and in some instances to look to Britain for training. Indeed, following a request by

---

[3] *Technical Assistance from the UK for Overseas Development.*
[4] TNA, OD 19/13, 'TPA 62 (i)', Committee on Training in Public Administration for Overseas Countries', Memo for Bridges Committee produced in DTC, 11 January 1962.

the Government of Pakistan that its officers might be allocated places on the training courses, Oxford began admitting Pakistani administrative probationers in the late 1950s, a move seen in Oxford as constituting a reversion to a form of the training entrants to the Indian Civil Service had received before independence and partition.[5] Admitting overseas entrants to public administration to the established Oxbridge training courses was also consistent with a broader commitment to encouraging colonial students to come to Britain to study. However, the evolution of these courses to become part of Britain's technical assistance programme was in no small degree the consequence also of a proactive approach by the universities and their associates, especially the University of Oxford.

This argument is pursued through an account of a series of distinct phases in the history of the courses. The first such phase occurred in the early 1950s and saw significant criticisms of the courses raise a question over their future. The threat averted, for the rest of the decade they catered to increasing numbers of colonial entrants to the Service. A second critical moment occurred in the early 1960s when African independence and the cessation of British recruitment to the courses led British officials once again to reconsider the future of the courses. They survived, albeit in a revised form and dependent henceforth on the recruitment of overseas students. Oxford finally ceased involvement in 1969, although it retained a role in training foreign diplomats. A final section explores the Cambridge course as taught in the 1970s, and the circumstances that led to its eventual demise in 1981. These latter sections show how over time the courses acquired new epistemologies, focused primarily on development studies. They nevertheless provide striking illustration of how Empire left legacies within the structures of British institutions long after most of the Empire had gone and thus of the colonial roots both of postcolonial development studies and practice.[6]

The Devonshire Colonial Administrative Service Courses

The principle that the Devonshire courses might cater to non-European recruits had been established at the outset.[7] As Table 3.1 shows, from 1946 a handful

---

[5] Bodleian, OUA, UR 6/Col/4/12, 'Proposal to admit officers of the Government of Pakistan to Oversea Service Courses A and B, or a combination of both', note by H. P. W. Murray, 6 June 1955; see also Hugh Braibanti, 'Introduction' in Ralph Braibanti and others, *Asian Bureaucratic Systems Emergent from the British Imperial Tradition* (Duke University Press, Durham, NC, 1966), pp. 3–22, esp. 4; Symonds, *British and Their Successors*, p. 90.

[6] On which see also especially studies by Kothari, Dimier and Hodge, discussed in the introduction.

[7] CO 877/22/13, 'An Inquiry into the system of training the Colonial Service with suggestions for its reform to meet postwar conditions', memo by Sir R. Furse, reproduced in Ashton and Stockwell eds., *Imperial Policy and Colonial Practice*, I, no. 5.

Table 3.1. *Students admitted at Oxford, Cambridge and London to the 'First Devonshire' training course, 1946–53*[a]

Year	Total	Local recruits[b]
1946–7	122	4
1947–8	140	–
1948–9	86	–
1949–50	87	4
1950–1	120	2
1951–2	95	5
1952–3	69	2

[a]Compiled from: CUL, UA, GBR/0265/CDEV 11/1, The Standing Joint Committee on Colonial Service Training, CST (53)3, Draft Papers for the Conference on Colonial Service Training, 'First Course – the problem of numbers'.
[b]The source did not differentiate between European and non-European cadets of 'local' domicile.

of what were described as 'local' recruits, both European and non-European, travelled to Britain to participate, although they were strongly outnumbered by British personnel recruited to an expanding Colonial Service.

In 1951 the Colonial Office, conscious of the growing number of local appointments being made to colonial public administration and of the fact that this trend would inevitably intensify, urged 'that every encouragement should be given to locally domiciled officers to come on these courses'. Officials argued that this was one of the 'most potent means' of ensuring the 'continuance of the British tradition and British ideals in administration in the Colonies'. The universities were encouraged to make small but necessary adaptations to cater to the local recruits, such as substituting new content for unnecessary language instruction.[8]

Yet the new courses were plagued from the outset by administrative and other problems. As we have seen, there were tensions between Oxbridge and London.[9] More significantly, by the early 1950s, the Colonial Office had concerns about their value. Like colonial governments, which bore about half the costs of their own administrative cadets, it was keen to reduce expenditure on training. There was a note of incredulity in a minute by one Colonial Office official on learning that his department was currently paying the salaries of 'no less than twenty-eight academics'.[10] Such worries might have acquired less

[8] Bodleian, OUA, UR 6/ Col/4/10, CST (51) 1, Note by the Colonial Office, 25 January 1951.
[9] See Chapter 1, pp. 37–8.
[10] TNA, CO 877/50/2, minute by D. H. Morris, 22 January 1951; CO 877/49/6, minutes by D. H. Morris and A. F. Newbolt, 24 November 1951, 5 December 1951.

traction if some officials had not also felt the first course to be 'doubtfully sound educationally', comprising a 'crowded syllabus' of 'scant practical value', including tuition in colonial history, geography, colonial systems of government, anthropology, 'native' languages and some practical instruction in other areas.[11] Colonial governments again shared these reservations.[12] There was a 'one-size-fits-all' approach to training, and some of the subjects taught were deemed irrelevant or of no practical application to administrators heading for very different destinations within the sprawling British Empire. For example, the government of Aden doubted that the time devoted to forestry was useful to administrators concerned only with a port and its immediate hinterland.[13] Most governments attached importance to language tuition, but were ambivalent about subjects such as economics, colonial history and geography. On his arrival in Nigeria in 1950 as a new administrative cadet, Anthony Kirk–Greene was questioned by his Resident as to what he had been taught. 'I told him about imperial history and comparative colonial policies, he said that sounded a more suitable fare for an about-to-be governor than a dogsbody cadet'; typing or accounting, his Resident observed, would have been more useful.[14] Some wanted the training to be even more practical. The British administration in the Seychelles argued for instruction in bricklaying and roofing, while the East African colonial governments together championed driving and car maintenance.[15] Among probationers themselves a year at Oxford or Cambridge was enjoyed as a pleasant interlude, particularly when it followed wartime service, a factor that was acknowledged as significant in encouraging post-war recruitment to the Service. 'Pure delight, utter bliss' judged one probationer.[16] But like their sponsors, some had reservations as to the practical relevance of their studies, regretting that they had not been taught more of the politics and history of the territories to which they were heading.[17]

[11] TNA, CO 877/51/9, no. 1, 'Colonial Service Training', memo by D. H. Morris, 11 April 1951.
[12] CUL, UA, GBR/0265/CDEV 2/5, Minutes of the Colonial [later Overseas] Studies Committee, 8 June 1953.
[13] CUL, UA, GBR/0265/CDEV 11/1, The Standing Joint Committee of Universities on Colonial Service Training, CST (53), annex I, Draft Papers for the Conference on Colonial Service Training, 'Summary of replies received from Colonial Governments to the Secretary of State's Circular Despatch No. 707/52'.
[14] A. H. M. Kirk-Greene, 'Public Administration and the Colonial Administrator' in *Public Administration and Development*, 19 (1999), no. 5, pp. 507–19, quotation 512.
[15] CUL, UA, GBR/0265/CDEV 11/1, The Standing Joint Committee of Universities on Colonial Service Training, CST (53), annex I, Draft Papers for the Conference on Colonial Service Training, 'Summary of replies received from Colonial Governments to the Secretary of State's Circular Despatch No. 707/52'.
[16] R. A. Hill, cited in A. H. M. Kirk-Greene, *Symbol of Authority. The British District Officer in Africa* (Frank Cass, London, 2006), p. 49.
[17] Ibid., pp. 50–3; Tony Schur ed., *From the Cam to the Zambezi: Colonial Service and the Path to the New Zambia* (I. B. Tauris, London, 2015), esp. John Theakstone, 'Mumbwa, Broken Hill, Mkushi', pp. 221–30.

Some colonial governments had already voted with their feet, recruiting British cadets without any training since they were in urgent need of new officers. Alarmed, Jerry Cornes, supervisor of the Oxford course and a former member of the Colonial Service himself, suggested that governments must be weaned away from direct appointments. An increase in the recruitment of locals to administrative posts appeared to reinforce this trend towards direct appointments. The Gold Coast government, the first to appoint Africans to its administrative service, had recently declined to send three such appointees to Britain on the grounds that the Devonshire courses were only relevant to expatriates who needed to learn about Africa.[18]

Many colonial governments also had reservations about the 'second' Devonshire course, which officers took after two years in the field.[19] Although 614 attended this between 1947/8 and 1952/3 (including some 116 'locally domiciled' officers), staffing problems made governments reluctant to release officers to attend for three terms, especially as they were still responsible for paying the officers' salaries and travel. As a result the course had initially been reduced to two terms preceded by a preliminary summer school.[20] In line with concerns about both elements of the Devonshire training system, the Colonial Office began to consider a variety of possible changes to the courses and even the abandonment of preservice training altogether.[21] In 1953 it convened a conference to explore the question.

The universities had their own worries. Margery Perham was concerned that only one 'black man' was registered for the next course. She feared that Africans seeking higher education were going to America or to a new colonial institution established by the Dutch, or indeed 'anywhere' but England. Perham asked the University's registrar, Sir Douglas Veale, whether Oxford could 'offer attractions to these black men which would counteract their tendency to seek their cultures from less desirable sources'. In turn Veale himself thought that the government failed to finance the courses properly. He queried caustically whether the United Kingdom was 'rich enough both in money and men to support both a welfare state and an empire'; at least, he concluded, it could be urged that higher education was 'much cheaper than groundnuts'

---

[18] Bodleian, OUA, UR 6/COL/16, file 1, 'Note on Future of Devonshire Courses', J. F. Cornes, 5 February 1953. John ('Jerry') Cornes had served in Northern Nigeria and Palestine. He was course supervisor, 1947–53. See obituary, *Daily Telegraph*, 25 June 2001.

[19] CUL, UA, GBR/0265/CDEV 11/1, The Standing Joint Committee on Colonial Service Training CST (53), annex I, Draft Papers for the Conference on Colonial Service Training, 'Summary of replies received from Colonial Governments to the Secretary of State's Circular Despatch No. 707/52'.

[20] Ibid., CST (53)1, Draft Papers for the Conference on Colonial Service Training, 'Basic principle of the Devonshire Scheme and subsequent modification'.

[21] TNA, CO 877/51/9, minutes by D. H. Morris, 6 November 1951; 'Colonial Service Training' memo by D. H. Morris, 11 April 1951.

(a reference to the notoriously unsuccessful flagship development project).[22] Sir Ralph Furse was equally anxious. He had retired from the Colonial Office but until 1957 remained a member of the Oxford Committee for Colonial (from 1956 Commonwealth) Studies, on which he had sat since shortly after its formation, and which provided an alternative platform from which to exercise some influence over colonial matters. Furse advised Veale that they might have to take measures to 'fortify' the position of the Devonshire courses in the 'face of possible faintheartedness in some quarters'.[23] In May 1953 he wrote that the issue was not just one of the 'survival of the course', but 'perhaps also of checking a possible disintegration' of the administrative service.[24] Whereas in the 1940s Furse had argued in favour of bringing London into the training in order to dispel claims that there was a class bias in recruitment to the courses, he now advised that the most 'important thing' was 'to drop London' from the first course, identifying the predominance of London 'products' going to Malaya as underlying some of the criticism,[25] and asserting the greater suitability of a 'residential university' on the Oxbridge collegiate model 'for Colonials'.[26] Cornes, the course supervisor, believed it would be best if the first course was concentrated entirely at Oxford, with Cambridge only retaining a footing via training agricultural probationers and in the second course. Oxford, he suggested, understood the vital role universities had to play in the 'drama of the new Commonwealth and Empire' and 'had taken steps to fit herself for her role'. In February 1953, Furse, Veale, Perham and Cornes concluded that the time was ripe for a resuscitation of the Devonshire Committee.[27]

Both Veale and Furse were strikingly confident of their capacity to shape imperial developments. Both sought to protect a training system which from the outset they had conceived to serve an ideological as well as a practical purpose – to assist probationers, in Veale's words, to appreciate the value of their work and see the Empire as generally a 'beneficient Institution'. Amidst on-going budgetary pressures and accelerating colonial political change, they came to see the university rather than the Colonial Office as best upholding this aspect of Britain's imperial mission. The Colonial Office, Veale feared,

---

[22] Bodleian, OUA, UR 6/COL/4, file 11, confidential note by Veale, 11 October 1952.
[23] Ibid., Furse to Veale, 26 January 1953.
[24] Bodleian, OUA, UR 6/Col 16/file 1, Furse to Veale, 9 May 1953.
[25] Gardiner, 'Sentinels of Empire', p. 81. Cadets destined for Malaya were generally taught at the LSE because of the way in which students were distributed between London, Oxford and Cambridge on the basis of their requirements for tuition in particular languages: OUA, UR 16, Col/ 4/ file 10, Note by Veale recording conversation with Furse, 15 February 1951; note addressed to Vice Chancellor, 24 January 1951.
[26] Bodleian, OUA, UR 6/Col/ 16/ file 1, Furse to Veale, 12 May 1953.
[27] Bodleian, OUA, UR 6/Col/4/file 11, Cornes to Veale, 5 May 1953; and 'Note of a discussion at dinner' [attended by Furse, Veale, Perham, Cornes, Mr Paterson, and Keith Murray, Rector of Lincoln College], 26 February 1953.

believing 'as it did a hundred years ago that the colonies are a burden and that the sooner we get rid of them the better', cared only to ensure a civil service that would prevent 'British rule from falling into disgrace'; resistance to this 'defeatist mood', would 'have to come from the universities if it is to come from anywhere'. 'Events', Furse observed of his own former department, always 'overtake the Col. [sic] Office, because it always starts too late'.[28] As we shall see, there are interesting parallels here to the Bank of England, where, a decade later, officials would express similar frustration at what they perceived as defeatism on the part of a Colonial Office concerned only, in their words, with 'shedding its responsibilities', and a comparable sense that it was left to others to maintain standards, in this case in relation to an orderly management of colonial currency boards.[29]

How far in practice Service training fulfilled the hopes Veale and Furse invested in it is, of course, a different matter. While some limited evidence suggests that what administrators learned shaped their working practices,[30] Christopher Prior's study of British colonial officials before the Second World War concludes that there were distinct limits to the impact of postgraduate preservice training, a reflection not just of what he identifies as 'imprecise' and generalized teaching, but of the diversity of the officials own views, conditioned by 'self-preservation, self-improvement and self-aggrandizement'.[31] What Veale and Furse aimed at was more ideological than educational, and at least in an earlier period their outlook was probably consistent with wider metropolitan mores and attitudes. Paul Deslandes' analysis of student journalism at Oxford and Cambridge before 1920 reveals how home undergraduates' reactions to non-Europeans and non-Christians arriving in their midst reflected their self-understanding as 'white, British, Protestant Christians, imperial leaders and gentlemen'.[32] But there were always multiple cultures of imperialism in Britain, and among entrants to the Colonial Service it seems likely that the diversity Prior identifies only increased in the post-war period, a consequence not just of a gradually widening recruitment pool, but also a product of the fast-changing political situations within the Empire.[33] Service memoirs and biographies reveal a wide variety of motivations and viewpoints among post-war entrants, and for some colonial political change appears to have enhanced the Service's appeal. Bruce Nightingale, determined on 'an outdoor life', applied

[28] Bodleian, OUA, UR 6/Col/16/ file 1, Brief for the Vice-Chancellor, 1 August 1953; Furse to Veale, 5 August 1953.
[29] See Chapter 4, p. 165.
[30] See e.g., Douglas Johnson, 'Political Intelligence, Colonial Ethnography, and Analytical Anthropology in the Sudan' in Tilley and Johnson eds., *Ordering Africa*, pp. 309–35, esp. 311.
[31] Prior, *Exporting Empire*, ch. 2, and p. 171.
[32] Paul Deslandes, 'The Foreign Element', p. 57.
[33] On attempts to broaden the social basis of the Service, see Jeppesen, 'Sanders of the River'.

to the Service in 1956. His interest piqued by what he refers to as the Colonial Office's attempt to explain its failures of policy in Kenya and Cyprus (where Britain was then engaged in counter-insurgency campaigns), Nightingale claims retrospectively to have decided that 'the right thing to do was to go and see what was happening on the ground'.[34] Others have written with enthusiasm about the opportunity to help colonies prepare for self-government. 'It seemed to us young-men', one early post-war recruit to Nigeria, N. C. McClintock, claims, 'starry-eyed idealists as we were, that this was something really worthwhile to which we could devote our lives. This was to be one of the great crusades of the twentieth century ... to free Africa ... and to lead her people towards the dignity of political independence.' Nevertheless, he admits, that he 'never imagined that it would fall to us to put the culminating touches to the work'.[35]

There is some irony in the fact that Veale and Furse's desire to preserve the Devonshire training system reflected an ambivalence about this changing colonial political climate, given that its introduction had corresponded to a wartime revival of imperial purpose inextricably bound up with new rhetorics of development and partnership. Nevertheless, by 1952–3 they were developing a plan of action, aimed at getting Cambridge on side, and shaping debate within the Colonial Office, not least via A. F. Newbolt, Furse's brother-in-law and conveniently also his successor as director of CAS recruitment. Newbolt was due to retire, and the pair sought to settle matters while he was still in post.[36] They were assisted by Oxford's vice chancellor, and chair of the University's Committee for Colonial Studies, Sir Maurice Bowra, well known for his liking for conspiratorial planning. A classical scholar, with elements of the radical, declaring himself 'anti-prig, anti-élitist, anti-solemn, anti-Balliol', Bowra was nonetheless a staunch defender of Oxford and its values.[37] Like Veale he was one of a handful of dons on a 'secret' list of those whom Furse relied for pre-interview information about candidates for entry to the Service, and, also like Veale, he had been involved in pre-war Service training and the Devonshire Committee.[38] In advance of the 1953 conference to discuss training, attended by representatives from all three universities and the Colonial Office, they

---

[34] Bruce Nightingale, *Seven Rivers to Cross: A Mostly British Council Life* (Radcliffe Press, London, 1996), pp. 32–3, 36, 42.

[35] N. C. McClintock, *Kingdoms in the Sand and Sun: An African Path to Independence* (Radcliffe Press, London, 1992), pp. 44–5.

[36] Bodleian, OUA, UR 6/Col 16/file 1, Furse to Veale, 9 May 1953, 12 May 1953; note by Veale, 18 May 1953.

[37] L. G. Mitchell, 'Sir Maurice Bowra', *Oxford Dictionary of National Biography*, accessed 5 October 2015.

[38] Gardiner, 'Sentinels of Empire', pp. 48–9, 87; Bodleian, Mss Perham, 245/5, Copy of 'Reflections on the Overseas Service Courses and their Club', E. G. Rowe, October 1969.

set out – in their words – to 'educate' its chairman, Lord Munster.[39] Suitably briefed, Munster opened the proceedings with a ringing endorsement of the value of training local recruits in Britain, not least as a way of 'strengthening the links which exist between the Mother Country and the Colonial territories'. It was not without significance that the conference was held in Oxford, enabling Bowra to deliver a lengthy opening address in which he pressed some of the arguments rehearsed beforehand with Veale and Furse.[40]

Although Veale and Bowra were powerful figures their interventions nonetheless beg the question of the degree to which they represented the wider University. For all that Oxford had a history of association to the Empire, those teaching, such as Margery Perham, had struggled to establish a secure base within the University for colonial studies; one reason why she had been so quick to seize upon the opportunities offered by funding associated with the Devonshire courses to establish the Institute of Colonial [later Commonwealth] Studies of which she became first director. The 'new' subject of colonial studies had a home within Nuffield College, founded as a base for social sciences, and while the training courses drew on, and had the support of, key faculty members, some of the posts created to support the courses lacked collegiate status and were among those the University termed 'non-don'. Even Veale had himself earlier warned Furse in connection with increasing demands for the 'loan' overseas of university staff, that his institution's resources were 'limited' and not every eminent scholar suitable for this 'kind of missionary work' within the Empire–Commonwealth.[41]

We should also note that both at Oxford and Cambridge the first appearance of nonwhite and non-Christian students had earlier given rise to tensions,[42] and some colleges had been reluctant to accept students of colonial origin. Even Balliol, notable for its connections to the Indian Civil Service, had operated an 'informal' quota system for Indian students.[43] That as recently as 1938 Cambridge had advised the Colonial Office that 'all Colleges were reluctant to accept coloured students and ... all would feel more difficulty in accepting Africans than others', illustrates the prejudice operating within the Oxbridge system.[44]

---

[39] Bodleian, OUA, UR 6/Col 16/file 1, Furse to Veale, 5 August 1953.
[40] CUL, UA, Papers of the University General Board, GB 760/939, file 1944–58, Extract from Lord Munster's Opening Address to the 1953 Conference to consider Colonial Service Training, 14–17 September 1953; Address by Sir Maurice Bowra.
[41] Bodleian, OUA, UR 6/ Col/6/1, Veale to Furse, 25 May 1943. It was no use he advised seconding those who suffered from 'ochlophobia, or is exceedingly ill-mannered, or enjoys poor health, or has a disagreeable wife, who insists on going with him'.
[42] Deslandes, 'The Foreign Element'.
[43] Perraton, *History of Foreign Students in Britain*, pp. 71, 75.
[44] *Report of the Colonial Students Committee*, 1938, 24, quoted in ibid., p. 163.

Yet even if the delivery of one-year courses sat uneasily within a system at this date overwhelmingly focused on undergraduates, and was undoubtedly marginal to the universities, in the immediate post-war era the views of men like Veale and Bowra certainly corresponded to a broad commitment to public service and to the Empire, as epitomized in Furse's own college, Balliol, and their well-established role in teaching and researching colonial administration (to which in the 1950s and 1960s, however, Oxford showed greater commitment than Cambridge, and greater willingness to assume financial responsibility for some of the associated activities and posts).[45] Dimier argues that what had been at stake in the interwar struggle for participation in the courses was no less than the 'place and legitimacy' of the universities in the 'production of the British elite'.[46] By the 1950s the issue was not just the production of a British, but also new colonial elites. As Oxford's Committee for Commonwealth Studies recorded in 1957, shortly before Furse ceased to be a member, delivering the one-year training courses was not without its costs, especially for the colleges in which the students matriculated. Nevertheless, they were also an investment in the 'people in whose hands lay the future of large areas of the Commonwealth'.[47]

Among those directly involved at Oxford there was nevertheless no unanimity of views. Strikingly, in 1953 those responsible for teaching the courses at Oxford were left out of some of the initial discussions about the future. Veale and Bowra agreed that they would explain to members of Oxford's Committee for Colonial Studies that they had not been consulted because the issue had arisen in the long vacation, although they acknowledged that Margery Perham, a key figure in the 1940s, whom they perceived as out of favour at the Colonial Office, must play some role.[48] Perham like some other lecturers was more sensitive to the political climate and the importance of moving away from colonial agendas if the universities were successfully to cater to local recruits. Indeed, although Perham and these academics supported the continuation of the courses, they did so for almost diametrically opposed reasons. Whereas Veale, Furse and Cornes believed the courses might prop up an ailing British colonialism, helping, as Cornes saw it, to propagate 'ties of a common culture and common values' among civil servants 'whether black, yellow or white' at a point at which 'it is all-important to counteract the centrifugal forces of

---

[45] Bodleian, OUA, CW 1/2, minutes 17 October 1950, 24 April 1951; CW 1/3, minutes 24 February 1970. Perhaps in the early 1950s this reflected Bowra's influence.

[46] Dimier, 'Three Universities', p. 355.

[47] Bodleian, OUA, CW 1/2, minutes CCS, 5 March 1957. Furse was still a member of the committee at this stage and the comments indicate his hand.

[48] Bodleian, OUA, UR 6/Col/16/file 1, brief for Bowra by Veale, 1 August 1953; Veale to Furse, 6 August 1953.

nationalism',[49] Perham saw them as important in the preparation of the colonies for self-government. In Perham's view with the colonies, 'on the verge of coming forward as communities fit to govern themselves', they were 'asking from us the one great essential, the training of their leaders and experts so that they may take back from us the control of their own affairs'. As a result, British universities now had a 'more important task than any handled by the Colonial Office itself'. Roland Oliver locates these views in a shift in Perham's thinking following the shock of the fall of Britain's far eastern colonies: from previously believing in the appropriateness of British officers – preferably public-school and Oxbridge educated – to administer African peoples, Perham had come instead to espouse a new educational mission.[50] At the 1953 Munster conference Perham argued for the importance of avoiding any colonial bias, and getting away from 'Colonial' studies.[51]

Whatever their different motivations, at the Munster conference delegates from Oxford and Cambridge not only succeeded in ensuring the survival of the Oxbridge role but also managed, as Furse had intended, to eliminate London from the delivery of the first training course except in relation to some language tuition at SOAS.[52] The decision was taken to continue the first course, now to be renamed 'Course A', at Oxbridge, to ignore calls for more practical training and to encourage local recruits to attend it. The second course, now 'Course B', was henceforth to be offered to officers from the Colonial Labour and Education Services as well as the Administrative Service, as a chance for them to concentrate on a specialist subject. 'Overseas Services Course (Short)' would provide an alternative form of post-selection training for those officers from the United Kingdom who had not taken 'A' before going overseas.[53] The following year the Secretary of State for the Colonies wrote to colonial governments inviting nominations of local candidates of suitable intellectual standard.[54]

Within London it was the LSE, 'heavily committed' to both Courses A and B, that was most affected. It was overwhelmingly the largest recipient of funds transferred to London from the Colonial Office to support staff and teaching, SOAS receiving only fee income for students,[55] although staff at SOAS

[49] Bodleian, OUA, UR 6/Col/4/file 11, Cornes to Veale, 5 May 1953.
[50] Cited in Roland Oliver, 'Prologue: the two Miss Perhams' in Alison Smith and Mary Bull eds., *Margery Perham and British Rule in Africa* (Frank Cass, London, 1999), pp. 21–6, citation p. 24.
[51] Bodleian, OUA, UR 6/Col/ 16/1, file 1, minutes of the Munster Conference for 15 September 1953.
[52] Ibid.
[53] CUL, UA, Papers of the University General Board, GB 760/939, file 1944–58, Summary of recommendations of the 1953 Conference to consider Colonial Service Training, 14–17 September 1953.
[54] Bodleian, OUA, UR 6/Col/4/file 12, Circulars 1232/53 and 318/54 from Oliver Lyttelton to colonial governments, 31 December 1953, and 7 April 1954.
[55] The estimates for London University expenditure on the courses for 1953–4 were: LSE £6,604; IoE, £3,133; UCL £890; King's College £358; Wye College £430; University Central Fund

were reportedly 'very sad' to lose the course.[56] The Institute of Education, the London institution with the next greatest financial stake in the Devonshire training scheme, was largely unaffected, since it was most involved in Course B, in which London continued to participate.[57]

How did the old universities succeed in getting what they wanted from the 1953 Munster conference, in the face of Colonial Office faint-heartedness and the sometimes conflicting demands from colonial governments? Both Veale and Furse illustrate the blurred boundary between 'state' and the universities and were well connected. In addition, both committees on colonial studies at Oxford and Cambridge reported directly to the universities' governing authorities and had high-level representation on them, although this was also true of the University of London, whose representatives at the Munster conference included the directors of both the LSE and SOAS. The three universities also had a role in policy formulation through representation on the Colonial Office's committee on Colonial Service training. Here Veale and Newbolt sat alongside Bowra,[58] and from Cambridge Dr J. A. Venn, former University vice-chancellor and master of Queen's College. In this context and others, they repeatedly asserted their own superior expertise. Their interventions were symptomatic not just of imperial hierarchies of knowledge, which placed western epistemologies over local, but also of internal British hierarchies as the universities claimed ascendancy over British officers in the field. As the Secretary General of the Faculties at Cambridge saw it, they, rather than colonial governments, were 'in the best position to know what the cadets could most profitably be taught'.[59] The universities persuaded the CO that many of the areas in which individual governments wished to see their recruits receive tuition were in fact already covered, if under a different name. 'What the Gold Coast government calls "Principles of Public Administration", Oxford explained, we probably already cover in "Colonial Government"'.[60]

£570. See LSE, Central Filing Registry, Box 327, 288/4/D, [Papers of] Special Advisory Board in Colonial Studies, 1951–8, meeting of special advisory board, 11 November 1953.

[56] Bodleian, OUA, UR 6/ Col/4, file 12, A. R. Thomas to Bowra, 9 September 1954.

[57] The IoE received twenty-five Course B students in 1953/4, eighteen the following year, and twenty-two in 1955/6, among whom were four Africans from the Gold Coast and three Malays. The LSE went on to become involved in ad hoc training for diplomats in new states. But in 1961 its Overseas Courses Committee was disbanded, having become largely inactive. By then the School was focused more on new courses designed for 'students from underdeveloped countries'. LSE, Central Filing Registry, Box 327, 288/3/D, [Papers of] Overseas Courses Committee, 1950–61, minutes 16 December 1953; note on file by Director, 5 May 1961.

[58] Membership from CUL, UA, GBR/0265/CDEV 11/ 1: papers of the standing committee on Colonial Service training.

[59] CUL, UA, GBR/0265/CDEV 2/5, CCS Minutes, 8 June 1953.

[60] Bodleian, OUA, UR 6/Col/4/file 12, Extraordinary meeting of the First and Second Course Sub-Committee, 16 September 1954, 'Overseas Course A. Comments by Educational Staff on the Recommendations by Governments', comments by F. G. Carnell.

In practice, the university delegates were also pushing at an open door. At the time British policy aimed to encourage students from colonial and new Commonwealth countries to come to Britain to study as a valuable means of spreading British influence. Otherwise, officials feared, students might go to communist countries instead.[61] In papers prepared in advance of the conference, Colonial Office staff argued that there was 'real value to anyone destined to occupy a responsible post in the Public Service Overseas in the opportunity to study the problems facing the Colonial Administrator in the impartial surroundings of a great British university against an informed background of study and discussion. the [sic] gain would be as much for locally recruited cadets as for those recruited in the United Kingdom and the Commonwealth'. Officials hoped that this would result in 'opportunities for a growth of understanding between this country and Colonial territories advancing to self-government, and between the Colonial territories themselves, which should bear fruit in the future'.[62]

Colonial governments took a similar view. Indeed, for all that some colonial governments had concerns about the value of the courses for British recruits, they were almost unanimous in their support for the proposition that *local* appointments to the senior levels of the Service study in Britain.[63] The hope that attendance at training at a British university would be a valuable means of broadening outlook and horizons among local recruits was commonly expressed. The Gold Coast, partially self-governing since 1951, was represented at the Munster Conference by one of the few senior African officials in its administration, A. L. Adu, as well as by the African ministerial secretary, Ohene Djan. However, although Adu emphasized, like Perham, that the courses must meet the needs of African officials, even the Gold Coast representatives did not significantly dissent from the British model for training in public administration.[64]

More specifically there was support for continuing to locate training at Oxbridge. Perhaps this reflects the fact that over half of all entrants to the CAS had undergraduate degrees from Oxford or Cambridge, alongside Oxbridge's on-going importance as a recruiting ground at a point when the Colonial Office struggled to find the new officers it needed.[65] But more than that it was widely held that, as a British representative from Nyasaland observed, Britain's oldest residential universities promised 'the settled atmosphere of an old institution' with a 'collegiate life' that would be especially fruitful for African

[61] Perraton, *History of Foreign Students*, pp. 98–9; see also Stockwell, 'Exporting Britishness'.
[62] CUL, UA, GBR/0265/CDEV 11/1, CST (53)3, Draft Papers for the Conference on Colonial Service Training, 'First Course–the problem of numbers'.
[63] See Circular Despatch No. 707/52, 14 July 1952.
[64] Bodleian, OUA, UR 6/Col/16/1/file 1, minutes of the Munster Conference, 15 September 1953.
[65] Gardiner, 'Sentinels of Empire', pp. 225–6, 263; Jeppesen, 'Sanders'.

recruits.[66] The subliminal message was that the antique surroundings of Oxford and Cambridge were a force for stability in a fast-changing world, and the ideal antidote to rapid change and impatient political ambitions. They offered practical advantages over London too, where there were problems with substandard lodgings, and with the poor impression that this generated among those one study termed Britain's 'disappointed guests'.[67] The Oxbridge collegiate model enabled students to be dispersed through different colleges and reside alongside British students. In turn, this related to contemporary (and long-standing) concerns about the radicalization of overseas students in London, not least in dedicated student hostels, and which led to increased surveillance of overseas students.[68] For London was not only an imperial administrative and financial centre, but also simultaneously a site of anti-imperialism, a meeting place for black intellectuals and anticolonial activists, where students might be brought into proximity with metropolitan, colonial and foreign political radicals.[69] Whether with an opportunist eye or from genuine concern, 'London' declared the Oxford course supervisor was 'unsuitable for Colonials'.[70]

Of course, Britain's governing classes, still overwhelmingly themselves the products of Oxbridge, had strong connections to the common rooms of Oxford and Cambridge, later satirized in Anthony Jay and Jonathan Lynn's 1980s BBC comedy, *Yes, Minister*. Furse later recalled that he 'never failed' to enjoy himself 'to the full at any Oxford high table or in any Cambridge combination room', especially on the 'almost indecently numerous occasions' when he was

---

[66] CUL, UA, GBR/0265/CDEV 11/1, The Standing Joint Committee on Colonial Service Training, CST (53), annex I, Draft Papers for the Conference on Colonial Service Training, 'Summary of replies received from Colonial Governments to the Secretary of State's Circular Despatch No. 707/52'.

[67] A. J. Stockwell, 'Leaders, Dissidents and the Disappointed: Colonial Students in Britain as Empire Ended', *Journal of Imperial and Commonwealth History* 36 (2008), pp. 487–507, esp. 492–3; Henri Tajfel and John L. Dawson eds., *Disappointed Guests: Essays by African, Asian and West Indian Students* (OUP for the Institute of Race Relations, London, 1965). Many of the contributors to this volume expressed a sense of bitterness at the prejudice and discrimination they encountered.

[68] Michael Lee, 'Commonwealth Students in the United Kingdom, 1940–1960: Student Welfare and World Status', *Minerva* 44 (2006), pp. 1–24, esp. 12–13. These dated back to the 1900s: see, e.g., Boehmer, *Indian Arrivals*, p. 209.

[69] As explored in a growing body of work: see, e.g., Jonathan Spencer, 'Anti-Imperial London: The Pan-African Conference of 1900' in Felix Driver and David Gilbert eds., *Imperial Cities* (Manchester University Press, Manchester, 1999), pp. 254–67; Susan Pennybacker, *From Scottsboro to Munich: Race and Political Culture in 1930s Britain* (Princeton University Press, Princeton, NJ, 2009); Hakim Adi, *Pan-Africanism and Communism: The Communist International, Africa and the Diaspora, 1919–1939* (Africa New World Press, Trenton, NJ, 2013); Kennetta Hammond Perry, *London Is the Place for Me: Black Britons, Citizenship and the Politics of Race* (Oxford University Press, Oxford, 2015).

[70] Bodleian, OUA, UR 6/Col/4/file 11, Cornes to Veale, 5 May 1953.

the guest of his 'old friend and ally', Veale.[71] To these elites the best preparation for entry to public administration meant education at Britain's oldest
universities and an association of the institutions with both cultural and political authority made them an inevitable accessory to any project that addressed
itself to state institutions and governance. Indeed, the preference for Oxbridge
over London for Course A must be understood not just with reference to contemporary concerns about London, but also to particular understandings about
an English bureaucratic tradition. This tradition included open entry to posts
via academic competition organized into grades according to function; a system of promotion based on merit and seniority; and adherence to a principle
of political neutrality that meant officials retained their posts irrespective of
party political allegiances.[72] These were features that went back to the 1854
Northcote-Trevelyan reforms, as well as to the reforms to the Indian Civil
Service that followed the Indian Revolt.[73] In *practice* nevertheless, the imperial services had departed from the British model in important respects. The
organization of colonial public services on grounds of race represented the
very opposite of a principle of an open, meritocratic system. Moreover, in the
colonies British public servants *were* the government as well as bureaucrats.
As Henrika Kuklick's study of the Gold Coast between the wars shows, even
those who occupied the lower ranks of administration 'did not realise the ideals
of bureaucratic neutrality',[74] although this did not stop the Gold Coast colonial
government trying to enforce a standard of political neutrality among African
civil servants after the war.[75] What is more, whereas entrants to the home civil
service received no specialist training, those joining the Colonial Service *did* –
in the form of the Oxbridge and, from 1946, Devonshire training courses.

   Yet, common nonetheless to both the imperial and home public services
was a shared ethos of public service and of the characteristics of the ideal
civil servant, one that privileged the academic rather than the practical, and the
generalist rather than the specialist.[76] As Dimier shows, this understanding had
informed earlier decisions that the training of Britain's colonial administrators
was best accomplished at a university rather than at a dedicated staff college.[77]

---

[71] Sir Ralph Furse, *Acuparius, Recollections of a Recruiting Officer* (Oxford University Press, Oxford, 1962), p. 72.
[72] Hugh Tinker, 'Structure of the British Imperial Heritage' in Braibanti ed., *Asian Bureaucratic Systems*, pp. 23–86, esp. 24.
[73] See p. 7.
[74] Henrika Kuklick, *The Imperial Bureaucrat: The Colonial Administrative Service in the Gold Coast, 1920–1939* (Hoover University Press, Stanford, 1979), p. 145.
[75] PRAAD, RG 3/1/67, Gold Coast circular no 51/1949 from R. Saloway to all heads of depart-
ment and Chief Commissioners, 2 August 1949.
[76] Correlli Barnett, *The Collapse of British Power* (Methuen Publishing, London, 1972), pp. 63–4;
Peter Hennessy, *Whitehall* (Secker and Warburg, London, 1989), pp. 7, 74–5, 194–9, 123–5.
[77] Dimier, *Le gouvernement des colonies*, p. 186; see, also, e.g., CUL, UA, GB 760/939, file
1942–45, 'Training for the Colonial Service', note of a meeting, 17 June 1942, between
representatives from Cambridge including the vice chancellor and Sir Ralph Furse.

By the mid-twentieth century the British generalist tradition could be seen as in tension with a growing reliance on specialist knowledge, and above all a Keynesian insistence on a planned economy; there were also long-standing concerns that the system privileged Oxbridge graduates over those of other universities.[78] Indeed the 'generalist' tradition was becoming increasingly controversial. Thomas Balogh was among the most notable critics. An emphasis on character and what he judged 'a purposefully, useless, somewhat dilettante, erudition', and a cultivation of 'powers of dialectical argument only' had had 'devastating effects' including in British colonies which lacked expertise in economic planning.[79] The criticism became more weighty in the 1960s, with the Fulton Committee on the civil service concluding that the cult of the generalist 'is obsolete at all levels'.[80] But in the 1950s only minor steps were taken towards more professionalization. Powerful advocates instead spoke in defence of established mores, not least Sir Edward [later Lord] Bridges, head of the home civil service 1945–56, and himself the very epitome of the generalist tradition.[81] Representatives of the universities successfully argued that a liberal, inter-disciplinary, academic training was now all the more important in a Keynsian era of the welfare, interventionist state. 'The modern world is a planned world', observed Veale, in which 'governments are bound to be more active and interfering than they have been in the past'. Civil servants, he suggested, 'must be better instructed, and in particular must learn how to use experts and expert knowledge'.[82]

While Balogh invoked Britain's colonial record in arguing for reform of the home civil service, in making a case for the continued salience of a liberal arts university education in their discussions about Colonial Service training British authorities were similarly intervening in contemporary debate about the domestic civil service, while also reflecting singular British ideas about the relationship of the state to civil society. Via tuition in a wide range of subjects as part of a liberal education, these overseas students would be equipped with the skills necessary to act as key mediators between politicians and experts. London's claims to expertise lay more in the social sciences and new area

---

[78] E.g., see evidence given to the 1929 Tomlin Royal Commission: R. A. Chapman, *Leadership in the British Civil Service: A Study of Sir Percival Waterfield and the Creation of the Civil Service Selection Board* (Croom Helm, London and Sydney, 1984), p. 18.

[79] Thomas Balogh, 'The Apotheosis of the Dilettante: The Establishment of the Mandarins' in Thomas Balogh, Dudley Seers, Roger Opie and Hugh Thomas eds., *Crisis in the Civil Service* (Anthony Blond, London, 1968), pp. 11–51, esp. 12, 16, 27–8. This was first published in 1959 in Hugh Thomas ed., *The Establishment*.

[80] *The Civil Service, Volume 1: Report of the Committee, 1966–68* (1968), PP 1967–8, XVIII, Cmnd. 3638, para. 15.

[81] Sir Edward Bridges, 'Administration: What is it? And how it can be learnt', in A. Dunsire ed., *The Making of an Administrator* (Manchester University Press, Manchester, 1956), pp. 1–36, esp. 15.

[82] Bodleian, OUA, UR 6/Col/16/file 1, Brief for the Vice-Chancellor, 1 August 1953.

studies, and the curriculum developed principally at the LSE reflected this. But the decision to continue Course A at Cambridge and Oxford rather than at the LSE probably reflected an on-going conviction among British elites in the salience for a career in public administration of more traditional subjects such as history, prominent within the course syllabi at both institutions.

The location of training in Oxbridge may have served other, more secretive, purposes too. Calder Walton, historian of British intelligence, observes that 'many senior officers' in British intelligence began their careers in the Colonial Service, although from the evidence he presents it seems that these were mostly in the Indian or colonial police services rather than the administrative branch.[83] Indeed before the Second World War, MI5, also known as the Security Service, which had responsibility for intelligence throughout Britain and overseas British territories, had little contact with British higher education, and until 1935 did not have a single graduate on its staff.[84] But both Oxford and Cambridge would become known as recruiting grounds for British intelligence, with a network of individuals throughout the colleges spotting talent among the student body. How far the presence of new elites from emergent Commonwealth African states presented new recruitment opportunities for British intelligence must be a matter for speculation, but at least one cadet, Zambian Valentine Musakanya, who joined the Cambridge course in 1961, was 'by all accounts except his own, recruited by the British intelligence services' while based at St Catherine's College, Cambridge.[85]

Catering to the 'Janus-faced' Imperial State: 1953–1962

The 1953 discussions consolidated an emerging policy that local entrants to the administrative service should attend the Oxbridge courses. Thus began a process by which one form of British technical assistance grew piecemeal out of existing colonial structures. In the uncertain transitional era of the 1950s, when the pace at which constitutional change would eventually occur was not yet apparent, the adaptation of existing structures indeed represented a logical way forward. As Table 3.2 shows, the decade in practice saw little 'localization'; the numbers of non-European students was very small (as evident also in Figure 3.1).

---

[83] Walton, *Empire of Secrets*, pp. 22–6, 143.
[84] Christopher Andrew, *The Security Service, 1908–1945: The Official History* (Public Record Office, London, 1999), pp. 7–8.
[85] Miles Larmer ed., *The Musakanya Papers: The Autobiographical Writings of Valentine Musakanya* (Lembani Trust, Lusaka, 2010), pp. 26, 35, 103–8; see also Valentine Musakanya, 'Chingola' in Tony Schur ed., *From the Cam to the Zambezi*.

Table 3.2. *Recruitment to Colonial Administrative Service Training Course A at Cambridge and Oxford, 1956/7–1963/4*[a]

Year	Cambridge: total intake on Course A	Cambridge: 'local' recruits on Course A	Oxford: total intake on Course A	Oxford: 'local' recruits on Course A
1956–7	33	9	29	7
1957–8	44	4	47	11
1958–9	37	3	25	9
1959–60	27	6	29	7
1960–1	22	8	20–22[b]	Unclear
1961–2	25	13	20	14
1962–3	11	6	10	Unclear
1963–4[b]	15	15	28	28 [?]

[a]Compiled from various papers in Bodleian, OUA, UR 6/Col/4/file 12 and UR 6/Col/4/13; and CUL, UA, CDEV 2/22, annual reports, CSC/OSC.
[b]There are discrepancies between figures given in one source and those in another, perhaps reflecting student withdrawals. In some instances the sources don't identify the number of non-British students. The figures for 1963–4 refer to a new course which combined the old A and B courses (see pp. 122–3).

Figure 3.1. Group photo, the Colonial Administrative Service 'First Devonshire' Course (Course A), the University of Cambridge, 1953–4

Domestic recruitment continued through the 1950s and, even as arrangements were put in place to assist with the resettlement of officers returning from those colonies approaching or having already attained independence, others were still being appointed as members of Her Majesty's Oversea[s] Civil Service. Indeed in the mid-1950s recruitment to Course A rose at Cambridge; the Colonial Studies Committee were gratified to see this 'steady increase in recruitment' at a time when 'African nationalism is so marked'.[86] Perhaps these expatriate recruits were inspired by the Colonial Office's recruitment literature: as late as 1955 this invited candidates to imagine their future in a 'white sun-helmet with a golden crest on the beaches of the Solomon Islands'. That the Colonial Service had recently been renamed Her Majesty's Oversea Civil Service hints at the dissolution of the Empire already underway, which the brochure also acknowledged in different ways;[87] but it still drew on standard tropes of colonial life, and reassured readers that the general picture was one of 'expansion and development'.[88] As Chris Jeppesen argues, for all the new rhetorics of partnership and development, and expansion of the technical side of the Service, the Colonial Office remained reliant on an idea of overseas adventure and travel associated with *Sanders of the River*.[89] The overwhelming majority were still men, although women were admitted to the Administrative Service from 1944 and there was at least one woman among overseas entrants to the course.[90]

These different dynamics – Africanization *and* on-going domestic recruitment – prolonged the situation in which Britons who still hoped for a career in Britain's colonial Empire sat side-by-side with small numbers of overseas students, initially nominated by the governments of Britain's colonies and under Colonial Office auspices, but augmented from the late 1950s by men from newly independent countries financed by their own governments or sent under various technical assistance schemes under the auspices of the British Council. In line with Colonial Office policy those supervising the courses and appointed by the Colonial Office were themselves all ex-colonial/HMOCS. Experience gained overseas was hence recycled not just to expatriate colonial administrators, but to their nonwhite successors. The Oxford supervisor, Jerry Cornes (1947–53), had served in Nigeria and Palestine, his successors

---

[86] CUL, UA, GBR/0265/CDEV 2/22, annual report, CSC, 1956–7.

[87] On this see also Chris Jeppesen, 'A Worthwhile Career for a Man who is not Entirely Self-Seeking': Service, Duty and the Colonial Service during Decolonization' in Andrew W. M. Smith and Chris Jeppesen eds., *Britain, France and the Decolonization of Africa: Future Imperfect?* (University College London Press, London, 2017), pp. 134–55. This has much of interest in it for the issues I discuss, but it was published after I had completed this book, and too late to engage with more extensively.

[88] Kenneth Bradley, *A Career in the Overseas Civil Service* (Colonial Office, 1955), p. 9.

[89] Jeppesen, 'Sanders'.

[90] Kirk-Greene, *Symbol of Authority*, pp. 181–2. Of the seven overseas or 'local' entrants to the course at Oxford in 1959–60 one was a woman from Jamaica.

H. P. W. Murray (1953–9) and E. G. Rowe (1959–69) in Northern Nigeria and Tanganyika, respectively. At Cambridge, Hugh McCleery (1953–69) had worked in Tanganyika, and Paul Howell (1969–82) in Sudan. Other old colonial hands were appointed to the lectureships including H. W. West, ex-HMOCS Uganda who joined the Department of Land Economy in Cambridge.

To begin with there was some concern that teaching the two very different cohorts together presented difficulties. At Oxford it was acknowledged that segregation was 'undesirable', but recommended that consideration be given to the 'special difficulties of a course in which colonial and British officers work together upon controversial problems which touch upon their emotions and their interests'. Some overseas entrants had what were described as 'psychological difficulties' arising from a sense of 'inferiority' and an 'attitude of antagonism to the whole imperial system'. They should be given as much attention as possible in 'an unobtrusive manner' through the allocation of a moral tutor or supervisor sympathetic to, or with knowledge of, their background.[91] However, although some overseas students arrived with what the authorities at Oxford described as a 'chip on the shoulder', they acknowledged that this was by no means universal.[92] Indeed in some cases the encounter might be a congenial one, centred around the colleges in which the students resided or each university's Colonial Service club. Anthony Kirk-Greene suggests that the experience of working alongside African civil servants on equal terms also led to the first loosening of social attitudes on grounds of race among expatriate officers.[93] From the vantage point of the late 1960s course supervisor E. G. Rowe remembered 'halycon' days in the 1950s when students of all races threw themselves into sporting and social events, and 'gentleman of mature years from the West Indies, Asia and Africa were frequently to be seen taking brisk walks around the University Parks on bitter, winter days and playing croquet madly all summer'.[94] Course alumni who attended the 1961/2 Cambridge course later recalled a sense of camaraderie among all participants, although – since by then the expatriate entrants realised they were, as one wrote, embarking on a 'suicide career' – white attitudes may well have been different to those of a few years before.[95] When Valentine Musakanya (shown far right, front row in Figure 3.2) and his wife found private landlords unwilling to take a black couple other members of the course rallied round to assist them and, when a

[91] Bodleian, OUA, UR 6/Col/ 4/file 10, CCS, Sub-Committee on Locally Recruited Officers, Interim Report, 31 March 1951.
[92] UoL archive, ICS 85/D/2, TPA (62)4, memo by Oxford University circulated to the Bridges committee, 26 January 1962.
[93] Kirk-Greene, *Symbol of Authority*, p. 162.
[94] Bodleian, Mss Perham, 245/5, Copy of 'Reflections on the Overseas Service Courses and their Club', E. G. Rowe, October 1969, ff. 7–8.
[95] Mick Bond, 'Mporokoso' in Schur ed., *From the Cam.* pp. 61–72.

Figure 3.2. Group photo, the Colonial Administrative Service Training Course A,
the University of Cambridge, 1961–2

fellow student married, Musakanya and another probationer joined them in
their new Cambridge house.[96] Nonetheless while E. G. Rowe recalled that
friendships 'spanning continents' were formed, many of the overseas students
congregated in what he described as 'groups of tribal languages', presenting a
somewhat different picture of relations between the races.[97]

That the courses fulfilled a dual purpose was of some practical consequence,
as the needs of the British and overseas students were almost diametrically
different. British officers still needed tuition in languages and law, with many
continuing to serve as magistrates in the colonies. Overseas students needed
some preparation for academic study and living in England. Concerned that the

---

[96] Jeremy Burnham, 'Mumbawa, Lundazi' in Schur ed., *From the Cam*, pp. 2–41, esp. 33–4;
Musakanya, 'Chingola, Elisabethville (Katanga), Lusaka', in Schur ed., *From the Cam*,
pp. 87–106, esp. 94–5; Wendy Bond, 'Mporokoso, Chinsali, Bancroft, Mongu, Lisaka, Kitwe'
in Schur ed., *From the Cam*, pp. 195–212.

[97] Bodleian Mss Perham, 245/5, Copy of 'Reflections on the Overseas Service Courses and their
Club', E. G. Rowe, October 1969, folio 9.

quality of locally domiciled officers had recently 'proved so poor', Cambridge contemplated beginning a pre-course in 'civics' for them. Oxford briefly experimented with an acclimatization course, and proposed in 1957 that each new Commonwealth government should give a member of its London staff responsibility for the discipline and welfare of administrative officers and probationers while they were studying at the University.[98] By the end of 1958 the Colonial Office had arranged for the overseas students to attend an induction course on 'Living in England' run by the YWCA Overseas Visitors Centre.[99] While in one year a Gambian achieved the best results on course A among a mixed expatriate and nonwhite cohort, there were also problems with fluency in English and variable levels of ability.[100]

Although there were still relatively few overseas or 'locally' recruited students, by 1957 their significance was deemed at Oxford 'out of all proportion' to their numbers',[101] not least because the overall size of the cohort had swollen as a result of contemporaneous requests that the University also provide some training for South Asian administrative officers,[102] as well as devise bespoke courses for entrants to the diplomatic service of new Commonwealth states. The admission of these additional colonial and Commonwealth students presented practical problems with finding college accommodation, especially as the increase coincided with a wider 'bulge' in admissions that the University authorities feared might be exacerbated by the end of British military service. It was hoped that discussions then underway for a new undergraduate college and postgraduate centre might ease the situation.[103]

The arrival of more non-Europeans in the 1950s also prompted further discussion at both universities of educational content. The issue was considered at Oxford at the start of the decade and then again in 1953 by some of those teaching on the course, who warned against focusing too much on the needs of the expatriate officers. Neither intervention led to change, not least because

---

[98] Bodleian, OUA, UR 6/Col/4/file 12, CCS, Sub-Committee on Overseas Administrative and Diplomatic Students under the CCS, 25 April 1957.

[99] CUL, UA, GBR/0265/CDEV 2/5, minutes of the CSC 17 June 1957, GBR/0265/CDEV 2/6, minutes OSC 26 January 1959, appendix VI. The source refers to the YWCA but it seems more likely that it was the YMCA. John Theakstone 'Mumbwa, Broken Hill, Mkushi' in Schur ed., *From the Cam*, pp. 221–30.

[100] UoL archive, ICS 85/D/2, TPA (62)4, memo by Oxford University circulated to the Bridges Committee, 26 January 1962.

[101] Bodleian, OUA, UR 6/Col/4/12, CCS, Sub-Committee on Overseas Administrative and Diplomatic Students under the CCS, 25 April 1957, and 'draft resolution'.

[102] From Pakistan, and later Ceylon and Burma: Bodleian, OUA, UR 6/Col/4/file 12, extract, CCS minutes, 30 April 1957; UR 6/Col/4/file 13, Education officer Ceylon High Commission to Registrar, Oxford, 30 April 1957; CCS, Courses Sub-Committee, 20 May 1958.

[103] Bodleian, OUA, CW 45, 'Memorandum of a discussion with representatives of the Nigerian Federation Government relating to suggested courses for Nigerian Officers', A. F. M. M[adden], 17 January 1957; CCS, Sub-Committee on Overseas Administrative and Diplomatic Students under the CCS, 25 April 1957, and 'draft resolution'.

the introduction of a parallel course for local recruits was incompatible with the desire to avoid segregation.[104] At Cambridge academics also contemplated syllabus reform.[105] A curriculum sub-committee was formed, which continued to report for some years, but, as at Oxford, the status quo prevailed. This was in part because the universities lived with a situation in which competing disciplines – which had from the outset advanced their claims to relevance, receiving funds from the Colonial Office – had become stake-holders in the training programme. Conversely attempts to develop new subject areas ran up against conservatism in the universities at large, evident in Cambridge in 1954 when the University's General Board was reluctant to support the appointment of new lecturers in African languages on the grounds that it was not clear these constituted a 'discipline' suitable for scholarly research.[106]

The curriculum, delivered to all cadets through dedicated lecture programmes and tutorials, consequently remained broadly unchanged, retaining its strong emphasis on imperial and economic history, law, economics and anthropology. This could create some curious situations, with, for example, new elites from emergent states attending lectures on the structure and practices of African societies by leading anthropologists such as Meyer Fortes and Audrey Richards (Cambridge) and E. E. Evans-Pritchard (Oxford). Audrey Richards' regional specialism was the Bemba of Northern Rhodesia. At Cambridge, Musakanya took exception to her analysis, and in 'retaliation' gave his own lecture entitled 'The Sexual Habits of the English Tribe'. It proved popular and was 'convincingly anthropological'.[107] During the 1960s accusations that anthropology characterized Africans as primitive while bolstering the position of colonial rule and traditional elites became common among African intellectuals.[108] For their part, British probationers were sometimes equally perplexed by the orientation of the curriculum, which reflected the preoccupations of the high colonial period rather than the emergence of new disciplines relevant to the probationers (including public administration) and most strikingly omitted analysis of the immediate political contexts to which they would be heading. In these circumstances some recollect that the presence of non-European students on their courses served as an alternative and welcome source of instruction.[109]

[104] Bodleian, OUA, UR 6/Col. 4, file 10, supervisor's report, 2 January 1950; report of Sub-Committee February 1953; CW 32, Kenneth Robinson to Professor R. H. Gibb 27 October 1953.
[105] CUL, UA, GBR/0265/CDEV 2/5, Minutes of the Colonial Studies Committee: 22 October 1956, appendix V, 'The Overseas Courses – Course A', memo by E. E. Rich, 3 October 1956; minutes, CCS, 28 January 1957.
[106] CUL, UA, GBR/0265/CDEV 2/5, CCS, 'Memorandum on the teaching of African languages at Cambridge', by H. H. McCleery [undated, but 1955], para. 11.
[107] Larmer, The Musakanya Papers, p. 26.
[108] For an account of these developments, see Kuper, Anthropology and Anthropologists, 64; Talal Asad Anthroplogy and the Colonial Encounter (1973).
[109] Kirk-Greene, Symbol of Authority, p. 53.

There is some, limited, evidence that some saw the courses as an opportunity to shape the thinking of overseas cadets in ways that might be useful politically. In discussions at Oxford in 1951 about possible adaptations to the first course to cater to the overseas cohort the hope was expressed that historical study of Britain, especially of the gradual evolution of British governmental institutions, might be the perfect antidote to 'impatient and perfectionist political ambitions' among overseas students; although it was acknowledged that British institutions and principles should not be presented 'as something approaching perfection which the backward peoples must endeavour to imitate'.[110] We should be careful, however, about assuming that those in charge consciously sought to embed particular ideas. The stated purpose of the course was to equip students to think for themselves, and, despite the concerns among some to promote British imperial values, those teaching the course professed themselves anxious to avoid 'indoctrination'. Even so, through course design and the construction of reading lists academic staff inevitably advanced particular perspectives and what they perceived to be relevant or canonical knowledge. Perham's course on 'Government' featured analysis of 'indirect rule', as well as, in one unspecified year, of the 'Development in Britain of a sense of responsibility towards dependent peoples'. In 1957 one tutor found that Nigerian cadets (in this case diplomats on an associated Foreign Service Programme (FSP), discussed later in this chapter) were keen to discuss 'major problems which seemed to be bothering them', such as whether Nigeria should follow India in pursuing nonalignment in international affairs. His four Nigerian students wrote essays on topics ranging from Nigeria's place in world affairs, to the 'problems' of exporting Westminster democracy, and Commonwealth politics.[111] But the heterogeneous character of the courses must complicate any claims about the straightforward transmission of ideas. Those teaching represented diverse disciplinary perspectives. For example, among economists there were those notable for their dissent from emerging development orthodoxies, such as Burmese economist Hla Myint (Oxford), and Peter Bauer (Cambridge, 1948–60)[112]; an illustration of the diversity or 'imprecision' in teaching Prior identified in an earlier era.

What is more, as others have shown, 'knowledge' did not travel in only one direction and imperial experience could be as profoundly constitutive of western practice and scholarly disciplines as the other way around.[113]

---

[110] Bodleian, OUA, UR 6/Col 4/file 10, CCS, Sub-Committee on Locally Recruited Officers. Interim Report, 31 March 1951. The sub-committee comprised Perham, Cornes and agriculturalist Mr Masefield.

[111] Bodleian, Mss Perham, 244/4, f. 1; Bodleian, OUA, CW 45, Francis [Rose?] to Freddie Madden, 4 December 1957.

[112] Douglas Rimmer, 'African Development in Economic Thought' in Douglas Rimmer and A. H. M. Kirk-Greene eds., *The British Intellectual Engagement with Africa in the Twentieth Century* (Palgrave Macmillan, Basingstoke, 2000), pp. 231–59, esp. 231.

[113] As e.g. recently discussed in Bennett and Hodge eds., *Science and Empire*, introduction.

The experience of teaching African and other non-European entrants to administration, and more generally their witness of events unfolding around them, informed the British academics' understanding in ways evident in their teaching as well as their research. Greater account gradually came to be taken of the changing political circumstances. New lectures and seminars were introduced, notably at Oxford in 1958 on nationalism in the Commonwealth, Africa and South and South-East Asia; and at Cambridge by Jack Gallagher on the 'Growth of Colonial Nationalism' in 1961.[114] Perhaps this encouraged the historians Robinson and Gallagher's reflections on managing transitions from formal to 'informal' empire in an earlier era? Conversely, it might not be too far-fetched to speculate that their thesis on informal empire may have fed into a discourse of 'influence' among British elites and especially entrants to the Service who attended their lectures. Even as the courses continued to provide a berth for an older generation of academics, a new generation was offering fresh understandings of their subjects (including Britain's imperial past) which represented radical departures from older epistemologies. For all that men like Veale showed a commitment to the Empire and Commonwealth, the views of those teaching may have been increasingly at odds with those initially associated with the project.

While the structure of Course A remained broadly as it had at the start of the decade, the names of associated committees and posts were updated, making the course more palatable to the 'local' recruits nominated by newly independent governments. Oxford's Institute of Colonial Studies was renamed the Institute of Commonwealth Studies in 1956, and the Committee for Colonial Studies became the Committee for Commonwealth Studies. Cambridge only took a similar step in 1958, when the Colonial Studies Committee, which managed the course, became the Overseas Studies Committee as a result of pressure from the Colonial Office. Ghana, the Colonial Office reported, was becoming 'rather suspicious of offers from the U.K. to nominate people for what are in effect the same courses which they attended in the bad old days of colonial servitude'.[115]

Feeling the Effects of the 'Wind of Change': The 1960s

More extensive changes to the courses followed in the 1960s as Britain's colonies were steered swiftly towards independence. The first comprehensive review of localization in Britain's colonial dependencies was a Public Services

---

[114] Bodleian, OUA, UR 6/COL/ 4/ file 13, CSC, Minutes of Courses Sub-Committee, 4 November 1958; CUL, UA, GBR/0265/CDEV 2/22, Annual Report OSC, 1961–2.

[115] CUL, UA, GBR/0265/CDEV 2/5, CCS, Minutes, 28 April 1958, and copy of letter E. G. Hanrott (CO) to H. H. McCleery, 7 February 1958.

Conference in March 1960. Following the conference governments were asked to exchange information on what they were doing to build up local civil services, and from September 1961 required to submit annual updates.[116] The United Nations was also showing greater interest in localization, the General Assembly having asked for more information on local training facilities for developing overseas public services. These developments, and the wholesale constitutional change which followed as the 'wind of change' swept through East and Central Africa, transformed the situation in ways which were not anticipated in late 1950s Oxbridge. In 1960, even after Macmillan had delivered his landmark speech in Cape Town, expatriate recruits were still being recruited on permanent and pensionable terms, and it was only in the academic year 1960–1 that the University of Cambridge cancelled its recruitment talk for the Service, due, it said in a masterly understatement, 'to the uncertainty' over its future.[117]

The impact on the profile of those attending the training courses was swift. As Table 3.2 shows, although the proportion of students on the course recruited locally (of unspecified race) had grown by 1960, it grew dramatically thereafter. For Course A at Oxford they accounted for 70 per cent of the total intake by 1961–2, and at Cambridge just over 50 per cent of the total intake. A majority of those attending Course B were also now predominantly 'local'. By 1963–4 all those enrolled on the courses were from overseas.[118] At Cambridge for the first time in 1965 these included a woman.[119] The 'rush of African independence' led initially to an overwhelming preponderance of African students, although by the late 1960s their numbers began to decline. In addition throughout the 1960s around one quarter of all students on the Oxford course were drawn from the West Indies.

Neither the universities nor Whitehall were well prepared for the breakneck pace at which political change had occurred. As officials scrambled to reconfigure Britain's established colonial development and welfare policies for a new postcolonial age, uncertainty surrounded the future of the Oxbridge training courses. If their survival had been in question in the early 1950s, the odds against now looked overwhelming. Their original constituency – expatriate officers – had become a 'dying species',[120] and, with the 'colonial apron-strings' cut, it proved harder to attract recruits to Britain.[121] The British were at risk of being left behind, supplanted by other external influences in

---

[116] *Report on the Public Services Conference,* Colonial No. 347.
[117] CUL, UA, GBR/0265/CDEV 2/22, Annual Report, OSC, 1960–1.
[118] Bodleian, OUA, CW 21, Annual Report, OSC, 1962–3; 1963–4; UR 6/Col/ 4/file 13, Col 798, 'The Future of the Overseas Service Courses A and B at Oxford University'.
[119] CUL, UA, GBR/0265/CDEV 2/22, Annual reports of the Overseas Studies Committee, 1965–6.
[120] TNA, OD 19/13, 'TPA 62 (i)', Committee on Training in Public Administration for Overseas Countries'. Memo for Bridges Committee produced in DTC, 11 January 1962.
[121] Bodleian, Mss Perham, 245/5, Copy of 'Reflections on the Overseas Service Courses and their Club', E. G. Rowe, October 1969, folio 11.

the former colonies. In December 1961, E. G. Rowe reported after a trip to Tanganyika (where until recently he had been Minister of Local Government) that the Ghanaian administrator, A. L. Adu, who also happened to be visiting, had warned that 'If British influence is to hold its own', 'it must "blitz" its way into what is now a competitive market, with substantial aid in cash and in kind'.[122]

Most importantly, by the early 1960s the issue was whether the Oxbridge model was relevant, and indeed whether overseas training was appropriate at all. In the early 1960s neither British officials in Britain's remaining colonies nor those attached to newly independent states were convinced it was. 'Too long and too general', was one complaint, in this case from the government of Sierra Leone, but echoed by others, including the British adviser to the Tanganyikan government, who noted the unfortunate association with 'the colonial regime'. In East Africa, a region where need for administrative training was most pressing of all, only the Kenyan colonial government still attached 'great value' to the courses, but even here the governor reported that it was 'hard to convince the Kenya politician that money spent on sending a Kenya civil servant to study in Europe is well used'.[123] Indeed sending some of their best for extended study at Oxbridge was a luxury that new states could ill afford, as a British official in Zambia acknowledged in 1967; it was a prospect that Zambia might 'seriously' consider in the mid-1970s or 1980s when there were 'more graduates to run our civil service'.[124]

Rather, amidst overwhelming pressure to Africanize, overseas governments believed the greatest need was now for the local provision of training, which was cheaper while also more acceptable politically. The importance of locating training in Africa was recognized in 1962 by the Commission for Technical Co-operation in Africa South of the Sahara, of which Britain was a member alongside other European and independent African countries.[125] The first local training courses had been inaugurated at Zaria in Northern Nigeria in 1957 and in Khartoum, but others developed in Kenya, Uganda, Nyasaland, Tanganyika, Northern Rhodesia, Ghana and the Nigerian city of Ife. As the acting director of the UN's Public Administration Division observed, most countries also

[122] Bodleian, OUA, UR 6/Col/ 4/file 13, 'Informal talks with representatives of East African Governments on basis of memorandum: The Future of Overseas Courses A and B at Oxford University', 31 December 1961.

[123] See evidence submitted to Bridges Committee: TNA, OD 19/34, 'Needs of the Sierra Leone Civil Service in Public Administration Training'; OD 19/35, Tang/TPA (62) 101, 'Training Information from the British High Commission in Tanganyika', appendix B, memo by Mr Anderson, Staff Department Adviser to Tanganyikan Govt; TPA (62) 87, 'Training. Memo from the Governor of Kenya', 15 May 1962.

[124] When offered the chance to nominate African civil servants for funded fellowships that had recently been established at Oxford's Queen Elizabeth House by the ODM: ZNA, CO 17/1/6, minutes by D. Jay, Cabinet Under-Secretary, 13 October 1967.

[125] TNA, OD 19/36, TPA (62), 122, 3 July 1962, 'Training of Middle Grade Personnel', extract from the recommendations and conclusions of the seventeenth session of the CCTA.

liked to obtain assistance from 'more than one direction' and disliked 'ideas and methods being pushed on them'.[126] In January 1962 the Ghanaian Cabinet, keen to avoid over-reliance on the United Kingdom, agreed that where possible all training in public administration should take place at home, with assistance sought at what was described as 'a more operative level' to enable local staff to work alongside British personnel for short periods.[127] It used UN help and appointed an Indian national to head up their new local training institution in public administration. That new states inherited systems modelled on those of their former colonial rulers meant, however, that even where new states turned to the United Nations rather than Britain for help they generally needed, and received, English-speaking experts familiar with British traditions. Indeed the persistence of distinct administrative and social traditions in new states frustrated the UN's own assistance in this field, which it had initially tried to concentrate at an International Centre for Training in Public Administration, as well as the delivery of regionally based programmes.[128]

As the last expatriate officers enrolled on the course, the new Secretary for Technical Co-operation, whose department now assumed responsibility for overseas administrative training from the CO, CRO and FO, appointed a committee under Lord Bridges, former head of the home civil service, to review the entire field of British assistance in the training of overseas public administrators. In Britain this included not only the Overseas Service Courses A and B but also courses taught at the Royal Institute of Public Administration and the University of Manchester.[129] Most of the evidence the Committee received from colonial and overseas governments underlined the case for local training and much of the report, published in March 1963, was dedicated to the contribution Britain might make to this. But the Committee's most striking recommendation was

---

[126] Kirk-Greene, 'Public Administration'; TNA, OD 19/34, information from British High Commissioner Accra to DTC, 9 January 1962; OD 19/21, TPA (62), eleventh minutes of Bridges Committee, appendix A, evidence by Mr F. J. Tickner; OD 19/35, 'United Nations Activities in the Field of Public Administration', paper by F. J. Tickner, 19 March 1962.

[127] PRAAD, RG 2/6/34, no. 236, minutes on notes of the UK Bridges report, incl. by 'Director, Organisation and Methods', 5–16 January 1962.

[128] Although in the early 1960s the Ghanaian government was among new states lobbying for a return to more regional methods presumably in line with its own pan-African vision: TNA, OD 19/21, TPA (62), eleventh minutes of Bridges Committee, appendix A, evidence by Mr F. J. Tickner; OD 19/35, 'United Nations Activities in the Field of Public Administration', paper by F. J. Tickner, 19 March 1962.

[129] From tentative beginnings in 1958 the latter had assumed a role in training overseas public administrators, initially in response to a Foreign Office request to one Australian researcher then based at the university that he assist with training government officials from South East Asia. With government funding the venture prospered and led eventually to the formation of first a Department of Overseas Administrative Studies, and later an Institute for Development Policy and Management: Ron Clarke, 'Institutions for Training Overseas Administrators: the University of Manchester's Contribution', *Public Administration and Development*, 19 (1999), pp. 521–33.

for the establishment of a new institution for training officials from developing countries. This would offer 'a wide, inter-disciplinary syllabus which goes far outside administrative training in its narrower traditional sense'.[130] This idea was seeded in the first instance by Ronald Robinson, who in a paper produced for the Committee cast an admiring look at the new French Institut des Hautes Études d'Outre-Mer in Paris. The French government footed the bill for students from former French colonies to attend, and the Institut was popular with overseas governments. 'Would we', Robinson asked, 'get the same response if we were willing to pay?'[131] At the DTC, the department's chief civil servant, Andrew Cohen, a former head of the Africa division within the Colonial Office and ex-governor of Uganda, was quick to seize control of what was recognized as the biggest hot potato in the Bridges report. Cohen's own preference for situating the new institute at the University of Sussex is apparent in the discussions that followed. Despite hopes at the University of Oxford that it would become the home of the new institute,[132] Cohen and other officials thought that in Oxford and Cambridge, with their 'powerful individual faculties, their rather cumbrous procedures and their deeply entrenched interests', the institute would be 'only a very small thing'. Robinson favoured London, but older resistance to basing overseas students in London persisted.[133] The Institute of Development Studies (IDS) duly opened at Sussex in 1964, an early manifestation of the way in which an initiative originally directed at training in public administration evolved into development studies.

The Bridges Committee saw 'little future' for Course A, which alongside other British courses it dismissed as of 'limited use' to countries whose need was 'most urgent' because it was 'so long'. It concluded also that, in view of the diverse and different circumstances to be found in developing countries, there was a 'deep-seated difference' between 'the needs of many overseas countries and the concepts of administrative training upon which this country relies'. Yet, perhaps against the odds, the report extended a lifeline to Course B, or a remodelled version already being offered at Oxford and Cambridge which had

[130] *Department of Technical Cooperation. Report of the Committee on Training in Public Administration for Overseas Countries* (HMSO, 1963), para. 86.
[131] TNA, OD 19/32, 'The Institut de Haute Etudes d'Outre-Mer', paper by R. E. Robinson.
[132] Although not necessarily as part of the University because of what was perceived as a risk that it might confuse an already complicated relationship between the University, QEH and the Institute of Commonwealth Studies, and also because the University was reluctant to become involved in anything essentially non-academic: Bodleian, OUA, CW 58, letter from L. C. W[ilcher?] and A. F. M[adden] to Mrs. E. M. Chilver, a member of the Bridges Committee, 22 June 1962; CCS. Comment on the Bridges Committee Report (prepared by the CCS Courses Sub-Committee in special meeting, 28 June 1963).
[133] TNA OD 19/62, Cohen to Sir Ronald Harris (T), 3 January 1964; see also BW 2/724, 'A special institution for research and training in Public Administration and Development Overseas', note by ODM for Cabinet Official Committee on Overseas Development, 6 January 1965; Symonds, *Oxford and Empire*, p. 290.

each recently combined the A and B courses into a single offering. In language that echoes the arguments of a decade before, the Report concluded that an Oxbridge course would be of value 'for an indefinite period' since it provided 'a valuable broadening experience for public servants who have never before been far from home'. For such people it offered 'the opportunity to exchange professional ideas with and make friends among administrators from other countries, and to have their thinking stimulated by university teachers who specialize in subjects of particular professional importance to them'.[134] Together with related courses, the Oxbridge ones were to be kept 'under review' and new coordinating machinery established in the form of a committee composed mostly of members of the DTC and the British Council. When this was established the University Grants Committee was represented on it, but not Oxford or Cambridge, and the Oxbridge courses apparently occupied little of its time.[135]

The lifeline extended to the Oxbridge courses surely reflected Lord Bridges' own experience and background, as well as that of some of the academic members of the committee. As well as a generalist administrator par excellence, Bridges was another 'Oxford' man, a historian as well as top civil servant, and a fellow of All Souls.[136] Of the two older universities Oxford presented the strongest submission to the Committee, noting that the university, 'rich in [relevant] resources', offered 'an intellectual climate hardly to be bettered'. 'An indigenous civil service cannot', the University's Committee for Commonwealth Studies claimed, 'just have handed on to it, ready-made, high standards of impartiality, reliability, incorruptibility and so on'. Instead, 'it must establish them afresh for itself. For this its officers need to learn how to read and to think; how to present a case and debate it; how to weigh conflicting arguments and reach a decision; how to apply that decision with realism and moderation; and how to recognize and use the lessons of experience ... nowhere can this be done better than in the older universities such as Oxford which, in effect, say to such students: "We cannot give you the answers to your future problems; but we can help you to acquire for yourselves the equipment with which you can usefully tackle them." '[137] The Cambridge Overseas

---

[134] *Report of the Committee on Training in Public Administration*, paras. 24–7, 75–6.

[135] TNA, OD 19/97 and 19/98, minutes of the Coordinating Unit for Training in Public Administration for Developing Countries, 1965–6.

[136] In the early 1960s he also chaired a committee at Cambridge charged with exploring how best to cater for visiting scholars and postgraduates within the University's collegiate structure. This recommended the establishment of a graduate college, and was followed in 1965 by the opening of University [later renamed Wolfson] College: Richard A. Chapman, 'Bridges, Edward Ettingdene', *Oxford Dictionary of National Biography*, accessed 1 December 2016; Brooke, *History of the University of Cambridge*, pp. 574–5.

[137] Bodleian, OUA, UR 6/Col/ 4/ file 13, COL/CP/789, 'The Future of Overseas Services Courses A and B at Oxford University' [undated, but 1961], memo submitted to the Bridges Committee, circulated 26 January 1962.

Studies Committee submission placed more emphasis on area studies, proposing that in future training should focus on the intensive study of underdeveloped countries, while expressing the hope that the University would continue to be able to 'use the staff, informed interest and experience' built up since 1946. For this they noted they would need funding 'on a somewhat larger scale'.[138] In contrast, the LSE, which had retained a role in Course B, proposed that training should now be local, and advocated focusing on deepening British links with the overseas institutions where this might take place.[139]

There was sympathy within Whitehall for continuing to offer Oxbridge training. The Foreign Office saw the advantages as two-fold: contributing towards the 'efficiency and impartiality' of overseas public services, and as 'a gesture of goodwill that may win sympathetic attention in the newly developing nations for our policies'.[140] Although officials in the Department for Technical Cooperation elected to encourage the trend towards locally based training, they nevertheless also pointed to the value of training in Britain for the development of 'character as well as of intellectual capacity', and proposed that such an education might continue to be provided for a select band of overseas students. With scarce resources, these should be targeted either at those best placed to spread 'the influence' of British training, or those earmarked for, or already occupying, senior posts.[141] This view may have been shaped by Furse's intervention during initial discussions at the new Department. On assuming responsibility for training, officials had sought his counsel, and he was predictably quick to defend the status quo: Oxford's part must be 'preserved at all costs' as the only institution which in his view had 'its heart in the business'.[142]

Moreover, if the unsettling climate introduced new questions about the future of the overseas service courses, the uncertainties and breakneck speed of change in this period nevertheless represents another key to explaining their survival. As British authorities responded to a fast-changing world they sought to adapt the existing colonial architecture and drew on those with relevant experience. In the new context the universities and the state had a symbiotic relationship: the universities were keen to maintain the courses and the funding stream; the British state assumed an on-going role in relation to training

[138] UoL, ICS 85/D/3, TPA (62) 5, 'Memorandum on Training Facilities in the Field of Public Administration and Related Subjects at the University of Cambridge', circulated to Bridges Committee, 26 January 1962, esp. paras 11–13.
[139] UoL, ICS 85/D/37, TPA (62) 70, memo submitted to the Bridges Committee by Richard Titmuss, Head of the Department of Social Science and Administration, LSE.
[140] UoL, ICS 85/D/5 and 6: TPA (62), 7 and TPA (62) 8, memo submitted to Bridges Committee by the FO and CRO, and circulated 26 January 1962.
[141] TNA, OD 19/13, 'TPA 62 (i), Committee on Training in Public Administration for Overseas Countries'. Memo for Bridges Committee produced in DTC, 11 January 1962.
[142] Bodleian, Mss Brit Emp s 415, 10/1, ff. 105–6, A. D. Garson (DTC) to Furse, 10 and 17 August 1961; Furse reply drafted on reverse.

administrators from former colonies, and also those states which remained under colonial rule. As global decolonization gathered pace and colonialism became increasingly toxic, connections between Britain and emergent states at a professional and institutional level, such as those offered by the universities rather than those of the state, were increasingly valuable. This was recognized by DTC officials, who had argued in their submission to the Bridges Committee that, while a staff college model might offer economies of scale, it could carry with it 'a suspicion, however, misconceived, of Government propaganda and indoctrination'. Courses taught within universities were unlikely to attract this critique to the same degree.

Such a consideration had led the Colonial Office in 1959 to propose that the University of Cambridge henceforth host the annual summer school in African Administration which since 1947 the CO had organized for members of the Colonial Service. This would make it more acceptable for delegates from newly independent countries to attend. The year before, the Ghanaian Cabinet had declined the British invitation to participate. As the conferences had previously concerned mainly European colonies, Ghanaian ministers concluded understandably that, 'it would not be proper for Ghana in her present status to participate'.[143] Conversely, civil servants from countries like Nigeria and Ghana were reportedly keen to attend, officials reported, if only a way round the political difficulties could be found. The Colonial Office proposed a sleight of hand to overcome postcolonial political sensitivities: the University would issue the invitations, but the Office would continue to undertake the administration. Despite some reservations among academics (notably Bauer) that the conference would be seen as what Sir Frank Engledow dubbed a 'façade' for Colonial Office 'colonialism', the conferences became a regular event, transformed under the chairmanship of Ronald Robinson into scholarly meetings, while continuing to serve a didactic purpose in relation to civil servants and policy practitioners.[144] The geographical remit was extended beyond Africa, and from 1961 the focus shifted from administration to development.[145]

The opening at Oxford in 1954 of Queen Elizabeth House (QEH), funded by a gift from Sir Ernest Oppenheimer and funds from the colonial development and Welfare fund, also illustrates this relationship between the Colonial

---

[143] PRAAD, ADM 13/1/27, minutes 10 June 1958, item 46.

[144] CUL, UA, GBR/0265/CDEV 2/6, Minutes of the OSC, 1958–61: 25 January 1960, appendix VI, 'Memo on Colonial Office Summer Conference on African Administration' and letter from the Provost of King's College to the Vice-Chancellor, 2 December 1959; H. H. McCleery, 20 February 1960 (reporting on a meeting between himself, Engledow, and Hudson of the CO); 13 June 1960, Appendix I, 'Action taken on the Minutes of 2 May 1960, item 2; 30 January 1961; Memo on the Colonial Office Summer Conference', 20 November 1961.

[145] CUL, UA, GBR/0265/CDEV 2/7, Minutes of OSC 20 November 1961; David Fieldhouse, 'Ronald Robinson and the Cambridge Development Conferences, 1963–70' in *Journal of Imperial and Commonwealth History* 16 (1988), pp. 173–99.

Office and the universities. The Colonial Office hoped that QEH would serve (in Richard Symonds' words) as a 'politically acceptable' link with colonies and former colonies, but was anxious that the initiative should appear to come from the University itself, so that it would not appear a 'neocolonialist' manoeuvre; Veale, on the other hand, emphasized the government role when laying the proposal before the University's Council and Congregation. QEH became the home of the Overseas Service Course, and later of the Institute of Commonwealth Studies [ICS], as well as a focus for development activities within the University. It would be beset with financial uncertainties, reliant as it was from funding from British and overseas governments, as well as other, private sources.[146]

The courses thus survived, but in increasingly perilous circumstances. What is more the wholesale change in student intake presented social as well as academic problems. Initially at least, few of the overseas students were graduates, and in the early years there was a long 'tail' with occasional students who failed to pass. Most, being already members of public services marked for rapid promotion, were also mature, and often married. Some brought their families to Britain. While this might help wives to acquire what British officials in the Gold Coast had patronisingly referred to in 1949 as a 'social manner' that might assist their partners' careers, it was feared that the presence of families would reduce the benefits of overseas study in a residential university by discouraging socializing.[147] In the later 1950s and 1960s as overall overseas student numbers rose, the issue became more significant. In 1969 the ODM warned students, referred to now as 'Study Fellows', that they should attend alone, but the failure to repeat the warning the following year, ensured that the problem was soon perceived to have reached 'crisis proportions'.[148]

Most difficult were issues around accommodation. The presence of wider family forced students out into private lodgings, where, as we have already seen, they might be exposed to racial discrimination; this also contradicted the goal of encouraging residential study within collegiate environments. Looking 'on the bright side', as the Cambridge course supervisor, Hugh McCleery, sardonically observed, 'an occasional dispute with an irate landlady' might prove an education 'in the British Way of Life [sic]' since so 'many of their contacts are handled with kid gloves, British Council Grants for Everything and grand tours with V.I.P treatment'. Conversely, as he complained to his counterpart in Oxford there were also 'landladies who express a preference' for 'an African

---

[146] Symonds, *Oxford and Empire*, p. 288.
[147] PRAAD, RG 3/1/572, no. 56, 'Married scholars in the UK', c. 1950; no. 6, 'Notes on a discussion held during the month of June 1949 between Mr G Hadow, Secretary for the Civil Service ...', extract.
[148] CUL, UA, GBR/0265/CDEV 11/4, 'Correspondence with the Ministry of Overseas Development, 1969–1980', letter prepared at Cambridge 18 September 1970 to ODM (but communicated by telephone).

because they can charge him more and push him around'.[149] Accompanying families brought problems with childcare and spousal occupation, as Jordanna Bailkin has discussed in relation to overseas students in Britain generally.[150] At Oxford authorities turned to wives and others associated with the academic staff for assistance in meeting their needs. Margretta Harlow, widow of the late Beit Professor of Commonwealth History, Vincent Harlow, and Alison Smith, a research officer and historian based at the Institute of Commonwealth Studies, were tasked with helping latter-day 'incorporated' wives combat the isolation and dislocation some experienced, while also offering practical assistance with maternity and health care, schooling and English.[151]

Problems with the admission of students from the colonies and Commonwealth to undergraduate colleges also clearly persisted after the war, with the Franks Commission into Oxford University reporting in 1966 that Oxford colleges treated overseas students badly. The problem was eased by the contemporaneous establishment of the new graduate colleges of St Cross and Iffley (later Wolfson), and the conversion of recently founded Linacre House to Linacre College. This took a large contingent of Commonwealth students, as well as offering a collegiate base for Oxford's non-dons.[152] Following the closure in 1969 at Cambridge of the Cambridge Overseas (formerly Colonial) Service Club opened in 1927, University (later Wolfson) College became the administrative and social centre for the course.[153] At Oxford the overseas cadets continued to make use of the old Club, although the course supervisor would later recall that the 'Club run on English lines without an English member lacked a little of the old sparkle'.[154]

Now that the courses were no longer serving domestic Colonial Service entrants, some of the pressures which had shaped the curriculum in the 1950s were removed. Those charged with delivering teaching could therefore undertake a more comprehensive review. At Cambridge Sir Frank Engledow, the professor of agriculture, and economist, Professor E. A. G. Robinson, argued in a joint memo that the needs of new recruits were 'antithetically different' from those of British officers, suggesting that Cambridge might best meet these by using methods associated with defence staff colleges.[155] As indicated earlier,

---

[149] CUL, UA, GBR/0265/CDEV 11/2, 'Correspondence with the Oxford Course, 1965', H. H. McCleery to E. G. Rowe, 10 December 1965.
[150] Bailkin, *Afterlife of Empire*.
[151] Bodleian, OUA, CW 5/4 and 6: reports on 'Welfare of Overseas Wives', for 1962–4, 1964–5, 1968–9.
[152] Colin Newbury, 'The Origins of Linacre College', *Linacre Journal* (June 1997), no. 1, pp. 5–27, esp. 22–3. Perraton, *History of Foreign Students in Britain*, p. 105.
[153] CUL, UA, GBR/0265/CDE2/23, Director's report, 1968–9.
[154] Bodleian, Mss Perham, 245/5, Copy of 'Reflections on the Overseas Service Courses and their Club', E. G. Rowe, October 1969, f. 11.
[155] CUL, UA, GBR/0265/CDEV 2/7, 'Draft memorandum for the Bridges Committee by Professor E. A. G. Robinson and Professor Sir Frank Engledow', and OSC minutes 8 January 1962, 22 February 1963.

both universities had now introduced a single course in place of 'A' and 'B': at Cambridge, a 'Course on Development'; and at Oxford the 'Overseas Course in Government and Development'.[156] Both courses were reconstituted to focus principally on key themes of governance, society and economics. There were also striking alterations to the mode of delivery and pedagogy, with greater emphasis on comparative analysis of the problems of developing countries, and more incorporation of examples relating to the countries from which the officers came. In 1964–5 the Cambridge Overseas Studies Committee declared the course 'an immediate success', buoyed by a small increase in numbers and an increase in the average academic standard of the cohort; a claim repeated in subsequent years, although the academic standards of intakes varied.[157]

Through the 1960s the courses nevertheless retained a strongly generalist element, with students at both universities offered a smorgasbord of optional subjects. Changes to curricula were incremental rather than sweeping, and subjects once the staple of British Colonial Service training – anthropology and imperial history – as well as economics, retained their place for some time. In Oxford in 1964 the Overseas Course in Government and Development comprised Government (including study of history as well as central and local government), 'Natural Resources' (including geography, tropical agriculture, tropical forestry, agricultural economics, and agricultural co-operation), Social Anthropology, Economics, Law and Regional Studies.[158] At Cambridge in the first year of the new course students chose from law, local government and education, but the list was subsequently expanded to include economics, land usage, international relations, history and anthropology.[159] In the academic year 1963–4 those lecturing to overseas administrators included not only Ronald Robinson, but also Sir Ivor Jennings, the lawyer and constitutional expert who had advised on the Ceylon and Malayan constitutions, vice-chancellor at Cambridge between 1961 and 1963.[160] As it was acknowledged at Cambridge, in the late 1960s the imperial origin of the courses cast a long shadow bequeathing a situation in which four faculties that had contributed to the old courses, namely Economics and Politics, History, Law, and Archaeology and Anthropology, still continued to do so in return for a stipend in the form of 'notional' lectureships from the UK overseas aid budget.[161]

---

[156] Oxford had reviewed the courses in 1961 in view of the increasingly diverse intake and this had led the University to direct some locally recruited cadets to a hybrid of Courses A and B: Bodleian, OUA, UR 6/Col/4/13, CCS, 'Review of Overseas Service Courses', E. G. Rowe, 15 September 1961.
[157] CUL, UA, GBR/0265/CDEV 2/22, Annual reports of the OSC, esp. 1964–5.
[158] Bodleian, Mss Perham, 244/6, item 5, Course booklet (1964).
[159] CUL, UA, GBR/0265/CDEV 2/22, Annual reports of the Overseas Studies Committee for 1963–4, and for subsequent years.
[160] W. A. Robson, 'Sir Ivor Jennings', Oxford Dictionary of National Biography, accessed 5 October 2015; CUL, UA, GBR/0265/CDEV 2/22, annual report of OSC, 1963–4.
[161] CUL, UA, GBR/0265/CDEV 2/23, OSC 197, 17 January 1972; GBR/0265/CDEV 2/9. OSC 219, papers for meeting 22 January 1973.

One of the criticisms commonly made of overseas technical assistance is that it was poorly adapted to the needs of developing countries.[162] What emerges from this case study is the makeshift and contingent nature of British training, reflecting more the relevant institutions' sense of their expertise, institutional cultures and priorities. In the 1960s those involved in administering the Oxbridge courses seemed unable to break away from a generalist model that was increasingly discredited. Entrenched interests appeared to hold back the development of new areas. When Jack Gallagher, since 1963 Beit Professor of the History of the Commonwealth at Oxford, proposed a new South Asian interfaculty liaison committee, part of a broader trend that simultaneously saw a similar initiative in relation to African studies, he was opposed by some on the Committee for Commonwealth Studies who feared a clash with their own functions 'in a wider and more general field'. Nonetheless, the rise of area studies in the 1960s increasingly pushed Commonwealth studies, once a source of prestige, to the margins within the universities. When in 1968 Oxford came to appoint a director of the ICS and warden of QEH, the selection of the economist P. P. Streeten, then acting director of the new IDS, was greeted with dismay by some, like the historian Max Beloff, who worried that the appointment would signal a sidelining of history, politics and administration; perhaps there was also a lingering wariness of the promotion of subjects that might be seen as vocational.[163]

The changed environment meant that both courses were now recruiting on the open market, while also taking students funded from the British aid budget. Through the 1960s Oxford especially began to seek, and to attract, significant numbers of students from the former colonies of other European colonial powers. In 1965–6 Commonwealth students were in a minority on the course.[164] As in the 1950s, catering to different constituencies imposed constraints. Many of those funded under the aid budget were not university graduates and struggled academically. Moreover, some had apparently been nominated for the programme in their home countries not on a straightforward basis of merit but for strategic reasons. Among the worst-performing students at Oxford in 1962 were Kalenjin students from Kenya (still at this stage under British control) whom the course supervisor believed had been selected in order to alleviate a preponderance of Kikuyu in government posts.[165] Concerned about maintaining the courses and protecting their income stream, it was difficult for the course supervisors to insist that recruits meet academic criteria. Both universities recognized that to be attractive to a

---

[162] See, e.g., Mende, *From Aid to Re-colonization*, p. 101.
[163] Bodleian, OUA, CW 1/3, minutes, 5 March 1968. The Chairman of the Board of the Faculty of History wrote to the chair of the Committee to object to the appointment: OUA, CW3/3, 12 March 1968 (copy).
[164] Ibid., minutes 12 October 1965.
[165] Bodleian, OUA, CW 5/2, 'Results of 1962 Course 'A' Examination', E. G. Rowe, 26 October 1962.

variety of applicants the courses needed to lead to some sort of qualification as evidence of attainment. When in 1967–8 the Cambridge Overseas Studies Committee introduced a Diploma in Overseas Development Studies to be awarded to those candidates showing 'sufficient merit' in the course examination, however, only four of twenty-eight students succeeded in attaining the requisite standard.[166] The introduction of the Diploma nevertheless appeared to have increased the appeal of the course, as the following year the number of applications exceeded available places.[167]

From the Devonshire Courses to Development Studies: The Long Working Out of the Administrative Service Courses at the Universities in the 1970s

By the late 1960s the immediate spike in African demand that had characterized the early to mid-1960s had subsided, and the case for British technical assistance was less compelling. Throughout the decade both Oxford and Cambridge faced continuing uncertainty over the future of state funding for the courses, and at the end of the decade the Ministry of Overseas Development embarked on a comprehensive reassessment. In 1969 it withdrew funding for the Oxford Overseas Course on Government and Development, and began an overhaul of that at Cambridge. The ODM's reforms not only brought to an end a tradition of teaching that had evolved continuously since the 1940s but marked the final stage in the emergence of development studies at Cambridge from the old Devonshire administrative training courses. At Oxford the end of the course led to the closure of Oxford's 'Commonwealth Services Club' and the reorganization of the Committee for Commonwealth Studies, which since 1946 had overseen the training courses as well as other related activity within the University, the ICS and QEH.[168] The University's General Board assumed responsibility for funding a lectureship in Commonwealth history previously paid for by the ODM.[169] Although at Cambridge the course survived, the new decade brought other changes that marked the end of an era. Robinson, appointed Beit Professor at Oxford in 1971, stepped down from the organization of the Cambridge development conferences in 1970. His departure provided the occasion for a minor reassessment. At a meeting with the ODM it was

---

[166] CUL, UA, GBR/0265/CDEV 2/22, Annual report of the OSC, 1967–8. Oxford contemplated the introduction of a certificate: OUA, CW 1/3, minutes 2 March 1965.
[167] CUL, UA, GBR/0265/CDEV 2/23, Annual reports of the OSC, 1969–81, report for 1968–9.
[168] Bodleian, OUA, CW 1/3, minutes 21 January 1969.
[169] Bodleian, OUA, CW 3/4, A. Barr (University Registry) to Ralph Feltham, QEH, 9 June 1969; CCS minutes, 24 February 1970.

agreed that the administration of the conference, now a biannual event, should be transferred to the University of Cambridge, although the ODM would continue to fund them. They would be chaired by an academic whose interests were closest to the conference subject.[170]

Oxford, with its long tradition of public service, was now asked instead to focus on a Foreign Service Course (later Programme) for training overseas diplomats in new states. The ODM agreed to pay an annual grant to the University and to QEH to fund a director and other posts in the expectation that around fifteen students would be recruited. The FSP had developed alongside the overseas administrative training course, initially in the form of bespoke teaching delivered in response to specific requests, beginning with Ethiopia in 1953, and subsequently from places such as the Gold Coast (1956), Nigeria (1957–8), the Caribbean (1960–1) and Tanganyika (1961–2). It shared some characteristics with its older sibling, the Overseas Course on Government and Development. In 1957 the FSP and Courses A and B were all described as providing a 'liberal education' rather than the kind offered at a 'staff college',[171] although a comparison of the content of the two programmes in the mid-1960s shows that the former was more focused, comprising (in 1964) only four units: International Relations, Diplomatic Practice, International Economics and International Law.[172] In the case of the colonies the costs of attendance were met under the development budget but independent Commonwealth governments picked up the tab for tuition and university and college fees. Students received some dedicated supervision but otherwise attended university lectures and seminars.[173] By the later 1960s recruitment to the FSP remained strong when the numbers on the Course on Government and Development were falling;[174] a former academic advisor on the latter recalls that by then its status within the University was 'nil', probably reflecting the comparatively low academic standards attained by many who took it.[175] The decision to close the Course to focus funding squarely on the FSP was therefore a logical one consistent with the balance of interests at Oxford.

At Cambridge, where there was more emphasis than at Oxford on development studies, the Course on Development (Figure 3.3) was significantly

[170] CUL, UA, GBR/0265/CDEV 2/8, minutes, OSC, 19 October 1970, 9 December 1970.
[171] Bodleian, OUA, CW 45, 'Memorandum of a discussion with representatives of the Nigerian Federation Government relating to suggested courses for Nigerian Officers', A. F. M[adden] 17 January 1957.
[172] Bodleian, Mss Perham, 244/6, item 7, Course booklet (1964).
[173] Bodleian, OUA, CW 45, M. Holdsworth to K. G. Ashton (CO), 8 June 1960.
[174] Bodleian, OUA, CW 1/3, CCS minutes 28 November, 1967.
[175] Interview with Colin Newbury, 9 October 2015. Newbury succeeded Freddie Madden as academic advisor to the OCGD in 1966.

Figure 3.3. Group photo, the University of Cambridge Course on
Development, 1970

reconstituted for the new era under the ODM's guidance. In 1970 the department asked Cambridge to include land administration within the course, a
source of some tension since this had a very different pedagogy and tradition.[176]
A new post of director was created, to which Paul Howell, an anthropologist and
former member of the Sudan Political Service with experience in development,
was appointed in 1969. Coming from the technocratic and professional side of
the imperial services rather than the old Administrative Service, his appointment underscored the change occurring.[177] The old 'notional' lectureships were
replaced by posts termed 'assistant directorships', initially in Economic Policy
and Planning, Land Policy and Development, and Sociology and Politics; by
1980 there were seven directly funded teaching posts. Although these equated
in salary terms to university lectureships, they could not be designated as such

---

[176] CUL, UA, GBR/0265/CDEV 2/7, OSC 137 (b), 'Supervisor's Comments on Professor
Hutchinson's Proposals', paper by H. H. McCleery, 4 July 1969.
[177] Interview John Toye, 9 October 2015, Oxford.

since the posts were funded on a five-year basis only, an indication of the on-going uncertainty surrounding state funding.[178]

Although the continuation of the courses offers a striking example of survival and institutional adaptation, in order to meet the criteria set by the ODM the courses evolved into a programme very different from those of the late 1940s, diverging from the liberal arts training previously favoured. This reflected not just the post-war emergence of development economics, but also the way in which in the 1960s British–Commonwealth relations came chiefly to be defined as developmental. The principal constituency for the course was identified as those responsible for planning and appraising economic and social development, and, in case anyone should be in doubt as to the changes that had occurred, publicity material described the course as '*not* [author's emphasis] a training course in public administration'.[179] Keen to reinforce the message, Howell was aware that he must emphasize that the character of the course was now 'totally changed', being related to 'real needs' rather than starting from the perspective of teaching 'what the natives need to know'.[180]

The course now became a vehicle for the transmission of a different kind of knowledge. It still provided a berth for some previously employed within the imperial services, like Howell and one of the new assistant directors, Henry West. The latter was a firm advocate of the merits of privatization of land in African societies and of cadastral land surveys to establish real property boundaries, an approach that even at the time was seen as problematic even by some of his colleagues, in view of concerns that it might have a destabilizing effect on societies in which access to common land underpinned social structures and practices.[181] But as this indicates, the course continued to be distinguished by its pluralism, and it also helped nurture scholars with emerging international reputations in development economics, including Edmund 'Valpy' Fitzgerald, whose research at the time focused principally on Latin America, and who joined the course on development in 1973,[182] or, who like John Toye, later head of the Institute of Development Studies at Sussex, would become preeminent within the field. Yet, for all that Howell sought to refocus the course on development, he seemed unable to break fully with earlier traditions. During discussions about the course reform in 1970 its primary purpose was still seen as to 'train the generalist administrator', thus differentiating it from what was on

---

[178] CUL, UA, GBR/0265/CDEV 2/12, papers circulated to OSC, 9 April 1980; GBR/0265/CDEV 2/9, OSC 235, draft OSC report, 1969–73.

[179] CUL, UA, GBR/0265/CDEV 2/9, course brochure, 1973–4.

[180] CUL, UA, GBR/0265/CDEV 2/23, P. P. Howell to Dr A. F. Robertson, Dr B. Van Arkadie, and Dr H. W. West, 19 October 1973. On Howell, see obituary, *The Independent*, 9 April 1994.

[181] Interview, John Toye, 9 October 2015, Oxford.

[182] John Toye, 'Valpy Fitzgerald: Radical Macroeconomist of Development', *Oxford Development Studies* 45 (2017), pp. 116–24.

offer at Sussex. Ultimately the continuing purchase of the 'generalist' tradition contributed to the demise of the course.[183]

Initially the outlook looked promising. In 1970 the Ministry of Overseas Development (which between October 1970 and 1974 and again from 1979 was incorporated in the FCO as the Overseas Development Administration (ODA)) was persuaded to fund more 'overseas study fellows', as those it supported had become known, and between 1973 and 1976 the number of ODA/ODM-sponsored students peaked at around forty per year.[184] The Course also recruited via the British Council a number of candidates sponsored by their own governments or by international agencies including the United Nations who paid course fees to the University through the ODA/ODM, as well as 'private' students who paid the University's standard home or overseas fees. Many came from countries outside the Commonwealth.[185] The majority were graduates in their twenties or early thirties and they included those holding posts in areas of public administration concerned with development, others in research positions and some drawn from an elite administrative cadre based in central or regional government secretariats. Finally, there was a sprinkling from nongovernmental organizations, including British ones.[186]

However, the course occupied a sometimes uneasy position, depending equally on the ODA/ODM for funding, and the University, where Howell struggled to dispel impressions that the course was '"extra-mural" and not quite respectable academically'.[187] When levels of attainment fell in the mid-1970s, steps were taken to develop a master's programme, lest the course 'become a rather second-rate affair'. Cambridge, it was observed, is 'hardly the place for that sort of thing'. The following year the decision was taken to offer an M.Phil., to be taught alongside the existing Diploma and Certificate, and with a view to eventually attaining full departmental status.[188] Offering a master's degree required that the Course be adopted by a Faculty Board, but those involved found those faculties with which they had the best 'fit' reluctant, probably because of a combination of the low academic standing of the programme and internal faculty politics.[189] After an 'unpleasant rebuff' by one unnamed faculty, and expressions of interest 'but regret' from Economics, the new degree found

[183] CUL, UA, GBR/0265/CDEV 2/8, minutes OSC, 25 February 1970.
[184] CUL, UA, GBR/0265/CDEV 11/4, Howell to D. T. Richards (ODM), 4 August 1970.
[185] CUL, GBR/0265/CDEV 2/23, OSC 397, 'Overseas Studies Committee. Director's Report for the Year 1979–1980', 22 October 1980; 'Overseas Studies Committee. Review of Activities and Progress 1969–74'.
[186] GBR/0265/CDEV 2/9, Director's Report for 1972/3, Table IV, Cambridge Course on development, List of Study Fellows, 1972/3.
[187] CUL, UA, GBR/0265/CDEV 2/23, Howell to C. R. O. Jones, FCO (ODA), 8 November 1973, in response to Ian Nance to Howell.
[188] CUL, UA, GBR/0265/CDEV 11/4, Howell to Eric Burr (ODM), 27 May 1977.
[189] Interview John Toye, 9 October 2015, Oxford.

a home in the Faculty of Archaeology and Anthropology.[190] Some progress was subsequently made towards the attainment of departmental status, with arrangements to relocate the Course to new premises in Trumpington Street, to be financed by both the University and the ODM. Initial results suggested that candidates for the M.Phil. were generally better, but problems with academic standards persisted. A tension emerged between privately funded students and those in receipt of funded study fellowships, nominated by their governments. The OSC found the ODM failed to do sufficient in its selection process to prioritize academic ability; although teaching staff reviewed applications, they had nonetheless to take a minimum number of study fellows in order to protect the position of the course. Once students were enrolled, staff seem to have been reluctant to remove them even where they lacked the requisite ability.[191]

By the later 1970s recruitment began to fall, and the programme team suspected it was suffering from the competition offered by the M.Phil. taught at Sussex.[192] There was also more competition from other institutions better suited to the development of modern and self-consciously modernizing disciplines. In all, between 1970 and 1979 the number of comparable development courses offered in Britain had risen from around eight at the beginning of the 1970s to some forty-five at the end, and state funding was now shared among a larger number of universities (including the Institute of Development Studies, the University of East Anglia's School of Development Studies and the University of Manchester),[193] which offered cheaper alternatives to the Oxbridge collegiate model. With its higher costs, the Cambridge course looked increasingly financially uncompetitive. The case Oxbridge had made in the 1940s and 1950s about the superiority of generalist knowledge now increasingly told against it, with the ODA at the FCO expressing a preference for more vocational and practical training.[194]

Twenty years after Harold Macmillan had declared a wind of change to be sweeping through Africa, the British ODA, facing sweeping budgetary cuts imposed by Thatcher's government, finally broke with this aspect of the colonial past, removing funding from institutions and initiatives that had first been conceived within the frame of colonial administration. Financial support was now withdrawn from the Cambridge Course and Oxford's FSP, by then also catering to a more diverse intake, with students funded by their own

---

[190] CUL, UA, GBR/0265/CDEV 11/4, 'Correspondence with Ministry of Overseas Development 1969–1980', Howell to Eric Burr, ODM, 27 May 1977.
[191] CUL, UA, GBR/0265/CDEV 2/12, OSC 359, minutes 15 June 1978; external examiner report, 29 July 1978.
[192] CUL, UA, GBR/0265/CDEV 2/10, OSC 281, minutes of meeting, 12 June 1975.
[193] CUL, UA, GBR/0265/CDEV 2/23, OSC 397, 'Overseas Studies Committee. Director's Report for the Year 1979–1980', 22 October 1980.
[194] CUL, UA, GBR/0265/CDEV 2/12, 'Cambridge Courses on Development: the Future', Appendix I, 'Background Paper', paper prepared by Howell, c. April 1980.

governments or international organizations studying alongside those paid for by the ODM.[195] Another casualty was the *Journal of Administration Overseas,* first published in 1949 as the *Journal of African Administration,* one of several ways in which alongside the new Devonshire courses, the Colonial Office had sought to boost Service morale and facilitate the exchange of ideas. It found a new home in the commercial journal sector, and in 1981 was renamed *Public Administration and Development.*[196]

At Cambridge the loss of ODA funding was greeted with understandable dismay. As director, Howell believed that the Course served important purposes, not just in educational terms, but also political and commercial, with alumni either already occupying or rising to important positions overseas. A prestigious institution like Cambridge should, he thought, be able to provide teaching in development, but it was nevertheless hard to demonstrate real 'impact' to the ODA.[197] Angry academics formed a 'battle group' to lobby for the survival of the course. But they were caught between a rock and a hard place, with the course perceived at the ODA as too 'academic', too 'theoretical' and too 'general', while the University's General Board refused to fund a course long regarded as academically inferior and marginal to university priorities. Howell felt badly let down by the ODA so soon after the M.Phil. had been welcomed in Whitehall, but had few allies in the University and proved unable to mobilize effective opposition to the plan.[198] The government duly withdrew funding in 1981, ending over fifty years of direct support.

Some legacies of the old Devonshire courses and the universities' role in service training remained. At Cambridge what had become the M.Phil. in Development Studies was taken over by the Department of Land Economy. At Oxford the FSP survived, probably because the University remained more willing than its fenland counterpart to assume financial responsibility for these relics of Empire. Other associated institutions also lived on. QEH was reconstituted as a centre for international rather than principally Commonwealth studies; in 1986 following merger with the ICS and the Institute of Agricultural Economics it became the International Development Centre, a department within the University's Social Sciences Faculty, and subsequently the Department of International Development.[199] In the twenty-first

---

[195] Bodleian, UA, CW 1/3, minutes 15 November 1977. The ODA undertook, however, to fund some scholarships places for the FSP: OUA, UR 6/Col/4/16, 'Report of the Director of Studies for 1984/5'.

[196] *Public Administration and Development. Special Commemorative Issue, 1949–1999,* 19, no. 5 (December 1999).

[197] CUL, UA, GBR/0265/CDEV 2/23, OSC 397, 'Overseas Studies Committee. Director's Report for the Year 1979–1980', 22 October 1980.

[198] CUL GBR/0265/CDEV 2/13, OSC 397, Howell's report for 1979–80, OSC 401, minutes of special meeting of the OSC, 11 December 1980; Interview, John Toye, 9 October 2015, Oxford; Toye, 'Valpy Fitzgerald: Radical Macroeconomist of Development'.

[199] www.qeh.ox.ac.uk/content/history: accessed 14 December 2016.

century, before the controversy over Rhodes' benefaction erupted in 2015, Oxford even trumpeted the FSP's colonial origins in its publicity for the course, invoking Rhodes as illustration of the University's 'proud history of encouraging those who ... "esteem the performance of public duties as their highest aim"'.[200]

Conclusion

Like other institutions which had assumed 'imperial' roles, the universities deployed their knowledge and expertise to reconfigure their activities for the postcolonial age. Their continuing role in overseas public service training into the 1970s shows that the processes by which the apparatus of the imperial and colonial state was localized or dismantled as new national institutions were constructed overseas could present new opportunities – or in some cases obligations – for British institutions operating on the boundaries of the domestic state and civil society. Indeed, it is clear that a perception of where the universities' 'best interests' lay may have changed over time, not least as a new cohort of administrators and academics succeeded the generation in place in the 1940s. We might speculate as to whether an on-going commitment to the courses and related activities may have been the result increasingly of a sense of obligation – or even 'burden', a term explicitly evoked in discussion at Oxford in response to the demands imposed by suddenly steeply rising course numbers in the late 1950s.[201] Even so, as this chapter has demonstrated, the perhaps surprising survival of the courses so long into the postcolonial era reflected the agency of key figures associated with the universities. It also derived from Whitehall officials, as they turned to questions of technical assistance after Empire, seeking to adapt Britain's existing institutions: the pluralism which characterized British colonialism was also a feature of British technical assistance in the postcolonial era.

The history of the Oxbridge courses in the 1950s and the early 1960s reflects the Janus-faced nature of the late British imperial state. Bits of it were focused on the still-functioning Empire; other elements were concerned more with adjusting to a world *after* Empire. In turn this reflects the protracted nature of British decolonization, especially relative to that of other European colonial powers. British technical assistance therefore served a dual purpose: it was designed to cater to both Britain's remaining colonies and to recently independent Commonwealth states. The Oxbridge courses saw British probationers trained alongside not just local administrators, but *postcolonial* locals.

---

[200] In relation to the FSP on its website, accessed May 2013; this has since been removed.
[201] Bodleian, OUA, UR 6/Col 4/file 13, CCS Courses Sub-Committee, 14 January 1958.

A manifestation of the pluralist British system, the universities' role reflected distinctive British views of the relationship between institutions in civil society and the state narrowly defined; this understanding was shared even by those within the state because they were themselves the products of these institutions and subscribed to the same values. British elites perceived a new African middle class – a nonpolitical elite of bureaucrats – as essential checks and balances to the raw political authority of new states. Studying at Oxbridge – in the settled atmosphere of the collegiate system – would be the best means of acculturating them to the values of a liberal education by broadening their outlook and horizons, fashioning African entrants to administration along the paths long trodden by the adaptable generalists so prized by the British civil service.

As Table 3.3 shows, students from nearly all Commonwealth countries attended the Oxbridge courses, and, if the number from any one country in any one year was small, the cumulative totals over a period of some years were more significant – albeit that the role the courses, and indeed any British-based initiative, could play in the enormous task of training the huge numbers of local administrators now needed to fill posts in overseas public services was limited. Thanks to the universities' recruitment strategies, not all the students were from former British dependencies, or indeed those of other European empires; one instance of how the break-up of overseas empires led to a diffusion of 'colonial' knowledge beyond the European colonial empires to other states in the 'south', increasingly conceptualized with former colonies as part of the 'third' or 'developing world'. Many of the course alumni held, or went on to hold, high office, especially in the period immediately following independence, when those selected for attendance comprised the top candidates from a small cohort meeting the educational criteria for appointment or promotion. As the courses evolved into more routine qualifications in development, candidates came through increasingly diverse routes funded by a wider variety of bodies, but they still included some destined for high office: students attending the Cambridge course in 1976 included Rupiah Banda, a future President of Zambia.

How far the courses proved a vehicle for the transmission of British ideas of public service, and, later, of development, is harder to ascertain. In the decades after decolonization there was growing scepticism among political scientists about the dividends of overseas study of all kinds for the development of less developed states, and appreciation that the needs of individuals studying abroad were not necessarily the same as the national interest of the countries from which they came. Studies from other regions and sectors show that the hope that overseas study or training would contribute towards successful institution

Table 3.3. *Geographical origin of overseas students attending the administrative training/ development courses at Oxford and Cambridge in the 1960s and 1970s*[a]

Anglophone Africa	Other Commonwealth states and former British dependencies or mandates	Other
Botswana	Aden	Argentina
Gambia	Anguilla	Brazil
Ghana	Australia	Chile
Kenya	Bahamas	Columbia
Lesotho	Bangladesh	Costa Rica
Malawi	Barbados	Ecuador
Nigeria	Belize (British Honduras)	Ethiopia
Sierra Leone	Brunei	France
Sudan	Canada	Indonesia
Swaziland	Cook Islands	Iran
Tanzania	Cyprus	Japan
Uganda	Egypt	Liberia
Zambia	Fiji	Mexico
Zanzibar	Guyana	Mozambique
	India	(preindependence)
	Jamaica	Nepal
	Jordan	Nicaragua
	Kuwait	Panama
	Malaysia	Peru
	Malta	Philippines
	Mauritius	Salvador
	New Hebrides	Saudi Arabia
	Pakistan	South Korea
	Papua New Guinea	South Vietnam
	Sabah	Thailand
	Sarawak	Turkey
	Somalia	United States of America
	Sri Lanka	Uruguay
	Trinidad	Venezuela
	St Vincent	

[a]Compiled from papers and reports of the Committee for Commonwealth Studies, University of Oxford, and the Overseas Studies Committee, University of Cambridge in Bodleian, OUA, UR 6/COL 2, UR 6/COL 4, CW5, and CW 19, and CUL UA, CDEV 2/22-3.

building was also all too often thwarted by the political and social circum-stances of the countries to which the students returned.[202] In the case of the

[202] Elinor G. Barber, Philip G. Altbach, and Robert G. Myers eds., *Bridges to Knowledge: Foreign Students in Comparative Perspective* (University of Chicago Press, Chicago, 1984), esp. 'Introduction', and essays by James Coleman, 'Professorial Training and Institution Building

Oxbridge courses, as E. G. Rowe lamented in his valedictory comments at the time of the closure of the Oxford Course on Government and Development, the evidence of impact was 'too scattered and fragmentary to support any precise evaluation'. He nonetheless noted that 'man after man, in conversation and later in letters, testified to the help' he had gained from his course and drew attention to how 'even in countries overtaken by violent upheavals, much of the credit for what has remained stable is said to accrue to their civil services – services largely British trained', with many of their senior officers alumni of the Oxford courses.[203]

Rowe can hardly be regarded as an objective source, but individual life histories bear testimony to the adoption of British ideas amongst some high fliers. Adu, the Ghanaian appointed to the Service during the war, remained committed to British ideals, at a cost to his own career. He became the first African Secretary to the Ghanaian Cabinet and head of the country's civil service, but found his position increasingly difficult as a result of the subordination of the service in which he had played such a significant role to the party machinery of Nkrumah's regime. With his experience in demand elsewhere, his later career advancement occurred principally outside Ghana. In the 1960s he also found time to write a history of the new civil services in Anglophone African states, in which he emphasized the importance of retaining political neutrality. Having spent his formative years in a service still dominated by expatriates, his outlook inevitably reflected the British public service ethos.[204] Like Adu, the Zambian Valentine Musakanya was instrumental in establishing his country's civil service, first as Secretary to the Cabinet and then Head of the Civil Service, in which capacities he was a key figure in discussions about sending other Zambian public servants to Britain for training.[205] His equal commitment to the principle of political neutrality set him on course for conflict with Kaunda's government, especially during a period of political radicalization in Zambia from the late 1960s that culminated in 1972 in the establishment of a one-party state under Kaunda's United National Independence Party. Officials in the President's own office, whose position increasingly challenged that of politically neutral civil servants, criticized the Cabinet Office as 'colonial',

in the Third World: Two Rockefeller Foundation Experiences' and Robert G. Myers, 'Foreign Training and Development Strategies'.

[203] Bodleian, Mss Perham, 245/5, Copy of 'Reflections on the Overseas Service Courses and their Club', E. G. Rowe, October 1969, folio 13.

[204] In 1960 he was appointed to a committee on localization in Nyasaland, and the following year served on the Salaries Commission in Tanzania. He became first Secretary General of the East African Common Services Organization between 1962–3 and later regional representative on the United Nations Technical Assistance Board in East Africa, as well as Deputy Secretary-General of the Commonwealth Secretariat: Adu, *Civil Service*, biographical note, and pp. 92, 141.

[205] See correspondence on ZNA, Cabinet Office files, CO 17/1/6, UK Training Abroad 1965–7.

and, following his appointment to a series of less senior posts, Musakanya resigned in 1970. He was later appointed and then removed from the post of governor of the Bank of Zambia, and in 1980 was probably one of several instigators of an attempted coup against Kaunda, leading to his arrest although he was eventually acquitted on the grounds that the evidence against him had been extracted under torture.[206] As these stories indicate, analysis of the bureaucracies of former states shows that while they retained distinctive elements of the British approach, most especially in the form of an elite administrative cadre,[207] governments in new states found ways to subvert traditions of political neutrality in the public services irrespective of the attitudes of the civil servants at their helm.[208]

By the 1970s the shifting dynamics had caught up with the British universities. The needs of emergent nations were changing, and there were also many new sources of technical assistance. The internal institutional motors were also now less significant in part because colonial and Commonwealth studies were increasingly eclipsed by the area studies stimulated by new sources of state funding in the 1960s.[209] Legacies of the earlier activities were left within the institutional structures, but the institutional energy and commitment had gone.

[206] Larmer ed., *The Musakanya Papers*, pp. 26, 35, 103–8; Miles Larmer, 'Enemies Within? Opposition to the Zambian One-Party State, 1972–80' in Jan-Bart Gewald, Marja Hinfelaar, and Giacoma Macola eds., *One Zambia, Many Histories* (Brill, Leiden, 2008), pp. 98–125; see also Valentine Musakanya, 'Chingola'.

[207] In South Asian states, which admittedly had a longer process of Indianization, almost twenty years after their independence from Britain the predominance of a generalist, administrative class was one of the most striking British legacies in relation to public administration despite an exodus of most remaining British officers at independence. Although they only constituted a small proportion of total members of their countries' public services, they nevertheless occupied key positions closest to the most senior politician, and the 'secretariat' remained paramount in all the bureaucratic systems of these former British colonies, as well as also in Malaya: Ralph Braibanti, 'Concluding Observations' in Braibanti and others, *Asian Bureaucratic Systems,* pp. 643–75, esp. 643–7.

[208] For example, early in Ghana's postcolonial history Kwame Nkrumah instituted a series of new posts that would be outside the public service, including 'district commissioners' for each district in the country's regions who would act as 'personal assistants' to ministers. In 1960 the government introduced fundamental changes to the public service commission as it had been established in 1957, including the substitution of a 'principal' for 'permanent' secretary. When the following year a branch of the CPP was inaugurated at the very heart of the public services in the Establishment Secretariat, it further eroded British traditions: PRAAD, RG 2/2/17, see correspondence from A. C. Russell (Kumasi Regional Office) to R. K. Gardiner, Establishment Secretary, 1957; and ADM, 13/1/27, Cabinet minutes 9 September 1958, item 2; 16 September 1958, item 6; RG 3/1/622, 'Establishment'; RG 2/4/27, Ohene Odame (sec/organizer, Establishment CPP branch) to V. C. Crabbe (CPP headquarters), 27 December 1961.

[209] Notably as a result of the 1962 Hayter report into area studies.

4   'Education and Propaganda': The Bank of
     England and the Development of Central
     Banking in African States at the End of Empire

At the beginning of July 1959 Cameron ('Kit') Cobbold, governor of the Bank of England, travelled to Nigeria to attend the official opening of the country's new bank.[1] The Central Bank of Nigeria had been established the previous year, but the celebration marked the commencement of its full operations and the issue of a new Nigerian currency in place of the old colonial notes and coins. To commemorate the occasion Cobbold presented the new bank with an engraved silver inkstand, a gift from the Bank of England.[2] As 'the mother of Central Banks', the Bank of England looked forward, he had declared during a visit the previous year, to 'welcoming the Nigerian Central Bank as the youngest member of the world wide family of Central Banks, and more particularly the family of Central Banks of the Commonwealth'.[3]

Central banks had become 'fashionable', and, as one of Cobbold's advisers recognized, they had 'glamour and appeal to the politicians for prestige reasons'. Perhaps equally compelling to governments, swept to office amidst public expectations of rapid economic development, was that central banks were known to be able to 'create money', and in the anticolonial climate of the time might be perceived as a means 'to rescue the communities and governments from the thraldom of London and London based banks'.[4] It was hence ironic – a reflection of the ambiguities of the decolonization process – that, as Cobbold's presence in Lagos in 1959 hinted, the Bank of England had played and would continue to play a formative role in the development of institutions that had become emblematic of independent statehood. In Nigeria, one moment in particular captures the ambiguities of the situation: the ceremonial presentation of the Bank's gift, when one white man, Cobbold, congratulated another white man, the Bank's new governor, on the achievement of this particular milestone in Nigeria's path to independence from Britain. The new governor,

---

[1] TNA, various papers in CO 1025/118; BoE, OV 68/13, no. 25, note, 'Central Bank of Nigeria', 18 June 1959.
[2] See BoE, G 1/532, papers relating to Cobbold's visit.
[3] BoE, G 1/531, no. 61, notes for speech at Finance Minister's dinner, 18 March 1958.
[4] BoE, OV 7/36, 'Some reflections on Currency Boards and Central Banks in the Colonial Context', paper by J. Fisher, 23 July 1958.

Roy Fenton, was one of a number of Bank staff recently transferred from Threadneedle Street; presiding over an institution formed in the Old Lady's image; its statutes based on recommendations by one of the Bank's employees. This chapter shows how, in Nigeria and elsewhere in British Africa, the Bank via 'education and propaganda', and a diaspora of its own personnel seconded as advisers and to fill senior posts within Commonwealth banks, sought, and sometimes managed to exercise oversight over the new banks. It thus was able to promote its own view of central banking, while also seeking to protect its interests, alongside those of sterling and the City.

Management of this process was concentrated within the Bank's department dealing with overseas matters. An 'Overseas and Foreign Department' had been established in 1932 to manage the growing work arising from its relationships with other central banks; this department became the Exchange Control and Overseas Department from 1941 until 1957, and in 1957 the Overseas Department. Between 1959 and 1964 the Overseas Department was folded into a newly established Central Banking Information Department, but, when this arrangement proved relatively unsuccessful, it was divided again, and a separate Overseas Department was created once again, the third in the Bank's history.[5] (In this chapter 'Overseas Department' may be used to refer to any of these iterations.) In the judgement of the Bank's official historian and a Bank insider, John Fforde, in the late 1940s the Bank had a capacity for managing external affairs, operating as an 'effective entity', able to devise and pursue coherent policies, which it lacked in relation to domestic post-war monetary policy. By the 1950s the Overseas Department was one of the largest and most significant within the Bank.[6]

To no small extent, the Bank's post-war activities relating to colonial and Commonwealth central banking must be understood with reference to an institutional culture formed under the Bank's long-serving interwar governor, Montagu Norman, and to continuities of outlook among a generation who had served their formative years under him. Cobbold, the governor from 1949 to 1961, was brought into the Bank by Norman in 1933 as an adviser on overseas matters, and had been acting deputy chief of the Overseas and Foreign Department, 1933–5.[7] Although Cobbold was followed as governor by Lord Cromer (1961–6), a Bank outsider and member of the Barings banking

---

[5] Hennessy notes this was partly in response to the Radcliffe Committee criticism of the Bank's statistical capabilities and what it saw as its failure to make the fruits of its research more available to the outside world: Hennessy, 'Governors, Directors and Management', pp. 205–7, and fig. 7.2, p. 208.

[6] Fforde, *Bank of England*, p. 316.

[7] Biographical information relating to Bank officials is taken from Appendix 2, 'Governors, Directors, and Senior Officials' in Kynaston and Roberts eds., *Bank of England*, pp. 244–96, as well as the biographical footnotes in Fforde, *Bank of England*.

dynasty, he was in turn succeeded by another official from Montagu's era, Sir Leslie O'Brien (1966–73), appointed to the Bank in 1927. Other senior advisers and officials in the post-war era had also played a key role in interwar overseas and Commonwealth banking developments. John Lennox (Jack) Fisher, head of the Exchange Control and Overseas Department from 1948 until 1950, when he became an adviser to the governor, was one of these. A key figure in the Bank's discussions in the 1950s, he had also been significant in an earlier phase of the development of Commonwealth banking as a member of the 1933 Macmillan Commission on Banking and Currency whose recommendations led to the establishment of the Bank of Canada. After the war, in addition to his role in Nigeria, he was also a member of a commission to advise and report on the establishment of a central bank in Libya (1954) and the Bank's representative on the colonial currency boards.[8] Guy Watson, from 1957, chief of the new Overseas/Central Banking Information Department, until 1963 when he also became an adviser to the governors, was another crucial figure in the development of the Bank's policies. He too had relevant experience of developing overseas central banking, having accompanied Sir Otto Niemeyer on a mission to Argentina in 1933, before becoming a Bank and Treasury representative in Latin America during the war. In 1956 he advised on the establishment of a central bank in Malaya.[9]

In their discussions of Commonwealth banking in the mid-1950s these men linked developments in the 'new' Commonwealth with pre-war developments in the 'old'. After the war, sterling lurched from the convertibility crisis in 1947 via that of devaluation in 1949 to a new balance of payments crisis that followed rearmament and the onset of the Korean War. The looming threat posed by enormous external liabilities, in the form of sterling balances held by British colonies, foreign and independent Commonwealth countries, was acutely problematic, while the establishment of new institutions like the World Bank and moves towards European integration had transformed the international landscape in which the Bank operated.[10] Yet notwithstanding these challenges, the cohort at the top of the Bank no less than before appeared to have every expectation that they would and should shape central banking within the Empire–Commonwealth, whether, initially, through resisting a development Bank officials deemed undesirable, or later through devising banking

---

[8] BoE, OV 21/25, schedule of Bank advisers and appointments to new central banks attached to note by G.E.H. (Overseas Department) addressed to Mr Parker, 18 May 1961.

[9] *Report on the Establishment of a Central Bank in Malaya by Mr. G.M. Watson and Sir Sydney Caine* (Kuala Lumpur, 1956).

[10] Although Schenk argues that the balances posed less of a threat to British financial stability in the 1950s than some contemporaries argued: Schenk, *Britain and the Sterling Area*, p. 48.

institutions that looked, as one adviser put it with reference to a new central bank in Ghana, 'fairly imposing' but which 'should not be too dangerous'.[11]

Indeed, Britain's greatly reduced financial situation only served to increase the importance for the Bank of exercising influence over central banking in the Commonwealth, enhancing the importance of the sterling area and of Britain's smaller dependencies, including its African colonies.[12] After the war the system agreed at Bretton Woods in 1944 entailed countries linking their currencies through fixed exchange rates to the American dollar (which alone among currencies was tied to gold). This still allowed for a continued global role for sterling as a 'secondary international currency', with the currencies of Empire–Commonwealth countries pegged to sterling rather than directly to the dollar.[13] With the failure of convertibility in 1947, Britain retreated into the sterling area, operating exchange controls against non-sterling countries. As net contributors of foreign earnings to the sterling area, the colonies, especially the trio advancing most rapidly to independence, Malaya, the Gold Coast and Nigeria, were crucial to its balance of payments. They had accumulated significant sterling balances, managed in London and invested in sterling securities. Catherine Schenk has argued that encouraging new banks in former colonies to maintain sterling reserves for their new currencies not only helped maintain investor confidence, but helped to insulate sterling at a point when older and south Asian Commonwealth states were seeking to draw down their reserves. Between 1950 and 1955 while Australian, New Zealand and South African balances halved in value from £640 million to £313 million, and those of India, Pakistan and Ceylon also fell, the balances of African colonies more than doubled in size, from £336 million to £720 million. Currency reserves comprised approximately one third of these colonial sterling balances.[14]

Given that the sterling area was largely coterminous with the geographical Commonwealth, and Commonwealth central banking cooperation underpinned sterling cooperation, it can be difficult to assess the relative significance of concerns about sterling and the City and of the idea of Commonwealth. Even so, the Bank showed a singular and striking commitment to the Commonwealth, although, as we shall see, this was not uncontested within the Bank. The Bank's initiatives also reflected the perceived value and superiority of its own expertise and models, inseparable (as we have seen was the case in relation to British ideas about training for public administration) from a wider British liberal political

---

[11] BoE, OV69/3, no. 61H, J. B. Loynes to Cyril Hawker (an executive director at the Bank), 7 March 1955 [should be 1956].
[12] On which see esp. Krozewski, *Money and the End of Empire*; Cain and Hopkins, *British Imperialism*, ch. 11.
[13] Schenk, *Decline of Sterling*, p. 417.
[14] Schenk, *Britain and the Sterling Area*, pp. 22, 417; Bangura, *Britain and Commonwealth Africa*, p. 44.

project, since the Bank hoped that new Commonwealth banks would operate autonomously of their governments, staffed by members of an emergent African professional and technocratic middle class, who would become part of an international cadre of professional central bankers. The bank aimed to foster a network of central bankers, an objective that must be understood in the context of American ambitions to achieve greater subordination of banks to governments.

These other, non-sterling objectives were of increased importance as the sterling area declined in significance following the restoration of sterling convertibility in 1958.[15] Successive changes beginning with devaluation in 1967 thereafter eroded the area's significance, culminating in 1972 when, following the collapse of the Bretton Woods system of fixed exchange rates to the American dollar, the pound was allowed to float and Britain imposed exchange controls on almost all other sterling area members. In 1979 the exchange control, which had brought the sterling area into existence in the first place, was removed altogether. By then sterling had ceased to be a significant reserve currency. Even before this, British policymakers had sought a reduction in sterling's international role, with Treasury officials concerned that Britain's short-term international liabilities might exceed Britain's available liquid assets. In the 1960s as this view became more widely accepted even the Bank 'stopped lobbying so hard for sterling's global role to be enhanced', and Schenk suggests that it instead sought to manage sterling's decline.[16]

Much of the Bank's activity in relation to the development of African central banks is discussed here for the first time. However, one area that has received attention is the Bank's role in the creation of new banks, the subject of an exhaustive, unpublished (and until recently inaccessible) in-house history by Eric Haslam.[17] Yusuf Bangura's history of economic decolonization in Commonwealth Africa offers as astute an overview as was possible before the archival sources were available.[18] My own and others' country case studies focus on the Bank's advisers' resistance to the development of central banks and (as I demonstrated for Ghana), later efforts to steer them along acceptable lines.[19] In Malaya and Nigeria, as Schenk and Chibuike Uche show, the British hand was forced by the recommendations of IBRD economic missions to them

---

[15] Schenk, *Britain and the Sterling Area*, p. 130.
[16] Schenk, *The Decline of Sterling*, passim, esp. pp. 271–2, 417, 423–9.
[17] BoE, OV 18/2: Eric Haslam, *Central Banks in the Making: The Role of the Bank of England 1948–74* (unpublished ms). At the time of writing only the chapter on Ghana had been declassified in response to a FoI request.
[18] Bangura, *Britain and Commonwealth Africa*, pp. 46–9.
[19] Stockwell, 'Instilling'; see also other studies of specific banks: Uche, 'From Currency Board to Central Banking'; Uche, 'Bank of England vs the IBRD'; Schenk, 'The origins of a Central Bank in Malaya'; see also Eric Helleiner, 'The Southern Side of "Embedded Liberalism". America's Unorthodox Money Doctoring during the Early Post-1945 years', in Marc Flandreau ed., *Money Doctors: The Experience of International Financial Advising, 1850–2000* (Routledge, Abingdon, 2003), pp. 249–75.

in the 1950s, which adopted a more positive approach to the part central banks might play in national economic development.

Beginning from a different perspective, Eric Helleiner agrees that the Bank of England obstructed the development of central banking in new Commonwealth states. This leads him to argue that the Bank of England's record after the war 'contrasted sharply' with its earlier promotion of central banking under Norman. As he shows, the British approach was also at variance with that of American officials, who, in the early post-war period, advised on the establishment of banks in several Central and Latin American states, as well as the Philippines, South Korea, and, to British dismay, Ceylon. Before the war the British and Americans had shared a common philosophy: a commitment to upholding the discipline of the gold standard. From the early 1940s, however, whereas British officials continued to adhere to a classical liberal orthodoxy, prioritizing external currency stability, those at the US Federal Reserve began instead to promote central banks that could pursue domestically oriented monetary policies and would facilitate domestic economic development, corresponding to a Keynsian economic model. Helleiner points out that while the British, opposed to the creation of banks with powers that might lead them to withdraw their sterling assets from the London market, had strong incentives to maintain the status quo as long as possible, the Americans perceived the promotion of central banking as a potentially useful means of winning influence among decolonizing states in the global south, including, potentially, former British colonies.[20]

It is not the intention in what follows to challenge the claim that the post-war Bank of England sought to resist the development of central banks in emergent Commonwealth states. The Bank, together with officials in Whitehall, *had* earlier opposed developments that it saw as contrary to the interests of sterling and the City, but also economically unnecessary (for existing arrangements for the issue and management of colonial currencies via regional currency boards worked to the Bank's own satisfaction, ensuring price stability). The colonies lacked the financial infrastructure and conditions which, in the Bank's conservative view of central banking, were necessary for the establishment of central banks. The Bank feared also that, as Jack Fisher put it, African central banks might become 'machines for inflation'.[21] Indeed what follows provides new evidence of the degree to which the Bank sought to delay the advent of Commonwealth central banking, and when this proved impossible,

---

[20] Helleiner, 'Southern Side of "Embedded Liberalism"', esp. pp. 249–52, 259; see also Helleiner, *The Making of National Money*, ch. 9.

[21] BoE, OV 7/36, 'Some Reflections on Currency Boards and Central Banks in the Colonial Context', paper by J. Fisher, 23 July 1958.

to exert control over the process so that the new banks would follow British rather than American banking orthodoxy, as well as to limit diversification away from sterling. When Cobbold referred to a 'family of central banks of the Commonwealth' at the opening of the Central Bank of Nigeria, it seems reasonable to suggest that he had in mind not only the Bank's hopes for strong inter-Commonwealth banking cooperation, but also that the new banks would show familial likeness to the British.

But such resistance must nevertheless be viewed in context of the Bank of England's other activities, in particular its provision of technical assistance to the new banks. This technical assistance shows the discontinuities between the interwar and post-war eras were not as great as Helleiner suggests. This was so not only because the Bank continued to exercise a form of financial imperialism, but more substantially because from 1955 to 1956 bank officials were planning for colonial central banks not only in Malaya, the Gold Coast and Nigeria, but more widely, and were preparing to offer significant help to the new banks. Officials themselves perceived their post-1945 advisory activities within the same frame as their pre-war advocacy of central banking, even where the advice offered was initially quite different. This is the context in which the Bank set in motion steps to supply staff to new Commonwealth banks and instituted its own training course.

In order to elaborate on this claim we will now consider the Bank's role in the establishment of new banks, before moving on to explore its contribution to their staffing and the training of Commonwealth central bankers.

'Potty Little Affairs': The Development of Central Banks in the Colonial Empire/Commonwealth

It was in the mid-1950s that the Bank began to revise its earlier opposition to the development of central banks in British Africa, as it became clear that if the Bank was unwilling to support the development of central banks, there were others who might. The American role in Ceylon represented one salutary experience, with the new Bank of Ceylon reflecting American rather than British orthodoxy.[22] In Nigeria, where the gradualist approach recommended by Fisher in 1953 was outmoded from the start,[23] the British found themselves forced into rear-guard action as a result of a visiting World Bank mission, ironically invited to the colony by the British and Nigerian governments to conduct an economic survey; an experience that led the Bank to try as far as possible to

---

[22] H. A. Gunasekera, *From Dependent Currency to Central Banking in Ceylon: An Analysis of Monetary Experience, 1825–1957* (London School of Economic and Political Science, London, 1962), pp. 260–2, note 8; Singleton, *Central Banking*, p. 167.

[23] *Report on the Desirability and Practicability of Establishing a Central Bank in Nigeria for Promoting the Economic Development of the Country* (Lagos, 1953), p. 18.

restrict the terms of future World Bank economic missions so that they did not stray into central-banking issues.[24] The IBRD team recommended swift progress on the development of national banking and currency institutions, including the immediate establishment of a state bank with currency-issuing functions.[25] Initially, Bank officials had tried secretly to dissuade the World Bank from proposing even a state bank, and the final report incorporated factual corrections the Bank had made on a draft,[26] a source of controversy within the World Bank.[27] But Fisher and others recognized further 'attack' might be counterproductive, especially if it became known that the British government had tried to influence the report.[28] Hence, when the Bank was asked by the Colonial Office on behalf of the Nigerian government to nominate someone who could advise on the establishment of a state bank, it decided to grasp the bull by the horns, persuading the Colonial Office that its brief should include the creation of a Nigerian currency so as to ensure that the British government was in a position to 'exercise influence to ensure that it was properly established'.[29]

In the Gold Coast, where a state bank had already been formed, developments were moving even more quickly. Already in 1954 Fisher had concluded that the Bank should no longer resist African moves for a central bank. But with the attainment of full internal self-government in 1954, and the appointment of a new Minister of Finance, Komlo Gbedemah, control of banking and currency issues was rapidly slipping from British hands, with Gbedemah and the expatriate managing director of the newly formed Bank of the Gold Coast, Alfred Eggleston, reportedly ambitious to become governor himself of a central bank, willing to act unilaterally.[30] By September 1955 Bank officials feared that Gbedemah would proceed with a bank based on statutes developed locally and which would not conform to what they perceived to be best central-banking practice. They were particularly appalled at the prospect that the colony might

---

[24] Uche, 'Bank of England vs the IBRD', p. 233.
[25] World Bank, *The Economic Development of Nigeria* (The Johns Hopkins Press, Baltimore, MD, 1955) pp. 97–8.
[26] Uche, 'Bank of England vs the IBRD', p. 235.
[27] The report's authors were criticized by others within the IBRD for their 'unquestioning' acceptance of some aspects of British colonial practice, including that a new currency be fully backed by sterling: Restricted report prepared for internal use within the IBRD. World Bank. 1956. *The reports of the Bank's general survey missions – a synthesis.* Central Economics staff series; no. EC 45. World Bank, Washington, DC. http://documents.worldbank.org/curated/en/1956/03/1558609/reports-banks-general-survey-missions-synthesis, p. 316.
[28] BoE, OV 68/2, 'Nigeria. IBRD Draft Report', 4 May 1954, note by Fisher.
[29] BoE, OV 68/3, no. 69 D, 'Note of a meeting held in the Colonial Office on the 22nd May [1956] to discuss arrangements for the setting up of a state bank in Nigeria'.
[30] BoE, OV 69/3, no. 57, Loynes' report on a meeting with Kenneth Tours, economic adviser to the Gold Coast, 25 January 1956.

end up with a central bank that had commercial banking functions, a situation that would lead to the new Bank competing with the aid of state funds with commercial banks in the country.[31] The 'basic essential', officials at the Colonial Office argued, was to ensure that the Gold Coast government did 'not set up a Frankenstein'.[32] There was a lot at stake. The Gold Coast was setting the pace for development elsewhere in Africa, and it also had some £200 million in sterling assets; it was a net contributor of dollar earnings to the sterling area, and an important location for commercial and financial interests. Having accepted that the unilateral action taken by the colony's new African Minister of Finance meant that the Bank could no longer afford to resist demands for a central bank, Bank officials advised the Secretary of State that Gbedemah must be encouraged to accept its assistance.[33]

At this stage the only comparable demands elsewhere in Anglophone Africa were from the settler-led Central African Federation. In this instance, the demand arose within the settler community in Southern Rhodesia, although the Bank of England had been reluctant here too to see the development of central banking, with a Bank adviser concluding against a proposal for a new central bank in 1949. But with on-going settler pressure a central bank was established in 1956.[34] No doubt influenced by the turn of events in West Africa, Fisher advised in 1958 that there was now little purpose in Bank advisers opposing central banks where these had become a political issue. Instead, he suggested, 'Our recommendations should be directed towards fashioning the safest form for the instrument which the politicians are demanding', even though the Bank's chief task was for the moment to 'improve the currency board system where possible and play long the central bank issue'. Whereas 'Whitehall have been and are very slow to act', Fisher thought that this transition was in fact 'rather easier' for the Bank, as it had a vested interest in dealing with other central banks, even if, as he put it, 'they are only potty little affairs'.[35] As Fisher's dismissive reference to 'potty little affairs' indicates, the Bank continued to regard the movement towards African central banking as intrinsically undesirable, and when pressures for central banking arose in other locations, sought to stall as it had done earlier in the case of Ghana and Nigeria. Yet not only had the Bank now moved from a position of obstruction to collaboration to ensure that it was able to exercise maximum influence, but also, as we shall

[31] Ibid., no. 55c, memo 6 September 1955.
[32] TNA, CO 1025/42, 'Gold Coast currency and banking', notes prepared in advance of a meeting with the Treasury and BoE, 14 September 1955.
[33] BoE, OV 69/3, 55 g, brief for the Secretary of State in advance of his meeting with Gbedemah, 15 September 1955.
[34] Sowelem, *Towards Financial Independence*, pp. 29–39.
[35] BoE, OV 7/36, 'Some reflections on Currency Boards and Central Banks in the Colonial Context', paper by J. Fisher, 23 July 1958.

see, it had begun developing plans for providing technical assistance to new Commonwealth banks.

More than any other, one man was instrumental in the Bank's efforts to exercise influence. John Barraclough (de) Loynes, from January 1960 Fisher's successor on the African currency boards,[36] had joined the Bank in 1924, becoming acting assistant adviser in 1948, and serving from 1949 to 1955 as assistant chief cashier of the Exchange Control and Overseas Department. From March 1955 he was appointed an adviser at the Bank.[37] Loynes's role in overseas central banking was by no means confined to Africa as in 1953–4 he had been seconded as a consultant to the Bank of Ceylon. From the mid-1950s, however, British Africa became his primary focus. Beginning in 1956 Loynes prepared reports or draft statutes that served as the basis for legislation leading to the introduction of new central banks or currency authorities in Ghana, Nigeria, Sierra Leone and the Gambia. He subsequently became head of the new Gambian Currency Board. Loynes was also instrumental in the transfer of the location and ownership of the EACB from London to the East African governments, and after in the creation of a separate currency authority for the Federation of South Arabia (which had previously been served by the EACB). Following the relocation of the EACB from London, Loynes served on the Board in a personal capacity, although the voluminous correspondence with the Bank about East African issues shows that he remained closely in touch with the Bank's Overseas Department. In the Bank's African country files, as well as in those relating to the currency boards, Loynes hand is to be seen everywhere. In June 1967 following a reorganization of the Bank's overseas work, the Bank's governor, Leslie O'Brien informed Loynes that his geographical areas of responsibilities now included all of Africa except for South Africa and the Arab countries of the north, as well as the exercise of 'general supervision of matters relating to central banking statues and currency board work throughout the world'.[38] This growing concentration of responsibility for African banking in one quarter probably reflects its dwindling importance within the Bank in line with shifting appreciations of the sterling area, but it also illustrates the significance of personal networks in handling African issues.

Loynes was in some respects an unlikely vehicle for the Bank's financial imperialism. In private he expressed a disdain for some locations to which

---

[36] Loynes changed his name by deed poll in 1965 to the old family name of 'de Loynes'.

[37] The information in this paragraph is based on his career notes and others papers on his personal file, BoE, G17/32. On Loynes see also, Chibuike Uche, 'J. B. Loynes and Central Banking Development in British West Africa', *South African Journal of Economic History*, 15 (2000), pp. 112–33.

[38] BoE, G 17/32, nos. 49 & 50, Leslie O'Brien (BoE) to Loynes, 8 June 1967; Loynes to O'Brien, 12 June 1967.

his work took him, writing on his appointment as an adviser to the governor in 1965 from Aden (then in the midst of the emergency) to say that he looked 'forward to getting back soon from these troublesome places', while he referred to the Gambia as a 'preposterous little country'.[39] Yet notwithstanding this he became the 'go-to' man on African issues, undoubtedly reflecting his own appetite for involvement in the affairs of so many countries as well as his accumulating expertise. The Bank's strategy turned in large part on developing working relationships with individuals – and in the very late 1950s and early 1960s Loynes was at the heart of these. He had developed an extensive network of contacts and secured information that sometimes Whitehall did not have. 'James Bond Loynes' was how one colleague in Threadneedle Street referred to him.[40]

Loynes' involvement with African banking began with his appointment to advise on banking in the Gold Coast in 1956, where the Secretary of State had succeeded in persuading Gbedemah to accept Bank of England assistance, followed by a similar mission to Nigeria the following year. In both countries he showed a strong appreciation of the need to accommodate local aspirations for central banks and national currencies, advancing specific recommendations that would satisfy local opinion, but which would endow the new banks with only limited powers, adhering to a sterling area system consistent with British conservative banking orthodoxy.

In the Gold Coast his primary task was to ensure a separation of commercial activities from central banking, in line with the Bank's own orthodoxy that central banks should never engage in the former.[41] This position was at odds with American thinking, which held that, to perform a developmental role in developing societies, new banks might have to engage in direct lending.[42] Loynes tailored his recommendations to what he declared appropriate to a 'small and undeveloped monetary system', for example by stipulating a fixed maximum fiduciary issue as opposed to the more normal mechanism of a varying percentage figure (as he suggested for Nigeria), which would rise and fall according to currency in circulation. He deliberately made no provision for the review of this maximum figure, thereby ensuring that it could only be changed by the country's new parliament.[43] His aim 'was to give the people here something that looks fairly imposing but which, if applied, should not be too dangerous'.

[39] Ibid., no. 38, Loynes to 'Maurice' [Parsons; an executive director at the Bank], 25 February 1965; no. 56B, Loynes to O'Brien, 5 June 1969 and enclosed note of his activities, dated 4 June 1969.
[40] BoE, OV 76/4, annotation, probably by Jasper St. John Rootham, an adviser to the Governor, on 'Record of discussion between heads of government in East Africa'.
[41] On the issues discussed in this section, see Stockwell, 'Instilling', and also the articles by Uche, especially, 'J.B. Loynes'.
[42] Helleiner, 'Southern Side of "Embedded Liberalism"', p. 253.
[43] BoE, OV 68/5, no. 56A, Loynes to H. L. Jenkyns (T), 18 February 1956.

In this instance, as also subsequently in Nigeria, Loynes adopted a strongly strategic approach, deliberately mentioning American banking practice to the Ghanaians so as to avoid accusations of bias and as a way of 'safeguarding our position in the most unlikely event of Americans or others coming this way'.[44] Loynes returned to the country in November, and again in January 1957, when he oversaw the drafting of relevant legislation and arrangements for the transfer of the currency from the WACB to the new Bank. In 1957 two bills were passed in the legislature, although not without some criticism: one to create the Bank of Issue, to be known as the Bank of Ghana, and the other to amend the ordinance of the existing state Bank of the Gold Coast to make this into a purely commercial bank, the 'Ghana Commercial Bank'.[45] When he returned to the country later in the year it was to attend the opening ceremony of the Bank, of which Alfred Eggleston became first governor.[46]

In Nigeria, although Loynes contended with the complications posed by the IBRD survey, he had a freer hand than in Ghana as he did not have to work within the confines of the plans already sketched by the government. Loynes expressed more confidence in the economic and political development of the country than in the Gold Coast, and recommended a central banking system that 'would have rather more elbow room and probably more permanence in its original form'.[47] With a view to ensuring the IBRD proposals were not resurrected, he commented on each 'crack-brained idea' advanced by the IBRD mission 'without mentioning' the IBRD itself.[48] Before producing the report, Loynes had advised colleagues at the Bank of England that it would be best to secure a 'reasonably early implementation' of any recommendations so that the Nigerians did not feel compelled to seek advice elsewhere.[49] With this objective in mind he incorporated a draft banking ordinance and statute for the new bank in annexes to his report.[50] To local politicians, that Loynes was willing not only to support the immediate creation of a central bank, but also provide detailed recommendations as to its structure and basis, must have cast him in a positive light. Such was his apparent popularity that the African Minister of Finance was keen to secure the services of Loynes himself as the Bank's first governor; colonial officials, however, wary of his wife's reputed

---

[44] Stockwell, 'Instilling', p. 110; BoE, OV 69/3, Loynes to Fisher, 23 February 1956.
[45] See papers in BoE, OV 69/4.
[46] See papers in BoE, OV 69/8.
[47] BoE, OV 68/5, no. 56A, Loynes to H. L. Jenkyns (T), 18 February 1956.
[48] BoE, OV 68/4, Loynes to Parsons, 30 July 1957.
[49] Ibid., 'Nigeria: Central Bank', note by Loynes circulated to M. Parsons, C. Hawker, and copied to Fisher, 17 October 1956.
[50] *Report by Mr. J.B. Loynes on the Establishment of a Nigerian Central Bank, the Introduction of a Nigerian Currency, and other Associated Matters* (Lagos, 1957).

racism, did 'not wish to run the risk of having Mrs. Loynes back in Nigeria',[51] and Roy Fenton was appointed instead.

In both Ghana and Nigeria Loynes aimed to replicate a British model. Both banks followed the structure of the Bank of England: they were headed by a governor and a deputy governor and given boards of directors with responsibility for policy and the general administration of office and business.[52] As in Threadneedle Street, separate departments were created to handle note issue and banking. The legislation establishing each of these new banks also preserved a strong tie to sterling, with the new banks required to keep the majority or even all of their currency reserves in sterling, British government securities or in gold held in London. As a result, the banks did little more than replicate some of the features of the currency board system. Limits were imposed on the degree to which they were permitted to employ reserves for developmental purposes.[53]

In addition to preserving sterling's role, these provisions served another purpose – ensuring that the new banks were not subject to excessive demands to supply credit to their governments. This corresponded to one of the Bank's key objectives: establishing central bank autonomy from government. One of the Bank's principal objections to the development of African central banking had been that African governments might use the banks as a source of easy money, giving rise to inflationary pressures.[54] The Bank of England had itself been nationalized in 1946, but adherence to central bank autonomy from government was a fundamental tenet of its officials understanding of sound central banking, and by extension, of a liberal political order. The founding statutes for the Banks of Ghana, Nigeria, as well as that of the Bank of Rhodesia and Nyasaland, hence departed from those of the post-war Bank of England, corresponding to its original, pre-nationalization, structure, with no provision made for their respective governments to be able to direct their activities.[55]

In Ghana and Nigeria, Loynes had successfully regained some of the influence the Bank and Whitehall appeared earlier to have lost. But in Ghana the part Loynes had played, and specifically his efforts to ensure separation of commercial and central banking, became a source of friction in British relations with the new Ghanaian bank, with Nkrumah reportedly keen to merge

---

[51] TNA, CO 1025/117, minute by R. J. Vile, 29 November 1957 on letter from G. G. Carlyle to the Nigerian Minister of Finance, 28 November 1957.
[52] Hennessy, 'Governors, Directors and Management', pp. 196–7.
[53] S. K. Basu, *Central Banking in the Emerging Countries: A Study of African Experiments* (Asia Publishing House, London, 1967), pp. 96–7.
[54] Uche, 'J.B. Loynes', p. 132.
[55] Basu, *Central Banking*, pp. 71–2, 76, 105; Erin E. Jucker-Fleetwood, *Money and Finance in Africa: The Experience of Ghana, Morocco, Nigeria, the Rhodesias and Nyasaland, the Sudan and Tunisia from the Establishment of their Central Banks until 1962* (George Allen & Unwin, London, 1964), pp. 58–9.

the Ghana Commercial Bank with the Bank of Ghana.[56] Opposition also arose in both countries to strict adherence to the sterling system. In these circumstances, as the Bank of England engaged in significant firefighting to maintain the arrangements devised by Loynes, it relied heavily on the interventions of its own men within the new banks: Douglas Stone, Eggleston's deputy at the Bank of Ghana, and Roy Fenton, first governor of the new Central Bank of Nigeria. Stone helped defuse initial pressure to adjust Ghana's reserves by recommending nothing be done at least until the new currency was issued,[57] while Fenton helped organize a secret meeting in September 1961 between the British Chancellor, John Selwyn Lloyd and Chief Festus Okotie-Eboh, the Nigerian Minister of Finance at the British High Commissioner's house in Accra to try to persuade Festus to limit a move away from sterling.[58]

Despite British efforts, both countries now modified the arrangements with which they had entered independence and between 1962 and 1963 both countries replaced the Loynes banking ordinances with new banking statutes. In the Nigerian case, this resulted in the Nigerian pound being redefined in terms of gold rather than sterling, which enabled the Central Bank of Nigeria to diversify away from sterling.[59] In Ghana the Bank was empowered to advance long-term credit to the government, to which the new legislation also subordinated the Bank. It dismantled the separation of the Bank's issue and banking functions, and ended the requirement governing the holding of reserves in sterling or in the securities of the British government.[60] The Bank's governor, Hubert Kessels, a retired German banker, sought and received Loynes' advice on the amendments, but even so the Bank felt the full force of anti-British, and more specifically anti-Bank, sentiment.[61] Developments in Ghana, and in particular the subordination of the Bank to the machinery of Nkrumah's one party state, were the very antithesis of what the Bank had sought, and in both Nigeria and Ghana the changes led to a reduction in their sterling reserves. Although both countries remained as members of the sterling area, these changes contributed to weakening the importance of the area. In part because of Ghanaian and

---

[56] The Ghanaian Cabinet agreed in principle to the amalgamation of the two banks in October 1958 but in the end this did not occur: PRAAD, ADM 13/1/27, minutes 28 October 1958, item 2.

[57] PRAAD, RG 6/5/14, 'Sterling Area Policy and Membership', D. Stone to J. C. Anderson (Ghanaian Ministry of Finance), 25 September 1957.

[58] BoE, OV 68/9, 'Note of a meeting held at the High Commissioner's House, Accra', 13 September 1961, with the Chancellor, Festus, Fenton and others. In the event Festus confirmed his intention to transfer 10 per cent into gold and up to 30 per cent into non-sterling currencies.

[59] Jucker-Fleetwood, *Money and Finance*, pp. 58–9; Bangura, *Britain and Commonwealth Africa*, pp. 99–102.

[60] Basu, *Central Banking*, p. 97.

[61] BoE, OV 18/2, Haslam, pp. 300–4.

Nigerian actions, the importance of African sterling reserves overall sharply declined, falling from £755 million in 1954 to £254 million in 1966.[62]

The early history of the banks in independent Ghana and Nigeria shaped the context in which later African central banks were formed in other ways. Even as the Bank of England was engaged with a process of financial devolution in other areas of British Africa, the experience in both states showed that overseeing the drafting of founding legislation for new banks was no guarantee against future amendment or diversification away from sterling, and could prove a source of tension in British–African central banking relations. Loynes became conscious of the need to 'be on our guard against Ghana-style criticisms'.[63] Moreover, developments in the two countries set precedents for new banks elsewhere in the continent, and Loynes feared that the revised as opposed to *original* statute of the Bank of Nigeria might be used as a model by some of those tasked with framing other new banks, 'irrespective' as Loynes complained, 'of their circumstances'.[64]

Ghana was also instrumental in changing the wider environment within which new African banks operated, encouraging both the IMF, which from the mid-1950s played a larger role in international economic relations,[65] and the World Bank, to develop new structures to address the interests of emergent African states. When Ghana became the first sub-Saharan African colony to become independent, it was the Fund's European and Australasian department that dealt with Africa. In 1960 Gbedemah proposed to both the IMF and the World Bank that they establish separate Africa departments, objecting to Africa's inclusion within the European and Australasian department. Gbedemah's proposal met 'with general approval' at the IMF, where discussion was already underway about the possible creation of separate machinery.[66] New Africa departments were established in both organizations and a post of African director created at the IMF for the first time in 1960–1. Three years later the IMF sought to expand its existing technical assistance, establishing in 1964 a Central Banking Service to supply experts to advise on the formation of new banks and their subsequent development, as well as fill senior posts within them, using staff transferred from experienced central banks, including

[62] Bangura, *Britain and Commonwealth Africa*, p. 97.
[63] He rejected a proposal for a full-time chair of the EACB on various grounds including that it might prejudice the chances of subsequently appointing a Threadneedle figure as head of a successor institution: BoE, OV 7/81, 'East African Currency Board', paper by Loynes addressed to Parsons, 11 May 1961.
[64] BoE, OV 68/10, Loynes to Fenton, 19 March 1963.
[65] Harold James, 'Who Owns "Ownership"? The IMF and Policy Advice' in Flandreau ed. *Money Doctors*, pp. 78–102.
[66] PRAAD, RG 6/3/4, 'Creation of a department of operation for Africa. IMF', nos. 7–10, letters from K. Gbedemah to Mr Omat Saadi Elmandjra, Exec. Director, IBRD, and to Mr Soetikno Slamet, IMF, 23 November 1960; nos. 21–2, Soetikno Slamet to Gbedemah, 24 February 1961.

the Bank of England, from 1961, under Lord Cromer, who had recently served as an executive director of the Fund as well as the World Bank. The IMF also established a training institute in order to expand its training activities for government and bank officials, for example, by introducing its first Francophone courses.[67] The IMF gradually became an important alternative source of assistance for new central banks. Some of the IMF's interventions in former British colonies dismayed Bank officials, while the Bank also on occasion sought to work through the IMF.[68]

The secession of the two more politically advanced territories from the WACB immediately raised the issue of whether Sierra Leone and the Gambia should continue to be served by the regional board. For all that the wider context was different, and despite the Bank's internal recognition it should no longer oppose local demands for central banks, Loynes continued to play the issue 'long', advocating a gradualist approach. He initially stalled the development of full-blown central banking in Sierra Leone and the Gambia, which he visited in 1961 at the invitation of their governments and the Colonial Office, producing a report dealing jointly with the two.[69] In Sierra Leone, as he had been in Ghana and Nigeria, Loynes was cognizant of the need to accommodate local political aspirations, anticipating that local political opinion was unlikely to be 'fobbed off' with a proposal being floated in the Colonial Office that Sierra Leone should establish its own currency board. But since he thought a 'central bank would seem to be nonsense', he favoured a 'currency board, but with another name and with trimmings', a monetary institute that would issue a new currency, linked to sterling, and undertake some central banking functions, but fall short of a full central bank.[70]

Although Loynes responded more imaginatively than the Colonial Office to the situation in Sierra Leone, and his proposals were initially accepted by the government of the newly independent state, he found that he was unable to shape developments as he had wished and in July 1962 Sierra Leonean ministers decided they wanted to move at once to the establishment of a central bank. With Loynes himself busy in Aden, another Bank of England man, Gordon E. Hall, was tasked with preparing legislation for the new Bank. In another illustration of the distinct limits to the Bank's influence, Hall chose not to follow a draft statute sent by Loynes, and instead sought to reflect Nigerian experience. In view of the 'strong desire here' to 'remove all traces of what

---

[67] *International Monetary Fund, Annual Report, 1961; Annual Report, 1964*, pp. 20–1; *Annual Report, 1965*, p. 37; *Annual Report, 1970*, pp. 47–8.

[68] As Uche also argues in relation to Sierra Leone, 'J.B. Loynes', p. 131.

[69] *Report by J.B. Loynes on the Problem of the Future Currencies of Sierra Leone and the Gambia* (Bathurst, 1961); see also Uche, 'From Currency Board to Central Banking', and 'J.B. Loynes'.

[70] BoE, OV 70/1, no. 11, 'Sierra Leone/Gambia', memo by Loynes, 22 July 1960 addressed to Parsons and Guy Watson.

is described as "Colonial domination"', he deemed it advisable that the new Bank hold sterling 'from choice and not because it is bound to do so'.[71]

For Britain's smallest, least advanced, West African colony, Loynes thought 'nothing more than a simple board, old style' was appropriate,[72] recommending the introduction of a new currency to be issued by a Gambia Currency Board. Since he proposed that this should be tied to sterling, and backed by 100 per cent reserves, these arrangements represented only a minimal departure from the old currency board system. In addition to being a practical necessity, Loynes hoped the new Board might serve a strategic purpose, obstructing the possible 'hasty absorption of the Gambia, in currency matters', by the French-controlled Central Bank in Dakar.[73] Loynes's proposals were initially generally well-received in the Gambia, with ministers reportedly 'most anxious' that Loynes accept the chairmanship of the new Board.[74] By 1968, however, there were mounting tensions between Loynes and the Gambian government over the extent of London's control. The following year the Minister of Finance, convinced that the Board no longer met the country's needs, approached the IMF for expert assistance with establishing a central bank.[75] Loynes died while preparations for the new bank were being made, but IMF officials liaised with those of the Bank of England, and used the currency authorities of Sierra Leone, Kenya and Southern Yemen as an initial model for the preparation of the legislation establishing the new Gambian Bank.[76] When the new central bank opened in 1971 it followed British lines, with a governor and small board of directors, while also continuing to hold all of its external assets other than special drawing rights with the IMF in sterling or sterling securities. The new currency, the Dalasi, remained initially pegged to sterling.[77]

In East Africa Loynes handled currency and banking matters with a similar pragmatic appreciation of the need to manage local aspiration. At the start of his period on the EACB he presided over its transfer from London to East Africa, advocating a transitional phase of localizing the EACB and making it into a quasi-central bank. His own position was now redesignated as a technical

---

[71] BoE, OV 70/2, 'Sierra Leone', memo prepared by Loynes, 17 July 1962; Loynes to Minister of Finance, 22 August 1962; Gordon Hall to H. R. Stobbs (Overseas Department, BoE), 15 November 1962; Hall to Loynes, 15 January 1963.

[72] BoE, OV 70/1, no. 11, 'Sierra Leone/Gambia', memo by Loynes, 22 July 1960, addressed to Mr. Parsons and Mr. Watson.

[73] BoE, OV 71/1, Loynes to Lord Cromer, 28 September 1964.

[74] Ibid., F. D. C. Williams (Gambia) to Arthur Galsworthy (CO), 25 January 1964.

[75] IMF Archives, Central Banking Department Immediate Office Advisory Technical Assistance Files, Box 18, file 5, The Gambia legislation 1969–73, S. M. Dibba, Minister of Finance, to Pierre-Paul Schweitzer, Managing Director, IMF, 23 June 1969; James K. Nettles to the Managing Director and Ag. Managing Directors, IMF, 12 August 1969.

[76] Ibid., see, e.g., James K. Nettles to H. J. Tomkins, 6 April 1970; memo from Robert C. Effros to James K. Nettles, 10 July 1970.

[77] Central Bank of the Gambia: Annual Report 1971–2 (Banjul, 1973), pp. 8–9.

adviser on a board whose other representatives were drawn from East Africa. Some weeks spent in East Africa in late 1960 convinced him that his task was now that of 'starting on the central banking road' and, although he 'had no wish to hurry matters unduly', he recognized that they could not 'stand still'.[78]

Yet Loynes would later regard East Africa as the site of his 'one failure'.[79] Determined to retain a common currency for the region, 'a prize worth preserving', the corollary to on-going and long-standing British ambitions for some form of regional political federation,[80] Loynes failed to secure his objective of an East African central bank and in the process to initiate a transition to full central banking in East Africa under British supervision. Instead, convinced that it would be disastrous to proceed with an East African central bank before political federation, Loynes sought to win over local opinion to his interim solution of the locally domiciled currency board.[81] This line became increasingly difficult to hold with Tanganyikan independence in 1961: not only because this made it more difficult to keep a grip on political developments, but as it now presented the anomalous situation of an independent country with a currency still issued by a board, whose authority derived ultimately from the Secretary of State in London. Loynes sought to remedy this through an agreement between the United Kingdom and Tanganyika, but his draft proposals were held up for months in the Colonial Office, preoccupied with managing a retreat from Africa at breakneck speed.[82]

On a variety of fronts Loynes engaged in constant firefighting to try to preserve the line until such time as the other East African colonies had caught up with Tanganyika, making it possible to achieve British ambitions for a regional federation. Loynes set out 'to cultivate' apparently sympathetic local politicians, as he did in the case of the Ugandan Minister of Finance, Amos Kalule Sempa, an 'agreeable little man'.[83] It became increasingly difficult, however, to keep a lid on developments on all fronts. By August 1962 Loynes feared, in his own colourful words, that 'there is not just one witches brew. Several cauldrons are beginning to bubble at the same time'.[84] One was the new East African Common Services Organization (which replaced the East African High Commission), which reflected the impact of Ghanaian decolonization, since in 1962 Ghanaian A. L. Adu was appointed its head, following his predecessor

---

[78] BoE, OV 7/81, Loynes (in Nairobi) to Maurice [Parsons], 5 November 1960.

[79] BoE, G 17/32, no. 38, Loynes to Maurice [Parsons] 25 February 1965; no. 56B, Loynes to the Governor and Deputy, 5 June 1969 and enclosed note of his activities, dated 4 June 1969.

[80] BoE, OV 7/82, Loynes to F. A. Reynolds (CRO) 30 April 1962.

[81] BoE, OV 7/81, 'East Africa and the Currency Board', report produced by Loynes for the Governor and Deputy of the Bank, 19 December 1960.

[82] BoE, OV 7/82, Parsons annotation on 'East African Currency Board', note by Loynes, 1 June 1962.

[83] BoE, OV 7/82, note by Loynes addressed to Parsons, 12 June 1962.

[84] Ibid., Loynes (in Nairobi) to 'Arthur' [possibly Galsworthy at the CO], 7 August 1962.

in simultaneously becoming head of the EACB. While there were hopes in the Bank that an African at its helm might help 'sell' the EACB locally,[85] Adu had his own ideas, proposing the appointment of some form of regional economic advisory board or advisor. There was also, Loynes opined, 'always Uganda'.[86] In the early 1960s the Bank persuaded a visiting World Bank mission to drop a recommendation that the Ugandan government initiate enquiries to develop a common central bank in advance of political federation,[87] but the Ugandan government proved unpredictable and inclined to embark upon its own initiatives. In 1963 it invited the academic and former economic adviser to the country, W. T. Newlyn, to lead an enquiry into central banking.[88] On this occasion Newlyn's recommendations corresponded to British plans, since he supported the idea of retaining some form of a regional currency union; but later Newlyn would prove another irritant, if a minor one.[89]

Tanganyika proved the most troublesome. A few months before independence, Ernest Vasey, the country's European Minister of Finance,[90] proposed an enquiry into banking and currency to be led by an expert from the Deutsche Bundesbank, the Tanganyikan government reportedly professing some admiration for the strength of the Deutschmark and a surprising 'sentimental attachment' to West Germany. Initially the British were relatively optimistic. Vasey had advised the Colonial Office that the enquiry would keep his African colleagues happy during the awkward stage before Kenyan and Ugandan independence and the achievement of federation, and, once the Colonial Office had persuaded Vasey to omit any consideration relating to a central bank and Tanganyikan currency from the terms of the enquiry, Loynes thought that it might offer 'valuable breathing space'.[91] He hoped 'to indoctrinate' the German adviser, Dr Pfleiderer, and keep 'a purely West German enquiry on sensible lines'. Although Loynes believed he had succeeded in persuading Pfleiderer of British aims, when Pfleiderer fell ill before he could travel to East Africa, a

[85]   Ibid., note on telegram from EASCO to Secretary of State for Colonies, copied to Loynes, 5 May 1962.
[86]   Ibid., Loynes (in Nairobi) to 'Arthur' [possibly Galsworthy at the CO], 7 August 1962.
[87]   The IBRD reported on Tanzania in 1961, Uganda in 1962, and Kenya in 1963. BoE, OV 7/81, 'East African Currency Board', paper by Loynes 11 May 1961 addressed to Parsons; OV 75/2, 'IBRD draft report on Uganda', by Loynes, 12 May 1961.
[88]   BoE, OV 7/83, Loynes to Sir Algernon Rumbold (CRO), 12 June 1963.
[89]   BoE, OV 76/3, Loynes to Lord Cromer, 14 July 1964, p. 3.
[90]   Vasey, a businessman, had served as Minister of Finance in Kenya, 1952–9. In 1959 he had been invited by Nyerere to go to Tanganyika where he was initially appointed Minister of Finance and economics, and from 1960–2 Minister of Finance: Sarah Stockwell, 'Sir Ernest Vasey', Oxford Dictionary of National Biography, www.oxforddnb.com/view/article/63463.
[91]   BoE, OV 76/3: 'Tanganyika', note by Loynes, 20 September 1961, addressed to Mr. Spiers; OV 7/81, 'East Africa: Currency', 27 June 1961 note by Loynes addressed to John Stevens (a director at the Bank, 1957–65), Parsons and the Governor and Deputy Governor.

second adviser, Erwin Blumenthal, was appointed instead.[92] Under Blumenthal the Tanganyikan enquiry morphed into a more general investigation of banking in East Africa, and the final report recommended a two-tier system in which each country would get a state bank linked to a central, regional organization.[93] Following the instruction of the Minister of Finance, Paul Bomani, the Blumenthal Report was submitted to the Tanganyikan government before the German had left the country to ensure, Loynes suspected, that it would not be 'twisted out of shape by the imperialists of Threadneedle Street'.[94]

To the Tanganyikan government the proposals held out the apparently attractive prospect of being able to have their own bank *and* a common currency. Now, in a striking illustration of the efforts he was prepared to go to in order to manage the situation, Loynes contemplated bringing in the IMF to produce an alternative report. He believed the Fund was 'rather anxious to have a finger in this pie', and, although Loynes arrogantly doubted that 'the Fund staff has much experience and competence in these matters', he saw the option as 'one of the few ways open to us for putting central banking proposals into some more sensible form', so long as they kept 'close' to those involved.[95] Promisingly, J. V. Mládek, the Fund's Acting Director in its new African Department, was also sympathetic to the idea of a common currency. But an IMF official would later comment on the dangers of close association with Loynes. 'Mr. Loynes and some of his proposals were being viewed with suspicion' in East Africa, he noted in 1964, worried that if Mládek were seen 'frequently' in Loynes' company this suspicion would extend to the IMF too and prejudice African attitudes towards the Fund's own advice on central banking.[96] In the event in 1963 the East African governments failed to agree at this stage either on a common appeal to the Fund for assistance or to any action on Blumenthal's report, although IMF representatives did travel to the region in the summer.[97]

When an IMF mission eventually visited after the three East African governments had finally agreed in August 1964 to invite the IMF to advise on

---

[92] BoE, OV 7/81, 'East Africa: Currency', 27 June 1961 note by Loynes addressed to Mr. Stevens, Mr. Parsons and the Governor and Deputy; OV 7/82, Loynes to A. N. Galsworthy (CO), 16 January 1962.

[93] BoE, OV 7/83, Loynes to Sir Algernon Rumbold (CRO), 12 June 1963.

[94] BoE, OV 76/3, Loynes to M. Parsons, 9 November 1962.

[95] Ibid., Loynes (in Aden) to M. Parsons 2 March 1963; 'East Africa and IMF', note addressed to Parsons, 4 April 1963.

[96] IMF Archives, Central Banking Department Immediate Office, Technical Assistance and Subject Files, Box 6, file 3, East Africa General 1964–75, memo from C. N. Isong to J. V. Mládek, 15 July 1964, reporting on visit to East Africa.

[97] BoE, OV 76/3, 'New Design Currency Notes', paper 27 May 1963; IMF Archives, Central Banking Department Immediate Office, Technical Assistance and Subject Files, Box 14, file 7, East African Mission Minutes, 1963.

the establishment of an East African central bank,[98] it quickly recognized that the regional project was over. Tanganyika (renamed Tanzania, following the country's merger with Zanzibar) declared its determination now to establish its own central bank,[99] even though Blumenthal, on a return visit the previous year, had not recommended this course (with his own bank, the Bundesbank, supportive of the idea of a common currency).[100] Plans for a common currency and central bank were abandoned, although a treaty of East African cooperation signed in 1967 preserved that part of the project that related to a common market in the region, and made provision for some collaborative arrangements relating to currency.[101] In June 1965 the finance ministers of the three countries each announced the collapse of a common currency system and their intention to establish their own central banks. This represented the final collapse of the strategy Loynes had pursued.[102] Even so the Bank, like the IMF, had been aware of the turn of events since February, and had been secretly preparing for this outcome.[103]

Following the collapse of plans for a common currency and bank, the Bank's involvement in the establishment of central banking in each of the three countries varied according to the domestic political circumstances. In line with its growing presence in Africa, the IMF drew up statutes for the new Central Bank of Tanzania. Loynes regarded this as 'a nasty prospect',[104] and his colleagues in Threadneedle Street feared the draft statutes for the new central bank had a 'slightly German flavour' and were 'unwieldy ... with little or no understanding of African conditions'.[105] In Tanzania, the Bank of England had now lost what influence it had had over developments, although one of its men was seconded as the new Banking Manager under the auspices of the IMF's new Central

[98] IMF Archives, Central Banking Department Immediate Office, Technical Assistance and Subject Files, Box 14, file 6, East African Central Bank, Paul Bomani to Mládek 21 August 1964.

[99] Ibid., Box 33, file 5, Request for CBS Assistance East Africa 1964–6, telegram Mládek to IMF, 13 February 1965.

[100] BoE, OV 76/3, Loynes to Mládek (IMF), 11 May 1964; Loynes to Lord Cromer, BoE, 14 July 1964.

[101] World Bank. 1971. *East African Community – Economic Developments: The Economic Report: East African Community, Kenya, Tanzania, Uganda.* Eastern Africa series; no. AE 16. Washington, DC: World Bank. http://documents.worldbank.org/curated/en/522051468202160344/The-economic-report-east-african-community-kenya-tanzania-uganda, pp. 1–2, 5–6. Eagleton notes that Kenyatta attributed the breakup of the EACB to Nkrumah's influence over Nyerere, but I have found no evidence to support this: Eagleton, 'Designing Change', pp. 224–5.

[102] BoE, OV 7/87, draft letter by Loynes (not clear to whom), 14 June 1965.

[103] Under another pretext the Bank loaned two experts on exchange control to Kenya in April to help prepare for the introduction of exchange control against sterling which it knew would come in all three East African countries: see various papers in OV 76/4.

[104] BoE, OV 7/87, Loynes to H. J. Hinchey, EACSO, 6 May 1965.

[105] BoE, OV 74/2, no. 132. 'East Africa', note by Loynes, 27 April 1965; Loynes note for Governor, 30 June 1965.

Banking Service.[106] The new statutes for the Bank of Kenya were also drawn up by the IMF, but the Bank had the opportunity to comment on them, and considered the governor designate, Dr Leon Baranski, a Polish man of wide experience in developing countries from the IMF, and former IBRD representative in Ghana, a 'friend'.[107] The Bank was most closely involved in Uganda. Ian Lewis from the Overseas Office was appointed deputy-governor designate and oversaw the preparation of the necessary legislation in close consultation with both Loynes and also S. W. Payton of the Bank's Overseas Department. Lewis did not have a completely free hand; V. C. Crabbe, a Ghanaian with a 'colonial chip on his shoulder', was brought in as a legal draftsman, and apparently drew inspiration from the revised statutes of the Ghanaian central bank.[108] The resulting draft was disliked at both the Bank of England and the IMF, whom the Ugandan ministry of finance also consulted, and the two institutions sought to direct the Ugandan authorities towards alternative models.[109] As they had been in West Africa, Bank officials in relation to both Kenya and Uganda were anxious to limit the degree to which new banks might fall prey to political interference, arguing against the inclusion of representatives from their ministries of finance on their governing boards.[110]

The developments in East Africa had repercussions for Aden, which had been served by the East African Currency Board, and here Loynes was instrumental in the creation and subsequent management of a new South Arabian Currency Authority, established in 1965, and in the operation of a successor institution, the Southern Yemen Currency Authority, formed in 1968 following independence for Aden and the former Aden Protectorate as South Yemen. Under his guidance, the new South Arabian dinar pound was pegged to the pound sterling, and all external reserves were held in either gold or sterling.[111]

---

[106] BoE, G14/299, 'Extracts from Committee of Treasury Minutes, 17 November 1965–9 April 1970'. G. R. J. Scott remained until 1970.

[107] BoE, OV 74/2.

[108] BoE, OV 75/3, Lewis to de Loynes, 20 January 1966. Lewis does not give Crabbe's initials, but it seems likely the Ghanaian was V. C. Crabbe, who served as constitutional adviser to the Ugandan government, and who is mentioned in an IMF account of a meeting between representatives of the IMF, Ugandan government and Loynes: see, IMF Archives, Central Banking Department Immediate Office, Technical Assistance and Subject Files, Box 14, file 8, East Africa Mission and Minutes 1965.

[109] IMF Archives, Central Banking Department Immediate Office, Technical Assistance and Subject Files, Box 44, file 7, Uganda, Central Bank of Uganda, 1965–69, A. J. P. M. Ssentongo to Mládek, 22 July 1965; 'Technical Assistance – Uganda; memo by San Lin, 29 September 1965.

[110] See BoE, OV 75/3, I. Lewis (Uganda) to Loynes, 26 October 1965; OV 74/2, 'Central Bank of Kenya: draft statutes', 16 September 1965.

[111] *South Arabian Currency Authority, Report for the Year 1966*; *Southern Yemen Currency Authority, Report 1967–8.*

While Loynes was struggling to hold the fort in East Africa pending some form of regional federation, the failure of the federal project in Central Africa propelled consideration of banking and currency in its constituent territories up the agenda. In mid-1963 the Bank of England discussed the possibility of incorporating Nyasaland, by far the poorest and least developed of the three territories, within the projected East African Federation,[112] but there were already moves afoot in both Nyasaland and Northern Rhodesia to create national banking and currency institutions, a relatively straightforward process since Zambian and Malawian branches of the federal bank had been opened in 1961 and 1962, respectively, that could serve as a basis for new central banks. Even before the formal end of the Central African Federation in December 1963, and independence for Nyasaland as Malawi and Northern Rhodesia as Zambia in July and October 1964, respectively, steps had been taken in both countries to establish national banking and currency institutions.[113] In Malawi preparations from late 1963 resulted in the issue of new Malawian coins in November 1964, and in Zambia in 1963 the Lusaka branch of the federal central bank had been converted into the Bank of Northern Rhodesia. In 1964 the Central Bank of Zambia was formed from this bank, while in 1965 the Reserve Bank of Malawi opened on the site of the former Blantyre branch of the old federal Bank.[114]

These new banks not only followed a British model with a governor (and sometimes a deputy) and boards of directors of varying size, but all the new banks established in the 1960s adhered to the sterling system, linking their new currencies to the pound. This was a logical choice in view of the prominence of Britain and other sterling countries in their external trade, especially for the smallest and poorest countries, and illustrates the constraints within which they operated. It was only in the 1970s after a series of sterling financial crises that they broke the sterling connection. The first major disruption occurred with sterling devaluation in November 1967. This resulted in a significant loss of external purchasing power for countries with a high proportion of sterling reserves, and, while Sierra Leone, Malawi and the Gambia chose to devalue alongside sterling, the three East African countries did not. The following year Britain concluded a series of bilateral arrangements with sterling area countries (the 'Basle Agreements') guaranteeing a dollar exchange rate in return for their agreement not to diversify sterling beyond a certain point.[115] In the 1970s,

[112] BoE, OV 76/3, 'Nyasaland and East Africa', memo by D. W. C. Allen addressed to J. Loynes, 18 July 1963.
[113] See, papers in ZNA, M[inistry of] F[inance] 1/3/41/225, Bank of Zambia information and legislation 1963–4.
[114] *Reserve Bank of Malawi: Tenth Anniversary 1965–1975*; website of the Bank of Zambia, accessed 16 September 2015.
[115] Schenk, *Decline of Sterling*, p. 429.

however, the new states, beginning with Tanzania in 1971, moved away from sterling, linking their currency either to the US dollar or to a new accounting unit introduced by the IMF in 1974, but by then the sterling area had ceased to be of any real significance.[116]

The Bank's stewardship of the currency boards continued even after the formation of the new central banks since it was necessary to ensure an orderly winding up of their business.[117] Managing these tasks fell principally to the Bank in the person of Loynes;[118] the Colonial Office, he observed in 1962, was no longer willing to give the system the attention it deserved.[119] On his formal retirement in 1969 he explained to the Bank's governor that 'It is unquestionable that I run both Boards and have done so for years', while also serving as the key figure in the currency boards of the Gambia and South Arabia/ Southern Yemen. There was a self-aggrandizing tone to Loynes's account, in part because he was seeking practical support from the Bank to enable him to continue these activities in a personal capacity on his retirement. As he explained to the Governor, if he were to relinquish his various roles 'we should lose the contacts'; no other Briton, he suggested, would be acceptable, whereas he had the confidence of local politicians, even where they had initially been suspicious of him or where there were strong sensitivities about the colonial connection. While the work had 'in the past been something of a burden', he felt that 'I ought to continue with it as long as this can be managed' as 'It would seem to be in the UK interest' and 'more specifically in the Bank's interest that I should do so' for 'as at present it would be my aim to keep the Bank in the picture'. The Bank might regard the continuing support for his roles as 'an aspect of help to the underdeveloped countries, which in essence, it is'.[120]

In August 1969, a month after retiring, Loynes died unexpectedly at the age of 60, drowned off Holkham beach in Norfolk while bathing with his family.[121] He left unfinished business, having been engaged in advising the new Currency Authority in South Yemen (where news of his death was met with astonishment as 'he used to be a good swimmer').[122] But in the main a process of financial decolonization in all the most important former British African

---

[116] *The First Ten Years: The Central Bank of Kenya* (1976), pp. 12, 25–8; *Reserve Bank of Malawi: Tenth Anniversary, 1965–1975*, p. 10.

[117] *Central Bank of the Gambia.* The last EACB centre closed in 1971; the WACB was still being wound up in 1971.

[118] Although he was technically responsible in East Africa to the East African representatives while the WACB, which remained based in London, was chaired by Sir Alfred Savage, second Crown Agent.

[119] BoE, OV 71/1, 'Gambia/Senegal', paper by Loynes, 18 September 1962.

[120] BoE, G 17/32, no. 56B, Loynes to the Governor, 5 June 1969 and enclosed note of his activities, dated 4 June 1969.

[121] *The Times*, 25 August 1969, p. 1.

[122] BoE, G17/32, Husein Hadi (secretary, the Southern Yemen Currency Authority) to Miss. J. M. Short, Loynes' secretary, 2 September 1969.

colonies was substantially complete. Guided principally first by Fisher and then by Loynes, the Bank had sought, and had in some cases achieved, oversight over the establishment of new central banks with a view at least initially to preserving a strong connection to sterling, as well as to replicating its own practices, and securing the development of central banks that might act independently of their governments. The Bank's advisers were dismissive of other sources of expertise, and confident in their own claims to shape developments. But as we have seen the Bank was often unable to do this, and even where it did, the British model rarely proved fully sustainable. Officials from the IMF also detected more suspicion among African authorities towards Loynes than was, not surprisingly, evident from his own portrayal of his role. Despite a tendency to hubris, after more than a decade working in new African states Loynes was, however, under no illusions as to the Bank's position. In 1967 a transcription error led his secretary to refer not to 'delineations' but to 'delusions of responsibility' in recording the Bank's role in South Arabia; it was not often, Loynes commented, that a misheard word commented 'so acidly'.[123]

Staffing the New Banks

From the mid-1950s, as the Bank dropped its outright opposition to the development of central banking and adopted a more cooperative approach, perceived as the best means of encouraging the adoption of a British banking model and of adherence to the sterling area, it also began considering what other forms of technical assistance it might provide to new banks in emergent Commonwealth states, with a view similarly to advancing British interests and their own central banking orthodoxy.

One area which officials started discussing in summer 1956 concerned what the Bank might do to help with staffing the new banks. This discussion was probably prompted by developments in the Gold Coast, since Alfred Eggleston, at this point governor designate of the new Bank, had requested that the Bank of England second several of its own employees to fill key positions within his new bank, including that of deputy governor. Loynes played a key role in the discussions that followed, establishing the likely requirements for assistance as 'far as they can be foreseen, over the next few years'. A table was put together setting out where demand was likely to arise.[124] At Governor Cobbold's suggestion, a list was also prepared of Bank employees deemed suitable for appointment to both 'top-level' and 'junior' posts in overseas central, as well as commercial, banks. The more junior men it was hoped might 'be

---

[123] Ibid., nos. 49 and 50, Leslie O'Brien to Loynes, 8 June 1967; Loynes to O'Brien, 12 June 1967.
[124] BoE, OV 21/25, 'Possible Requirements of Staff for Posts Abroad' (Draft), 19 June 1956.

most valuable in providing a leavening of experience and in setting standards of trustworthiness just where the top level people would like to have it in the early years of a new Central Bank'. The list comprised midcareer employees, mostly in their thirties, experienced but still youthful. Among those listed as suitable for senior posts were Loynes himself, Douglas Stone, and Roy Fenton.[125]

In a further illustration of the importance attached at the highest levels within the Bank to this issue, Cobbold also began considering how those identified as potential candidates for employment overseas might best be given appropriate experience, proposing that the bank should have two 'potential high-flyers' 'out' at any one time working in clearing and foreign and Commonwealth banks, respectively.[126] In line with this prescription Bank officials explored the possibility of sending staff to a variety of institutions within the Commonwealth such as the Commonwealth Development Bank of Australia.[127] Enhancing knowledge of development finance was identified as a particular priority by Loynes,[128] and the Bank also now considered sending men to courses run by the World Bank and the LSE.[129] Although the deputy governor, Humphrey Mynors, thought the World Bank course too elementary for Threadneedle staff, remarking in one revealing exchange that he assumed it was 'a child's guide (for black children)', this was nonetheless the option eventually determined upon after Eugene Black, President of the World Bank, proved reluctant to agree to Cobbold's alternative suggestion that one of his staff might be seconded to the World Bank for up to a year in order to acquire experience in development finance. But the first man to attend the course did not think the experience worthwhile, and the issue consequently continued to concern senior figures at the Bank. In 1960 the step change in political development in Africa underscored the importance of, in Cobbold's words, getting 'our people a bit of training in "development"'.[130]

While these discussions undoubtedly reflected a sense of obligation in Threadneedle Street to assist banks likely to struggle to find suitable personnel, senior officials saw the installation of the Bank's *own* men rather than other expatriates as important, and another means of spreading the Bank's influence. As Loynes said, 'I assume that, in principle, we should prefer the

---

[125] Ibid., no. 22A, 'Central Bankers', 9 September 1956; no. 27, 'Supplementary Staff', note by Watson, 22 September 1956.

[126] Ibid., note by Governor, 21 May 1957; colleagues noted that in practice the Bank already did this: draft reply by Watson, 'High Flyers', 24 May 1957; subsequent draft 'Training in Commercial Banks', 13 June 1957.

[127] Ibid., minutes at nos. 69 and 72, by Mynors, 22 May and 2 July 1958; no. 149, 'Training in Development Finance', Mr. Heasman, 28 June 1960.

[128] Ibid., no. 63, Loynes to the Governor, 22 March 1958.

[129] Ibid., note by Watson, 14 May 1958.

[130] Ibid., no. 82, Cobbold to Black, 13 August 1957; no. 96, M. Parsons to Cobbold, 9 October 1958; 'Economic Development Institute', 26 April 1960; Cobbold annotation, 4 May 1960.

colonies to approach us rather than to go elsewhere'.[131] Preventing the 'infiltration of American ideas on monetary theory' was one reason for this,[132] and when it proved difficult to identify members of the Bank's own staff to second overseas, the Bank expressed a preference for finding other candidates from within the Commonwealth. Not all personnel from elsewhere in the old Commonwealth, however, were considered ideal, as it became evident when the Bank was seeking a candidate for a senior position in Nigeria. Treasury and Bank officials considered but rejected the possibility of appointing a Canadian, concluding that 'excellent as the Canadians are', their ideas on central banking were too far removed from the British model. Perhaps because Canada was not in the sterling area, they deemed the introduction into the colonies of a 'Canadian philosophy' undesirable, but thought an Australian might be satisfactory.[133] For the Bank a diaspora of staff transferred overseas could also serve as an important source of intelligence on the policies of the new governments. Officials were nevertheless aware that, where this was the case they needed to tread carefully, and ensure that, as one official commented in relation to the Bank's man in the new Bank of Uganda in 1966, that this did not become widely known.[134]

By the early 1960s Bank officials had been appointed to posts in a number of new banks in former colonies, including Roy Fenton as governor in the Central Bank of Nigeria, and Douglas Stone to the role of deputy governor in Ghana. To avoid a possible 'division' of loyalties both men stepped down from their posts in London,[135] although since they continued to enjoy the same pension and rights as if they had remained in the Bank, they were as good as seconded, and their resignation from the Bank was something of a technicality.[136] Fenton was guaranteed the option to return within five years on terms at least as favourable as those on which he left. When in the summer of 1963 he eventually did exercise this right, he was appointed Deputy Chief of the Central Banking Information Department on a salary more than twice that he had received before his departure for Nigeria.[137] In Ghana Cabinet opposition to reliance on the Bank of England ensured that only one other Briton was appointed alongside Stone. When Gbedemah had raised the issue of staffing

[131] Ibid., 'Colonies: Bank of England assistance to monetary authorities', memo by Loynes, 27 April 1956.
[132] Evident in discussions about Malaya.
[133] T.N.A., CO 1025/117, minute by Sir H. Poynton, 24 October 1957, on secret savingram from Nigeria, 9 October 1957.
[134] BoE, OV 75/14, 'Uganda', 13 September 1966.
[135] BoE, OV 21/25, 'Gold Coast', confidential note addressed to the Chief Cashier and Deputy Governor, 19 October 1956.
[136] Details from Fenton's case: BoE, G17/17, no. 6, A. W. C. Dascombe (BoE) to Fenton, 17 July 1958 (copy); papers relating to employment on return.
[137] Ibid., 'Mr Roy Pentelow Fenton, C.M.G'.

in Cabinet, his colleagues had urged that the recruitment field 'should be widened if possible'.[138] Nkrumah suggested that to balance Stone's appointment a second deputy governorship be created to be filled by an appointment from a different overseas central bank. Gbedemah himself resisted this proposal as contrary to the Bank's statutes and likely to cause friction within the leadership team, but with the Cabinet determined to accept only two British men, it was decided to fill a third key appointment by recruitment from elsewhere, perhaps from the Reserve Bank of India.[139] There were more British men at the new Central Bank of Nigeria. In addition to Fenton, four other staff from the Bank of England were in post when the new Bank opened, and between 1958 and 1964 a total of eleven men and women from Threadneedle Street were employed at the new Bank, as well as three from the Reserve Bank of Australia, and, between 1960 and 1966, five staff from the US Federal Reserve Bank.[140] Fenton's first two secretaries were among those from the Bank of England. This was probably crucial in enabling Fenton to correspond confidentially with Threadneedle Street. By May 1961 there were also five Bank employees at the Bank of Rhodesia and Nyasaland, an additional nine had worked, or were still working, in the new central bank in Libya, one in Malaya, two at the Bank of Jamaica, eight in Iraq, four in Ceylon, and one in Burma.[141]

The second wave of banks created in the 1960s had equally significant staffing needs, and were similarly reliant on external assistance to see them through a transitional period. In Sierra Leone Gordon Hall became the first governor of the new Bank of Sierra Leone when it opened in September 1963, while several other staff from Threadneedle Street were seconded to fill other senior posts.[142] In its first year 24 of 148 staff employed at the Bank of Kenya were expatriates, and they comprised most of the Bank's senior officers, although within ten years the Bank had succeeded in appointing Africans to all but one of these positions.[143] Staffing presented especially acute problems in countries lacking a reservoir of locals educated to a higher level. Some ten years after the Reserve Bank of Malawi had opened only 34 of its 134 staff possessed university degrees or diplomas.[144]

---

[138] PRAAD, ADM 13/1/26, minutes of Cabinet meetings, 12 February 1957 (item 2); 26 February 1957 (item 2).

[139] Ibid., minutes of Cabinet meetings, 2 April 1957 (item 43); 3 December 1957 (item 8); ADM 13/2/43, C. M. 787 (57), Cabinet memo by Minister of Finance, considered in Cabinet, 3 December 1957.

[140] *Twenty Years of Central Banking in Nigeria: 1959–1979* (Research Department, Central Bank of Nigeria, Lagos, 1979), appendix 1, pp. 220–4.

[141] BoE, OV 21/25, schedule of Bank advisers and appointments to new central banks attached to note by G.E.H. (Overseas Department) addressed to Mr. Parker, 18 May 1961.

[142] BoE, OV 70/3, 'Sierra Leone', 19 September 1963; draft memo, 'Sierra Leone', 17 July 1964.

[143] *The First Ten Years: The Central Bank of Kenya*, appendix 2, p. 33.

[144] *Reserve Bank of Malawi*, p. 13.

By then, there were more sources of technical assistance available. In particular, the IMF's new Central Banking Service played an increasingly prominent role in meeting African staffing needs, supplying a growing number of experts. In the financial year 1964–5 it supplied eleven experts to fill advisory and senior posts, including a governorship, in developing states; in the year 1969–70 this had risen to more than seventy-one experts, recruited from twenty-one countries, for assignments in thirty-six countries, although as demand for the most senior posts began to wind down, it reported a shift towards more specialized and technical assignments.[145] When the Bank of the Gambia was formed, it drew entirely on the assistance of the IMF's Central Banking Service in filling its key posts, and those appointed – two experts from Burma and Pakistan respectively – reflected the IMF's new strategy of appointing experts from developing states to posts in other developing states. But in the mid-1960s, the Bank of England still played a significant role. In Uganda, as we saw earlier the Bank's Ian Lewis became deputy governor, and in Malawi, Bank officials served as the first two governors of the new bank.[146] Tanzania, perhaps in keeping with its political stance, accepted assistance from the IMF's Central Banking Service instead, but, as already noted, L. J. Scott, appointed under the auspices of the IMF to the senior position of banking manager was one of the Bank's own men.[147]

The experience of those transferred or seconded overseas varied greatly, reflecting the different political trajectories of the countries to which they went, as well as the financial problems they encountered. In Uganda Lewis found coping with the country's tricky financial situation difficult, and his relations with Joseph Mubiru, the Bank's first governor, trying. As an added complication, he was aware that, because Mubiru came from Buganda, a monarchical subnation only poorly integrated within the new unitary Ugandan state, Mubiru's own position was vulnerable, and neither he nor the Bank of Uganda consequently enjoyed close relations with the government of Uganda.[148] A few years later Mubiru is thought to have been murdered while in police detention, after he annoyed Idi Amin in a letter to the press written following his resignation.[149]

Few British staff had as quite as hard a time as Douglas Stone in Ghana. His relations with Alfred Eggleston were frequently poor.[150] Eggleston's successor, Hubert Kessels, proved easier to work with, but the respite was short-lived.

---

[145] *International Monetary Fund. Annual Report, 1965*, p. 36; *Annual Report, 1969–70*, pp. 147–8.
[146] *Reserve Bank of Malawi*, pp. 15–18; *Central Bank of the Gambia*, p. 13.
[147] BoE, G14/299, 'Extracts from the Committee of Treasury Minutes, 17 November 1965–9 April 1970.
[148] BoE, OV 75/14, 'Uganda' note 13 September 1966.
[149] Singleton, *Central Banking*, 173.
[150] BoE, OV 18/2, Haslam, pp. 268–70.

When Ghana became a republic in July 1960, Nkrumah increased the number of party men in the bank. A member of the CPP's Central Committee, Kwesi Amoaka-Atta, in Stone's assessment, an 'ultraleft-wing moron', pledged to rid the Bank of the influence of the Bank of England, was promoted as deputy over Stone.[151] By 1962 the Bank of Ghana was completely run by Ghanaians with the exception of one Bank man, seconded to work in the Exchange Control Department. Those sent to Nigeria fared better. They contended with heavy workloads, and knotty issues, but had the advantage of working alongside other members of a numerous cohort of expatriates. Fenton had a strong working relationship with his Minister of Finance, as did his colleagues in Threadneedle Street. For one man employed as currency officer in Nigeria between 1958 and 1960, the 'launching of the Central Bank, with raw staff, a new building, and a new currency, in a period of nine months' was a hectic experience, but 'immensely satisfying to all of us who took part in it'. He found the Nigerians appreciative of British help; 'the "Mandarin approach"' had 'had its day', but 'Technical or managerial assistance offered in this spirit will be readily accepted'.[152]

The Bank of England and Training: The Commonwealth Central Banking Course

The secondment of external experts was a short-term solution, and, as well as advising on the establishment of new banks and assisting with their staffing, a third significant strand of the Bank's approach to the development of central banking in new Commonwealth states concerned initiatives to train non-European staff. Personnel from overseas banks already visited the Bank on an ad hoc basis, and occasionally arrangements were also made for overseas staff to spend time in other British banks. But the almost complete absence of trained personnel in emergent Commonwealth states, especially in Africa, indicated that a new approach was required. Once again, it was the Gold Coast that provided an early indication of the problem, in this instance following the establishment of the Bank of the Gold Coast, the state bank that opened in advance of the central bank under Eggleston's management. As he grappled with the training issue, Eggleston proposed to Achimota College in the colony that they might institute banking studies, and he also arranged for African trainees to gain experience through placements at the small private bank of

---

[151] OV 69/6, 'Republican Ghana', memo by Stone, 15 November 1960; BoE, OV 18/2, Haslam, pp. 290–1.
[152] BoE, OV 68/7, no. 183, personal reflections by P. B. Edgeley, 25 January 1961, addressed to Messrs. Heasman, Watson and Parsons.

Glyn, Mills and Co.[153] The connection to Glyn, Mills & Co proved lasting, with several Ghanaians travelling to Scotland to receive some form of bespoke training in the mid-1960s.[154] The Central Bank of Nigeria faced similar problems and in January 1959 a six-month training course ran ahead of the Bank's formal opening, followed by on-the-job training. In general, placing African trainees for periods within commercial and overseas central banks became a common practice.[155]

In the light of the staffing needs of new central banks Guy Watson, a head of the Exchange Control and Overseas Department, in 1956 suggested that a more 'positive approach' to training was needed. He proposed that the Bank begin its own Central Banking Course, aimed at those who had reached junior administrative grades in Commonwealth central banks, those serving, or about to serve on currency boards and banking commissions in the Commonwealth, and those 'in other ways marked for the new Central Banks'. Although the costs of travel and accommodation of attendees would be met by their sponsoring institutions, the Bank would pick up the tab for outside lecturers and all administrative costs.[156] As one senior official commented, this 'would involve a formidable burden'; he nonetheless thought 'it would be a worthwhile investment'.[157] The course was inaugurated in 1957 and ran thereafter on a biannual basis. Attendees at the inaugural course included the first African delegate, Ghanaian Adam Adomakoh. Initially lasting some six weeks, but later extended to nine, the course became the Bank's most significant contribution to overseas training. It was very much an independent initiative, with Bank officials only reluctantly conceding that they would need to inform government departments of their plans. A suggestion that the Bank might invite a representative from the Colonial Office was dropped because the Bank's Chief Cashier, L. K. O'Brien, wondered if they could then 'refuse to receive a Treasury man' if 'H.M.T. think it would be useful for their people to come and sit at our feet?'[158]

While inaugurated with an eye to the training requirements of new banks, the course was another vehicle by which the Bank of England aimed to advance its own views and interests. 'We want to sow the proper central banking doctrine early in Colonial minds', observed one official. 'If we can catch such

---

[153] BoE, OV 69/2, 'Gold Coast', confidential memo by W. J. Jackson (BoE, Overseas and Foreign Office) addressed to Kershaw, Fisher and O'Brien, 31 January 1953.
[154] Royal Bank of Scotland Archives GM/2074/2, GM/2074/2: 'Training Programme for Mr T.E. Anin'; memo from Mr. R. C. Homes to Mr. L. P. de Gerdon, 23 August 1965.
[155] BoE, OV 7/83, correspondence with various banks early 1963.
[156] BoE, OV 21/26, Commonwealth Central Banking Summer School by G. M. Watson, 1 October 1956.
[157] Ibid., Minute by Deputy Chief Cashier, H. Q. Hollom, 1 October 1956.
[158] Ibid., Minute by L. K. O'Brien on 'Central Banking Course', G. M. Watson, 15 January 1957.

people early, it may save trouble later on'.[159] As he subsequently explained, 'The object would be to inculcate sound ideas of currency and credit and some conception of how London works in the minds of those who will play a large part in shaping future colonial financial policies'.[160] The course was thus conceived as a form of 'education and propaganda', although the Bank was clear the latter should 'not be of an overt kind'. It was 'essential', Watson argued, 'to attract visits from good men' and 'to have them with us when they are young and receptive'. The Bank aimed the course at high-fliers in their thirties and forties, although by the mid-1970s it was admitting delegates in their late twenties too.[161]

From its inception the course was conceived very much as a Commonwealth affair. Although Humphrey Mynors, the Bank's deputy governor, argued that 'education and propaganda' was 'as important for South Americans as for South Africans', it was agreed initially at least to confine participation to Commonwealth member states or British colonies and make it by invitation only. Before its launch the Bank had also canvassed opinion among the central bank governors from the old Commonwealth states as well as from India, Pakistan and Ceylon, but preferred neither to publicize the course, nor to mention it to foreign central banks, or to the IMF, the IBRD, the European Payments Union or the Bank for International Settlements (BIS, effectively the bank for central banks).[162]

More than anything, this 'propaganda' aimed at the promotion of the sterling area. 'The Sterling Area', wrote Watson, 'is a living entity with, we believe a real value to all members ... It is not, however, sufficient for us to preach this gospel ... a true appreciation can only be obtained if their representatives come to London to see for themselves how the mechanism works'. Attending the course in London would enable representatives from developing countries to see 'in action' the 'full range of facilities available within the sterling area system'. As had also been the case in the 1930s in relation to the looser sterling bloc formed after sterling's departure from the gold standard, Commonwealth central banking networks old and new were perceived as an important means of supporting sterling and facilitating this sterling cooperation. Alongside this imperative, there were other considerations, including

[159] Ibid., 'Central Banking Course. Colonial Candidates', note by Eric Cranshaw, 1 November 1956.
[160] Ibid., 'Central Banking Course. General Plan', unsigned paper probably by Cranshaw, 15 January 1957.
[161] Ibid., 'Commonwealth Central Banking Summer School', memo 1 October 1956, G. M. Watson. On the age of participants see: ibid., 'Central Banking Course 1975', memorandum by R. Fenton, 27 June 1974.
[162] Ibid., Mynors cited in no. 11A, 'Central Banking Course', memo by G. de Mowbray, 31 March 1960 [the original memo by Mynors appears to be missing from the file]; 'Central Banking Course', minute by Eric Cranshaw, 7 February 1957.

'selling the City' as a whole. Demonstrating first-hand the 'wide variety of facilities which London has to offer' to emergent markets in Commonwealth states was one of the overt aims of the central banking course,[163] and the curriculum provided for visits to other key City institutions, including the Royal Mint (until its 1969 move to Cardiff).

The content of the courses and the time apportioned to particular subjects provides further evidence of the objectives behind the Bank's 'education and propaganda'. As well as introductory lectures on such matters as the balance of payments, financing foreign trade and the roles of deposit and merchant banks, officials proposed discussion of a variety of different markets. There were also to be sessions on the practice of central banking in selected Commonwealth countries and on the operation of colonial currency boards.[164] There would be lectures on the sterling area, as well as the Bank of England itself, and on other institutions within the City of London.[165] In all over three weeks – 59 per cent of available time – was to be devoted to the sterling area, the Bank of England and the City of London. Lectures on these subjects were to be given by the Bank's own staff or by others from the City. A further seven to nine days were to be devoted to Commonwealth central banking, ideally (to avoid the risk that the Bank was presuming to speak for central banks in older Commonwealth states) to be led by representatives of the banks themselves. In contrast, one week sufficed for discussion of the principles of central banking and consideration of economic indicators under the heading of 'General Principles'. The Bank hoped that notable economists such as Richard Sayers, Dennis Robertson, Alec Cairncross or Redvers Opie, might be persuaded to do these particular lectures.

The emphasis was hence overwhelmingly on the Bank as well as the resources and institutions of the City and the Commonwealth-sterling area. The content was also orientated towards the practical rather than the theoretical. This reflected the prevailing culture within the Bank at a time when there were still few professional economists on its staff; a position that changed after the publication of the Radcliffe report, which was critical of the Bank's capacity for statistical analysis and its record in economic research and publication.[166] A preponderance of lectures on the sterling area, the Bank itself, and the City, areas within the Bank's own field of expertise, was probably also necessary to ensure that the Bank was in a position to deliver the course.

The course itself constituted a form of financial diplomacy, an occasion on which the Bank welcomed representatives from Commonwealth states, and, who simply through their presence there as delegates from

[163] Ibid., 'Commonwealth Central Banking Summer School' by G. M. Watson, 1 October 1956; 'Review of the Central Banking Course', memo 11 March 1970 (by S. W. Payton).
[164] Ibid., 'Commonwealth Central Banking Summer School' by G. M. Watson, 1 October 1956.
[165] Ibid., 'Central Banking Course. Syllabus', 5 November 1956.
[166] Singleton, *Central Banking*, pp. 144–5.

the Commonwealth, helped project a sense of Commonwealth cohesion. Alongside timetabled lectures, the Bank organized a programme of external visits to prestigious British sites such as Stratford-upon-Avon, the birthplace of William Shakespeare, and the old university towns. Bank staff were also encouraged to offer evening entertainment to their visitors;[167] an acknowledgement of the important role that hospitality might play in fostering Commonwealth relations, and, as others have shown, in the 'performance' of Commonwealth unity and friendship.[168]

Following the inaugural course in 1957 some revisions were made to content. Bank officials unsurprisingly discovered that delegates were more interested in subjects relevant to their own countries, as well as in American, Canadian and some western European banking practices, than they were in those of other countries within the Commonwealth.[169] Sayers, a professor at the LSE, and the preeminent historian at the time of colonial and Commonwealth banking, had been an obvious choice of lecturer, but had proven a 'disappointment to most people and was not well liked'.[170] Perhaps the Bank also had other concerns about Sayers. In his writing he had not been uncritical of the Bank's conservative approach to central banking in the colonies. In a book published in the year of the first Bank of England course, he had also advanced a line at odds with the Bank's own central banking orthodoxy, suggesting that it might be acceptable for central banks to engage in commercial banking if this were confined to a transitional period until commercial banking had reached a sufficient stage of development[171]; a thesis subsequently cited by Ghanaian critics of the ordinances on which their new Central Bank was based.

In the late 1960s and the 1970s significant changes were made to the course. There was now less attention to Commonwealth central banking practices and the sterling area in line with the dwindling importance of the latter. Correspondingly, more time was now spent on training in central banking principles and techniques, as greater education in a variety of technical subjects relevant to the local needs of participants was now considered appropriate. These changes were in part a response to the criticisms that the course was too 'City', as well as British, in its orientation.[172] Whereas proposing the

---

[167] BoE, OV 21/26, 'Central Banking Course. General Plan', 15 January 1957, and appendix [with annotations].

[168] On which see, Ruth Craggs, 'Hospitality in Geopolitics and the Making of Commonwealth International relations', *Geoforum*, 52 (2014), pp. 90–100.

[169] BoE, OV 21/26, 'Central Banking Course', Leslie Whittome, 11 June 1957.

[170] Ibid., note by E. Cranshaw, 12 June 1957.

[171] Jucker-Fleetwood, *Money and Finance*, pp. 60–6. R. S. Sayers, *Central Banking after Bagehot* (Oxford University Press, Oxford, 1957), pp. 108–33.

[172] BoE OV 21/26, 'The Commonwealth Central Banking Course', by S. W. Payton, 6 February 1969; 'Report on Central Banking Course, 1969', 14 July 1969, prepared by R. P. Edgley; 'Review of Central Banking Course', paper by C. W. McMahon, 23 April 1970.

course in 1956 Watson had suggested the promotion of the sterling area as the principal objective, in 1970 an introduction to the City as a commercial and financial centre and the Bank's role in the City was seen as the Bank's top priority.[173] As this indicates, officials at the Bank apparently continued to imagine Commonwealth states as potentially valuable markets for British financial services, perhaps reflecting the continued importance of Britain in their trade and finance more generally.

In the early years, although intended as a course for delegates from new central banks, representatives from the older Commonwealth and South Asian countries outnumbered those from the newly independent countries or other colonies fast approaching independence. The central banks of India, Pakistan and Ceylon had all responded enthusiastically when first informed of the Bank's plans, although the Bank was warned that Pakistan would protest at any mention of 'dominion' (the status with which the South Asian colonies had originally entered independence). The Bank of Canada had initially been less keen. The Governor was advised that 'No Canadian would be interested in attending any course with a "Commonwealth" label', whereas a course organized at perhaps the LSE with Bank participation 'would be a different matter'.[174] Although the Bank dropped the title it originally proposed for the course – 'the Commonwealth Central Banking School' (a characterization which showed an extraordinary lack of self-awareness of the political sensitivities and realities of London's relations with central banks in the old Commonwealth) – and adopted instead 'Central Banking Course', the Governor of the Bank of Canada still cavilled at the implied reference to 'tuition', and at first declined to participate.[175] From 1963, however, the Canadian bank was represented at every course with the exception of that in 1985. Australia, New Zealand and South Africa had almost unbroken records of attendance, each only missing one or two meetings also in the 1980s. After South Africa's departure from the Commonwealth in 1961, the Bank agreed to continue inviting South African participants, also extending an invitation to Eire as a fig leaf to disguise the special arrangements being made for the apartheid state.[176] The possibility of also including Burma, which had not joined the Commonwealth at independence, was considered and rejected on a number of occasions.[177]

[173] Ibid., 'Review of Central Banking Course' (draft), 11 March 1970.
[174] Ibid., Central Banking Course', 19 October 1956, note by H. C. B. Mynors of governor's discussions at meeting of Commonwealth central bank governors.
[175] Ibid., J. E. Coyne, Bank of Canada, to H. C. B. Mynors, 7 February 1957. Within the Bank the course was sometimes referred to as the Commonwealth Central Banking Course and sometimes just as the Central Banking Course.
[176] Ibid., 'Central Banking Course, 1963', memo 23 May 1962.
[177] Ibid., 'Central Banking Course, 1973 invitations', 24 August 1972.

One explanation of this Commonwealth focus is that the inclusion of older Commonwealth countries alongside newer recruits helped to provide what one official referred to as 'a leavening of sophistication in the syndicate discussions with the newer brethren'.[178] While considerations to do with the sterling area were still important, it also enabled the Bank to include others who might add their weight to emphasizing the advantages of the sterling area: the experience of the first two courses suggested that when participants from a former colony questioned elements of the sterling area system 'it is the Australasians who often do battle – while the UK just sit back and hold the ring!'.[179] But Canada was not a member of the sterling area, and the presence of representatives of a country which had opted to tie its currency to the dollar might appear to have undermined the objective of promoting the sterling area. Its inclusion is particularly striking in the context of concerns expressed elsewhere in the Bank that Canadian influence might serve as a Trojan horse for American influence. Equally one might speculate as to whether the Bank hoped that the inclusion of countries that had been independent for some time might help dispel any concerns among emergent nations that the course represented a form of on-going colonialism.

Alongside the tactical motives for their inclusion, it seems that the decision to invite all Commonwealth states to send representatives to the course reflected a genuine sense of the Commonwealth as an organic whole, which in turn corresponded to the Bank's own history and its pre-war role in and liaison with dominion central banking. Generation was important in reinforcing this Commonwealth mission. In retrospect we can see the writing on the wall for the 'idea of Commonwealth' as a significant vehicle for post-imperial British collaboration with its old colonies, but to contemporaries the 'new' Commonwealth was the means not only for the perpetuation of British ties but also the refurbishment of imperial mission in ostensibly more egalitarian terms. In practice, officials nevertheless acknowledged limits to Commonwealth unity. They ensured that invitees to the inaugural course would know which other countries had been invited to participate in view of potential 'colour difficulties'. With 'so many antipathies between white and black, Indian and Pakistani, and South African and Indian', the Bank also made arrangements to accommodate the participants in the first central banking course in different locations rather than bring them all together in one site. In subsequent courses the very different economic circumstances of participating countries also presented problems with accommodation, with

[178] Ibid., 'Review of Central Banking Course', final version 10 April 1970.
[179] Ibid., 'Central Banking Course', memo by G. de Mowbray, 31 March 1960.

some finding the hotels recommended by the Bank too expensive, while for others they were too basic.[180]

With repeat invitations sent to all countries that had previously participated, the number of delegates climbed steadily over the years and by the second half of the 1960s the Bank debated knocking down an internal wall in order to create a larger lecture room that could accommodate them all.[181] Officials also considered leaving some countries off the guest list. Tanzania was one of these. In 1966 Bank officials debated whether the country should be included in its list of invitees in the light of the 'political antics' of the country, which in December 1965 had broken diplomatic relations with Britain following the UK's failure to stop Rhodesian UDI. That neither of the Tanzanians who had attended previous meetings had, as yet, been appointed to posts within the country's central bank inclined one Bank official to regard further invitations to Tanzania as pointless; whereas to another official this made the task of 'cultivating a third student' so as to try to get 'an old boy' in the country's bank all the more important.[182] In the event an invitation was sent. Between 1963 and 1979 Tanzania had an unbroken record of attendance. After UDI the Bank did cease to invite Rhodesia, although Zimbabwean representatives attended from 1981. More generally, however, as Table 4.1 illustrates, the pattern of attendance was not disrupted by political upheavals in Commonwealth states or by conflict between Commonwealth members. Most countries continued to send participants throughout periods of military rule or following military coups, and delegates from both India and Pakistan continued to participate during the Indo-Pakistani wars. By the 1970s the pressure on numbers was so great that the Bank's invitation had become distinctly lukewarm, advising that the Bank would regard it 'in no sense as a discourtesy if, on occasion, our invitation is declined'. It was forced to warn some states that if the uptake for the course was too great it might have to ask them to stand down, and emphasized that delegates must be of high calibre.[183]

For all this, between the inauguration of the course in 1957 and 1989 many newly independent Commonwealth countries with local central banks or currency authorities participated in almost every biannual course. In Ghana, perhaps because of London's strictures about ensuring the academic calibre

---

[180] Ibid., no. 24, 'Central Banking Course', memo 11–12 November 1956; 'Future Central Banking Courses. Reappraisal and Recommendations', by P. B. Edgeley, 14 July 1969.

[181] Ibid., annotated minute, 30 October, on 'Tanzania. Bank of England Course', 28 October 1966.

[182] Ibid.

[183] Bank of Ghana [BoG], Accra, Corporate Records Management, TRG 20, 'Courses at the Bank of England', no. 4, Bank of England to Amon Nikoi, Governor of the Bank of Ghana, 24 September 1976.

Table 4.1. *Attendance at the Bank of England Central Banking Course 1957–89 (the dates given after former African colonies indicate when they became independent and when their central banks were established)*ᵃ

Commonwealth Sterling Area	57	59	61	63	65	67	69	71	73	75	77	79	81	83	85	87	89
Australia	*	*	*	*	*	*	*	*	*	*	*	*		*	*	*	*
Bahamas		*	*					*		*		*	*		*		*
Bangladesh													*				
Barbados										*	*	*	*	*	*		*
Belize													*	*			*
Botswana												*		*		*	
Canada				*	*		*	*	*	*	*	*	*	*	*	*	*
Cyprus						*		*					*	*		*	*
East Caribbean										*	*	*	*		*	*	*
Fiji								*		*	*	*		*	*	*	*
Gambia (65/71)	*					*		*	*	*	*	*	*	*	*	*	*
Ghana (57/57)		*	*	*	*	*	*	*	*	*		*	*	*	*	*	
Guyana						*	*					*	*	*			
India	*	*	*	*	*	*	*	*	*	*	*	*		*	*	*	*
Jamaica		*	*	*	*	*	*	*	*	*		*		*		*	*
Kenya (63/66)					*	*	*	*	*	*	*	*			*	*	*
Lesotho																	
Malawi (64/65)						*		*	*	*	*	*	*	*	*	*	*
Malaysia	*	*	*	*	*		*	*	*	*	*	*	*	*	*	*	*
Malta							*	*		*		*	*	*		*	*
Mauritius							*							*			
New Zealand	*	*	*	*	*	*		*	*	*	*	*	*	*	*	*	
Nigeria (60/58)		*	*	*	*	*	*	*	*	*	*	*	*	*	*	*	*
Pakistan	*	*	*	*	*	*	*	*	*	*	*	*	*	*	*	*	
Papua New Guinea													*				

(cont.)

Table 4.1. (*cont.*)

	57	59	61	63	65	67	69	71	73	75	77	79	81	83	85	87	89
Commonwealth Sterling Area																	
Seychelles													*	*	*	*	
Sierra Leone (61/64)		*	*	*	*	*	*	*	*	*		*		*	*		*
Singapore	*			*	*	*	*	*	*	*	*					*	*
South Africa	*	*	*	*	*	*	*	*	*	*	*	*	*	*	*		*
Sri Lanka	*	*	*	*	*		*	*				*	*	*			*
Swaziland										*			*			*	*
Tanzania (61/65)				*	*	*	*	*	*	*	*	*	*	*	*	*	*
Trinidad & Tobago				*	*	*	*	*	*	*	*	*		*	*	*	
Uganda (62/66)					*	*	*	*	*	*	*			*	*	*	
Zambia (64/64)					*	*	*		*	*	*	*		*	*	*	*
Rhod/Zimb	*	*	*	*		*	*	*	*	*		*	*	*	*	*	*
Europe																	
Denmark										*				*			
France									*		*						
Germany									*		*		*				
Ireland				*	*	*	*		*				*				
Italy									*			*					
Netherlands										*							*
Belgium														*			
Spain																	*
Middle East																	
Saudi Arabia										*	*						
UAE										*				*			

[a] Information provided by the Bank of England.

of participants, the selection of able nominees was taken very seriously. By
the mid-1970s heads of department in its bank were asked to propose potential candidates, who were then grilled by a panel of senior colleagues on their
knowledge of banking and related matters. The selection process was maintained and refined over the next few years, with candidates awarded a numerical score. Most of those considered for participation were of managerial or
deputy managerial level. The nominee would in effect serve as a representative of the Bank of Ghana alongside representatives of other Commonwealth
central banks. It was no doubt important to the Bank of Ghana that it should
present a professional image in this international forum. Dress and behaviour
would be important and the successful nominee was given a relatively generous 'kit allowance'. This was common practice, with similar provision made
for those attending university courses in the United Kingdom as well as members of the armed forces to equip them for England's cool climate, but it seems
likely that for the Ghanaian Bank – especially in economically turbulent periods – appearance was especially important.[184]

The Commonwealth focus did not go uncontested within the Bank of
England. Periodically officials debated whether it should open the course to
delegates from other states, especially non-Commonwealth sterling area countries with whom the Bank's relations were perceived as 'almost as close', and
from Latin America, a region in which in the interwar years the Bank had
played a prominent part, and where officials feared the Bank now risked losing ground to other organizations offering training, which might 'minimize
the role of sterling' and present a more American point of view.[185] In March
1960 one senior figure canvassed the idea of a *non*-Commonwealth course that
might run in alternate years, but the proposal was rejected because of the burden this would place on the Bank's staff.[186] Later in 1960, a tumultuous year in
African decolonization, with the precipitate withdrawal of both Belgium and
France from their sub-Saharan African colonies, Loynes also warned against
'overconcentration' on solely Commonwealth countries in Africa.[187]

By the late 1960s it had become clear that the Commonwealth had not lived
up to the hopes attached to it. Loynes acknowledged in 1968 that the Course
had been 'conceived as a Commonwealth effort in the days when this concept
held out more promise and attracted more interest and support than seem logical today'. With more representatives from African and Caribbean states than

[184] Ibid., no. 13, 'Bank of England – Central Banking Course for 1977, note by P. K. Enchill,
Training Office (Admin Dept)', 21 February 1977; and subsequent papers dealing with the
selection process. There are no records relating to the period before 1976; no. 29, P. K. Echill
to Bank's participant for 1977, 15 March 1977.
[185] BoE. OV 21/26, 'Central Banking Course', memo by G. de Mowbray, 31 March 1960.
[186] Ibid., 'Central Banking Course', 23 May 1962.
[187] BoE, OV 138/1, no. 47, 'Africa', paper by Loynes, 27 July 1960.

any other region, Loynes observed that the composition of the Course had become 'increasingly negroid'. In view of what he perceived as falling standards, Loynes thought some participants would benefit from plain instruction. While he argued that Commonwealth central banks would continue to be of importance to Britain not least because of their bearing within their own countries on commercial banking, in many cases predominantly British, he nonetheless suggested the Bank needed to 'look more critically at the Commonwealth and especially at the concept of one Commonwealth entity'.[188] The nature of the City of London was also changing with the growth of foreign-owned large corporations, while the Bank's own position and independence of government weakened. In the 1960s the City became increasingly cosmopolitan, playing a significant role in the development of the Eurobond market. Indeed, Cain and Hopkins argue that, as 'the good ship sterling sank, the City was able to scramble aboard a much more seaworthy young vessel, the Euro-dollar'.[189] Loynes now argued in relation to the Central Banking course that the Bank must 'look more closely at Europe'.[190] The question of European participation in the course was repeatedly raised over the next few years, especially following a reappraisal of the purpose of the course following Britain's successful application to the EEC, leading to the participation of a handful of European states from 1973.[191]

As news of the course leaked out beyond the Commonwealth, the Bank had also began to receive requests from other monetary authorities and countries wishing to attend. In 1967 the Bank declined one such request from Hong Kong. It had earlier determined against inviting representatives from the territory because of concerns about the position of the 'Hongshai' Bank, a reference to the Hong Kong and Shanghai Banking Corporation that (in the absence of a local central bank) issued the territory's bank notes and managed its currency balances; presumably this was because the Bank of England did not want to see delegates from the Hong Kong bank participate alongside those from central banks.[192] Hong Kong's request also came after a period of growing tension between the Bank and the territory, which had seen Bank officials increasingly worried about the possibility of a large-scale sterling exodus through Hong Kong, identified as a weak spot within the sterling system because of the

---

[188] BoE, OV 21/26, Memo by J. B. Loynes, 20 September 1968.
[189] Cain and Hopkins, *British Imperialism* (3rd edn., 2016), pp. 679, 718–19.
[190] BoE, OV 21/26, Memo by J. B. Loynes, 20 September 1968.
[191] Ibid., 'Central Banking Course 1975. Invitations', 20 September 1974. In late 1972 the Bank also explored the possibility of attaching staff to European Central Banks: OV 21/25, no. 123, 'Attachments to European Central Banks', 3 November 1972, by J.G.W.D.
[192] Ibid., papers concerning the 1967 course, inc. 'Central Banking Course', 23 January 1967; 'Central Banking Course', 9 August 1967.

absence of local financial and banking regulation.[193] Other requests to attend generally came from countries which had a historic link to the sterling area or which carried out most of their transactions in sterling, notably within the Middle East. Despite their historic and contemporary connections to Britain and the sterling area, and their strategic importance to the United Kingdom, in the 1960s the Bank refused these requests partly on grounds of space, but also because they were aware that if they started accepting delegates from some states it might complicate the Bank's relations with banks elsewhere. In 1974, however, the Bank revised this position and issued invitations to three Arab states, including Saudi Arabia. This U-turn occurred at a time when the steeply rising price of oil on world markets had led to significant growth in the sterling assets of these Middle Eastern states.[194]

All considered, the Bank's commitment to the Commonwealth was to prove remarkably steady. It was probably sustained by returning Bank men who had been seconded to positions in the new Commonwealth banks. By the 1960s some of these returnees were occupying key posts in Threadneedle Street. Having returned to the Bank of England from Nigeria in 1963 Roy Fenton saw rapid promotions end in him becoming in 1965 Chief of the Bank's Overseas Department, a position he held until 1975. His deputy was S. W. Payton who had recently returned to the Bank after spending some five years as Governor of the new Bank of Jamaica. With Fenton's retirement in 1975, the role of those with direct experience in the Commonwealth was maintained with Payton's appointment as his successor.

Perhaps because of their influence, the Central Banking Course not only survived reappraisals in the late 1960s and early 1970s but continued throughout the 1980s. During the 1970s the Bank's Commonwealth connections continued to be perceived as an important way of generating 'goodwill and understanding'; to Fenton, the prospect of British entry to the EEC in fact rendered the importance of this task as 'great as ever'.[195] Although some Commonwealth central banks took the Bank's warnings about numbers to heart and 'stood down' in some years, many ex-colonies that had begun to send representatives on the opening of their new central banks had unbroken records of attendance – one suspects not least because this was a popular junket for those attending. In 1989 Commonwealth representatives outnumbered those from Europe by

[193] Catherine Schenk, *Hong Kong as an International Financial Centre. Emergence and Development, 1945–1965* (Routledge, London, 2001), p. 15. Valeria Zanier and Robert Peruzzi, '1967 as the Turning Point in Hong-Kong British PRC Economic Relations' in Priscilla Roberts and Odd Arne Westad eds., *China, Hong Kong and the Long 1970s: Global Perspectives* (Palgrave Macmillan, Basingstoke, 2017), pp. 233–56.

[194] BoE, OV 21/26, papers concerning the 1967 course; 'Central Banking Course 1975', memo by Fenton, 27 June 1974; Schenk, *Decline of Sterling*, pp. 358–9.

[195] Ibid., 'The Commonwealth etc., Central Banking Course', memo by R. P. Fenton, 4 November 1971.

more than ten to one.[196] In 1990 the Bank embarked upon a new educational initiative in the form of a Centre for Central Banking Studies aimed principally at the states of another collapsing empire, this time in Eastern Europe. At this juncture responsibility for the Commonwealth course was transferred within the Bank to the new Centre.[197]

As these discussions illustrate, as sterling area matters declined in importance the course functioned to an increasing degree as a form of financial diplomacy. New banks remained hungry for assistance and there was still demand for help from the Bank of England. In the 1970s, 1980s and 1990s the Bank of Ghana requested that the Bank provide short-term attachments for staff for training purposes, sometimes proposing that these be added on for participants after the end of the Central Banking Course. The Bank of England generally acceded to these requests, although it commonly proposed that the attachments might be of shorter duration than suggested by the Bank of Ghana.[198] By the 1960s, however, alternative forms of training became more readily available, with the IMF Institute offering courses that were longer than the Bank of England's and of greater technical specialization.[199] Local banking courses and institutes were also established, including in Ghana under the auspices of the College of Administration.[200] In London the training needs of developing countries were perceived as now 'less urgent'. Alongside the continued importance of promoting the City, the course could thus be reconceptualized as a 'well balanced "finishing school"', offering an 'unrivalled experience for any young central banker with the ability and temperament for a senior post'. Just as in an earlier period, the Bank was committed to facilitating interbank collaboration, and its initiatives in relation to central banking must be viewed in the context of the continued desire of its senior staff to retain independence from the state at a time when there were attempts to see professional bankers brought more firmly under the control of sovereign governments. While acknowledging these were difficult to quantify, Bank staff thought 'close and good central bank relations' remained as 'important to our Overseas functions as they

---

[196] Ibid., information was provided by the Bank of England, as the papers relating to the Course after 1974 are closed.

[197] BoE, 4A73/1, Extract from Financial Report, April 1991; and 'Centre for Central Banking Studies', confidential memo 28 June 1991.

[198] BoG, Corporate Records Management, TRG 20, 'Courses at the Bank of England', nos. 92–3, correspondence between Y. O. Adjepong-Boateng and B. A. Kwaaning, 22 and 26 February 1979; G. N. Fagg (Overseas Visitors Liaison Manager, BoE) to H. N. O. Quao (Director, Admin Dept, BoG), 29 June 1984.

[199] *International Monetary Fund. Annual Report, 1967*, p. 140; *Annual Report, 1968*, p. 109.

[200] See e.g. Basu, *Central Banking*, pp. 241–2.

ever were, and on this score alone we would judge that the Courses have more than paid their way'.[201] In the late 1960s the Bank estimated that at least half of all those who had at some stage attended the Central Banking Course had been appointed to senior positions. Fifteen had become governors, deputy governors, directors or chief executives in their own central banks, including twelve in African countries. The majority of other alumni had been appointed to posts as assistant heads of department or above. Some had moved on to work for other organizations including the IMF, ensuring that the Bank's networks were remade within new contexts.[202] Among course alumni was the Ghanaian Adam Adomakoh, an economist, lawyer and banker, nominated for the first course by Eggleston as 'a very promising African'.[203] In 1965 he became the fourth, and the second African, governor, of the Bank of Ghana, and in that capacity he sought a return to more British central banking orthodoxy, curbing government borrowing and asserting the importance of central bank autonomy from the government.[204] Alhaji Aliyu Mai-Bornu, the first Nigerian governor of the Central Bank of Nigeria (1963–7), was also an alumnus of the Central Banking Course, having attended in 1961, before being appointed as Fenton's Deputy in 1962. His participation in the course had led to useful connections, which both he and the Bank of England actively sought to maintain.[205] Mai-Bornu's Deputy, Dr Abai Njoku Abai (1963–7), was another alumnus, as were other members of his staff.[206] By 1969 the diaspora of course 'graduates' included Samuel B. Nicol-Cole, first African governor of the Bank of Sierra Leone, who had attended the course in 1963, as well as his General Manager and Assistant General Manager who had participated in 1965 and 1967, respectively. John Robert Elangot, Secretary of the Bank of Uganda, attended in 1967, while Bitwell Kuwani, at one time deputy governor of the Bank of Zambia, and M. J. Katundu, assistant to the General Manager, Bank of Zambia and Goodall Gondwe, Assistant Adviser at the Reserve Bank of Malawi, were among other African participants.[207]

---

[201] BoE OV 21/26. Review of Central Banking Courses' (draft), 11 March 1970.

[202] Ibid., 'Training of Overseas Visitors', 29 January 1969.

[203] BoE, OV 18/2, cited in Haslam, p. 262.

[204] Edward S. Ayensu, *Bank of Ghana: Commemoration of the Golden Jubilee* (Bank of Ghana, Accra, 2007), pp. 39–40.

[205] See e.g., BoE OV 68/10, 'Nigeria. Visit of Chief Festus and Mallam Aliyu Mai-Bornu', 14 May 1962; and note 17 May 1962 on Mai-Bornu's visit.

[206] BoE, OV 68/13, see various papers including no. 94, 'Central Bank of Nigeria', 27 October 1960; no. 167, A. Mai-Bornu to Loynes, 8 August 1963. *Twenty Years of Central Banking in Nigeria*, ch. 3, and appendix 1.

[207] BoE, OV 70/3, 'Sierra Leone', 19 September 1963; BoE, OV 21/26, 'Training of Overseas Visitors', 29 January 1969, appendix. Biographical information from: Magbaily C. Fyle, *Historical Dictionary of Sierra Leone* (Scarecrow Press, Lanham, MD, 2006); Owen. J. Kalinga, *Historical Dictionary of Malawi* (4th edn., Scarecrow Press, Lanham, MD, c. 2012).

It is difficult to quantify the extent to which this diaspora of Bank personnel and alumni was in practice useful in the promotion of British banking models and commitment to the sterling area. However, within the Bank the Central Banking Course was seen as at the very least an important form of financial diplomacy, a means of forging new professional connections and friendships with emergent Commonwealth states, and an occasion on which the Bank could advertise the City of London's financial services,[208] albeit that it was recognized that such advantages which might follow from these were by nature long term.[209]

Conclusion

We have seen that in ways perhaps more commonly associated with its activities in the interwar era, the Bank of England was a key player in the development of overseas central banking, not only, but most obviously, in British Africa. The initiatives of the 1950s, 1960s and 1970s reflect a continuing sense of vocation which bears comparison to ideas of civilizing mission and development in earlier eras – or even 'burden', a word used at the Bank when educational measures were first discussed, albeit one that, as we have seen, the Bank concluded would be 'a worthwhile investment'. One might speculate that this sense of mission was increasingly to the fore as the importance of the sterling area declined.

In offering forms of technical assistance both the Bank and Whitehall officials clearly perceived their role in part as discharging an obligation to the countries concerned, by helping ensure their financial security within the Commonwealth. But it is equally apparent that developing forms of technical assistance was a means for the Bank of promoting its own goals. Indeed, the Bank's repeated use of the word 'propaganda' in relation to the Central Banking Course shows how self-consciously it carved out a role after Empire with a view to serving its own interests. In East Africa the Bank pursued the particular objective – ultimately unsuccessfully – of creating a single East African central bank and currency, and more generally to promote the interests of the City of London. However, in the mid-1950s the most obvious considerations here concerned sterling and the sterling area. The advisers the Bank sent out sought to ensure that the legislation establishing each of the new banks preserved a strong tie to sterling, with the

---

[208] BoE, OV 21/26, 'Review of the Central Banking Course', memo 11 March 1970 (by S. W. Payton).
[209] Ibid., untitled memo reviewing the Central Banking Course by J. B. Loynes, 20 September 1968.

result that in some respects the earliest banks did little more than replicate some of the features of the currency board system.

Alongside the interests of sterling and the sterling area, the Bank promoted its own preferred model of central banking. The Bank's 'mission' aimed to promote not a generic western capitalist system of finance but reflected a belief in *British* banking models – especially as distinct from American – as best practice. The Bank's advisers to new African central banks sought to replicate features of the Bank of England, aimed to separate commercial from central banking functions, and to ensure the autonomy of the new banks from their governments. This was logical in relation to developing countries, but also consistent with the cultivation of 'close and good central bank relations' in line with the Bank of England's own agenda of developing a class of international professional central bankers who might interact independently of their governments.

As we have seen these initiatives were far from an unalloyed success. The development of African central banking was an on-going process, and the structures and ordinances of the new banks, in which the Bank of England, had played such a key role, by no means fixed. The new banks were expected not just to be symbols of monetary autonomy but to play a dynamic part in the economic development of their countries, assisting in the creation of new money and capital markets and sponsoring the construction of financial structures appropriate to developing countries, such as development banks and institutions.[210] Most significantly for the Bank they developed in ways that were the very opposite of what its officials had hoped, with central banks subordinated to their governments, supplying inflation-fuelling credit to bridge the gap between state revenue and state expenditure; although in the 1980s and 1990s in most cases this emphasis was replaced by greater commitment to maintaining instead price stability.[211]

But if the Bank's immediate objectives were of at best limited success, they may have helped ensure some adherence to sterling and the sterling area in a period in which this still mattered. Perhaps equally significantly, however, the Bank's investment in technical assistance contributed to the development and mobilization of networks of individual contacts among an emergent professional African banking middle class. In the late 1950s and 1960s John Loynes became the 'personal face' of the Bank of England in Africa. With a wide range of contacts among African politicians, he had proven generally able to ride out anti-British sentiment, remaining acceptable – almost indispensable.

[210] See, e.g., Jucker-Fleetwood, *Money and Finance*, pp. 51–2, 112–13, 172–5; Basu, *Central Banking*, pp. 198, 205–6.
[211] Maxwell J. Fry, Charles A. E. Goodhart, Alvaro Almeida, *Central Banking in Developing Countries: Objectives, Activities, and Independence* (Routledge, London, 1996), pp. 112–13; 138.

Through a diaspora of advisers, seconded staff, and alumni from the bank-ing course, the Bank also built contacts with new African elites, nurturing a generation of central bankers who might serve as interlocutors between Threadneedle Street and their governments. Working alongside the diaspora of British bankers, they might absorb a British public service ethos, and atti-tudes. P. B. Edgeley, working in Nigeria, observed this approvingly among young Nigerian banking staff, whom he described as 'Nigeria's emergent middle class'. 'We need not fear', he thought, for the long-term future of Nigeria, 'once the middle class becomes sufficiently distinct to exercise an effect on public opinion and politics'.[212] As Stone's troubled time in Ghana shows, the networks the Bank cultivated were inevitably disrupted by the turbulent politics of the postcolonial era, which sometimes saw the margin-alization or departure of those the Bank had courted and the subordination of banks to political party machinery. External influences diluted that of the Bank, while the old colonial connections were supplemented by new regional initiatives, such as the Association of African Central Banks, and its subre-gional groupings. Formally inaugurated in 1969 at a meeting of twenty-five African central banks, the Association quickly began sponsoring its own train-ing activities.[213] But the Bank also played a long game and, as the example of Adomakoh in Ghana shows, it sometimes saw those it had sponsored acced-ing to positions of influence even in countries where the circumstances had initially looked unpromising.

The extension of hospitality, gifts and the politics of 'gesture' played a role in sustaining contacts developed via the course and relations with new African banks. Entertaining the heads of African central banks in Threadneedle Street became a common courtesy, although not always a duty contemplated with enthusiasm within the Bank of England. For example, in 1975 senior officials reluctantly accepted that they needed to extend some hospitality to the visiting governor of the Bank of Uganda 'for the sake of relationships', but feared that not only was the governor 'heavy going', but that Uganda did not provide 'easy subjects for small talk'. Lunch seemed 'easily the least painful way of coping'.[214] The Bank generally sent telegrams to congratulate the new banks on their opening, and, as it had done on the occasion of the opening of the Central Bank of Nigeria, the Bank presented inkstands to other new African

---

[212] BoE, OV 68/7, no. 183, personal reflections by P. B. Edgeley, 25 January 1961, addressed to Messrs, Heasman, Watson and Parsons.

[213] IMF Archives, Central Banking Department Immediate Office, Technical Assistance and Subject Files, Box 6, file 3 East Africa General 1964–75, memo from Moeen A Qureshi to Managing and Deputy Managing Directors, IMF, 5 January 1970 about the inaugural meeting of the Association.

[214] BoE, OV 75/14, 'Bank of Uganda, note by PNM (Overseas Department) to Fenton, McMahon and Governor's private secretary; note by C W M (?), 1975.

central banks as well.[215] Sometimes there was confusion over etiquette. When one overenthusiastic official in the Bank's overseas department suggested the 'presentation' of a gift following the opening of a new bank building in Uganda, he was advised that the Bank did not offer gifts just for building extensions.[216]

For all the other competing influences, the Bank's connections to new Commonwealth central banks proved, perhaps surprisingly, enduring. From 1990 the Bank's new Centre for Central Banking Studies hosted a greater variety of courses aimed at a wider audience. By 2017 over 27,200 delegates from 177 central banks and 42 regulatory authorities had participated in the Centre's events.[217] Yet Commonwealth states remained core attendees. In 1993 those attending one course comprised a mix of Eastern European states, the Republic of China, and developing states within the Commonwealth. Perhaps more pertinently in the 1990s the Centre continued the Commonwealth tradition by offering courses that, like those earlier, were described as 'Commonwealth Central Banking Courses', albeit of shorter duration than before. These covered central banking techniques and principles as well as international finance and economic and monetary policy, but, like the predecessor courses, made particular reference to 'the role of the Bank of England and the City of London as a commercial and financial centre' while also aiming to 'further cooperation and understanding between participating central banks'.[218] In 1993 the Centre also began producing newsletters to keep in touch with course alumni.[219] In 1995 representatives from over forty-four banks were invited to a symposium on central banking in developing countries in London. The participants were drawn, in the words of the Governor, Eddie George, who had joined the Bank in 1962 at the height of the decolonization era, from the 'erstwhile Sterling Area'.[220] The participants, who included the governors of central banks in *all* former British African colonies, as well as senior figures from banks in countries in the Middle East and a few other foreign states, were described in the book that resulted as 'the Bank of England group'.[221] For the Bank, an institution that was

---

[215] Ibid., note, 30 December 1969.

[216] Ibid., note, 28 January 1976, by P.N.M.

[217] 'Foreword from Mark Carney', *Centre for Central Banking Studies: Prospectus 2017* (Bank of England), p. 2.

[218] BoG, Accra, Corporate Records Management, TRG 20, Michael Hewitt (Director of Central Banking Studies), BoE, to Dr G. K. Ayuma, Bank of Ghana, no legible date, but about a course 8–19 March 1993; and also 25 February 1993.

[219] Ibid., correspondence from Manager, Centre Central Banking, BoE, to BoG about course newsletter, 20 May 1993.

[220] This was a follow up to an earlier meeting focused on banking in developed countries, organized as part of the Bank's tercentenary activities.

[221] Fry, Goodhart, Almeida, *Central Banking in Developing Countries*, foreword by George, pp. x–xi, table 1.1, p. 2. The former Anglo-Egyptian condominium of Sudan did not, however, attend.

not itself 'imperial' but which had assumed significant imperial interests, the end of Empire had become the source of new institutional connections and dynamics, and a redirection of 'imperial mission', an illustration of the on-going purchase of the Commonwealth idea in this corner of British society. Through its continued support to new banks, the Bank of England had a long imperial 'afterlife', maintaining initiatives devised in the 1950s and framed by a culture formed in an earlier period.

5   Making Money: The Royal Mint and British Decolonization

In April 1966 the Royal Mint, Britain's oldest manufacturing organization,[1] was given the new Queen's Award for Industry for Export Achievement, the first of a number of occasions on which it would receive this accolade. The award followed a period of notable growth in both output and staff that coincided with a decade of African decolonization. This was no coincidence. By the mid-twentieth century, national currencies, although a relatively recent phenomenon, had become potent symbols of independent statehood, a form of 'banal nationalism' by which the nation is 'flagged' in the day-to-day lives of its citizens.[2] Within emergent Commonwealth states, where colonial currency boards issued notes and coins that were in practice little more than local variants of sterling, politicians were now keen to have their own currencies issued by new central banks.[3] National currencies were a means of differentiating the postcolonial present from the colonial past, of projecting the new regime's authority, and important tools of national economic management, crucial for the orderly administration of taxation and financial systems. They were also a means of securing for the new polities the profits from currency issue.[4]

For the Mint the introduction of new national currencies presented business opportunities, but also risks, since it entailed the loss of its established business of producing coins for tied customers. A minor department of state that also engaged in commercial activities, the Mint – like other institutions discussed in this book – hence also aimed to maintain its connections to

---

[1] *The Royal Mint. Annual Report 2014–15*, p. 14, available at https://www.royalmint.com/globalassets/the-royal-mint/pdf/annual-reports/ar_2014_2015.pdf, accessed January 2016.

[2] Michael Billig, *Banal Nationalism* (Sage Publications, London, 1995), p. 6.

[3] Although there were exceptions to the pattern, including in the Caribbean, where some of the smaller island territories continued to participate in a form of currency union: Guyana, Trinidad and Tobago withdrew from the British Caribbean Currency Board, established in 1950; the other states created an East Caribbean Currency Authority in 1965. Other exceptions include the Pacific (where Australian, New Zealand or American currencies are used in small states) or in Lesotho and Swaziland where the South African Rand was still allowed even after the creation of national currencies: Helleiner, *Making of National Money*, pp. 208–9, 215–16.

[4] Ibid., pp. 19–37, 46–51; Gilbert and Helleiner eds., 'Introduction', *Nation States*, pp. 3–9.

the former Empire, obtaining the business of emergent states. This chapter argues that the Mint's success in winning this business was critical to its transformation from an 'imperial' institution to a 'global' one. Its role in producing and in some cases designing the coins as well as independence medals for new states constitutes another compelling example of the ambiguities of the decolonization process. The Mint, like the Bank, British universities and the Army, also became a source of technical assistance to new states, in the African context to Nigeria, which established its own mint. In the Mint's case such activities reflected a hard-nosed commercial impulse rather than a cultural or strategic imperative, although negotiations over the production of new coins for emergent nations sometimes also revealed persistent 'cultures of imperialism'.

What follows first illustrates the determination with which the Mint set out to secure this Commonwealth business. It then goes on to consider the factors behind the Mint's success, identifying as crucial its skilful navigation of the uncertain and rapidly changing landscape of constitutional change in the British Empire, as well as its ability to draw on networks of British personnel in emerging states. The diaspora of Bank of England officials embedded in the new banks of emergent states was particularly useful. The Mint's capacity in design was also fundamental to its success, and a further section considers how far the accession of economic might that the Mint's success represented was reproduced in cultural terms. Although there has been only very limited scholarly analysis of the sector in which the Mint operated, the manufacture of metallic and paper security and currency products, there has been a little more discussion of the symbolism of currency design of British manufactured coin used in Anglophone African states.[5] Here I want to suggest that although the cultural politics of imperialism and decolonization are certainly evident in both the designs and discussions, for the Mint at least, the acquisition of new African orders was unquestionably about business opportunity, and its history primarily interesting as a manifestation of an economic rather than cultural imperialism. A final section shows that the favourable conditions the Mint enjoyed during most of the 1960s were fading by the end of the decade and provides the basis for the conclusion that, because the Mint was initially able to draw on legacy networks of British personnel, it was only from the later 1960s that the force of decolonization was more fully felt in terms of open competition.

---

[5] Lutz Marten and Nancy Kula, 'Meanings of Money: National Identity and the Semantics of Currency in Zambia and Tanzania', *Journal of African Cultural Studies*, 20 (2008), pp. 183–98; Harcourt Fuller, *Building the Ghanaian Nation State: Kwame Nkrumah's Symbolic Nationalism* (Palgrave Macmillan, Basingstoke, 2014); Eagleton, 'Designing Change'.

Capturing New Commonwealth Trade

By the early 1950s the Mint was significantly involved in export production. Under an earlier Deputy Master, Sir Robert Johnson (1922–38), the Mint's export business had expanded, rising from the production of 28 million coins in 1927 to 157 million in 1937, and then, under Johnson's successor, to 357 million in 1943.[6] On the Queen's accession to the throne the Mint estimated more than 100,000,000 people around the world were using coins with the royal image. In that year, although the percentage fell thereafter, overseas business accounted for 91 per cent of the Mint's production. Foreign customers included Libya, Iraq, Nicaragua and Bolivia (whose order the Mint had received after two years of 'patient negotiation').[7] The following year the Mint also produced coins for the first time for Paraguay and Uruguay.[8] Nevertheless, orders from British colonies and for independent Commonwealth countries had become – in the words of the Mint's Deputy Master Sir Lionel Thompson – 'by far the most important' of all the Mint's overseas business.[9] In 1952 they accounted for nearly two-thirds of its export production. Africa's part in this expanding business was at this point driven by strong export earnings, greater African adoption of colonial coin (which finally saw an end to the parallel currency systems that had prevailed in the interwar era), and a tendency among some Africans to hoard coin.[10] Changes to constitutional and financial arrangements were also significant. These included the extension of the geographical scope of the East African Currency Board to include Aden and Somaliland in 1952, and the creation of the Central African Federation in 1953, which led to the introduction of a new Central African currency to replace the old Southern Rhodesian and British coinage used previously.[11]

The Mint's first responsibility was the production of coin for domestic use, as well as commemorative coin and the manufacture of other products including medals for a variety of British organizations, civil and military. The Deputy Master and Comptroller of the Royal Mint was also ex-officio Engraver of the Queen's Seals; a minor function except at the time of the royal succession.[12] Because the Mint collected the seignorage – the difference between the face value and production cost – on all domestic coin sold to British clearing banks the Mint's manufacture of British coin was generally very rewarding in financial terms. However, the Mint's export business – both

---

[6] *85th Annual Report, 1954* (HMSO, 1956), p. 4. *100th Annual Report, 1969* (HMSO, 1970), p. 7.
[7] *83rd Annual Report, 1952* (HMSO, 1954), p. 8.
[8] *84th Annual Report, 1953* (HMSO, 1955), pp. 7–10.
[9] TNA, MINT 20/2563, Sir L. Thompson to Sir Herbert Brittain (T), 11 July 1955.
[10] See pp. 48–9.
[11] *83rd Annual Report*, pp. 1–2, 9–10; *86th Annual Report, 1955* (HMSO, 1956), pp. 5, 11. TNA, MINT 20/2068, minutes of 131st meeting of the RMAC, 10 November 1954.
[12] *84th Annual Report, 1953*, pp. 7–10.

colonial and foreign – played a crucial part in supporting this domestic role, enabling the Mint to operate at capacity whatever the fluctuations in domestic demand, and thereby helping the Mint to operate as cost effectively as possible. In the early 1950s producing for the overseas market had an added advantage for the Mint. The purchase of metal is the most significant single expenditure in the manufacture of coin, and needs to be carefully managed to minimize risk from exposure to changing metal prices and exchange rates. In the 1950s cupro-nickel had become the most common coinage alloy, formed from 75 per cent copper and 25 per cent nickel. Silver coinage was abandoned in Britain itself following the Coinage Act of 1946 and a recovery programme introduced to reclaim silver to use as repayment of the US lend-lease debt. A shortage of nickel, however, forced the Mint to suspend its domestic programme of substituting silver coin with cupro-nickel. Because overseas demand was principally for bronze coins, which contained no nickel, or for nickel brass (with 1 per cent nickel), the Mint had been able to keep producing coin while reducing its demand for virgin nickel.[13] By the mid-1950s, buoyed by its expanding business, plans were afoot to acquire additional land adjacent to the Mint's existing site in Tower Hill for the construction of new factory buildings. These plans were later put on hold by the Treasury during a period of economic difficulties, and, when a move finally took place in the late 1960s, the Tower Hill site was regarded as too small, and the Mint moved instead to Llantrisant in Wales. But from the perspective of Mint officials in the mid-1950s, retaining the business of manufacturing coins for former colonies was seen as crucial to its London redevelopment plans.[14]

In view of the Mint's already extensive overseas business the claim that decolonization saw the Mint's transformation from an 'imperial' to a 'global' institution might appear to attribute undue importance to a largely semantic distinction. However, within the Empire and Commonwealth the Mint benefited from what Jack James, Deputy Master of the Mint from 1957 to 1970 later admitted had been a 'tied' market, whereas independent countries could exercise sovereignty in their choice of where to place orders for coin. Under the established arrangements in which seignorage provided the Mint with easy profit, there had also been little incentive to innovate or improve efficiency. By the mid-1950s the changing colonial-political situation confronted the Mint with the choice of either 'becoming more competitive' or of being left with meeting only 'home and vestigial colonial demand'. The decision was taken to 'to go all out to capture the trade, not only in the Commonwealth but in

---

[13] *83rd Annual Report, 1952*, p. 1; *88th Annual Report, 1957* (HMSO, 1958), p. 3; *90th Annual Report, 1959* (HMSO, 1960), pp. 6–7.

[14] TNA, MINT 20/2563, letters from Sir Lionel Thompson to A. N. Galsworthy (CO) and Sir Herbert Brittain (T), 11 July 1955.

the world at large'.[15] It was 'rather important', Sir Lionel Thompson, James's predecessor as Deputy Master, emphasized to the Colonial Office in 1955, that British officials 'should make every effort' to ensure that the Royal Mint retained the work of producing coinage for former colonies. The Treasury, the Mint's parent department and also its principal customer, Thompson suggested, would 'attach as much importance as I do to ensuring that everything possible is done to maintain our connection with the newly enfranchised Territories'.[16]

The Mint's bid to 'capture' this trade in British Africa was first evident in relation to the Gold Coast. Although at this juncture the territory remained under British rule, the colony had had full internal self-government since 1954, and, as we saw in Chapter 4, the country's new African government sought its own currency as well as an independent central bank.[17] The colony became the focus of a dogged Mint campaign to secure the contract to produce the colony's new coins, illustrating the importance the Mint attached to retaining African business. From the outset, however, the Mint, like the Bank of England, struggled to keep abreast of the developing situation as it related to currency. News that – after some initial communication about the manufacture of coins – an order for the production of new bank notes for the country had been placed with a private British firm while the Mint had itself heard nothing, provided an early warning of the difficulties the Mint might encounter in trying to retain the business of new African states in the transitional phase from colonialism to independence. The ensuing Mint campaign is also a demonstration of the weapons in the Mint's arsenal.

Concerned that the Mint might lose out in the Gold Coast, Thompson adopted a multipronged strategy. This included lobbying the Colonial Office directly, while attempting to work through the Treasury as well.[18] He also adopted a more direct approach, sending his chief clerk, Harry Stride, to the colony in November 1955.[19] Perhaps in his desire to ingratiate himself with the Gold Coast's African ministers, Stride exceeded his brief, recommending that a fiduciary issue might yield a windfall for the colony of around £12 million; a prospect understandably attractive to Komlo Gbedemah, the country's Minister of Finance, but one that dismayed officials at the Treasury which like the Bank of England preferred to see the currency backed by 100 per cent

---

[15] *95th Annual Report, 1964* (HMSO, 1965), pp. 4–5.
[16] TNA, MINT 20/2563, Sir L. Thompson to A. N. Galsworthy (CO), 11 July 1955.
[17] See Chapter 4, pp. 152–3.
[18] TNA, MINT 20/2563, Sir L. Thompson to A. N. Galsworthy (CO), 27 July 1955, enclosing note on the services of the Royal Mint.
[19] Ibid., Sir L. Thompson to T. J. Bligh (T) 21 October 1955; 'Gold Coast Currency', a report produced by Stride following his visit to the Gold Coast, 22 November 1955; T. M. Kodwo Mercer to Sir L. Thompson, 29 December 1955.

reserves.[20] When, Gbedemah travelled to Britain the following month, he and T. M. Kodwo Mercer, the first Ghanaian High Commissioner to Britain, visited the Mint, before being wined and dined by a senior British official at his London club.[21] During negotiations Thompson sought to swing the case by promising that the Mint was prepared to develop coins of all shapes, sizes, colours and denominations so that coins would be easily identified and hard to counterfeit, while also playing what he thought was a trump card: images of the Queen already used on coins were the property of the Royal Mint. Although the Mint had supplied an image of the uncrowned Queen to dominion and branch mints, the Mint, he explained, was not prepared to allow these images to fall into the hands of a foreign competitor. The Gold Coast government was informed that only the Royal Mint could execute coinage bearing the Queen's effigy.[22] In so arguing Thompson was rehashing arguments previously used by Johnson in the 1930s when it looked as if an order for a new Mauritian coinage might be placed with the mints in India rather than entrusted to Tower Hill.[23] In the event, since the Gold Coast became the first of many African states to buck Commonwealth tradition and elect not to use the royal image, it became clear that this particular claim would not play to the Mint's advantage at least in an African context. Stride's diplomacy and commercial approach was probably more effective. Concerned that it might lose out to other producers of coin, notably the Pakistan Mint, which the Mint feared was also trying to secure the contract for the Gold Coast coinage, the Mint had also been obliged to offer the Gold Coast highly competitive rates.[24]

Despite all the Mint's efforts, a hiatus ensued, the result of changing policy decisions and local political considerations, on which the Mint, for all its connections, struggled to keep a grip, as the country's African ministers weighed up the advantages and disadvantages of decimalization. Gbedemah favoured decimalization and was initially willing to defer the issue of a new Ghanaian coinage until such time as the arrangements for this might be made. In January 1957, however, shortly before independence, Nkrumah's Cabinet decided that the continued use of the old currency board coins in the interim, especially in regions dominated by the opposition, might lead to an eventual rejection of the new currency in favour of the old.[25] When Stride made a further visit in March 1957, just after the country had achieved independence as Ghana, Gbedemah was ready to proceed with the introduction of a new coinage and to drop plans

---

[20] Ibid., 'Secret. Note on recommendations made by Mr Stride of the Royal Mint for the introduction of a new coinage in the Gold Coast' (November 1955).
[21] Ibid., Mercer to Sir L. Thompson, 29 December 1955.
[22] Ibid., Sir L. Thompson to Galsworthy, 27 July 1955, enclosing note on the services of the Royal Mint.
[23] Dyer and Gaspar, 'Reform', p. 564.
[24] TNA, MINT 20/2563, 'note', 30 September 1955.
[25] PRAAD, ADM 13/2/35, [unnumbered] Cabinet memorandum, 'The Introduction of a Decimal Coinage', by Minister of Finance; discussed in Cabinet, 18 January 1957: ADM 13/1/26.

(a)   (b)

Figure 5.1. Ghana 10 shilling coin, 1958

Figure 5.2. Image of Hastings Banda (by Paul Vincze) on the obverse of the
first coins produced for Malawi, 1964

for immediate decimalization. The Cabinet's desire to issue coins as quickly as
possible hence favoured the Mint, with its pre-existing contacts in the country.
The order for 240 million coins for Ghana was received in 1957.

This was a significant feather in the Mint's cap. Ghana was a standard bearer
for African decolonization, and thereafter the Mint could cite its role when
soliciting the business of other colonies approaching independence or newly
independent countries. It could also show examples of the coins already produced. Paul Vincze, who produced the first image of Nkrumah (Figure 5.1b),
was also entrusted with creating the portraits for use on new coins of Hastings
Banda (Figure 5.2) and Sekou Toure, the leaders of Malawi and Guinea,
respectively, each of whom had an association with Nkrumah. This was surely
no coincidence, and suggests that Ghana's example may have been influential
in their decision-making process.

Thompson retired as Deputy Master of the Mint in 1957, succeeded by
Jack (later Sir Jack) James, the 'least bureaucratic' of public servants, who
provided dynamic leadership during his long tenure from 1957 to 1970.[26] On
his arrival at the Mint James took up where Thompson had left off. He emphasized to the Colonial Office the importance of bringing the services offered
by the Mint to the attention of colonies and former colonies with new coinage
needs 'as early and as often as possible'; he specifically mentioned Malaya,

---

[26] Dyer and Gaspar, 'Reform', p. 561; Interview, Graham Dyer, 20 January 2016.

Borneo, Brunei and Sarawak, on which the Mint had received 'no news'. In the absence of 'news', continued rumours about competition from other quarters, especially from the Pakistan Mint, made British officials jumpy, although they were sceptical as to whether the Pakistan Mint had the capacity to deliver on large orders, or to secure the materials to do so.[27]

Most immediately important was Nigeria. As it had done in the Ghanaian case, the Mint asked the CO to act as an intermediary and set out to woo relevant individuals, inviting the Nigerian Minister of Finance, Chief Festus Okotie-Eboh, to visit the Mint while in London.[28] An order for 1,000,000,000 coins, the largest single order the Mint had ever received, was actually achieved with relative ease, in comparison to the effort required to secure some much smaller orders.[29] The Mint also successfully bid to produce the Nigerian independence medal. In this case its quotation was not the cheapest, but it won the contract on the grounds that its quality was perceived as higher; an illustration of the prestige associated with the British mint.[30]

Having secured the contract for producing coins for the largest and most populous of all former British African colonies, senior figures at the Mint were dismayed to discover early in 1962 that the Nigerian government intended to establish its own Mint, and as a result would cancel the remaining 340 million of its original order yet to be despatched. Their strong reaction, which saw them try to block this unwelcome development, reflected their determination to secure African contracts. For the Mint, the issue was not so much the cancellation of the remaining part of the Nigerian order, to which the Mint had not yet fully committed resources, but the potentially 'far-reaching' consequences for the Mint's market of the loss in the future of 'a potentially valuable customer' and 'the possible entry on the African scene of a competitor for the business of the expanding African states'. Equally worrying was the possibility of emulation by other states anxious not to be outdone in 'the development of self-sufficiency', Ghana came first to their minds.[31]

In its opposition to the Nigerian project the Mint had past form, Johnson having previously dissuaded New Zealand from setting up a mint, in an effort to protect the Mint's exports to colonial markets.[32] But the response of Deputy Master Jack James to the Nigerian proposals reveals how the Mint, as well as some other British commercial organizations, continued to regard new states in

[27] TNA, MINT 20/2774, J. James to A. N. Galsworthy, 5 December 1957; J. Fisher (BoE) to J. James, 18 March 1958; James to Fisher 18 March 1958.
[28] Ibid., James to Galsworthy, 24 April 1958.
[29] Interview, Dyer; Dyer and Gaspar, 'Reform', pp. 594–5.
[30] TNA, MINT 20/2833, S. Leadbetter (CRO) to S. J. G. Fingland (UK High Commission, Lagos), 21 September 1960.
[31] RMM, Nigeria boxes, file 249/9, C. Hewertson to J. Macpherson (T), 'Coinage for Nigeria', 12 January 1962. Hewertson succeeded Harry Stride as chief clerk at the Mint.
[32] Dyer and Gaspar, 'Reform', p. 564.

a colonial light, expecting that the Mint, and British personnel, should be able to shape outcomes favourable to British interests. That despite the appointment of the Bank of England's Roy Fenton as first governor of the Central Bank of Nigeria the Mint had received no prior warning of the Nigerian plans infuriated James. Although Fenton had written to inform the Mint of the reasons for the cancellation of the remainder of the Nigerian coinage order, James clearly thought that his fellow Briton, whom in a telling phrase he referred to as 'the Bank [of England]'s representative', should have been more on side: 'Why', he railed, 'Fenton could not have written a more co-operative *confidential* letter I can't think'. James now proposed that the Mint raise the 'danger' presented by the Nigerian plans with the Treasury and Bank of England, with a view to discouraging Fenton 'from doing anything positively or negatively to prejudice the Mint's markets'.[33] It was 'unfortunate we have had no inkling of what was being proposed', a Mint official wrote. 'Whether we could have brought any influence to bear is a matter of speculation but we would at least have used what arguments we could muster on the advantages of having a ready-made supplier only too anxious to meet Nigerian requirements'.[34]

In this, however, the Mint found itself out of step with opinion in both the Bank and in Whitehall. Initial enquiries led one official in the Mint to inform James that Fenton had had 'to sever all links' with the Bank of England when he took up his Central Bank of Nigeria appointment; no 'influence could be brought to bear on him either through the Treasury or through the Bank to disclose more information than he has already given'.[35] This was partially true: as we have seen Fenton did act independently, and the Bank had determined that Fenton should not be seconded temporarily, but resign from his position at the Bank. It seems likely, however, that in this case the interests of the Bank did not align with those of the Mint. To James's irritation, the CRO for its part advised treading softly. To James this seemed to rub salt into the wound: the CRO, he complained, 'do not seem to understand that it is preferable on all grounds except materialistic ones for the Nigerians to go on having their coins minted by us'.[36] But the Treasury, a department to which the Mint had to defer, advised that the Mint should not 'try to swim against this tide'.[37] Fenton had already asked the Bank of England's advisor, John Loynes, to send him a list of companies in Britain and elsewhere that might be invited to send proposals to 'participate' in the establishment of the security printing works and mint,

---

[33] RMM, Nigeria boxes, file 249/9, note by J. James addressed to C. Hewertson, 19 March 1962 on letter from Roy Fenton, 15 March 1962.
[34] Ibid., C. Hewertson to Macpherson, 'Coinage for Nigeria', 12 January 1962.
[35] Ibid., file 249/8, minute by C. Hewertson on letter from Fenton, dated 15 March 1962.
[36] Ibid., minute by J. James, 12 June 1962.
[37] Ibid., file 249/9, minute by C. Hewertson, 22 January 1962.

and rather than oppose a project that the Nigerian government had determined upon, the Treasury advised James to focus on the procurement opportunities the new venture might yield.[38]

Other British interests began to mobilize to exploit this possible opportunity, and sought to persuade the Mint to join its interest with theirs. The banknote manufacturers Bradbury Wilkinson and Co., and the Birmingham engineering firm Taylor & Challen Limited, proposed acting in concert to persuade the Nigerian Government to agree to a contract requiring that it accept the British provision of partly printed notes and coin blanks over 'a long period'.[39] Whether James disapproved of this attempt to form a cartel or regarded it as unlikely to serve the Mint's best interests is unclear, but for whatever reason the Mint declined to participate. Instead, on the very same day James wrote separately to Chief Festus offering the Mint's technical assistance in setting up the Mint. Like the Bank, the Mint had past experience of providing technical assistance to other mints within the Commonwealth or in former British dependencies. In 1953 a representative from the Pakistan Mint had spent some weeks at the Royal Mint studying its processes, and around the same time the Mint had also advised on the possible creation of a mint in Egypt, a former customer for its services.[40] In the Nigerian case, however, the offer of technical assistance was aimed more at 'finding out what they have in mind without asking in so many words'. Should the Nigerian Government take them up on their offer – for example soliciting help with staff training – the Mint judged that it might be an 'inconvenience', but this was a risk worth taking, since if the government should prove 'not entirely committed' to the project it was hoped it might realise the disadvantages of running its own establishment.[41]

This was not to be the case. The initiative was officially launched by Chief Festus in April 1963 under an agreement signed in May with the De La Rue Company Limited.[42] De La Rue's own salesman at the time, Alex Napier, later claimed that the firm had seeded the idea of the Nigerian Mint in the first instance, after concluding that Nigeria's size and population made it a suitable location for the establishment of a new facility, offering to develop a new security printing works while also negotiating to print the new bank notes.[43] Within the Mint it was noted that De La Rue's competitors had 'made themselves unpopular by bribing the wrong people', while De La Rue itself had 'played it

---

[38] Ibid., file 249/8, R. W. Phelps (T) to C. Hewertson, 18 January 1962; C. Hewertson to R. C. Barnes (CRO), 9 February 1962; BoE, OV 68/9, no 162, Fenton to Loynes, 14 December 1961.

[39] RMM, Nigeria boxes, file 249/8, Director of Taylor Challen Limited to the Mint, 24 July 1962; James's reply, 10 August 1962.

[40] *81st Annual Report, 1950* (HMSO, 1953), p. 6; *84th Annual Report, 1953*, p. 201.

[41] RMM, Nigeria boxes, file 249/8, minute by C. Hewertson, 8 August 1962.

[42] Until 1958 it was called Thomas De La Rue & Company, Limited.

[43] Peter Pugh, *The Highest Perfection: A History of De La Rue* (Icon Books, London, 2011), pp. 179–80.

quite straight'.[44] This is the only indication in the sources of payments to secure contracts in relation to currency matters, although it suggests that backhanders may not have been uncommon in this sector, as also in others, if not paid by the Mint itself.[45] De La Rue would hold 40 per cent of the shares in the new printing company, the Federal government 55 per cent and the Central Bank of Nigeria 5 per cent, an arrangement similar to one De La Rue had signed with the government of Pakistan. Although provision was made for an eventual buy out of De La Rue's share, a ten-year technical advisory contract gave De La Rue extensive powers, including the right to appoint a managing director for the duration of this period. Construction of the new facility began in 1964 at an estimated total cost of £1.5 million; a Colonial Development Corporation loan contributed £0.5 million. Trading under the name Nigerian Security Printing and Minting Company Ltd., the mint made Nigeria the only country in Africa with complete facilities for printing bank notes and other security documents such as Treasury Bills, cheques and stamps. The Nigerian government hoped that this might enable it to obtain contracts to produce security documents and notes for other countries.[46]

When the new facility began operation the Nigerian government took the Mint up on its offer of technical assistance, hoping to secure the services of its technicians for six- or twelve-month periods.[47] Since the Mint continued to produce coins for Nigeria until 1965, and thereafter on an occasional basis, this investment was probably worthwhile for the Royal Mint, although the Mint's association with De La Rue from the mid-1960s, discussed later in this chapter, was probably of greater value in ensuring that Nigeria remained a customer. From 1965 the Mint also began producing the blanks ready for striking in the Nigerian Mint together with the dies, steel tools used for striking images on the obverse and reverse sides of the coin) and collars (that held the blank in place, and which determined the size of the coin when, under the pressure of the striking process, the metal flowed outwards); thirty years later it was still supplying the Nigerian mint with blanks, dies and collars, although for a few years in the 1980s it lost this business to a competitor.[48] Indeed, despite the pessimism

[44] RMM, Nigeria boxes, file 249/9, J. James to Festus, 10 August 1962; and J. S. Sadler to K. Taylor (BoT), 5 March 1963. De La Rue took over one of these other firms, Bradbury, Wlkinson and Co., in 1986.

[45] As I showed in *Business of Decolonization*; see also for the early postcolonial period, esp., Dimier, *Invention*, p. 74.

[46] BoE, OV 68/10, W. B. J. Dobbs to J. M. Reilly (BoT), 20 May 1963; OV 68/11, no. 29 A, D. L. S. Coombes to Reilly, 28 April 1965.

[47] RMM, Nigeria boxes, file 249/4/2, 'Nigeria', note by J. E. Lucas addressed to A. R. Fisher, 26 November 1970. Fisher was Superintendent of the Operative Department at the Mint.

[48] Ibid., from various files in Nigeria boxes, 'Nigeria 1/2d. Coinage dies and collar', 9 September 1965; 'Coins struck at Mints in the United Kingdom for Nigeria, 1959 to 1966'; copies of order forms in Nigerian boxes; 'A Report on the visit of Mr E. E. Sideso, Director of Currency, Nigerian Security Printing and Minting Company Ltd., at Llantrisant, 2 September 1988'.

that the news of the Nigerian plans had provoked in London, the Nigerian Mint proved unable to meet the country's need for coin, and it remained reliant on the importation of supplementary coins. Other African central banks which needed to be sure that their supplier could deliver on schedule and also meet the security needs of their coinage preferred not to purchase from it. That Ghana or other countries would follow suit was also unlikely on any other than prestige grounds given the high and recurrent costs both of running a mint and of remaining abreast of technological advances, not to mention the very problem which made the Royal Mint value its own external business: that of maintaining production during periods of low domestic demand.

If the creation of a Nigerian Mint appeared as a potential obstacle to the Mint's plans, over the course of the next few years the Mint went on to acquire the business for producing new coinages for most former British colonies in Africa and elsewhere. These included new coinages for Sierra Leone and for the Gambia when in 1966 it became the last of the British West African colonies to abandon the coinage of the West African Currency Board.[49] After plans fell through for a possible regional federation in East Africa (which had seen the Mint involved in discussions about a possible common East African currency to be issued by a regional central bank),[50] the Mint was tasked instead with producing coins for each of the three East African countries. Orders were placed at the Mint via the Crown Agents for 34 million coins in five different denominations for the Kenyan government[51]; for 174 million coins for Tanzania in four different denominations, and for Uganda in six denominations.[52] At much the same time the Mint also secured contracts to produce coins for Malawi and Zambia after the dissolution of the Central African Federation and the consequent demise of the common Central African currency first issued in the 1950s. Only Rhodesia – to the relief of staff at the Mint – did not become a customer, turning instead to South Africa to source its coins following its illegal unilateral declaration of independence. In the 1980s after the overthrow of white minority rule the Mint began producing for Zimbabwe.[53]

Securing an initial order with new states gave the Mint future advantage over other mints. Once a coinage had been issued, the Mint held on behalf of the customer the master tools and dies to be used in the production of additional coins; new states were effectively tied to the Mint for repeat orders of either additional or replacement coin until the introduction of an entirely new coinage. Moreover, where changes were made to designs, they tended to be incremental rather than comprehensive, with countries retaining elements of the

[49] 97th Annual Report, 1966 (HMSO, 1967), p. 4.
[50] TNA, MINT, 20/2978, H. R. Hirst, secretary to the EACB, to J. James, 26 February 1964.
[51] TNA, MINT, 20/3036, Crown Agents to Mint, 15 September 1965.
[52] 97th Annual Report 1966, pp. 2–4.
[53] RMM, Zimbabwe boxes.

original style. For example, when in 1967 Ghana issued a new decimal coinage and removed Nkrumah's image from the obverse of its coins, the government chose to retain the distinctive five-point star on the reverse. Such continuity acknowledged the fact that societies have confidence in familiar coins, and that establishing trust in new currencies especially in rapidly changing societies could be difficult. Even feel and weight could be significant, and since these could vary between the products of different mints, it may have predisposed overseas central banks to continue to purchase new coins from established sources.

The Mint had, then, an inbuilt advantage in securing repeat orders. Further, in the 1960s and 1970s new orders were received not just for additional and replacement coin, but as a consequence of the turbulent political and economic history of postcolonial African states. Regime change, devaluation and changes to currency systems all led to sudden and frequent adjustments in currency requirements. Ultimately some of these factors were to work to the Mint's disadvantage as run-away inflation transformed some societies into note-only economies. But in the 1960s they brought new, if erratic and unpredictable, orders to the Mint's door.[54] The Mint's approach was determinedly commercial, managing whatever opportunities came its way in a fashion that decades earlier had led Winston Churchill, then Chancellor of the Exchequer, to lambast James's predecessor, Johnson, as too 'commercially minded' when in 1924 the Mint began producing coins for the Soviet Union.[55] The same political detachment was evident in the mid-1970s when the Mint was advised by the FCO that, in view of the current suspension of diplomatic relations between Britain and Uganda, the Mint might supply coins on a commercial basis to the country but should not openly publicize its dealings there by marketing coins on Uganda's behalf.[56]

Other contracts related to the Mint's production of commemorative coin and medals. Some countries, including Ghana, Nigeria and Sierra Leone, commissioned commemorative medals to be issued at their independence: a transaction that seems a particularly striking illustration of the ambiguities of the transition to independence by former British colonies. Further coins were requested to mark significant anniversaries, such as those commissioned by the government of Sierra Leone in 1966 on the occasion of the fifth anniversary of independence,[57] as well as to commemorate other notable transitions and dates. The Ghanaian government placed orders for commemorative coins to mark Republic Day in 1960 (Figure 5.3a and b) and the Conference for the

---

[54] *98th Annual Report, 1967* (HMSO, 1968), p. 1.
[55] Cited in Dyer and Gaspar, 'Reform', p. 564, note 278.
[56] RMM, Uganda box, file 3/377/8, note, G. J. Watkins, 20 September 1976.
[57] *97th Annual Report, 1966*, p. 4.

(a)   (b)

Figure 5.3. The reverse (a) and obverse (b) of the two pound Ghanaian coin issued
in 1960 to commemorate Republic Day

Organization of African Unity in 1965; the Malawian government did the same
in 1966 on the first anniversary of its transition to republican status,[58] as did
the Irish government to mark the fiftieth anniversary of the Easter Rising.[59]
Producing what were often small orders at short notice could be challenging
for the Mint, but, for this one domestic institution, commemorating the demise
of British colonialism brought good business.

Beyond British Africa, the Mint also received the contract to produce a coinage for independent Cyprus as well as for the South Arabian Federation.[60] The
secession of colonies from the old British Caribbean Currency Board led to
orders for coins for Trinidad and Tobago and Guyana,[61] and in the later 1960s,
there were new orders for Malaysia to replace the Malayan currency, as well as
from Singapore, Brunei, Western Samoa and Somalia.

The Mint sought additional opportunities in the colonies of other European
empires. Although the Mint had in the past produced coins for non-British
dependencies, as it did for French West Africa during the Second World War,[62]
the French withdrawal from all their sub-Saharan African colonies in 1960
transformed the African political landscape, and raised the prospect that the
Mint might again produce coins for the region. Most former French colonies retained strong links to metropolitan France, not only joining the French
Community formed by De Gaulle in 1958, but also as members of the CFA
franc zone created after the war and of a regional central bank formed under
French management, the Banque Centrale des États de l'Afrique de l'Ouest. In
January 1961, however, the Mint learned of a rumour that the former French
colonies of Guinea (which declined to remain in the CFA franc zone) and Mali
(which left the CFA zone after only a short period) were likely to establish
their own central banks, and might soon be introducing their own currencies.

[58] See correspondence in MINT 20/3104; *97th Annual Report, 1966* (HMSO, 1967), p. 14.
[59] *97th Annual Report, 1966*, p. 5.
[60] See papers in TNA, MINT 20/3103.
[61] *97th Annual Report, 1966*, pp. 2–4.
[62] RMM, French West Africa box, letter G. P. Dyer to Mr Michel Martière, 1 April 1996 (in
response to an enquiry).

The head of the Mint's General Section, Alan Dowling, a close colleague of James, advocated an approach anticipating that adopted shortly after in response to the Nigerian Mint project: 'In cases like these ... I think it will be less a matter of asking for information than of offering in the first instance the advice and help of the Royal Mint in all the problems involved'.[63] Guinea, which in 1958 had entered into a loose regional union with Ghana, looked most promising.[64] Guinea already had its own currency, but its authorities were unhappy with the quality of coins produced in eastern Europe, and, with De La Rue acting as agents in secret negotiations, the Banque de la République de Guinée placed an order with the Mint in 1962.[65] The Mint later produced coins for some other former French colonies, but at least for the time being the opportunities in relation to Francophone states were limited by the strong association most retained to France. Former Portuguese colonies, which won their independence from Portugal in the mid-1970s, presented further opportunities, especially in view of the strength of British interests in Lusophone Africa. The Mint won initial contracts for the production of coin for Mozambique, although it appears that this currency was never circulated.[66] In the early 1960s the Mint also picked up orders to produce coins for the Philippines when the US Mint was unable to do so, and for Ethiopia,[67] while continuing to attract other foreign orders, especially in Central and South America and the Middle East.

By 1966, when it received the Queen's Award for Industry for Export Achievement, the Mint's production had grown enormously, a consequence above all of its great success in securing orders from emergent Commonwealth states. Between 1956 and 1966 – a decade which saw the independence of numerous new African states – production rose from 500 million to 1,400 million coins per annum as Table 5.1 shows. Whereas in the decade 1948–58 annual exports had averaged 300 million pieces, they rose to 800 million in the following decade, peaking in 1967 at more than 1,500 million coin with an invoice value of £6.5 million. The Mint was now devoting more of its capacity to export than any other world mint, and its share of the available overseas coinage market had reached over 80 per cent, supplying fifty of the sixty counties calculated regularly to import coin.[68]

[63] Ibid., A. J. Dowling to A. R. Everett, BoT, 24 January 1961.
[64] Mali joined the union in 1960. The states aimed eventually at a currency union but in the event the regional grouping proved short-lived.
[65] RMM, French West Africa box, correspondence between the Mint and the Banque, May 1961; 93rd Annual Report, 1962 (HMSO, 1963), p. 3.
[66] It appears the issue was produced in secret in view of the delicacy of the situation in Portugal. Bank of England files make no mention of this issue although they do refer to De La Rue's contract in Mozambique. See Stockwell, 'Exporting Britishness', pp. 166–7.
[67] 95th Annual Report, 1964, p. 3.
[68] Fifth Report from the Estimates Committee, 1967–8. The Royal Mint, PP 1967–8, IX (Cmnd. 364), paras. 27–8; ibid., Minutes of Evidence taken before Sub-Committee D of the Estimates Committee, para. 51.

Table 5.1. *Total annual Royal Mint coin production for export, 1954–69*[a]

Year	Total annual Mint production (in millions)	Production for overseas (in millions)	Production for overseas subcontracted to Birmingham Mints (in millions)	Total coins produced for overseas at either Mint or in Birmingham (in millions)
1954	506.2	251.6	Not specified	251.6
1955	505.5	207.6	Not specified	207.6
1956	499.5	159.5	Not specified	159.5
1957	507.7	208	Not specified	208
1958	593.2	293.7	88	381.7
1959	709.6	465.5	89.4	554.9
1960	707.2	401.7	158.8	560.5
1961	836.3	538	213.7	715.7
1962	774.6	282	157.2	439.2
1963	796.5	296.2	102.3	398.5
1964	1,044.6	603.4	282	885.4
1965	1,258	757.1	458.6	1,215.7
1966	1,400.4	774.4	615.4	1,389.8
1967	1,366.7	925.3	593.2	1,518.5
1968	1,357	456.2	328.3	784.5
1969	2,685.5	310.7	257.4	568.1

[a]Constructed from information in *Annual Reports*. Figures rounded to the nearest 100,000.

The Mint was not keen to advertise to its competitors (or the Birmingham mints to which it subcontracted some overseas production) the degree of profit obtained from these sales. Instead, in its trading accounts and in estimates submitted as a minor department of state to Parliament, it made no distinction between its production of UK coin and coin for export.[69] In 1968, probably in response to a request from the parliamentary estimates committee that the Mint might introduce greater financial transparency, the Mint experimented with producing 'alternative' accounts that provided more detail of profits from its commercial business, the source for Table 5.2. However, although the Mint charged a percentage of overheads to overseas customers (in line with loose instructions provided by the Treasury in 1930), the fraction arrived at was notional rather than real, because the overheads entailed for the Mint in running its establishment were constant regardless of how much coin it

[69] Ibid., paras. 5–6.

Table 5.2. *Profits on the Royal Mint's Commercial Account, 1963–4 to 1967–8*[a]

Financial Year	Profits from 'Commercial Account'
1963–4	£149,903
1964–5	£474,021
1965–6	£661,572
1966–7	£702,233
1967–8	£638,959 (subsequently revised downwards to £531,984)

[a]From MINT 20/3782, 'Alternative form of accounts'. Whether the 'Commercial Account' includes any returns from commercial sales of UK products is unclear, but the source implies that it refers solely to overseas business.

produced for overseas customers. The accounts are not therefore necessarily a 'true' reflection of costs and profits of the Mint's overseas business.[70] Nonetheless, Table 5.2 reveals that between the financial years 1963–4 and 1967–8 the Mint's export success brought significant returns. In 1967–8 the Mint's gross return from commercial sales of coins, medals and dies was £5,964,769; its costs of production on this trade were calculated at £4,888,030 and of overseas distribution at £437,780. This means that in 1967–8 the Mint made a profit on its commercial sales of some £531,984. Although this sum was small in comparison to seignorage earned on the production of coin for domestic use (which in the same year was about £7.32 million), the Mint regarded seignorage not as 'profit' but as in effect an 'extended loan to the state' from the public, generally sufficient to cover the costs of running the Mint, while generating a surplus for the Treasury.[71] To secure its return on its commercial account the Mint aimed to charge its overseas customers profit on manufacture of 30 per cent to yield an actual profit of 15 per cent. In practice the returns fluctuated, although they generally increased in the early to mid-1960s, with the rate of return on capital calculated within the Mint as rising from 9 per cent in 1962–3 to 17 per cent in 1963–4, 16 per cent in 1964–5, before reaching a very healthy 22 per cent in 1965–6.[72] In all between 1964–5 and 1967–8 annual

[70] Ibid.; TNA, MINT 20/3242, extract of Treasury letter, 3 March 1930.
[71] *Fifth Report*, para. 10; ibid., Minutes of Evidence taken before Sub-Committee D of the Estimates Committee, paras. 299–321, evidence of Mr James, Mr Dowling, Mr Howell and Mr Kitcatt. The Mint also had an obligation to buy back coin from UK clearing banks as well as supply coin to them, although where the value of coin appreciated beyond face value as a result of an increase in metal prices, the Mint could also profit on the recovery of metal from coin taken out of circulation and returned by British clearing banks: ibid.; evidence of Mr B. C. Sharp, Chief Accountant, Barclays Bank Ltd.
[72] TNA, MINT 20/3879, analysis done in 1967 in response to US competition; 'Pricing Policy Taking into Account Estimated Commercial Costs in 1968–9', G. F. Howell, finance branch, RM, 12 November 1968.

'profits' on the Mint's home and overseas activities, payable to the Exchequer, averaged £11 million. Such was the strong state of the Mint's finances that for more than thirty years it received no subvention from the state; a situation that only changed in 1968–9 when it was voted nearly £6.5 million in order to prepare for decimalization in the United Kingdom.[73]

This commercial success, in which African decolonization played a critical part, rendered the Mint's position within Whitehall increasingly anomalous, and led the parliamentary estimates committee to recommend that the Mint's status be reconsidered.[74] In 1975 following the recommendations of the Mallabar Committee on government industrial establishments and the introduction of the Government Trading Funds Act of 1973, the Royal Mint became only the second government department or agency after the Royal Ordnance Factories to start operating as a 'trading fund'.[75] Designed to facilitate commercial activities by government establishments, this change of status enabled the Mint to retain its trading income to cover its own expenditure, and released it from the 'supply estimates' process, by which Parliament approves the allocation of funds to government departments.[76] Further refinements to its legal position followed, and since 2010, the Mint has operated as the Royal Mint Ltd., a company wholly owned by the Treasury.[77]

'Novel Efforts and Competitive Strokes'

How did the Royal Mint succeed in capturing such an enormous slice of new Commonwealth, as well as other foreign, business? As we have seen, the Mint sometimes struggled to keep on top of developments in new states, and feared that newly independent countries might look to other world mints to meet their coinage needs. In practice, however, most did not initially seek to assert their independence in this way, and instead drew on established connections to Britain. Although this reflects an on-going imbalance in power, and, as discussed below, the continued presence of British officials and others in former colonies, it was also a consequence of the leadership of the two deputy masters at the Mint at the time: Sir Lionel Thompson (1950–7) and, especially the dynamic Jack James. Thompson and James acted on their own initiative

---

[73] *Fifth Report*, para. 10.
[74] However, the issue was already under consideration by a sub-committee appointed to report to the Chancellor on the Mint's relationship to the Treasury: ibid., paras. 7–8, Appendices to the Minutes of Evidence taken before the Sub-Committee D of the Estimates Committee, appendix 2, para. 2c.
[75] Challis, 'A new beginning'. p. 669.
[76] *Guide to the Establishment and Operation of Trading Funds* (HM Treasury, 2004), accessed online at: webarchive.nationalarchives.gov.uk, 21 December 2016.
[77] *Annual Report 2015–16*, p. 7, available at https://www.royalmint.com/globalassets/the-royal-mint/pdf/annual-reports/ar_2015_2016.pdf, accessed 6 September 2016.

rather than at the direction of the Treasury: although the Chancellor had been *ex-officio* Master of the Mint since 1870, and the Treasury appointed senior officials to posts at the Mint, it treated the Mint like any other department and had no insider role.[78] Both men were proactive in securing business and lobbying government departments for help. Their hard-nosed commercial approach resembled that of longstanding interwar Deputy Master, Sir Robert Johnson, who had been instrumental in seeking out overseas business, including some in new states that emerged after the First World War. While neither Thompson nor James had been in the Mint during Johnson's period, his long incumbency had shaped its culture: for example, Harry Stride, instrumental in securing the Ghanaian order, and very much Thompson's 'right-hand man', had joined the Mint in 1920, rising to the position of chief clerk.[79] Historians of the Mint regard James as the more significant of the two post-war deputy masters: Challis locates a transformation from 'the passive to the active' in the Mint's approach under his leadership.[80] James himself played up his reputation in a series of discursive and historically minded contributions to the Mint's annual reports. If Thompson's vigorous campaign to obtain the Ghanaian order belies Challis's description of the Mint under his stewardship as 'passive', it is nevertheless clear that James in particular, recalled as dynamic and influential,[81] was willing to innovate across different fields. He was also not shy of courting controversy, canvassing, for instance, the introduction of a plastic coinage in one of his annual reports.[82] It was under James management that in 1960 the Mint was represented at a large overseas exhibition when it participated in the British Exhibition in New York, an illustration of his commercial approach. As we have seen, under James the Mint was also prepared to produce prototype coins before orders had been placed.

Perhaps most importantly James determined that the Mint should never decline an order on grounds of capacity. His approach contrasts with that of the US Mint, which for a few years from 1964 retreated from exporting coin to focus solely on a domestic recoinage. James recognized that the particular nature of the sector made securing the first contract crucial, and under his leadership the Mint refused very few orders even where these were likely to yield little profit. In 1967, for instance, the Mint accepted a low-value order for commemorative proof sets from Kenya, since it was keen not to 'offend' 'an important customer'.[83] Yet at the same time the Mint had an overriding com-

[78] *Fifth Report*, para. 3; ibid., Minutes of Evidence taken before Sub-Committee D of the Estimates Committee, paras. 136–9.
[79] Interview, Dyer.
[80] Challis, 'A New Beginning', quotation p. 663.
[81] Interview, Dyer.
[82] *90th Annual Report 1959*, p. 9.
[83] RMM, Kenya boxes, File 203/7, minute on file (1967).

mitment to first meet its obligations for the domestic market. Manufacturing the enormous Nigerian coinage while also delivering on the Mint's other commitments was particularly challenging.[84] To reconcile these sometimes conflicting imperatives James took steps to increase production that set the Mint up for on-going development. The claim that African decolonization was 'transformative' for the Mint rests not just on the Mint's success in acquiring new African business, but on the changes to institutional practice and culture that were adopted to enable it to do so. Some of the 'innovations' discussed here had been tried before, but they were implemented on a greater and more continuous scale, and older, self-imposed, ideas about the limits to the Mint's operational capacity were discarded. Thus, whereas in 1951 the Mint had regarded 500 million coins as the maximum it could produce annually,[85] in 1958 James determined that the Mint should aim to increase its output to 800 million coins per annum, far exceeding its previous production.[86] In 1959 the quantity of overseas coins produced was greater than in any previous year, with about one third destined for Nigeria.[87]

The most important means open to the Mint of exceeding capacity was through the subcontraction of business to two private mints in Birmingham: the Mint, Birmingham, Ltd., and Imperial Metal Industries (Kynoch) Ltd., a subsidiary of Imperial Chemical Industries. Some export manufacturing (including the production of coin in the early 1950s for the African currency boards) had already been outsourced to these mints, but subcontracting now became more routine and extensive. By the early 1960s in order to meet overseas orders where governments 'expected delivery the day before yesterday and on the nail', a significant part of total production was subcontracted.[88] In 1966 the Birmingham Mints produced 615 million coin on top of the 1,400 million struck within the Mint itself, all of which were destined for export since British coin had not been struck under subcontract since 1919. The private mints had come to depend on the Mint's custom.[89] Although outsourcing probably reduced the Mint's own margins,[90] the practice enabled the Mint to meet growing overseas demand while continuing to fulfil its domestic obligations.

The Mint retained some control over its subcontractors, supplying dies to the private mints and conducting inspections. However, when the Mint was forced to subcontract to meet the order for the new Ghanaian currency, it was keen

---

[84] TNA, MINT 20/2774, J. James to A. N. Galsworthy, 24 April 1958.
[85] *95th Annual Report, 1964*, p. 5.
[86] *89th Annual Report, 1958* (HMSO, 1959), p. 4.
[87] *90th Annual Report, 1959*.
[88] *Fifth Report*, Minutes of Evidence taken before Sub-Committee D of the Estimates Committee, Evidence by Mr James, Mr Dowling and Mr Knight, para. 26.
[89] Ibid., para. 34; *97th Annual Report, 1966*, p. 1.
[90] Implicit in the evidence given by James and Mr Dowling: *Fifth Report*, para. 3; ibid., Minutes of Evidence taken before Sub-Committee D of the Estimates Committee, paras. 492–7.

not to advertise the fact to its new African client, perhaps because it feared that the government might perceive the products as inferior, or because this undermined their own singular claims to expertise.[91] The Mint's desire to keep outsourcing secret from its African customer may also reflect problems experienced the year before with coins produced by Imperial Metal Industries for Malaya and Borneo, with what the Mint worried might be possible detrimental consequences for its own reputation.[92]

In 1958 faced with an order for 240 million coins for Ghana and 1,000 million for Nigeria, the Mint also introduced a night shift, although not an entirely novel departure, to meet the new Nigerian order.[93] The night shift became common practice thereafter and crucial to the massive expansion in the Mint's business that occurred on James's watch. Alongside the subcontracting and the use of nightshifts the Mint's staff doubled in size, rising from 736 at the end of 1958 to 1,858 in 1969.[94] Additionally the Mint purchased more presses and replaced older machinery with faster models.[95] It engaged in constant technical innovation to ensure that its operation was as effective as possible, exploring new technologies, for example the introduction of powder metallurgy and semi-continuous casting.[96] With these innovations the Mint aimed to meet the exacting demands of banks in emergent states, which frequently sought currency to very tight schedules. In 1966, for example, it quoted a timetable of between 8 and 14 weeks (the difference depending on the individual coin) from design to delivery to the Bank of Zambia when the latter sought currency urgently.[97]

The manufacture of entirely new coinages posed particular challenges, entailing the preparation of new designs. Each denomination had to be easily distinguishable from another, as well as from coins already in circulation, and not permit easy counterfeiting. The design had to lend itself to the reducing process and be suitable for small coins, and be of even depth. The Mint needed also to keep the production cost below the face value of the coin, and this could be tricky in relation to the low denomination of some overseas coins.

The Mint was prepared to adapt its practices to try to ensure the best results on the design front too. Since the nineteenth century hand engraving of original coinage tools had been replaced by a 'reducing machine'. This was used to prepare 'punches' of coin size in different denominations from a nickel-faced

---

[91] TNA, MINT 20/2802 and MINT 20/2775, esp. H. G. Stride to W. F. Brazener (The Mint Birmingham), 3 March 1958.

[92] TNA, MINT 20/2300, J. James to A. V. Iliffe, 10 December 1957.

[93] *90th Annual Report, 1959.*

[94] *89th Annual Report, 1959*, p. 13; *100th Annual Report, 1969.*

[95] *Fifth Report*, para. 55.

[96] *95th Annual Report, 1964*, p. 7.

[97] TNA, MINT 20/3106, 'Zambia', memo from G. M. Fletcher to Superintendent (Mint), 18 July 1966. It appears that the delivery was subsequently delayed.

copper electrotype produced from a plaster cast of approximately 8 inches diameter prepared by the artist. Under the artist's supervision the Mint's crafts-men formed matrices, working punches and dies for the different denomina-tions. Use of this technique was essential to production in the modern era, but had long attracted criticism that it resulted in less pleasing an appearance than older, more laborious methods. In response the Mint sought to re-engage designers in the production process in order to 'bridge' the design and manu-facturing phases. An early deployment of the reformed methods came in the creation of a new image of President Nkrumah on the commemorative coin introduced to mark Republic Day; James hoped that it restored some of the high standards associated with the older technologies.[98]

In 1964, when gross earnings on overseas exports amounted to £2.5 million, Jack James allowed himself a metaphorical clap on the back, striking a self-congratulatory note in his annual report. 'It is not easy', he wrote, 'for a minor department of the State to move purposefully from the very shallow end of occasional production for tied or suppliant clients into new techniques in deeper waters, needing novel efforts and competitive strokes'. 'Apart', he added 'from our traditional inertia, civil servants (not necessarily confined to the Mint) even today often find it more politic to curb rather than to spur and the systems of control to which they are accustomed and pay homage do not stimulate transitions to adventure. There are no profit motives and encourage-ment is hard to come by'. Yet he claimed the 'Mint has managed so far to capture about two thirds of the available overseas trade'.[99]

James here suggested that the Mint's success was in spite of rather than *because* of its position as 'a minor department of state', a parastatal, com-mercial organization, of a kind that, like the paper and metallic currency and security products market, has hitherto attracted little attention from historians. Studies of British business and decolonization show British firms could not rely on the unconditional support of either colonial authorities or the British government, since national strategic and financial interests sometimes eclipsed the importance for the state of narrower concerns of particular companies in particular locations or sectors.[100] As the episode of the Nigerian mint shows, the Mint too found that its agenda was not necessarily shared by officials, even at the Treasury. Within some limits, however, it is apparent that the Mint enjoyed advantages in new Commonwealth states that other suppliers of coin did not. James himself suggested that overseas ministries and central banks probably preferred to deal with a government organization 'whose image is

---

[98] *91st Annual Report, 1960*, p. 16.
[99] *95th Annual Report, 1964*, p. 7.
[100] Stockwell, *Business of Decolonization*; White, *Business, Government and the End of Empire*.

primarily of public service and non-commercial'.[101] From his experience, De La Rue's managing director believed that it was the 'Royal' imprimatur that was especially important: there was a 'certain mystique in attaching it to the Crown' in the eyes of the 'average foreigner', making the Mint's name of unique value to the brand.[102]

Most obviously, however, the Mint was a Whitehall insider. The Mint recruited its staff through the same channels as other home civil servants. Before James (who came to the position from the Admiralty), deputy masters were generally appointed to the Mint from the Treasury. Some of the familial and social connections which Peter Cain and A. G. Hopkins argue produced an affinity of interests between Britain's 'gentlemanly capitalists' and Whitehall and Westminster were amplified in the case of the Mint.[103] Crucially, in securing orders the Mint was exceptionally well placed to draw on a range of contacts within Whitehall and the Crown Agents, and through these, within colonial administrations and, in new Commonwealth states, British high commissions. Common language and culture shaped tendering processes in relation to business opportunities in new African states where European officials still had a role, as Véronique Dimier demonstrates was the case with the European Commission's award of contracts for development projects in Africa.[104]

More than their links to Whitehall, the Mint's connections to the Bank of England and the security note manufacturer De La Rue were especially useful. The Mint was able to exploit their networks, receiving early information about likely currency requirements before central banks or finance ministries put these out to open tender. The Bank of England was most valuable in the 1950s and early 1960s when the Mint was able to benefit from the Bank's own attempts to spread influence among new central banks in decolonizing states. As noted earlier, the Bank of England arranged a visit to the Mint for participants on its central banking course until the Mint's relocation to Llantrisant made this impractical.[105] Of greatest value was the expanding diaspora of Bank of England men in former British colonies both as advisors and filling senior positions in central banks. If the Mint's experience in the case of the Nigerian mint shows that these officials might not always act in the Mint's interests, they were nevertheless often instrumental in directing business to the Mint.

[101] *Fifth Report*, paras. 7–8, Appendices to the Minutes of Evidence taken before Sub-Committee D of the Estimates Committee, Appendix 2, para. 2c. De la Rue's Managing Director disagreed: Minutes of Evidence taken before the Sub-Committee D of the Estimates Committee, paras. 357–60.

[102] Ibid., Evidence given by P. F. Orchard, Managing Director, De La Rue: ibid., para. 3; ibid., Minutes of Evidence taken before Sub-Committee D of the Estimates Committee, paras. 333–74, esp. 357–61.

[103] Cain and Hopkins, *British Imperialism*.

[104] Dimier, *Invention*, ch. 4, esp. p. 614.

[105] BoE, OV 21/26, 'Report on Central Banking Course 1969', R. P. Edgley.

Most significant was John Loynes. It was Loynes who in March 1958 was the source of intelligence that Nigerian ministers were considering placing orders with another mint.[106] Four years later advanced notice of Loynes' recommendations about new currency for Sierra Leone and the Gambia enabled the Mint, worried that it might face 'severe competition', to be proactive in its efforts to secure the orders. Mindful that newly independent states tended to be 'suspicious of approaches through diplomatic channels', the Mint approached the Sierra Leonean Minister of Finance directly, emphasizing its long involvement in producing West African currency. The Mint commissioned an artist to produce a selection of possible coin designs before it had received any formal instruction from the government of Sierra Leone and then proceeded to despatch these to the country where their favourable response helped ensure the Mint won the contract.[107] Loynes' attitude towards a tendering opportunity in East Africa is instructive of his approach even though it relates to a new East African note (to be issued by the EACB). Sensitive to the possible political repercussions of being seen to favour British interests, he briefly wondered whether it might be politic to ask the Crown Agents to open the tendering to foreign note printers. But being 'not anxious for the order to go outside' Britain, he decided against the move, preparing instead 'our excuse' in the event of complaints being made to African ministers.[108] It is not surprising that back in London James perceived Loynes as important, affording him 'red carpet' treatment on a visit to the Mint in the 1960s.[109]

By the mid-1960s it was De La Rue that had become most useful to the Mint. The two institutions already had an established record of collaboration. Between about 1950 and 1962 De La Rue had been instrumental in helping the Mint secure orders to the sum of about £1.9 million in foreign states for which De La Rue had received 'agency fees'.[110] The majority of these countries were in South America. Here the assistance of De La Rue's 'man in Latin America', John Innes, fluent in Spanish and Portuguese, who would 'bore the backside off the customer' until he secured orders, contributed to the Mint's export success in the early post-war era. The company was quick to exploit opportunities in other regions, including in Africa, with its staff busy 'chasing' key figures in states about to become independent. However, in the early 1960s, the relationship between the two institutions suffered when De

[106] TNA, MINT 20/2774, J. Fisher (BoE) to J. James (communicating Loynes observations), 18 March 1958; James to Fisher, 18 March 1958.
[107] TNA MINT 20/3067, various correspondence, but esp. G. Hewertson (Mint) to R. C. Barnes, 9 February 1961; Mint to M. S. Mustapha (Minister of Finance, Sierra Leone), 27 April 1962; and A. J. Dowling (Mint) to M. G. Rizzello (artist), 15 February 1963.
[108] BoE, OV 7/103, minute by J. Loynes, 9 October 1962.
[109] Interview, Dyer.
[110] TNA, MINT 20/3468, J. James to A. J. Platt (Treasury), 31 January 1962; C. Hewertson to A. J. Platt, 14 February 1962.

La Rue branched into coin supply itself, purchasing them from whichever mint, including non-British ones, that would manufacture at the best price.[111] When the Mint's former chief clerk, Harry Stride, who had been instrumental in securing the first Ghanaian order, was poached by De La Rue to lead a new department concerned with the sale of minting machinery and possibly even coin manufacture for export, James feared that the 'special knowledge' Stride had would now be used to enable De La Rue to enter into direct competition with the Mint. James hoped that the Treasury might intervene to stop a move he claimed constituted a 'threat' to employment at the Mint, but the latter saw no objection to Stride's employment with De La Rue.[112] The Mint continued to be suspicious of De La Rue's intentions, fearing, for instance, that in Guinea, where De La Rue had helped the Mint win its order, the company might now either assist the country with the construction of its own mint or try to secure the contract for producing its future coinage itself.[113] The company's extensive holding and role in the creation of the Nigerian Security Printing and Mint Company may also have fuelled these concerns. By 1965, however, De La Rue had abandoned its ambitions of entering into coin manufacture itself and, at its instigation, the two institutions entered into a consortium.[114] De La Rue became procurement agents acting solely for the Mint, serving, in the words of its Managing Director, as the Mint's 'sales department'. In cases where it helped secure orders it sometimes drew up the contracts, and it accepted some liability for the successful delivery of coinage. In return, De La Rue received a commission on such orders on average of 2 per cent. The Mint began from a negotiating position that assumed a commission of 3 per cent, but this was lowered where the Mint had to reduce prices in order to remain sufficiently competitive to secure the order.[115]

From the mid-1960s De La Rue represented the Mint in areas of the world where the latter believed that the company could be useful to them. In 1968 De La Rue estimated this was the case in around forty-five countries; it is unclear how many of these were in Africa, as the Mint continued to deal directly with

[111] Evidence given by P. F. Orchard, Managing Director, De La Rue: *Fifth Report*, para. 3; ibid., Minutes of Evidence taken before Sub-Committee D of the Estimates Committee, paras. 333–74; Pugh, *Highest Perfection*, pp. 175–8; Interview, Dyer.
[112] Stride retired as chief clerk in 1961 and finally left the Mint in 1962: TNA Mint 20/3468, J. James to W. Armstrong, 12 June 1961; A. J. Platt to J. James, 12 February 1962; Interview, Dyer.
[113] RMM, French West Africa box, file 172/4/2, 'Guinea. Coinage Orders, 1963–6', minute by C. Hewertson, 9 May 1963.
[114] Pugh, *Highest Perfection*, p. 201, dates the agreement with the Mint to 1967, but Orchard's evidence to the select committee indicates that it predated this.
[115] The relevant Mint file dealing with this is reported by the TNA as 'lost' so the following comes mostly from evidence given by Orchard to the parliamentary estimates subcommittee: *Fifth Report*, para. 3; ibid., Minutes of Evidence taken before Sub-Committee D of the Estimates Committee, paras. 333–74.

territories where it had either particular historic or other links. Nonetheless, in the postcolonial era, as the Mint's ability to utilize older colonial networks dwindled, De La Rue's overseas resources and contacts in foreign central banks were probably of enhanced importance even in areas where the Mint had established business. The company's managing director and later chairman, Peter Orchard, claimed that De La Rue was in continuous contact with 'all the central banks throughout the world', and had salesman who 'spend their life in aeroplanes' as well as local agents. The latter were carefully selected for their connections 'with the people who matter', such as politicians and those in central banks, rather than their particular commercial expertise. 'In an awful lot of countries', especially developing ones, he noted that there were about twenty 'famous' families – 'the people we want'. Whether there was immediate business available or not, through its peripatetic salesmen the company kept in constant touch with this network of agents to ensure it would always be first on the spot and know not just 'who was who' but who was likely to be the next Minister of Finance or his equivalent. Through this network of contacts the company operated what it described as an 'intelligence service', political as much as commercial.[116] In London favour was curried through regular 'diplomatic dinners' for influential diplomats, businessmen and as 'often as not the Prime Minister and one or two Royals' at which guests were presented with unique, often personalized gifts. From the 1970s the company also began opening manufacturing plants overseas including in Kenya, Malta, Singapore, Hong Kong and Sri Lanka.[117]

These connections could be a valuable asset. This was evident in 1978, when the Royal Canadian Mint, keen to expand into export production, wrote advertising its services to the Nigerian Security Press and Minting Company. Brian Shapcott, managing director of the Nigerian company, alerted De La Rue, which in turn advised the Mint of the potential threat. 'Brian will, of course, do his best to ensure that the Royal Canadian Mint make no progress', De La Rue reassured the Mint. De La Rue advised that in Ghana it would now try to expedite a currency order before the 'Canadians arrive on the scene'.[118] As well as access to the company's extensive sales network, the Company also provided forecasts of demand and market trends for the Mint, helping it anticipate its possible production demands, thereby enabling the Mint also to predict its likely consumption of raw materials, important because of the volatility of metal prices. Between them the Mint, De La Rue and the Bank of England's network of personnel constituted a powerful combination. De La Rue's official

---

[116] Evidence given by Orchard, *Fifth Report*, para. 3; ibid., Minutes of Evidence taken before Sub-Committee D of the Estimates Committee, paras. 333–74.

[117] Pugh, *Highest Perfection*, pp. 4, 216.

[118] TNA, Mint 20/3879, Dennis Paravicini (DLR) to A. R. W. Lotherington, 6 April 1978. Paravicini managed De La Rue's relations with the Mint: Pugh, *Highest Perfection*, photo. 2.19.

historian claims that the relationship with the Mint was not in fact especially profitable for the company, but admits there were exceptions, such as the occasion when De La Rue persuaded an Arab monetary authority led by a Briton to purchase one million gold coins worth £32 million; the authority is unnamed, but was likely the South Arabian Monetary Authority, in which John Loynes was a key figure. The deal brought in £800,000 for the company and 'millions' for the Royal Mint, while the monetary authority also profited since it subsequently capitalized on rocketing gold prices when it sold off coins, the vast majority of which were excess to its requirements.[119]

However, seen from the Mint's perspective the relationship retained its competitive elements. With De La Rue inclined to claim superior knowledge about currency export markets (including in correspondence with the Chancellor), the Mint had in turn to assert its own authority. James was also reluctant to see publicity given to the consortium's arrangements, not only because of the possible criticism it might bring from rival firms, but also because it might lead to De La Rue being seen as the 'principal' in currency matters. A comment – that this might leave De La Rue 'well poised to take over' the Mint's export markets should the Mint's own situation change – indicates that James had suspicions about the note manufacturer's long-term ambitions.[120] In the mid-1970s, when Uganda become an entirely note-based economy, staff within the Mint even attributed this to De La Rue's influence, although the shift must be understood in the context of the country's high inflation.[121] Whatever these initial worries, the collaboration nevertheless endured, and in the financial year 1982–3 the two organizations formed a joint venture company, 'Royal Mint Services Ltd.', to sell the Mint's expertise in producing and supplying coinages internationally.[122]

Both the Bank of England's and De La Rue's connections worked to the Mint's advantage because orders for currencies were handled in the first instance by overseas central banks and within finance ministries. By being first in the door and anticipating a client's needs, sometimes before they had themselves appreciated them (as we saw in the case of Sierra Leone), they

---

[119] Pugh, *Highest Perfection*, p. 201. Pugh doesn't name the Briton either but it seems probable he was from the Bank of England. The story needs, however, to be treated with caution as a source at the Mint Museum comments that an order for 1,000,000 gold coins cannot be located prior to 1976.

[120] TNA, MINT 20/3881, 'The problems of selling in overseas markets – 1967', De La Rue paper sent by Orchard to Chancellor; 'The problems of selling in overseas markets', Mint paper by N. P. Howard in response, 26 October 1967; correspondence between Mint and Chancellor.

[121] RMM, Uganda box, 'Note of a meeting held with the Central Bank of Uganda in Kampala, 27 March 1974', by D. Martin Jones.

[122] Interview, Dyer; Dyer and Gaspar, 'Reform', p. 594; Challis, 'A New Beginning: Llantrisant' in Challis ed., 607–72, esp. 664, and 664, note 1; Eagleton, 'Designing Change', p. 227.

prevented business being put to worldwide tender.[123] Contracts might also be agreed and orders placed before the issues were considered at Cabinet level in overseas states; this caused concern in Ghana in August 1958, when Nkrumah was unhappy that an order for a commemorative coin had already been placed with the Royal Mint and a contract issued before his Cabinet had had a chance to discuss the matter.[124] Personal networks were important in relation to business in which 'trust' was crucial. Purchasing banks had to be confident that the supplier would deliver on schedule, often at short notice, and to a high standard that would minimize the risk of counterfeiting. Between 1966 (when, alongside the Mint, De La Rue also won a Queen's Award for Export) and 1968,[125] De La Rue estimated that it had won export business worth about £7 million for the Mint. By 1968 the two institutions produced about 70 per cent of the world's 'available' paper and metal coinage, respectively, and the collaborative relationship was hailed as having worked 'magnificently' in bringing about 'a united British effort for the export of coin'.[126]

Design and the Cultural Politics of Decolonization

As the Mint gained momentum from African decolonization it might appear inevitable that the resulting accession of economic muscle this represented would have been replicated in cultural terms. The Mint offered its clients a 'complete service' involving design as well as manufacture, commissioning designs from its established circle of freelance artists for review by its advisory committee.[127] In securing orders, the Mint was exporting a form of cultural capital, which derived not just from the Mint's exceptionally long history, its established position in overseas markets and its capacity to deliver on large orders, but also from its expertise in both the technical and the artistic aspects of coin design. For new states, as Harcourt Fuller observes with reference to Ghana, access to international experts and artists might serve to legitimize new regimes 'within the global order of nation-states'.[128]

The Royal Mint Advisory Committee on the Design of Coins, Medals, Seals and Decorations was central to the Mint's claims to expertise and prestige. Its members, who were unpaid, included such luminaries of the British artistic

---

[123] Evidence given by Orchard, *Fifth Report*, para. 3; ibid., Minutes of Evidence taken before Sub-Committee D of the Estimates Committee, paras. 333–74.

[124] PRAAD, ADM 13/1/27, minutes 12 August 1958.

[125] Pugh, *Highest Perfection*, p. 199.

[126] Evidence given by Orchard, *Fifth Report*, para. 3; ibid., Minutes of Evidence taken before Sub-Committee D of the Estimates Committee, paras. 333–74, esp. 371; and TNA, Mint 20/3881, 'The Problem of Selling in Overseas Markets – 1967', De La Rue paper sent by P. F. Orchard to the Chancellor.

[127] *Fifth Report*, Memorandum submitted on behalf of the Chancellor of the Exchequer, para. 53.

[128] Fuller, *Building the Ghanaian Nation-State*, pp. 7, 40–2.

establishment as Sir Kenneth Clark, Sir John Betjeman and Sir Hugh Casson. In 1958 there were fourteen members in total, with Jack James acting as chair and Stride as secretary.[129] Although the Mint claimed to employ local artists where possible, designs were generally solicited for review from a relatively small group of freelance artists with the requisite skill and experience. When more than one artist had been asked to produce initial drawings, the Committee would adjudicate.

The Committee was reconstituted in 1952 when Prince Philip, Duke of Edinburgh, accepted the specially created position of president, undoubtedly enhancing the Committee's already high prestige. With Philip as President, it met generally at St James' Palace. This was the first occasion that an outsider had chaired the committee; his appointment one of a number of initiatives to provide the Duke with meaningful roles following the Queen's accession and his consequent retirement from the navy. Prince Philip continued in the position until 1999 and was far from simply a titular head. Former colleagues comment that he proved an able and engaged chair; he himself regarded his own contribution as principally to get the committee to reach a common viewpoint, although he also sometimes expressed personal views over matters of design.[130] For example, he expressed a personal preference for moving away from the traditional vertical design of coins, with an obvious top and bottom, suggesting that images selected for the first Nigerian currency would lend themselves to a 360-degree treatment.[131] As well as an interest in art (he was an amateur painter), Prince Philip brought to the role first-hand experience of the colonies and dominions both as a young naval officer, and as the Queen's consort and President of the Commonwealth Games. In the years after the Queen's coronation he travelled extensively, sometimes with the Queen (beginning with a six-month tour of the Commonwealth in which the couple took in Uganda as well as the Caribbean, Mediterranean, Australia and Ceylon) and sometimes on his own (as to Tanganyika and Kenya on the occasions of their independence).[132]

The design of coins is a highly technical process, with plenty of opportunities to inscribe meaning and power into what are literally symbols of the government's legal and financial authority. In both the coins produced and the discussions surrounding them we can see some of the cultural politics of imperialism on display. However, where this was the case it was generally not the result of crude cultural assertion, but a more subtle and nuanced phenomenon, reflecting western aesthetic judgements framing a process in

[129] *89th Annual Report, 1958*, p. 13.
[130] HRH the Duke of Edinburgh, 'Foreword', in Clancy ed., *Designing Change*, p. 6.
[131] TNA, MINT 20/2563, Minutes, 137th meeting, RMAC, 20 March 1958; MINT 20/2774, letter from James (surname unclear) (Buckingham Palace) to C. L. Powell (Mint), 28 April 1958.
[132] Murphy, *Monarchy*, pp. 56, 79–84, 120.

which emergent states, as Catherine Eagleton has also recently shown in relation to East African coin, seem to have been able to exercise considerable agency without any significant resistance either from the Mint or its advisory committee.[133]

This was most evidently the case in relation to discussion surrounding the retention of the Queen's effigy on the obverse of new Commonwealth coins. The use of the Queen's image provided visual demonstration that British colonies were entering independence as members of the Commonwealth, although India had ceased to use the royal image on coins and notes after it became a republic.[134] When Ghana became the first African state to elect not to use the Queen's image, proposing instead to portray the country's first prime minister, Kwame Nkrumah (Figure 5.1b), there was some initial dismay in Whitehall at this failure to follow 'Commonwealth practice', before it was recognized that 'Ghana will be master in her own house'.[135] As Harcourt Fuller argues in his account of Ghanaian symbolic nationalism, Kwame Nkrumah was adept at using his position as head of the ruling party to exercise control over potent symbols of the state to reinforce his own authority; but the move was controversial in Ghana among opposition parties who feared it presaged 'first steps towards dictatorship' and was 'discourteous to the Queen'.[136] In defence, Nkrumah argued that in a society with a high level of illiteracy the new coin would provide visual demonstration that the country was 'now really independent'.[137] Ghana, nevertheless, also saw one of the most surprising postcolonial designs: a new £2 coin commissioned in 1958–9 to celebrate an upcoming visit by the Queen which was intended not only to carry a new image of the monarch, but strikingly the phrase 'Queen of Ghana' (Figure 5.4). In the event it was never struck, since the Queen's visit was postponed when she became pregnant, and by the time the visit finally took place Ghana had become a republic.[138] But the model is a curiosity in numismatic as well as political terms since the image of the Queen, by Humphrey Paget was a new one specially commissioned for the occasion.

A majority of other African states opted to follow Ghana's example and to use images of their own leaders rather than the Queen on their new coinages. This followed the precedent of the iconography of postage stamps issued by

---

[133] Eagleton, 'Designing Change'.

[134] TNA, MINT 20/2563, Sir L. Thompson to A. N. Galsworthy, 27 July 1955, enclosing note on the services of the Royal Mint.

[135] J. Chadwick, Commonwealth Relations Office, quoted in Fuller, *Building the Ghanaian Nation-State*, pp. 73–4.

[136] TNA, MINT 20/2633, telegram from Gold Coast parliamentary opposition, 21 February 1957.

[137] Kwame Nkrumah, 'Why the Queen's Head Is Coming Off Our Coins', quoted in Fuller, *Building the Ghanaian Nation-State*, pp. 76–7; see also Fuller, pp. 22, 40–2, 47.

[138] RMM, Ghana Boxes, C5/59, 'Ghana. Commemorative Gold Coins', 21 January 1959; RMAC, minutes, 138th meeting, 22 October 1958; 139th meeting, 12 November 1959.

Figure 5.4. Plaster model with effigy of the Queen by Humphrey Paget for
Ghanaian two pound coin, 1959, commissioned to celebrate the
Queen's planned visit to Ghana

former British African colonies, all of which carried images of new leaders.[139]
British or other European international designers, both from the Mint's stable of regular artists and also new, younger men, were entrusted with captur-
ing the likenesses of the continent's emerging leadership. Because there were
few artists with the requisite skills in portraiture several were responsible for
capturing the likeness of a number of different figures.[140] As indicated earlier,
Paul Vincze (1907–94) produced the first coin portraits of Nkrumah, Hastings
Banda, and Sekou Toure (Guinea). Michael Rizzello (1926–2004), born in
London to Italian parents, created the images of Sir Milton Margai (Sierra
Leone), President Sir Dawda Kairaba Jawara of Gambia, King Sobhuza II
(Swaziland), President W. R. Tolbert Junior (Liberia) and President Mobutu
(Zaire). Christopher Ironside (1913–92) depicted Julius Nyerere (Tanganyika);
Norman Sillman (1921–2013) modelled Jomo Kenyatta (Kenya) and President
Kaunda (Zambia), as well as Kenyatta's successor, Daniel Arap Moi. Generally
the artists worked from photographs. As with British royal portraits, arriving at
images deemed accurate and attractive, and which pleased their subject as well
as meeting with the approval of the Committee and the governments concerned,
could be tricky. Objections from the Malawian government that Vincze's first
attempt to capture Hastings Banda gave 'an impression of harshness' which
his government was keen to avoid nonetheless seems particularly prophetic.[141]
    Nigeria and the Gambia were the two exceptions to this trend away from
retaining the Queen's image (Figure 5.6b). Nigeria was not only more
Anglophile in outlook than some states, but the use of an external monarch

[139] Agbenyega Adedze, 'Commemorating the Chief: The Politics of Postage Stamps in West
Africa', *African Arts* 37 (2004), pp. 68–73.
[140] Unless other sources are indicated, the information in this and subsequent paragraphs comes
from the Royal Mint annual reports; Fred Reinfeld and Burton Hobson, *Catalogue of the
World's Most Popular Coins* (New York, 10th edn., 1979); http://worldcoincatalog.com/
(accessed 11 February 2016); www.worldofcoins.eu (accessed 11 February 2016); www.royal-
mintmuseum.org.uk/history/people/artists/ (accessed 11 February 2016).
[141] TNA, MINT 20/3101, H. Robertson (Sec. to Treasury, Nyasaland) to A. J. Dowling (RM), 6
June 1964.

was a 'neutral' choice in view of the country's strong regional political differences.[142] Uganda, where the complex politics surrounding the monarchical Bugandan 'state within a state' made the selection of a local leader sensitive, opted for a different form of politically neutral image, in this case a coat of arms.[143]

If officials had been dismayed at the decision of the Ghanaian government their position on the general issue changed in line with thinking about republicanism within the new Commonwealth. Since India had become a republic in 1949, a common head of state in the person of the British monarch had ceased to be a unifying factor within the Commonwealth, with the London Declaration establishing a new formula, of the Queen as head of the Commonwealth, to accommodate the change. Some hoped that new states would retain the Queen as head of state, but as Philip Murphy has shown, Whitehall officials soon decided that it was better for royal and British prestige that new states enter independence as republics, after Tanzania had been persuaded to retain the Queen as head of state at independence only to become a republic within a year. It would look bad if new states immediately discarded the British monarch or – as in Kenya – used the British monarchy as a short-term expedient only until alternative arrangements relating to a new office of president could be worked out. Murphy also argues that officials came to believe it better that new African states became republics rather than risk the Queen becoming embroiled in African politics although there was no consensus on this, particularly among Conservative politicians.[144]

Perhaps such ambivalence explains why there is little sign – at least after the initial discussion of Ghana – of any sentimentality among members of the advisory committee around the use of the royal image. Rather it was the prospect that the Queen's image *might* be used that could prove potentially most embarrassing. In 1964, to the Mint's dismay, Rhodesia seemed likely to be the first country to use a portrait by Arnold Machin, the first to be produced since the Coronation.[145] In the immediate aftermath of Rhodesian UDI the Queen's position as head of state remained unresolved, only being finally settled in 1970 when the white minority regime declared itself a republic.[146] Such discussions led to curious situations in which members of the 'Royal' advisory committee, including Prince Philip, engaged in discussion of the aesthetic merits of coin which not only constituted decolonizing statements, but in some cases also republican ones. This was the case when the Duke proposed that the inscription 'Republic Day' on a medallion commemorating

[142] TNA, MINT 20/2563, Minutes, 137th meeting RMAC, 20 March 1958.
[143] Eagleton, 'Designing Change', p. 226.
[144] Murphy, *Monarchy*, pp. 89–94.
[145] Interview, Dyer.
[146] Murphy, *Monarchy*, pp. 103–6.

Ghana's transition to republican status follow the curve of the coin to enhance its appearance;[147] a proposal that was not adopted.

Nonetheless, although it did not overrule choices made by new states, the Advisory Committee might approach the design of new Commonwealth coin from an on-going imperial perspective. During the interwar era it had become common practice that the royal image should be crowned in the case of the colonies, and uncrowned in the case of the United Kingdom and dominions.[148] This practice continued after the Queen's succession: seven coinages (the British, Canadian, Australian, New Zealand, Ceylonese, South African and Southern Rhodesian – and after the creation of the CAF, those circulating in Northern Rhodesia and Nyasaland) bore an uncrowned effigy by Mary Gillick, while twelve colonial coinages carried a common crowned effigy based on a portrait by Cecil Thomas. This division was maintained until the 1960s when a new image was produced based on Machin's portrait approved in 1964 show-ing the Queen wearing a coronet rather than a full crown. The new portrait was adopted in Canada, Australia and New Zealand in the 1960s, and, although some places continued to use the old crowned effigy, the Queen advised that it might be used by any territory that wished to do so.[149] When it came to discuss the new Nigerian coinage the Advisory Committee briefly toyed with alert-ing Nigeria to the availability of alternative images of the monarch. However, although Nigeria was shortly to become independent, the Committee was unanimous in its preference for the crowned effigy 'as used on all colonial coinages'.[150]

On the reverse of coins, depictions of flora and fauna were common, such as the celebrated image of a crocodile that Rizzello produced on the new Gambian coins, the rabbit, ostrich and saltfish on the designs by Ironside for the Tanzanian currency, and the corn, elephant and rooster created by Vincze for the Malawian (Figure 5.5a–c). Lutz Marten and Nancy Kula argue that images of animals and landscapes depicted Africa as 'primeval', its nature 'to be admired, protected, tamed and conquered'.[151] Certainly the images departed from the more tra-ditional heraldic designs of British coins, although coats of arms were used on the reverse of several African coins, including the Malawian half crown (Figure 5.5d).[152] But images of animals can also be seen as modernizing. The Irish coinage, seen as the classic modern coinage, showed a variety of animals, and when in 1936 Edward VIII expressed a desire for his new coinage to be more modern, a series of designs were created of birds and animals which could

[147] RMM, RMAC, minutes, 140th meeting, 17 May 1960, item 9.
[148] See Chapter 1, p. 49.
[149] McLoughlin, 'Crowned and Uncrowned Effigies'.
[150] RMM, RMAC, Minutes, 136th meeting, 16 July 1957.
[151] Marten and Kula, 'Meanings of Money', p. 185.
[152] See also the reverse of the Kenya, the Sierra Leonean, and several of the Ugandan coins.

(a)   (b)   (c)   (d)

Figure 5.5. Images by Paul Vincze on the reverse of the first Malawian coin, 1964

be claimed to have some royal association, although his abdication meant the coins were never issued.[153]

A number of the new national coinages departed only minimally from the older currency board designs. As already indicated, continuity could be regarded as a means of instilling confidence in the currencies. The new Nigerian coinage, incorporating images of groundnuts, cotton plants, cocoa beans and palm trees (Figure 5.6a), designed before independence, was among those that most closely resembled the old colonial currency.[154] Palm trees and products were also depicted on the coins of Sierra Leone and the Gambia, and groundnuts on the Gambian. The British representative on the Sierra Leonean monetary authority objected that 'what would perhaps be the most suitable design for our coins with a local flavour, namely local produce' had 'already been appropriated by Nigeria', and noted that, while palm products were not especially representative of Sierra Leone, local opinion favoured them because they were a link to the WACB coinage.[155] Groundnuts, cotton, cocoa and palm oil were all key commodities in the colonial economies of the region, and their prominence in the coin designs suggests how the new states were conceptualized within the global postcolonial economic order.

Other coins, however, carried a bolder decolonizing message. In the case of Tanzania, which Loynes had anticipated would want to eradicate all outward

<hr/>

[153] *102nd Annual Report*, 1971–2, appendix XVI, G. P. Dyer, 'The Proposed Coinage of King Edward VIII', pp. 80–93; Additional material from RMM, RMAC, minutes 93rd meeting, 27 May 1936.
[154] TNA, MINT 20/2563, RMAC, Minutes 137th meeting, 20 March 1958.
[155] TNA, MINT 20/3067, G. E. Hall, Sierra Leone Monetary Authority, to J. James, 14 March 1963.

(a)   (b)

Figure 5.6. The reverse (a) and obverse (b) of the Nigerian one shilling coin, 1959,
incorporating portrait of the Queen by Cecil Thomas

signs of the colonial past,[156] they depicted the torch of freedom. Ghana also
sought to differentiate the postcolonial present from the colonial past in
choosing a five-point star for the reverse (Figure 5.1a); a reflection of what
Fuller observes was the country's preference for 'symbols of an African-
adapted modernity' over 'traditional motifs'.[157] This is also evident on the
Mint-manufactured official independence medal. The Ghanaian Cabinet opted
for a statement of cultural decolonization, showing Nkrumah in 'national' as
opposed to western dress. But in a further direction that speaks to the absorption of western racial ideas, it objected to the Mint's first attempt to capture
Nkrumah's image on the grounds, as reported by the British officer in charge
of the independence celebrations, that it made him appear 'more negroid'
than they thought was in fact the case: 'the face appears rather "deadpan"
instead of extremely mobile, as it is in fact. His lips are not quite so thick
nor is his nose so flat'.[158] Some political statements were more subtle, and, as
Eagleton argues in her discussion of the design of new coins for East Africa,
might reflect regional as much as anti-colonial political dynamics. Uganda,
for example, opted for only subtle deviation from the old EACB coins, replacing the old mountain and lion with a crane and volcano, representing 'separation from Kenya and Tanzania' rather than independence from Britain.[159] The
rooster, depicted on the Malawian six pence coin, was the symbol of the ruling
Malawian Congress Party.

  While most commissioning banks and governments issued instructions as
to the subjects they wished to see depicted, in colonies or new states where
British officials still occupied key positions the latter could still have significant input into the decision-making process. Even where this was not the
case those charged with translating their requests into attractive and func-
tional design subjects were generally European – and in some cases had also

---

[156] BoE, OV 7/103, no. 91, 'East African Currency Board', 5 June 1962.
[157] Fuller, *Building the Ghanaian Nation-State*, p. 67.
[158] TNA, MINT 20/2633, Captain Everard (Gold Coast Independence Day Celebrations Officer)
   to Sir L. Thompson, 25 September 1956 and 3 November 1956.
[159] Eagleton, 'Designing Change', pp. 226, 236–7.

designed old colonial coins. Paul Vincze, whose work was featured on coins issued by the Central African Currency Board, had, as discussed above, created the designs for the first Ghanaian and Malawian coins, and was responsible for half the designs of the first Nigerian coinage, a responsibility shared with Humphrey Paget (1893–1974), who had produced both a highly regarded portrait of George VI for used on his coinage and an image of Cecil Rhodes for the Central African currency.[160]

The Committee and artists often worked from photographs or other objects available in Britain to produce designs, sometimes supplied by the countries concerned. During meetings of the Advisory Committee, Prince Philip would occasionally retrieve objects from his personal or palace collections when the Committee came to discuss them as possible subjects; his knowledge of local environments was considered very useful by other Committee members.[161] Norman Sillman worked from photographs of a stuffed Oribi in his attempt to fulfill a brief provided by the Zambian government. His first attempt was judged inaccurate by the Zambian authorities who sent him photos of a live Oribi to work from instead.[162] Where necessary the Mint would draw on the assistance of organizations such as the Royal Botanic Gardens at Kew and the Royal Zoological Society.[163] For example, when Committee members felt 'rather out of our depth' in determining whether Zambia's proposed flower was in fact native to the country, it turned to Kew to resolve the matter.[164] Representations of fauna and flora or distinctive cultural artefacts were thus sometimes quite literally viewed through a colonial lens, before being re-imagined by the artists for re-export to the countries concerned.

Value judgements on artistic or other sensibilities among African peoples indicate an on-going cultural imperialism of a different form. When the Ghanaian finance minister expressed concern that the new coins (made from an alloy of 95.5 per cent copper and 4.5 per cent tin and zinc) might tarnish, the Mint's man suggested in response that 'brownish, yellowish and even the carbonate-greenish patinas on bronze are much admired by artistic and cultural people'; but, he went on, the 'dark skinned' had a weakness for 'bright colourings and trinkets'.[165] In response to Kenyan complaints that his first design of a lion did not sufficiently resemble that on the Kenyan coat of arms

---

[160] Michael Rizzello was responsible for the Sierra Leonean and Gambian, Norman Sillman for those for Kenya and Zambia and Christopher Ironside for Tanganyika.

[161] Interview: Dyer. For example, in 1971 he produced the fruit of a coco-de-mer to assist discussion of the design of the coinage of the Seychelles.

[162] TNA, MINT 20/3106, G. M. Fletcher to Sillman, 1 April 1964.

[163] *Fifth Report*, Minutes of Evidence taken before Sub-Committee D of the Estimates Committee, Memorandum submitted on behalf of the Chancellor of the Exchequer, para. 53.

[164] TNA, MINT 20/3106, G. M. Fletcher to C. E. Hubbard, 4 March 1964.

[165] TNA, MINT 20/2563, D. F. Stone to H. Stride, 14 November 1957; note by Stride addressed to Dr Watson, 18 November 1957, commenting on Stone's letter.

on which his image was supposed to be based, Sillman revised his original drawing but thought the result now looked more 'like a circus turn ... It is completely naturalistic and I fear they will prefer it'.[166] The British represent-ative on the Sierra Leonean monetary authority thought 'Birds and animals, would, I think, hold little attraction' for the local population since they 'are not naturalists, in any sense'.[167]

Although an issue beyond the Mint's immediate purview, the nomencla-ture of new coinages presented further opportunities for political statements. Most African states in fact initially followed a British pattern in using crowns, florins, shillings, and pence as their units. Zambia was an exception. Its new coins issued in 1968 were known as 'kwacha' and 'ngwee', which translate as 'dawn' and 'bright' in the country's leading Bemba and Nyanja languages. Marten and Kula suggest that, having adopted English as their official lan-guage, the choice of these terms enabled Zambians nevertheless to make a gesture of cultural nationalism; 'dawn' had an additional symbolic meaning having been used as a popular slogan in the independence movement.[168] Only Sierra Leone introduced a decimal coinage from the outset, based on the Leone and cents. When other countries followed suit in the 1960s and 1970s, this was generally the occasion on which they also adopted names for their coins that broke more clearly from the colonial period.

By the late 1960s the Mint's expertise in design no longer played as much to its advantage. More countries chose to submit their own designs. Producing the coins for both Tanzania and Zambia provided an early experience of this. The Tanzanian coins were approved and had entered production before the Committee met, while the Mint commissioned Cecil Thomas and Norman Sillman to work on ideas that Zambia had already submitted.[169] Although through the 1970s the RMAC continued to advise on the designs for some overseas coinages – particularly for some smaller island nations such as the Solomon Islands and Tuvalu – the urgency with which some orders were placed and the importance of speed for the Mint if it were to secure orders in the face of other competition did not allow time for referral to the Committee. It also became increasingly common for the Committee's proposals to be refused.[170] The rejection of advice from its high-powered committee was of some embar-rassment to the Mint, and in the early 1980s it was decided that the RMAC

---

[166] TNA, MINT 20/3036, N. Sillman to Fletcher, 2 March 1966.
[167] TNA, MINT 20/3067, G. E. Hall, Sierra Leone Monetary Authority, to J. James, 14 March 1963.
[168] Marten and Kula, 'Meanings of Money'.
[169] RMM, Zambia boxes, A. J. Dowling to Cecil Thomas and Norman Sillman, 12 and 13 February 1964; for Tanzania, see Eagleton, 'Designing Change', p. 231.
[170] RMM, RMAC, minutes 170th and 172nd meetings, 24 October 1974 and meeting, 31 October 1975; minutes 176th meeting, 10 May 1977, and memorandum on procedure by Sir Hugh Casson and additional note by Deputy Master.

would cease to advise on overseas coinages, although the Mint's engravers were still involved to ensure that the designs submitted by overseas clients were technically fit for purpose.[171]

The 1970s and Beyond

In 1966–7 the Mint's export business peaked. In retrospect it is apparent that, despite the Mint's anxieties about capturing the business of emergent states in place of its colonial export role, and for all the real difficulties the Mint had sometimes experienced in keeping track of developments in decoloniz-ing states, decolonization had provided the opportunity for notable overseas expansion. In the first decade of African decolonization the Mint had been able to benefit from the last vestiges of British rule and from a diaspora of British officials. New states in a hurry were inclined to draw on established linkages and place orders with the Mint. However, in the early postcolonial era, although the Mint held many, it did not have all the cards. Under strong leader-ship the Mint was determined in its pursuit of this business, and willing where necessary to pull the stops out so as to accommodate orders from new states.

By the end of the 1960s, however, it was apparent that the overseas envi-ronment was becoming less favourable. Although sterling devaluation in 1967 assisted exports to non-sterling markets, reducing prices relative to the Mint's competitors by a few per cent, the Mint now expected its returns to fall. New states were still emerging on the world stage, as the decolonization process continued, but the immediate rush of African independence had subsided. Moreover the Mint was ill-positioned to meet an increasing demand among developing countries for cheap coin of no recovery value (sought as a means of combating the difficulties high-inflationary countries faced where the face value of coins might fall below recovery value) since it had generally dealt hitherto in the manufacture of copper, nickel or silver coin.[172] As export orders fell, and the Mint's need for the services of the Birmingham mints declined, the Mint spec-ulated too that the latter might seek business elsewhere, becoming competitors rather than clients of the Mint. Moreover, at home the adoption of a decimal coinage in the United Kingdom introduced some complications, not least asso-ciated with the Mint's move to Llantrisant to accommodate its expanding pro-duction, a site chosen on political rather than economic grounds to comply with the government's desire to see the facility located in a 'development' area of the United Kingdom. The move seemed likely to increase overheads, such as those

---

[171] Interview, Dyer; Information from Kevin Clancy, director, Royal Mint Museum.
[172] TNA, MINT 20/3882, 'The problems of selling coin in overseas markets – 1967', paper by Mr P. F. Orchard (DLR); *Fifth Report*, Minutes of Evidence taken before Sub-Committee D of the Estimates Committee, para. 337.

relating to coin distribution,[173] and provoked trade union opposition.[174] For a short period following the opening of the new facility the Mint had to operate on split sites, retaining some production at Tower Hill, although by early 1971 the new plant was producing all coin intended for circulation.

Most importantly, however, newly independent countries which had initially looked to Britain for their currency needs increasingly turned to other suppliers. In 1967 a Mint official noted (in one rather telling comment) that Commonwealth states are 'beginning to realise they are not in fact "tied" to us', and were likely to 'shop around' seeking competitive tenders.[175] African independence had thus had a delayed effect. Between September 1966 and September 1968 the Mint lost out on eighteen orders in fourteen countries, mostly on grounds of price.[176] The Mint's competitors at this stage included mints in Germany, and, to a smaller degree, France, and also Australia, where a new national mint had opened at Canberra in 1965. The irony that the Australian branch mints, which at this point remained formally under the Mint's control (although by then this meant little in practice), might also come to represent a 'serious threat' in the region was not lost on staff at the Royal Mint.[177] In 1968 the Melbourne branch closed and that at Perth ceased to operate as a branch of the Mint.[178] Of the old Commonwealth countries only New Zealand still purchased its coin from the Royal Mint; but in the early 1970s the Mint lost out to the Australians for an order for coinage from what had been Britain's most loyal Commonwealth state.[179] By the mid-1970s the Canadian Mint, which like the Australian, could trade under the useful 'royal' label, had emerged as one of the Mint's principal competitors. Anxious to 'meet the requirements of African countries because of our vulnerability there to competition from Canada', the Mint strove to meet Ugandan currency needs at a time when the United Kingdom itself had broken diplomatic relations. If one country was 'driven to turn to the Canadian Mint others might quickly follow'.[180]

Although there was no immediate risk, the Mint also anticipated that into the future it would face more competition from mints in new states. A number of other Commonwealth countries had followed Nigeria's lead and established their own mints, including Malaysia. In Africa it predicted that new nations

---

[173] Ibid., para. 10, Minutes of Evidence taken before Sub-Committee D of the Estimates Committee, paras. 587–99.
[174] Challis, 'A New Beginning', pp. 637–41, 658.
[175] TNA, MINT 20/3881, 'The problems of selling coin in overseas markets – 1967' paper by N. P. Howard, 26 October 1967.
[176] TNA, MINT 20/3879, B. W. Tucker to J. E. Lucas, 'Commercial Coinage Cost 1968/9', 18 September 1968.
[177] TNA, MINT 20/3882: minute by N. P. Howard to G. M. Fletcher, 11 January 1968.
[178] 99th Annual Report, 1968 (HMSO, 1969), p. 9.
[179] TNA, MINT 20/3879, A. J. Dowling to J. E. Lucas, 4 May 1971.
[180] RMM, Uganda Box, file 3/377/8, 'Uganda' memo by A. J. Dowling, 20 August 1976.

might collaborate following a similar trend in South America. The United Nations had recently given its blessing for mints in Khartoum, Cairo and Nigeria to work together producing coins designed by African artists to African traditions. A further mint was believed to be in prospect at Kitwe, Zambia.[181]

But in the late 1960s it was the US Mint which appeared to pose the greatest threat. The American mint, like the Royal Mint controlled by its country's Treasury, had been a significant coin exporter until about 1964, principally serving markets in South and Central America, the Philippines and Korea. In 1968, to the Mint's dismay, the Americans re-emerged as competitors, not only trying to re-establish themselves in America's traditional markets, but also attempting to move into others such as those in the Caribbean where the British had only narrowly secured a Jamaican order put out to open tender. In Africa the US Mint was extending its sales effort to Central Africa and Nigeria, where a re-coinage was anticipated after the end of the civil war. The American Mint was at an immediate advantage since it was offering to produce overseas coins at cost. In London the Royal Mint objected that the Americans were acting 'uncommercially', and possibly in contravention of American legislation passed a century earlier (which the British believed permitted the production for overseas governments at cost, but not if the contracts had been actively solicited on this basis). With the support of the Treasury, CRO and Board of Trade, the Mint requested that the British Treasury and Supply delegation in the British American Embassy make representations on its behalf to the American government.[182]

When in 1967 the Chancellor requested a study of future trends in export markets in response to concerns articulated by the Mint and De La Rue, the Mint anticipated that in the next five-year period its exports might average 900 million pieces per annum.[183] In 1971 a new Marketing and Sales Division opened at the Mint under the direction of Alan Dowling, leading to an 'intensification' of the Mint's export efforts. In its first year members of the new department made twenty overseas visits, mostly to Latin America, the Middle East and South East Asia, and Dowling hoped that in the course of the next few years staff would travel to all the countries for which the Mint produced coin. The following year the Mint was once again awarded the Queen's Award to Industry; a recognition of the Mint's success in the export market, including in

[181] TNA, MINT 20/3881, 'The problems of selling coin in overseas markets – 1967', paper by N. P. Howard, 26 October 1967.
[182] Ibid., 'US competition', paper prepared by RM and DLR, enclosed J. James to E. Maude, 31 December 1968.
[183] TNA, MINT 20/3882: P. R. Baldwin to J. James, 24 November 1967; minute J. E. Lucas to J. James, 18 January 1968, see various drafts of paper.

relation to proof coins and medallions.[184] But thereafter the Mint experienced a sharp slowdown in demand. A low point was reached in the financial year 1973–4. As the demand for new British decimal coin declined, the Mint found that it was facing the combined challenge of falling domestic *and* falling international demand. Consequently the Mint could no longer compensate for fluctuating domestic demand through export sales. In that year only 350 million coins were produced for export, the lowest figure for sixteen years, and less than a third of the previous year's production.[185] The Mint was also facing other problems. It had an obligation to buy back coin from its regular customers but in the mid-1970s found that it could not absorb all the overseas coin withdrawn from circulation, since nearly all coin produced for overseas markets before 1976 had a high lead content.[186]

The Mint was becoming uncompetitive in increasingly competitive world markets. In response to the 1967 review of future trends, the Chancellor had proposed aiming at a return of 10–11 per cent on export orders as perhaps more realistic than the previous target of around 15 per cent.[187] Even so, by the early 1970s, the Mint's estimates, designed to yield a profit of 12 per cent, were as much as 25 to 30 per cent higher than those of the Birmingham Mint and about 15 per cent higher than those of Imperial Metal Industries. In several cases the Mint found it had to reduce prices in order to secure orders. Although orders rose again in 1974–5, a change in the Mint's approach was called for. In late 1975 Dowling proposed that the Mint must adopt a new strategy entailing differential pricing. For those regular customers not regarded as 'particularly price conscious', he advocated estimating costs based on a profit return of between 8 and 12 per cent or even higher still if the Mint's past experience with the client suggested that this might be possible. For other established clients known to be 'sensitive to price', however, Dowling recommended that the Mint now quote prices that represented an increase over the last order by an amount proportional to the rise in the relevant wages index, but be prepared to come down to the lowest prices acceptable to the Birmingham Mint, to whom the Mint would then subcontract the business, even if this entailed the Mint making little or no profit on the transaction. This was preferable to the risk of losing these customers, since he believed that if the Mint lost 'a single one the rest immediately become more vulnerable'. As for 'occasional customers', Dowling proposed a

[184] *102nd Annual Report, 1971–2* (HMSO, 1973), pp. 3–6; *103rd Annual Report, 1972–3* (HMSO, 1974), p. 2.
[185] *104th Annual Report, 1973–4*, pp. 4–5.
[186] TNA, MINT 20/3879, 'Stocks, Purchase and Consumption of Scrap Coin', J. E. Cussen to D. C. Snell, 21 September 1976.
[187] TNA, MINT 20/3882: P. R. Baldwin to J. James, 24 November 1967; minute J. E. Lucas to James, 18 January 1968, see various drafts of paper; P. J. Kitcatt (Treasury) to J. James, 1 March 1968.

more flexible policy, with the Mint going all out 'for all business', but in better times perhaps allowing some work to go to competitors rather than diverting attention from their more important regular clients.[188] Whether because of the change in strategy or not, the Mint attracted some fresh customers in that financial year, with first orders received from Botswana, Tunisia and Equatorial Guinea.[189] But increasingly the 'loyal' cohort of regular customers was dwindling. In October 1983, on learning, for instance, that the Kenyan Central Bank had received visits from the Brazilian, German, Canadian and Singaporean mints, staff at the Mint concluded that Kenya would in future require 'competitive tenders' and could no longer be regarded as a tied customer.[190] When in 1996 the Mint lost to Canada the tender for two new high-value coins for Ghana, the acquisition of whose business had been regarded as so important during the first wave of decolonization,[191] it illustrated how much things had changed from the early postcolonial era.

Conclusion

Today the Royal Mint claims to be the world's leading export mint. In 2015–16 it supplied 2.4 billion coins and blanks to forty countries around the world, including twelve in Africa, more than in any other region of the world.[192] The revenue generated from this activity, as well as from the sale of other products such as collectors coins to dealers, was significant: in five years from 2010–11 until 2014–15 revenue from overseas always exceeded that from the United Kingdom, accounting for an average of nearly 60 per cent of total revenue.[193] In 2014–15 although Asia was the source of the greatest proportion of revenue at 30 per cent, and the United States was a close second at 29 per cent, revenue from business in Africa totalled £12,378 million, some 8.5 per cent of all overseas sales; the previous year it had been £17,276 million, just over 9 per cent of the total.

The more challenging circumstances in which the Mint traded from the late 1960s show that there was no simple progression for the Mint from its acquisition of the business of new African states to this global export success. But we have seen that decolonization was nevertheless crucial to the Mint's transformation from a financially successful imperial institution to a global one.

---

[188] RMM, Liberia box, file 213/1, memo by A. J. Dowling, 24 September 1975; 'Pricing of Ordinary Coinage', memo by A. J. Dowling, 20 November 1975, addressed to Deputy Master.
[189] *106th Annual Report, 1975–6* (HMSO, 1978), p. 2.
[190] RMM, Kenya boxes, 'Note of a meeting with the Central Bank of Kenya, Nairobi, 17 October 1983' and handwritten note on this.
[191] RMM, Ghana boxes, copy of fax from John Kelly to H. Elsaser, 4 April 1996, 'Ghana'.
[192] *Annual Report 2014–15*, pp. 12, 29; *Annual Report 2015–16*, pp. 15, 62.
[193] Calculated from *Annual Report 2014–15*, p. 29, 'Financial Summary'.

For African political change, which presented risks as well as opportunities to the Mint, forced it to adapt. That it did so was a consequence of dynamic leadership, the Mint's own agency and its hard-nosed commercial approach. Yet its experience of decolonization was not only revealing of on-going cultures of imperialism, but also underscores the importance of cultural capital.

In its determined pursuit of the new business of emergent states the Mint was assisted by legacy networks of British personnel as well as by De La Rue, easing the Mint through what might otherwise have been a more difficult period. For this reason although we should not deny the very real economic and political significance of the moment of independence for expatriate businesses (especially for those domiciled in new states, where they sometimes faced nationalization and more punishing taxation and regulatory regimes), for the Mint, which had no formal presence in African states, the full effects of decolonization were only felt some years after the event. Decolonization was a staggered process in which flag independence marked a starting rather than an end point in a European retreat.

In the late 1960s as the legacy networks of British officials declined, the Mint experienced the full impact of African political change and found itself operating in a more competitive market. But it was nevertheless assisted in negotiating these new more challenging circumstances by the linkages to postcolonial states it had built in the immediate postcolonial years and by the new practices and strategies that it had adopted in the immediate aftermath of African independence when it had set out with such singular determination to capture the business of emergent Commonwealth states. A decade of African decolonization saw changes to the Mint's culture and practice, and its more commercial character was recognized soon after by its change to a trading fund. The Mint's handling of African decolonization was thus of long-term significance to its on-going commercial success, and current position as the world's leading export mint.

6 'Losing an Empire and Winning Friends': Sandhurst and British Decolonization

Visiting the Royal Military Academy at Sandhurst in spring 1978, General Sir Frank King was delighted to see 'so many' overseas students 'still gracing the parade ground'. There was an implied note of surprise that, long after Harold Macmillan had called time on Britain's African Empire, there was such a large cohort present from Britain's former colonies, including its African ones, as well as from foreign states. 'Britain may have lost an empire', he observed, but 'it would be good to feel she is still gaining friends'.[1] King was taking the Sovereign's – or 'passing-out' – Parade, which still marks the end of each term, a key moment in Sandhurst's calendar when officer cadets march before the sovereign, or, more commonly, his or her representative, on Old College Square. In a striking finale, the Adjutant ascends the steps of the Grand Entrance of Old College on his charger. In 1978 as now, tradition structured Sandhurst life; but as King's comments convey, Britain's place in the wider international order had changed significantly.

When the new Academy opened in 1947 there were huge numbers of British men in arms, and many officers saw service somewhere in Britain's Empire either with colonial regiments or in fighting late colonial insurgencies. Major-General Sir Hugh Stockwell, who arrived at the Academy as its second Commandant in June 1948, provides one example. Like many of his generation, he had extensive overseas and colonial experience. He had been seconded to the Royal West African Frontier Force at Ibadan in Nigeria and had commanded the 30th East African Brigade in campaigns in Madagascar and Burma, before being appointed commanding officer of the 82nd (West African) division.[2] Immediately prior to what was to him a surprising posting to Sandhurst, he had served with British forces in Palestine.[3]

While many newly commissioned British officers passing out from Sandhurst were destined to serve in the colonies, the 1940s and 1950s also

---

[1] *The Wish Stream*, XXXII, no. 1 (Spring, 1978).
[2] Liddell Hart Military Archive, King's College London, papers of Gen. Sir Hugh Stockwell, GB 0099 KCLMA, Stockwell, 6/39, nos. 1 and 2; file, 5/6/39, no. 1.
[3] *The Wish Stream*, ii, no. 1 (August 1948), p. 6.

saw significant traffic in the other direction as growing numbers of colonial
and Commonwealth cadets travelled to England to train at Sandhurst. The second part of this chapter shows that the admission of overseas cadets to the
Academy on a large and unprecedented scale complicated and sometimes
threatened to undermine Sandhurst's primary task, producing officers for the
British Army. As discussed in a third section, it also risked some of the racial
and anti-colonial politics of an era of global decolonization being played out in
the intense environment of the Academy.

As the Empire shrank, together with Britain's own capacity to sustain an
extensive military presence around the globe, Sandhurst came under critical
scrutiny, as considered in the fourth section below. In 1972 imperial decline
and retrenchment, coupled with wider transformations in British society and
higher education, led to the co-location of Mons Officer Cadet School (which
after the war provided training for those seeking national service and later
short-service commissions) at Sandhurst, and, despite the combined opposition of Sandhurst's military and academic staff, to fundamental re-organization
at the Academy. But even as a shrinking British Army ceased to operate on
a global canvas, with huge consequences for the Academy, Britain's military training establishments had attained a new international prestige, and, as
explored in a fifth and final section, new states continued in the 1970s and
1980s to seek places at the RMAS. Sandhurst had become, in the words of one
senior officer, 'an instrument of foreign policy acting on behalf of the Foreign
and Commonwealth Office', a means by which the British state exercised soft
power overseas,[4] and one way in which Britain sought to substitute influence
for imperial rule. As this chapter shows, making this transition was not without
difficulties and challenges.

There are parallels between this experience of decolonization and that of
the other institutions we have considered, not least in relation to the provision of technical assistance to new states. In Sandhurst's case this principally took the form of the admission of overseas cadets, and the support the
Academy provided to new military academies established in former colonies. However, unlike the other institutions, Sandhurst did not seek this role,
although the Academy's officer and permanent academic staff had a common
pride in the education they provided and a public service ethos not unlike
that found in other institutions. In negotiating the new landscape, staff at the
Academy had much less control of their own fortunes than was the case in
our other institutions. Sandhurst was controlled by the Army and the War
Office, and, from 1964, by a new unified Ministry of Defence. The most
senior positions at Sandhurst were held by serving officers, including at the

---

[4] RMAS, [Room] A12, Box 457, file 4192, 'overseas students, 1987–1992', no. 21 minutes of a
meeting to discuss arrangements for overseas cadets, 20 February 1989.

top, the Commandant, a Major General, as well as an Assistant Commandant and the Adjutant. Sandhurst represented a relatively short interlude in these officers' Army careers. Between 1946 and August 1979 there were twelve commandants; each remained at Sandhurst for on average a little under three years. Those appointed as Regimental (from 1960 Academy) Sergeant Major held their posts longer and were often the individuals who made the greatest impression on cadets.[5]

There was also greater continuity among the teaching staff, appointed on a permanent basis. These were academics, although many had army experience either from the war or as a result of national service. Some transferred from Woolwich or had been at Sandhurst in the 1930s, and between them might constitute a repository of institutional memory. The most senior was the director of studies, directly responsible to the Commandant. Between September 1948 and January 1962 one man, T. S. J. Anderson, held this post, and, although his successor was in the job only a few months, the historian Kenneth Ingham, who was next appointed to the role, remained in it for five years.[6]

The revolving door of military appointments to Sandhurst did not necessarily equate to an absence of institutional culture either. On the contrary, life at the RMAS was highly ceremonial and structured, modelled on British regimental practice, although the institution had also developed distinctive traditions of its own, maintaining customs associated with both the RMA Woolwich and the old RMC. Commandants controlled the day-to-day running of the Academy and could and did seek to shape developments there, stamping their own authority on the institution. Unlike officers in charge of other British Army divisions, they did not come under area command, but instead reported directly to the War Office (and later the Ministry of Defence) and in particular to that branch that dealt with officer training, and through this to the Army Council (from 1964 known as the Army Board), the executive managerial organization of the British Army. Comprising senior politicians and soldiers, including the Chief of the (until 1964, Imperial) General Staff, the Council was chaired by the Secretary of State for War or from 1964 of Defence. A smaller Executive Committee of the Council dealt with much of the Council's routine business.[7] As we shall see, while Sandhurst officers and civilian staff might oppose changes planned in Whitehall, on the rare occasions when they actively resisted centrally agreed initiatives they were given relatively short shrift.[8] Alongside broader and more significant issues relating to the fundamental

---

[5] Pugsley and Holdsworth, *Sandhurst*, pp. 140–2; Sheppard, *Sandhurst*, pp. 217–8, appendix.
[6] Ibid.
[7] French, *Army, Empire and Cold War*, p. 15.
[8] Interview with British officer, formerly at Sandhurst, 10 May 2016.

reorganization of officer training in the period, the admission of overseas
cadets sometimes generated friction both within the Army and between the
WO/MoD and other Whitehall departments.

The Post-War Academy

When the new combined Royal Military Academy Sandhurst opened in 1947
Britain's imperial and military commitments stretched round the globe. British
forces were deployed in the restoration of European colonial rule in South East
Asia following the Japanese surrender; in Palestine in suppressing a violent
Jewish uprising; in North Africa; and in policing the post-war settlement in
Europe, principally in the deployment of men to Germany. Other than western
Europe, immediately post-war the War Office expected the Army's principal
fields of operation to be in the Middle East, an area of crucial British strategic
interest, where huge numbers of British men were stationed in the Suez Canal
Zone in Egypt under the terms of a 1936 treaty, until a negotiated withdrawal
was agreed in 1954. Alongside these commitments, the British Army also now
faced new tasks that David French argues changed Britain's officer requirements in two important respects. First, the onset of the Cold War raised the
prospect that Britain might need to mobilize a large-scale army rather than
the small professional one on which it had historically relied in peace time.
Second, Britain's post-war continental role was extended indefinitely, and
Britain committed to a long-term military presence in Germany as part of the
defence of western Europe and in line with Britain's obligations as a founder
member of NATO.[9] To meet these needs, in 1947 the post-war Labour government passed the National Service Act, introducing national service just before
the demobilization of the wartime army was complete. By 1952 there were
440,000 men in the British Army, half of whom were national servicemen or
on the new 'short-service engagement'.[10]

A high-quality British officer class of an estimated 25,000 men was required
to train and lead what Field Marshal Bernard Montgomery, the Chief of the
Imperial General Staff from 1946 to 1948, called his 'New Model Army' of
conscripts. They were to be trained principally at Sandhurst, although officer
training for short-service commissions took place at Eaton Hall near Chester
and at Mons at Aldershot, and high fliers could later join the Staff College at
Camberley. At the outset there was a shortfall of almost 10,000 in the number
of officers required. Efforts were hence made throughout the late 1940s and
the 1950s to expand recruitment and to attract applicants of high calibre from
a wider social base by abolishing fees (which had been paid by most cadets

[9] French, *Army*, p. 7.
[10] Smyth, *Sandhurst*, p. 177.

before the war) and introducing pay for training. In 1953 in one attempt to widen recruitment the Army opened Welbeck School to provide a two-year sixth form education for boys preparing to enter Sandhurst with a view to serving in the Army's technical corps. In practice, however, change was slow and, initially, officer cadets were overwhelmingly recruited from Britain's public schools, although the concentration on the most exclusive institutions diminished.[11]

The new RMAS constituted a strange hybrid of school and army: 'boarding school with guns' as one described it.[12] Cadets were normally aged eighteen and arrived at Sandhurst having already committed to a particular regiment or corps, although competing regiments might seek to win over the best during their time at the Academy. They entered one of four companies attached to each of Sandhurst's three colleges, each presided over by a lieutenant-colonel: Old College, New College and Victory College. The companies became the cadets' main focus of loyalty, equivalent to a regimental attachment, and were led by an officer of the rank of major, usually supported by a senior captain and a company sergeant major. Several 'senior cadets', those in their last two terms, were designated senior or junior under-officers.[13] Within each company there were three platoons, one from each intake over the two-year course, each commanded by a captain and a colour sergeant.

The course at the new Academy, taught over eighteen months, aimed to deliver a 'broad general education with a distinct military bias'.[14] The 'Chief Instructor' (from 1952 re-designated 'Assistant Commandant'), a Brigadier in rank and second in command to the Commandant, was responsible for all military instruction. Company officers instructed cadets in areas such as tactics, staff duties, military law, map reading and administration, and NCO instructional staff taught drill and weapon training, signal communications, vehicle servicing and physical training. A sizeable contingent of permanent lecturers delivered the academic half of the course. After the war there were forty-four civilian lecturers and six officers on the teaching staff, organized into departments of mathematics, science, modern subjects and languages; in the first twenty years most had been educated at Oxbridge, contributing to the Academy's academic environment.[15] By the 1950s each department had its own head, a principal lecturer and around sixteen further senior lecturers. Military history was taught by the officers, but they did so under the guidance

---

[11] French, *Army* pp. 43–4, 60; Strachan, *Politics of the British Army*, p. 195.
[12] RMAS [Room] D56, Box 307, 'Sandhurst – A Tradition of Leadership', papers and correspondence, comments by former cadet.
[13] Written information provided by Anthony Clayton to the author.
[14] RMAS, D56, Box 108, file papers for Commandant, paper 1A 'Army College Curriculum', para. 4A (1946).
[15] Written information provided by Anthony Clayton to the author.

of an academic, and teaching eventually passed solely into the hands of the civilian staff in a special new department.[16] In 1956 the course was extended from eighteen months to two years, and changes were made to the curriculum. By the early 1960s all cadets took an obligatory course in military history taught by members of the new Department of Military History, and also an academic study of the Malayan emergency. This had quickly become established as the model counter-insurgency campaign, in which Britain employed minimum force while 'winning hearts and minds', an interpretation that had long-term traction in academic literature, although recent scholarship has shown how in reality British regiments were involved in the use of 'exemplary' force that targeted and intimidated civilians.[17] The more academically able also undertook additional studies of the English Civil War, the French Revolutionary and Napoleonic Wars and the American Civil War.[18]

Above all the course aimed to inculcate qualities of leadership. As Assistant Commandant Brigadier J. H. Page put it in 1971, the training was not so much directed to what an officer should know, but 'what he should be'. 'It is', he wrote, 'far more difficult and time consuming to broaden the intellect or to develop a sense of leadership of responsibility in a young man than to give him a smattering of military knowledge'.[19] 'Leadership' was taught with reference to past examples of discipline, courage, loyalty and endurance, although from the early 1960s, in the hands of an academic member of staff, a more conceptual, managerial approach was adopted.[20] It was in the early 1960s also that the RMAS began organizing overseas expeditions in vacations to locations from Greenland to the Middle East as a further means of inculcating qualities of leadership. These also provided an opportunity to conduct zoological, geological and other research, and had the additional benefit of reinforcing British familiarity with, and knowledge of, overseas terrain and forces. The expeditions ranged in scale from very small affairs involving only a handful of participants to much larger undertakings. Colonel John Bashford-Snell, whose name would later become synonymous in the public mind with overseas travel as a result of his founding role in Operation Raleigh, an educational venture aimed at young people, and through published accounts of his exploits, was designated 'Adventure Training Officer'. Given a 'global brief', the world map sourced for Bashford-Snell's new office was soon covered with pins, and he was instructed to 'get as many as

---

[16] Pugsley and Holdsworth, *Sandhurst*, p. 150.
[17] French, *Army, Empire and Cold War,* ch. 5.
[18] RMAS, D56, Box 246, file 'Dept of Mil. Hist. Syllabus etc.', Syllabus, 24 January 1961.
[19] RMAS, A12, Box 369, file RMAS 229/4/Gword, paper submitted to Tillard working party by J. H. Page, 7 August 1971.
[20] Anthony Clayton, *The British Officer. Leading the Army from 1660 to the Present* (Pearson, Harlow, 2006), p. 190.

possible of the officer cadets on worthwhile projects for the benefit of their character' and, in a rather opaque instruction, with 'the least possible detriment to the Empire'.[21]

'Over-Loaded with Non-British Cadets': The Competition for Places at Sandhurst in the 1950s

The War Office conceived the new Academy principally with a view to the development of a high-quality British officer class. However, from the outset it proposed setting aside 100 places for cadets from the Empire and Commonwealth who met the basic educational criteria for entry as well as for some from foreign states nominated by their governments. Reflecting its recent experience of world war, the occasion of an impressive show of Commonwealth military solidarity and collaboration, the War Office hoped by bringing Commonwealth and overseas officer cadets to Britain for training to spread British practice among overseas officers in ways that might result in 'mutual understanding' in the event of future war. In its first year the Academy took three cadets from South Africa (although none in following years) and seven from Jordan, a British mandate until 1946 and thereafter a significant regional ally. At this stage the War Office saw Sandhurst's role through an imperial lens in relation to an on-going British imperialism. It consequently emphasized that the allocation of places for overseas cadets was 'NOT [sic] intended to provide a local substitute for the British officer'. Indeed, in June 1948, the Army Council advised that it was considering the position of 'men of colour' who might be recommended for a commission, but for the time being instructed that these should not be admitted to Sandhurst unless they were from forces that no longer had, or were likely to have, British officers – presumably because the Army feared this might compromise the cultural authority of British officers who out-ranked their local counterparts, but who had shared the same training. Given that this effectively ruled out all non-whites from British colonies the Colonial Office concluded that it was not worthwhile passing on details of the vacancies to colonial governments.[22]

The re-opening of the Academy, however, coincided with the British withdrawal from South Asia. The first Burmese cadets arrived in 1948, from Ceylon (Sri Lanka) in 1950 and Pakistan in 1952, as well as from 1950 from the colony of Malaya, where the counter-insurgency had commenced in 1948 following the declaration of a state of emergency. From the early 1950s these were joined

---

[21] Cited in Pugsley and Holdsworth, *Sandhurst*, pp. 105–7.
[22] TNA, WO 32/12017, no. 26c Circular despatch no. 23 from DO to UK commissions in the Dominions, 24 June 1947; no. 48A, 'draft note for inclusion in 42B'; no. 49A, 25 June 1948, G. A. Rimbault to Lt Col JC Liesching; CO reply to Rimbault, April 1949.

Figure 6.1. West African cadet in front of Old College, RMAS, 1954

by Africans from Nigeria and the Gold Coast (one of the first of whom is shown in Figure 6.1), as well as by cadets from Fiji.[23] From almost the very beginning the Academy began, then, to serve a second purpose – training cadets from new Commonwealth states as well as from British colonies to create a local officer class, a function diametrically at odds with the War Office's initial objectives.

By the mid-1950s Sandhurst was admitting increasing numbers of non-European cadets. A ratio of one in ten was set for overseas to British cadets, but by 1954 increasing applications had led to the actual proportion rising. The problem came to a head in 1955, exacerbated by the impending extension of the RMAS course from eighteen months to two years. By early 1955 the Commandant thought the 'absolute limit' had been reached in terms of the

[23] From information in *The Wish Stream*.

overall numbers of overseas students admitted to the Academy.[24] Sandhurst, however, had by then become the vehicle for the delivery of distinct, and sometimes competing, objectives formulated in different Whitehall departments, not just in the War Office, but also in the Foreign, Commonwealth Relations and Colonial Offices.

At both the Foreign and Commonwealth Relations Offices the admission of foreign and Commonwealth cadets to British military training establishments was seen as a valuable means of spreading influence, especially, as far as the former was concerned, in the strategically important Arab states, and, from the CRO's perspective, to bolster Commonwealth unity. Both departments had clout within Whitehall to promote their goals, especially since refusals to grant foreign and Commonwealth countries the places they sought risked injuring Britain's standing overseas. Requests from Commonwealth states for places at Sandhurst were generally submitted to the British defence advisers attached to overseas British high commission offices, while requests from foreign states were made via the British defence attaché in the country concerned or through other diplomatic channels. At the War Office the Director General of Military Training found that, when he refused some of these requests, 'some extremely high-ranking person or organization' within the British establishment would order him to accept them after foreign ambassadors and high commissioners had intervened at ministerial level.[25]

The hope that a British military training would help foster British influence and practice was also an important consideration behind the admission of colonial cadets, but in other respects the case for training a colonial officer class at Sandhurst was different to that shaping policy in relation to foreign and Commonwealth cadets. Whereas the Foreign and Commonwealth Offices sought vacancies at Sandhurst for overseas cadets to offset some of the effects of decolonization and the change in Britain's world position, the Colonial Office, War Office and senior figures in the British Army did so in order to *advance* a decolonizing process.

By the mid-1950s, as we saw in Chapter 2, the rapid transition of the Gold Coast and Nigeria towards independence had propelled the issue of the future of the RWAFF – and hence of training for an African officer class – up official agendas. At the same time, a need to relieve increasing demand for British officers to serve with colonial forces reinforced interest in African officer training. By then the colonies constituted the Army's principal theatres of armed engagement (aside from its involvement in Korea), tying down British men and resources as Britain embarked on a series of lengthy and difficult colonial

---

[24] TNA, WO 32/17829, no. 50A, minute by Lt.-General Sir James Cassels, DGMT, 24 February 1955. The Commandant thought that there should be no more than thirty-five overseas cadets admitted per intake; a number that had already been exceeded.

[25] Ibid., no. 50A, minute by Lieutenant-General Sir James Cassels, 24 February 1955.

counter-insurgencies. In addition to the Malayan emergency (1948–60), a military campaign was fought in Kenya against the Mau Mau insurgency and a state of emergency was in force from 1952 to 1960, although the insurgents were largely defeated by 1956. In Cyprus an emergency lasted from 1955 to 1959 in the face of violent action by a Greek Cypriot guerrilla organization that sought union with Greece. Writing in the Academy's journal, *The Wish Stream*, at the start of the Malayan emergency, one new officer wrote that news that he was to be posted to Malaya had excited in him visions of the 'glorious East'. At 'long last' he would be visiting 'the happy writing ground of Somerset Maugham'.[26] The reality was surely somewhat different, and although the counter-insurgencies were successful, the Malayan emergency at least exacted a high toll in terms of military casualties.[27] In Kenya especially news of the abuse of Mau Mau detainees inflicted reputational damage that contributed to the government's reappraisal of Britain's role in Africa.[28]

By the mid-1950s there were some 1,700, or 5 per cent of all, British officers on transfer to command colonial forces, 2 per cent more than before the Second World War. Deployment to a colonial or Commonwealth force continued to be regarded as a useful part of the on-going development of officers after they had passed out from the Academy, and secondment to either the RWAFF or the KAR generally brought an accelerated chance for command, alongside other attractions. In 1955, two years after he passed out from Sandhurst, Mike Scott was appointed a captain and platoon commander in the 3rd KAR in Kenya; he later looked back on the period as one in which he had 'never lived as well' while having 'TOTAL "job satisfaction"'.[29] But Africa tended to be regarded as a backwater in career terms, and there were difficulties attracting high-calibre officers for overseas roles.

Faced with the combined circumstances of colonial political change and the growth of demand for seconded officers, the Cabinet Committee on Security, chaired by General Sir Gerald Templer, then Chief of the Imperial General Staff, recommended that colonial cadets should be brought to Britain for military training to facilitate the transfer of colonial forces to local control. Templer acknowledged that Sandhurst was already 'becoming overloaded with non-British cadets', but he saw no viable alternative to training this successor African officer class at the Academy.[30] The implications of this recommendation concerned several of the Army's other most senior figures, including Lieutenant General

---

[26] *The Wish Stream*, IV, no. 2 (August 1950).

[27] The figures are: 1201, Malaya; 94, Kenya; 1135, Korea: Richard Vinen, *National Service. A Generation in Uniform, 1945–1963* (Penguin, London, 2015), p. 419, appendix III.

[28] On which see esp. David Anderson, *Histories of the Hanged: Britain's Dirty War in Kenya and the End of Empire* (Weidenfeld and Nicolson, London, 2005); Caroline Elkins, *Britain's Gulag: The Brutal End of Empire in Kenya* (Jonathan Cape, London, 2005).

[29] Bodleian, Mss Afr. s. 1715, Box 16, file 241, ff. 4, 20-1.

[30] TNA, CAB 129/76, CP (55) 92, Cabinet. Security in the Colonies', July 1955, incorporating 'Report by the Committee on Security in the Colonies', 1955, paras. 16, 272–81, 288.

Sir William Oliver, the Vice Chief of the Imperial General Staff and General Sir Cameron Nicholson, the Adjutant General, who believed that Britain's own training requirements must override those of other places, but they acknowledged that Templer's prescription for colonial forces made this difficult.[31]

In an attempt to negotiate between these conflicting domestic, colonial, Commonwealth and foreign policy needs, the Executive Committee of the Army Council and the Cabinet Defence Committee established an order of priority for the allocation of vacancies at Sandhurst to overseas entrants.[32] Those, such as the Gurkhas and Maltese, whose role (because they were commissioned directly into a British Army corps) related directly to the needs of the British Army, would take precedence, but the Secretary of State for War proposed to the Cabinet that colonial cadets should also be prioritized over other Commonwealth and foreign cadets. This was in line with Templer's recommendations, assisting with the development of local officer corps within British colonies and reducing pressure within the British Army for seconded personnel.[33]

Despite these efforts to manage demand, to the Commandant's dismay the proportion of overseas cadets at Sandhurst continued to rise, reaching 15.9 per cent in the January 1957 intake, and being projected to exceed 20 per cent by January 1959. This was partly because the War Office could not in practice allot vacancies on a percentage basis since the need for trained colonial officers was greater than ever.[34] But it also reflected the fact that, in the late 1950s, despite the priority which the Army Council had assigned to the colonies, the pressure to admit cadets from new Commonwealth countries was growing rather than diminishing. Indeed, during the 1950s, as Table 6.1 shows, although there was a sizeable cohort from Malta, most overseas cadets came from either newly independent states in South Asia, especially Ceylon and Burma, or from Jordan, Iran and Iraq, with somewhat smaller numbers from Saudi Arabia. Malaya (which became independent in 1957) supplied more than any other colony or Commonwealth nation. The move by the Commonwealth Relations Office in spring 1959 to secure new funding to support cadets from the five Commonwealth countries that had attained independence since the war, India, Pakistan, Ceylon, Malaya and Ghana, at British military training establishments only intensified this demand – although India, which had its own military academy, sent only one

---

[31] TNA, WO 32/17829, ECAC/P(55) 37, 'Allotment of overseas vacancies to the RMAS', draft paper, 31 May, 1955; Extract from minutes of Executive Committee Army Council, 3 June 1955, item 67.

[32] Ibid., 'Allotment of Vacancies at RMAS to non-British cadets', Cab. Defence Committee memo by Secretary of State for War, 30 June 1955; no. 89B, 'Vacancies at Sandhurst' draft paper, August 1955.

[33] Ibid., 'Allotment of Vacancies at RMAS to non-British cadets', Cab. Defence Committee memo. by Secretary of State for War, 30 June 1955.

[34] Ibid., no. 217A, Commandant to Under-Secretary of State, WO, 4 October 1957; no. 220A, WO response, 29 October 1957.

Table 6.1. *Overseas entrants to Sandhurst by country and year 1947–60*

Country	1947	1948	1949	1950	1951	1952	1953	1954	1955	1956	1957	1958	1959	1960	Total
Afghanistan								1							1
Albania											1				1
Bahrain											1				1
Burma		12	4	7	8	10	6	8	7	2					64
Ceylon				15	14	11	8	8	8		8	7	8	8	95
East Africa[a]												1	4	2	7
Egypt								1							1
Ethiopia	1							1			2	2			6
Fiji				1	1	2	1								5
Gambia												1			1
Ghana							1	1	1	6	2	13	8	10	42
Guyana							1								1
India									1						1
Iran									1				1		2
Iraq								3	5	6	4	4		3	25
Jordan	7	8	3	4	14	1		1					2		40
Kenya														2	2
Kuwait						1					1				2
Libya									2						2
Malaya				11	15	11	25	20	23	32	29	2	5	4	177

(*cont.*)

Table 6.1. (*cont.*)

Country	1947	1948	1949	1950	1951	1952	1953	1954	1955	1956	1957	1958	1959	1960	Total
Malta		4	4	3	7	3	4	4	8	6	3	3	3	2	54
Nepal[b]						1	1		3	1	2	4	2	6	20
New Zealand											2	2	1	2	7
Nigeria					2	3	1	2	7	3	4	6	13	9	50
Oman														1	1
Pakistan						2	2	2	2	2	2	2			14
Rhodesia								5	9	7	10	2	5	5	43
Saudi Arabia		1		1				4			1	1			13
Sierra Leone							1	1		3				2	7
Singapore								1	1						2
Syria	9														9
Somaliland								2					2		4
Tanganyika												1	2		3
Thailand				3	1		1	2	2	4	1	3	6	4	27
Turkey	2														2
Uganda														1	1
West Indies												2	2	5	9

[a] Some cadets from East Africa were listed as 'East African' rather than by country.
[b] Includes seven Nepalese in the Brigade of Gurkhas.

cadet to Sandhurst after the war. As we saw in Chapter 2, this initiative evolved into the Commonwealth Military Training Assistance Scheme (CWMTAS), and, as more states entered independence, the sums provided through the scheme steadily grew.[35] Only weeks after the CRO launched the CWMTAS, Alan Lennox-Boyd, the colonial secretary, complained that the colonies were losing out to cadets from newly independent states and 'not getting their fair share' of Sandhurst vacancies.[36]

At this date growing anxiety about new states looking to other, 'undesirable', quarters to fulfil their training needs, probably informed by concerns about the first independent Commonwealth African state, Ghana, reinforced the case for the admission of Commonwealth cadets. In May 1958 the Ghanaian Cabinet agreed that the policy of sending Ghanaians to RMAS would continue, but decided that arrangements should also be made to send some officers to other countries for training, especially as Ghana was unable to secure all the Academy places it sought.[37] British officers were dismayed when some Ghanaians were sent to Pakistan, which had opened its own military academy on the Sandhurst model, even as a small number of Pakistanis also continued to attend Sandhurst. Only a 'short step to elsewhere', as Sir Lashmer (Bolo) Whistler, the last Colonel Commandant of the RWAFF, noted.[38] Indeed, it was acknowledged within the War Office that Sandhurst had to accept the overseas cadets because if Britain did not 'they will go to Russia'.[39] Yet, the Ghanaian case illustrates that, while newly independent states began to diversify their associations, especially where they sought to break their strong reliance on Britain, they mostly also continued to utilize training opportunities in Britain, reflecting their urgent need for a local officer class. Because their new armies were created from the old British colonial regiments, maintaining structures and practices associated with the British Army, there was a strong argument for training in Britain. In practical terms, continuity assisted the maintenance of cohesion within new national armies, preventing the importation of too many different traditions.[40] Other circumstances also acted to reinforce a British orientation, evident again in the case of Ghana, where Nkrumah cancelled the country's training agreement with Pakistan after a military coup there in 1958. Somewhat ironically (since the coup had been led by General Ayub Khan, who had himself trained at Sandhurst) the episode apparently underscored for

[35] See pp. 81–2.
[36] TNA, WO 32/17829, Alan Lennox-Boyd to Christopher Soames, Sec. of State for War, 30 July 1959.
[37] PRAAD, ADM 13/1/27, Cabinet minutes, 27 May 1958, item 7. On sending cadets to Russia, see Gutteridge, *Military in African Politics*, p. 103.
[38] TNA, WO 216/913, no. 42B, Whistler to Festing 23 February 1959.
[39] TNA, WO 32/17829, 248A, DMT to DMI, 9 September 1958.
[40] Written answers to author's question provided by Ghanaian Army officer, a cadet in the 1970s.

Nkrumah the value of an allegedly British apolitical military tradition. Nor when some Ghanaians were sent to Russia did the Ghanaian military regard this as a success, and the cadets themselves were reportedly unhappy.[41]

Simultaneously, other contemporaneous circumstances fuelled demand within the British establishment to admit overseas cadets. Access to places at Sandhurst appears to have been perceived almost as an elastoplast that could be utilized to patch over other developments of an adverse kind. In the 1950s the greatest blows to Britain's world standing came in Egypt, when the departure of the final British soldiers in summer 1956 under the terms of the agreement reached two years before was followed swiftly by Nasser's nationalization of the Canal Company, and the humiliating Suez Crisis. With sterling under huge pressure, and Britain facing almost universal international condemnation, Anthony Eden's government was forced to withdraw troops only days after they had reoccupied Egypt in alliance with the French and secret collusion with the Israelis. Suez was swiftly followed by the 1958 revolution in Iraq against the reigning monarch, a British ally, sweeping away what influence Britain had retained in the area, and increasing the importance of the Gulf states. In this context the War Office became concerned about access to Sandhurst for nationals from Kuwait; not only a crucial source of oil but also a valuable member of the sterling area. As Britain sought, in Simon Smith's words, to 'insulate' the Gulf states from the 'shock waves' produced by the Iraqi revolution, the War Office was anxious lest difficulties securing training places prejudice both Britain's relations with Kuwait and the efficiency of its army. Since Kuwait was at this point renegotiating its ties to Britain, leading in 1961 to the termination of the 1899 treaty which had allowed Britain to control its external affairs, Britain's future position in this key state and the region generally depended more than ever on goodwill.[42] In the event, although two Kuwaitis had attended in the 1950s the next did not arrive until 1965, and it was only in the 1990s and 2000s after the Gulf War that they did so in large numbers. In contrast, although no Iraqis were admitted in 1959, there were three entrants in 1960 and six in 1962.[43]

By the beginning of the 1960s, then, amidst a fast-changing colonial and international situation, demand for places at Sandhurst was growing from all directions. The intensifying Cold War added to these pressures, with a committee established in the Ministry of Defence to coordinate how Britain's training

---

[41] Gutteridge, *Military in African Politics*, pp. 99, 133; information from Tony Clayton.
[42] TNA, WO 32/17829, no. 322A, F. E. Kitson (WO), about Kuwaiti students, 18 May 1960. Simon C. Smith, 'The Wind that Failed to Blow: British Policy and the End of Empire in the Gulf', in L. J. Butler and Sarah Stockwell eds., *The Wind of Change: Harold Macmillan and British Decolonization* (Palgrave Macmillan, Basingstoke, 2013), pp. 235–51, esp. 239.
[43] Data provided by RMAS.

schools might potentially be deployed as 'a cold war weapon'.[44] By January 1961 overseas students comprised approximately 13 per cent of all cadets at the Academy.[45] By the end of the year almost 800 overseas cadets from nearly 40 countries had attended the new Academy since 1947.[46]

The repeated assertions by the Sandhurst Commandant that the number of overseas students should not exceed an agreed ratio was not simply a reflection of the impossibility of accommodating both overseas and home cadets, as evident from a disinclination to address the number problem by simply constructing new accommodation blocks. Moreover, the Commandant's protests that the numbers of overseas cadets at Sandhurst had reached unacceptable and critical proportions in fact coincided with a fall in domestic applications for Sandhurst, from just under 700 in 1953 to under 600 in 1956 (although this was a situation that the Army was keen to remedy).[47] Rather, it spoke to a wider range of concerns about the impact of overseas cadets, and, specifically, those of colour, with the Commandant suggesting in 1957 that white Commonwealth cadets could be excluded from official discussions of the problems posed by the percentage of overseas cadets at the Academy.[48] Tellingly, in private the proportion of overseas to British cadets was referred to as the 'dilution' ratio.

Several key considerations lay behind this concern to limit the impact of the non-white overseas element, not least of which were persistent worries about their academic standard. Overseas applicants did not sit the same Regular Commission Board and tests that British candidates did. In colonial forces potential entrants to the officer class were chosen by British-officered selection panels. But as we saw in Chapter 2, British officers struggled to identify candidates from the colonial forces who met what they perceived to be adequate standards. In independent states the 'applying authorities' were responsible for the initial selection of candidates so long as they met the minimum age and entry requirements and passed security clearance. Publicly the RMA was at pains to deny that overseas cadets underperformed.[49] But despite some striking successes by notable high flyers (like West Indian cadet R. K. Barnes, who became the first senior under-officer born outside the United Kingdom to lead a company in the march past on the Sovereign's Parade,[50] or Ghanaian A. K. Sam, who took more or less a full sweep of all prizes for overseas cadets

[44] TNA, WO 32/17829, 368A, minute addressed to DMT, 19 January 1961.
[45] 'Africans seeking pips on their shoulders' *The Times*, 31 January 1961, p. 11.
[46] Calculated from data supplied by RMAS.
[47] French, *Army*, p. 66.
[48] TNA, WO 32/17829, the Commandant to the Under-Secretary of State, War Office, 4 October 1957.
[49] 'Africans seeking pips on their shoulders', *The Times*, 31 January 1961.
[50] RMAS, D56, Box 2, RMAS press cuttings 1950–60, report probably from 1957.

as well as several others in 1972)[51] overseas cadets were generally perceived within the Academy to be among their weakest. The first African cadets at Sandhurst, all from West Africa, passed out towards the lower end of their intake: one was eventually placed 170, a second 200 and a third 235 of a total of 238 cadets in the final order of merit.[52] Overseas cadets were underrepresented among prize winners, including for the ultimate accolade, the sword of honour. Perhaps for this reason a specific overseas prize was instituted, the 'Certificate and Stick' (later the 'Stick') as well as subsequently other prizes aimed solely at the overseas cadets.[53]

With the entry requirement set at five passes at O level, the standard of educational attainment among the British school leavers arriving at Sandhurst in the 1940s and 1950s was also by no means consistently strong. But for precisely this reason the authorities worried that the presence of significant numbers of overseas cadets adding to an existing tail might jeopardize efforts to raise standards within the post-war British Army,[54] and lessen the 'appeal' of Sandhurst to 'parents, headmasters and boys'. In turn, this would weaken recruitment at a point when the Army was struggling to build its officer class and applications to the Academy were falling.[55] To overcome the perceived problem with standards among overseas students, the War Office proposed the introduction of an English test. This went ahead, but the CRO's insistence that it should not apply to newly independent countries in the Commonwealth meant that its effect was undermined,[56] and instead the British authorities were reliant on reminding sending countries that unless candidates had received a good secondary education they would not benefit from the academic instruction.[57] To add to these difficulties, once overseas cadets had been admitted, the Academy found it tricky to deal with those who underperformed or in some other way presented problems. With overseas cadets accepted for colonial and foreign policy reasons rather than military ones, the Director General of Military Training told the Commandant in 1961 that there would be some cases among overseas cadets, such as the son of a ruler or another important figure,

[51] *The Wish Stream*, XXVI, no. 1 (Spring, 1972).
[52] RMAS, A12, Box 14, Commissioning List, December 1956'; Box 13, file 2, 'Confidential intermediate grading – intake 16'.
[53] *The Wish Stream*, XXV, no. 1 (Autumn, 1972), pp. 10–11; XXVII, no. 2 (Autumn, 1973), p. 91.
[54] Clayton, *British Officer*, p. 191.
[55] TNA, WO 32/17829, no. 268A, Commandant to DMT, 22 May 1959.
[56] Ibid., no. 111A, Commandant to Under-Secretary of State, War Office, 9 December 1955; no. 201A, extract from minutes, 608th meeting of the ECAC, 31 May 1957.
[57] RMAS, A12, Box 460, File 1800/G, Vol. 1, June 71–December 73, no. 7, 'Administrative Instructions for Candidates sent from Overseas Countries to the United Kingdom for Training for Commissions' (MoD, October 1971). Revised instructions were regularly sent to Sandhurst and Mons.

where strict attempts to police the Academy's standards might do 'more harm' than to commission a cadet who did not otherwise make the grade.[58] Behind the Academy's efforts to maintain a strict ratio were also concerns to protect Sandhurst's own culture and the character of the training delivered. Since the British Army authorities aimed at acculturation to Britain's own traditions, overdilution threatened to undermine the logic for the admission of overseas cadets, since it would reduce the opportunities for close 'touch' with their British counterparts.[59] In accepting overseas cadets, the British government was also exporting a form of cultural capital, and fundamental changes to this might weaken its international appeal.

'Blown Together by the Wind of Change': Overseas Cadets at Sandhurst in the 1950s and Early 1960s

As at other institutions, the uneven political trajectories of different regions of the British Empire in the 1950s, when the speed with which the Empire would unravel was not fully apparent, were, thus, reflected in apparently contradictory developments. Despite his 1955 recommendations, in 1956, only months before Ghana's independence, Templer urged cadets at Sandhurst to study the 'problems of our great Colonial Empire where one day most of you will almost certainly serve'.[60] With its emphasis on character-building and exploration, the 'adventure training' commenced in the early 1960s superficially also seemed to hark back to an earlier imperial age, but it seems likely that it also reflected Britain's changing role. A small expedition in the winter of 1962–3 to the Hadhramaut, Saudi Arabia, received secret orders to carry out local reconnaissance at the borders of the western and eastern Aden protectorate and the Yemen and to make contact with the local security forces of the eastern Aden Protectorate. The expedition coincided with a period of acute instability in the region, as resistance grew to the British presence in Aden from an Egyptian-backed National Liberation Front and the Front for the Liberation of Occupied South Yemen. An emergency was declared in Aden in December 1963.[61] Some of Sandhurst's overseas cadets participated in these expeditions, and their presence produced some striking situations. When a Kenyan cadet, a member of the Sandhurst expedition to Aden, became involved in firing on

---

[58] TNA, WO 32/17829, Lieut-Gen. J. B. Ashworth, DGMT to Commandant, 12 May 1961.
[59] Ibid., no. 217A, Commandant to Under-Secretary of State, WO, 4 October 1957.
[60] Speech reproduced in *The Wish Stream* XI, no. 1 (February 1957), p. 6.
[61] Similarly, a three-man 'adventure training expedition' to Muscat and Oman in 1970, which spent three weeks in Southern Arabia attached to the Sultan of Muscat's armed forces (to which the British government had been providing financial and material assistance since 1958), aimed to obtain knowledge and experiences of serving with an Arab force. RMAS, post-expeditionary reports held in central library, Sandhurst: 'The Hahramaut, Saudi Arabia December–January 1963'; 'Adventure Training Expedition to Muscat and Oman. A Report [1970]'.

rebels, Bashford-Snell was advised to ask the cadet to forget the incident, but recalled that years later when the cadet had become a senior officer in the Kenyan Army, he himself enjoyed retelling the story of his role in repelling 'the Imperialists' enemies'.[62]

Templer's reference to 'one day' hence invoked a picture of a future that was even then incompatible with the changes already underway, of which the presence of overseas cadets at Sandhurst was one manifestation. Colonial pressures were growing in ways that some feared were spilling over to the Academy. Publicly the British authorities hoped that friendships between cadets could be 'the most potent force for good in the Commonwealth and Empire'.[63] To facilitate integration, overseas cadets were dispersed evenly through different companies and within these to the platoons, formed from each intake within a company. Some platoons had a pair from one country, but cadets of the same nationality were not otherwise grouped together, with most platoons generally comprising some twenty-five British cadets and four from overseas, at least one of whom would be appointed to the company's cadet officer class.[64] Mons later experimented with consolidating overseas students together but the arrangement was not regarded as a success, with the 'overseas' platoon forming 'an all-black' clique. The Director of Army Training acknowledged that replicating this arrangement carried the risk of alienating 'our older [overseas] customers' who 'would be greatly offended by any degree of segregation', and might well also attract 'bad publicity' at home. Segregation also undermined one of the main advantages to be gained from foreign students training in Britain: the 'mixing and exchange of ideas' with their British contemporaries.[65] Nevertheless, the integration led to some friction within platoons when some of the weaker cadets had to be 'carried' by others.[66] Aware of difficulties, some platoon officers tended to go easier on the overseas students than their British counterparts.[67]

The dispersal of overseas cadets of different origin could also result in some odd associations, with the first black African cadets in the same company as whites from the settler-dominated Central African Federation. *The Times* speculated optimistically that while British cadets might learn from close proximity to African cadets, 'White Rhodesians and East Africans' might 'learn even

---

[62] Cited in Pugsley and Holdsworth, *Sandhurst*, p. 107.
[63] *The Wish Stream*, VII, no. 1 (April 1953), p. 1.
[64] Information received from Tony Clayton.
[65] RMAS, A12, Box 460, file 1800/G, Vol. 1, June 71–December 1973, no. 70, 'Overseas vacancies at RMAS', Col D. E. M. Earle (for Director of Army Training), MoD, 6 August 1973.
[66] RMAS, A12, Box 456, file RMAS 124/OC, folio 140, 'minutes of a meeting to discuss arrangements for overseas cadets', 28 February 1991.
[67] Interview, British officer, 10 May 2016.

Figure 6.2. Intake 25 Normandy Company, RMAS, September 1958, including
Ghanaian Officer Cadets Afrifa and Akuffo

more from this experience of being blown together by the wind of change'.[68]
But while one ex-cadet, the Ghanaian, Akwasi A. Afrifa (seen Figure 6.2), who
was instrumental in the successful coup against Nkrumah in February 1966 and
in 1969 become head of state, recalled that he encountered 'no discrimination
whatsoever', with the Academy 'an institution which teaches that all men are
equal',[69] other evidence points to the existence of significant racial tensions.
Relative social isolation led the earliest African students to stick together, with
consequently more mixing between senior and junior cadets than was usual,[70]
and the Commandant reported that overseas cadets at the Academy tended to
'segregate themselves'.[71]

Indeed, in private some painted a bleak picture of race relations at the
Academy. In the late 1950s, when anxieties were high about the number of
colonial cadets, the War Office's Director of Military Instruction reported that
the 'foreigners' group together in the canteens, where 'such gatherings are
referred to as "the bazaar" by the British cadets'. Speaking shortly after the

---

[68] 'Africans Seeking Pips on Their Shoulders', *The Times* [London, England] 31 January
1961, p. 11.
[69] Akwasi A. Afrifa, *The Ghana Coup, 24 February 1966*, (Frank Cass, Guildford and London,
1966), pp. 50–1.
[70] Luckham, *The Nigerian Military*, p. 132; written answers provided to author by anonymous
Ghanaian officer, a cadet in the 1970s; evidence from RMAS files.
[71] TNA, WO 32/17829, no. 217A, Commandant to Under-Secretary of State for War, WO, 4
October 1957.

revolution in Iraq, he expressed concern that the anti-British sentiment of two Iraqi officers, rumoured to have been British trained, might stem from the treatment they had received in Britain. He believed, that with British cadets 'not renowned for tolerance towards those who do not conform to the normal British pattern of behaviour', cliques and antagonisms had developed. Nevertheless, he himself was suspicious of the overseas cadets. Reflecting contemporary ideas about overseas student radicalism, he complained that throughout Africa and Asia '"students" are now exerting an improper political influence', and 'are filled with an aggressive nationalism'. 'Those who come to Sandhurst are probable [sic] typical of these' he claimed, their heads 'filled with reckless, muddled and intransigent ideas'.[72]

As the reference to the 'bazaar' implies, cadets of Middle Eastern origin appear to have been the least popular. The War Office's Director of Military Training did not accept all aspects of his colleague's assessment of the state of race relations at the Academy, but admitted that while some 'cadets of colour, like the West Africans' did well and were popular, those from the Arab states were 'not at all easy to get on with', in part because of problems resulting from their poor English, but also because recent developments in the Middle East were generating tensions between some Arab and British cadets.[73]

Although neither man explicitly made the connection it was also surely significant that this exchange occurred only days after race violence erupted in Notting Hill, West London, on 1 September 1958, after West Indians who had settled in Britain in growing numbers since 1948 were targeted by white gangs. Stories of Britain's 'race war' filled the press and attracted attention around the world. In their aftermath, colonial and Commonwealth governments sought reassurance from British officials that they would ensure the protection of their nationals in Britain, and in telegrams sent to British representatives overseas, the British government sought to play down the significance of the clashes and questioned the characterization of them as 'race riots'.[74]

At this acutely sensitive moment in the history of British race relations, as well as delicate juncture for Britain overseas, officials considered taking new steps to improve race relations at Sandhurst. However, procedures already existed to prevent possible friction between British and overseas cadets and to support the latter at the Academy. British cadets were 'discreetly briefed' on their relations with those from overseas, and each national cohort was assigned a member of staff to 'look out for them'.[75] Sandhurst's own staff were carefully

[72] Ibid., 245A, CR Price, DMI to DMT, 22 August 1958; 248A, DMT response, 9 September 1958; no. 253 A, DGMT to DMI, 30 September 1958.
[73] Ibid., 248A, DMT response, 9 September 1958; no. 253 A, DGMT to DMI, 30 September 1958.
[74] Hammond Perry, *London Is the Place for Me*, pp. 89–106.
[75] TNA, WO 32/17829, no. 253 A, DGMT to DMI, 30 September 1958.

chosen.[76] There were several – like Kenneth Ingham, historian of Africa, and Antony Clayton, who had served in the Kenyan colonial administration in the 1950s and in London working with Kenyan students – who were brought into teaching posts in the Academy. From 1952 the lion's share of managing the welfare of overseas cadets at Sandhurst, however, was shouldered by a volunteer, Miss Margaret Jones. While she was never formally on the pay role, Sandhurst provided accommodation and paid her expenses.[77] An 'institution within an institution',[78] she quickly became indispensable, and, more than any other individual, played a key role in relation to the pastoral care of overseas students. She came to know individual cadets well, hosting lunches at her home, and also interviewing them for vacation placements. Although very different from the Bank of England's John Loynes, or Oxford's Margery Perham, Jones became a personal face for her institution, developing a diaspora of connections at home and overseas. She drew on her 'own personal' contacts with embassies and high commissions and travelled extensively in countries from which the cadets came 'as guest of their army officers', thereby reinforcing her credentials for dealing with the cadets at the Academy.[79] During the following decades she acquired extraordinary influence with successive generations of cadets, securing her own otherwise somewhat anomalous position at Sandhurst itself. The generous response of various overseas countries to a call for donations to a fund in her memory following her death in 2017 demonstrates the continuing affection with which she was still held by overseas cadets, and guests at her memorial service included diplomatic representatives from Afghanistan, Bahrain, Jordan and Qatar.[80]

Sport played a key role in the success or otherwise with which overseas students integrated at the Academy. It was a crucial part of Sandhurst life: success in sporting competitions and in drill determined the selection of the 'Sovereign's Company', which received the Colour to be presented by the Sovereign's representative at the Sovereign's Parade at the end of the summer term from the existing 'Sovereign's Company'.[81] In the 1950s and 1960s Sandhurst remained a conservative place. Horse riding, polo, rifle shooting, fox hunting, rowing, sailing, rugby and cricket were all popular. Some overseas cadets were better equipped to participate in these activities than others. Nigerian cadet Hassan Katsina, the second son of the Emir of Katsina, 'a fine

---

[76] TNA, WO 32/17829, no. 253 A, DGMT to DMI, 30 September 1958.
[77] RMAS, A12, Box 460, file RMAS 224/A, 'Responsibilities towards Overseas Student Officers and Cadets', Lt. Col. K. J. Davey, GSO 1, 2 August 1978.
[78] O/Cdt Azmi Hamid Bidin, in Pugsley and Holdsworth, *Sandhurst*, p. 77.
[79] RMAS, A12, Box 451, file with broken cover, no. 25, 'Responsibilities towards Overseas Student Officers and Cadets', Robin Crawford, 11 February 1975.
[80] Information provided by the Academy. Miss Jones's papers are now being sorted but it was not possible to consult them for this book.
[81] Pugsley and Holdsworth, *Sandhurst*, pp. 177–81.

polo player', though fitted in well.[82] Nonetheless overseas cadets were prominent in other sports, especially boxing and athletics, in which the Academy came to 'depend on the Commonwealth element' for success. In 1961 a cadet from Tanganyika, Mrisho Sarakikya, set a new Sandhurst record for the mile that ten years later remained unbeaten.[83] As well as running intercompany competitions, Sandhurst participated in occasional athletics meetings with western European military academies. At some of these African students representing Sandhurst competed against cadets at St Cyr from Francophone African states, reproducing old imperial associations within Europe.

Yet for overseas cadets, plucked out of their normal environment, adjusting to their new situation might still be difficult.[84] One commandant who arrived at Sandhurst in the early 1990s direct from a posting in Zimbabwe remembered the transition from the 'informality of Africa to the traditional pomp and ceremony of Sandhurst' as 'stark'.[85] For African cadets a generation earlier the contrast must have been all the greater and potentially quite bewildering. 'Lots of unnecessary shouting and doing things which have no meaning or/and importance' recalled one; while, for another former overseas cadet, 'bullying/polishing boots' was an overwhelming memory. Even the most well-connected overseas cadets appeared to be subject to the same discipline. 'Mr King Hussein sir – are you an idle king, sir – What are you?' demanded his Regimental Sergeant Major when the monarch, enrolled as an officer cadet in 1952, failed to respond to an instruction quickly enough.[86] Although, as we have seen, for diplomatic reasons not all cadets *were* always treated equally, episodes of this kind, coupled with the fact that all cadets were addressed as 'sir' by the drill sergeants, may lie behind Afrifa's perception that they were.[87]

For overseas cadets some of the difficulties adjusting may have been mitigated by the familiarity of drill and physical training. In the 1950s and early 1960s British officers in colonial regiments also provided some preparation for African cadets selected for Sandhurst in the form of a short training course to give them some military training prior to their departure.[88] In East Africa the British officer in command of the Training Company and the Military Training School, at the suggestion of an Asian officer recently graduated from the Academy, even experimented with organizing pre-Sandhurst training on manners. More fin-

---

[82] Bodleian, Mss Afr. s. 1734, Box 2, file 83, appendix 1, ff. 63–4, Major William Catcheside; Gutteridge, *Military in African Politics*, p. 63.
[83] *The Wish Stream*, XXVI, no. 1 (Spring, 1972), p. 31; RMAS, A12, Box 450, Lt. Col. K. J. Davey to Col. R. K. Barnes, Jamaican High Commission, 21 June 1978.
[84] Written information provided by Anthony Clayton to the author.
[85] RMAS, D56, Box 306 'Sandhurst – a tradition of leadership': Papers and correspondence, box 3', questionnaires completed by staff.
[86] Pugsley and Holdsworth, *Sandhurst*, p. 90.
[87] See above p. 253.
[88] Bodleian, Mss Afr. s. 1715, Box 3, file 42, f. 65 (Lt. Col. H. K. P. Chavasse).

ishing school than military training, this involved basic instruction on how to use a knife and fork before a final dinner where some thirty sat down to eat.[89] But even where they had experienced some acclimatization, many overseas cadets found England an alien environment. For those who had come from warmer countries the British climate proved particularly challenging. Field exercises during the British winter could be uncomfortable and potentially the most difficult aspect of training at Sandhurst.[90] For some it was even debilitating. The family of a Jamaican cadet were 'extremely frightened' to learn their son was hospitalized with frostbite, 'rather like people here would have been on learning that one of their officers was down with malaria in Jamaica', explained the military attaché at the Jamaican High Commission in London.[91]

Among post-war overseas cadets there was not, however, the same attrition rate that had characterized the experience of Indian cadets at Sandhurst in the 1920s.[92] Only a minority, notably those from Gulf states, came from the same privileged backgrounds as the Indian cadets had done, and for some of these withdrawal would have meant a loss of face, especially when several of their own monarchs had stayed the course. Otherwise the majority of Commonwealth cadets were not self-funded and came from very different backgrounds. That RMAS provided accommodation and catering and kept cadets fully employed except at weekends, and in recess periods meant it could shelter overseas cadets from some of the challenges of living in an alien country. One cadet from Mozambique (admitted in a later period) told his lecturer how easy life at Sandhurst was, with its three meals a day and roof over his head, in contrast to his former existence as a guerrilla insurgent.[93] It was 'perhaps the best time in my life as a young man', judged a Ghanaian officer, from a middle-class family background.[94]

'Changed Out of All Recognition': Sandhurst in a 'Post-Imperial' Age

While decolonization delivered more and more overseas cadets to Sandhurst's gates, it also changed the British Army's geographical field of operations. By the 1960s only a smattering of smaller island dependencies and the African high-commission territories remained. In line with the shrinking Empire, as

---

[89] Ibid., Box 6, file 146, pp. 19–20 (Lt. Col. Charles Ivey).
[90] Written answers to author's questions provided by Ghanaian officer, a cadet in the 1970s.
[91] RMAS, A12, Box 450, Jamaica file, Col. R. K. Barnes, Jamaican High Commission London to Lt. Col. K. J. Davey, RMAS, 7 June 1978. Barnes had been the Academy's first high-performing overseas cadet, see p. 249.
[92] See p. 54.
[93] Pugsley and Holdsworth, *Sandhurst*, p. 152.
[94] Written answers to author's questions provided by Ghanaian officer, a cadet in the 1970s.

well as Britain's weakened economy, the British Army was also pared back. In 1957 a defence review by the Secretary of State, Duncan Sandys, placed more emphasis on building up a nuclear deterrent, and proposed a corresponding reduction in conventional forces. National service was ended and when the last conscripts were finally demobilized the Army reverted once again to its peacetime role as a small, professional all-regular force, a transition of which Templer as CIGS was a principal architect.[95]

Britain's senior military men were outwardly bullish. Templer's successor as CIGS, Field Marshal Sir Francis Festing, reflecting on the end of national service, suggested that the regular army was more in accord with 'the national genius of our race' than a 'continental' conception of conscription; moreover it had twice in recent times saved the British nation, Commonwealth and 'our race'.[96] But in reality Britain's senior military figures now had a much smaller army on which they could draw. David French argues that Sandys' promise that he could reduce the size of British forces without a reduction in Britain's operational capacities was proven empty when interventions in Jordan, Kuwait, Indonesia and, following the mutinies, East Africa, left Britain without the means or appetite for intervention in Rhodesia after the declaration of UDI. The British Army had become, he suggests, a 'Potemkim Army', designed to have just enough capability to create the illusion of strength.[97]

Between 1966 and 1968 the East of Suez cuts signalled the end of a world role that dated back to the previous century. More than any other, the change demonstrated to the rest of the world Britain was no longer a global impe-rial power. It did not go unnoticed in Britain's former colonies. The Zambian President, Kenneth Kaunda, writing to the British Prime Minister, Harold Wilson, to explain that his country would no longer use loaned service per-sonnel, expressed the hope that his country might instead recruit on contract those he pointedly described as the 'unfortunate' British military personnel made redundant as a result of cuts stemming from the recession in the United Kingdom.[98] Coincidentally, only weeks before this exchange, Kaunda's own son, Panji Kaunda, had joined young British cadets beginning an army career, having entered Sandhurst in January 1967.

Britain's main military spheres of operation were now the Rhine in Germany and, from the early 1970s, Northern Ireland, where the onset of the Troubles saw British troops deployed on the streets. Ashley Jackson argues persuasively that aspects of the 1970s, a decade of domestic crises and cuts when Britain 'chose

---

[95] French, *Army*, pp. 156–71.
[96] *The Wish Stream* XIII, no. 1 (Spring, 1959), pp. 4–5.
[97] French, *Army*, pp. 300, 306–7.
[98] ZNA, CO 17/1/7, 'UK Technical Assistance and Aid', 1965–1967, no. 21, A. S. Masiye (Permanent Secretary, Office of the President) to Major-General C. M. Grigg, Commander Zambian Army, 28 February 1967.

the European club over the Commonwealth', can distract from the 'hardy survival of Britain as an international player that never ceased to seek a global role', especially with the 'resurgence of an interventionist Britain from the Falklands War'.[99] Nonetheless, in the late 1960s and early 1970s, British economic decline and the withdrawal from East of Suez produced very real changes for the Army and for Sandhurst. 'Whole generations' of soldiers were growing up and assuming positions of responsibility, opined Lt Col. P. G. T. Bates, 'who have no experience other than Northern Ireland and BAOR'. 'Our ability', he thought, 'to intervene in third world problems must be becoming increasingly restricted as a result of our increasing lack of experience in any theatre of operations other than North West Europe'.[100] When the opinion of Sandhurst's cadets was canvassed in 1966 they articulated growing dissatisfaction at the 'gradual emasculation of the Armed Forces' and the lack of new roles to 'compensate for the loss of the old combat ones'.[101] Taking the Sovereign's Parade that year, General Sir Charles Jones acknowledged that the situation was 'grim in many ways'. He hoped to bolster the morale of those just embarking on their army careers. 'This country will wield its influence in the future in some great way – not in the same way as in the past, but in some way', and for that, he reassured them, Britain would still need an army.[102] When the Chief of the Naval Staff, Admiral Sir Varyl Begg, spoke on the same theme the next year after the announcement of the East of Suez withdrawal, he betrayed bemusement – even bewilderment – at the dizzying speed with which Britain's role had changed and the emergence of 'fifty five, but it could well be fifty-six or fifty-seven, so quickly is the process going – fifty five new independent countries who are responsible amongst other things for their own defence'. Britain, he asserted, would nevertheless still need its army.[103] Despite the assurances, the following year the fall in British intake forced the Academy to close Inkerman, Somme and Normandy companies and, in one very visible indication that economies were the order of the day, cheaper paper was used to produce the Academy's journal *The Wish Stream*.

The effects of British imperial and economic decline, coupled with the transition in British defence policy from a focus on conventional warfare to greater reliance on nuclear deterrence, interacted with other dynamics in British society to make the wider environment increasingly less hospitable for Sandhurst. Interest in pursuing a career in the Army as members of an officer class fell. In particular, the expansion of higher education saw more school leavers aspiring to attend university, and the numbers of British applicants seeking a regular career commission rather than a short service one slumped, often because

[99] Jackson, 'Empire and Beyond', pp. 1350–2.
[100] Bodleian, Mss Afr. s. 1734, Box 1, file 27, ff. 1, 13.
[101] Results of a poll among intakes 37–40: *The Wish Stream*, XX, no. 2 (Autumn, 1966), p. 99.
[102] Reproduced in *The Wish Stream*, XXI, no. 1 (Spring, 1967).
[103] Reproduced in *The Wish Stream*, XXII, no. 1 (Spring, 1968).

cadets knew they could convert to regular commissions while in service. At the time of its relaunch, the War Office had been clear that the Academy should be organized as a school rather than a university,[104] but as more young people in Britain began to go to university the position of the Academy became increasingly anomalous. With more of the population now receiving degrees an independent review into Britain's service colleges completed in 1965 recommended that the services should cease to be largely officered by men who had received no formal non-military education after the age of eighteen.[105] This position was rendered more problematic by other social change. Between 1947 and 1967 the number of cadets from elite public schools fell from 26.4 per cent to under 10 per cent.[106] By 1963 as much as half the intake was from grammar schools.[107] But as more officers came from grammar rather than the elite public schools, the class and social difference between a British officer and non-officer class potentially shrank, and it became more important that officers had received a higher education if only to differentiate them from the Army rank and file. Equipping officers to deal with the complexities of modern weapons and equipment provided a further need for higher education.[108] Sandhurst's own staff harboured ambitions to deliver a university-style education, especially with the inauguration of the two-year course that more closely resembled a degree. However, the 1965 review was not only critical of aspects of Sandhurst's training, but squashed these ambitions, emphasizing that the Academy should focus instead on developing collaborative relations with Britain's expanding university sector.[109]

In 1972 the effect of these changes in the wider environment came home to impact on the Academy with force. Mons was relocated to Sandhurst and with the Academy now the site for training for both short *and* regular service commissions, the Director of Army Training established a committee under the chairmanship of Brigadier F. B. Tillard into the future of the RMAS course. Both the military and academic staff at Sandhurst, as well as a new RMAS Academic Advisory Council, established the previous year to assist the Director of Studies and academic staff and chaired by the military historian Michael Howard who had coauthored the 1965 independent review, staunchly resisted the cuts now on the table. The outgoing Director of Studies, Geoffrey S. Sale,

---

[104] RMAS, D56, Box 108, file 'papers for Commandant', paper 1A, 'Army College Curriculum', para 3 (1946).
[105] RMAS, A12, Box 372, file RMAS/1A Comdt., Howard-English, para. 9.
[106] French, *Army*, pp. 60–4.
[107] Parliamentary answer by John Profumo (Secretary of State for War), *The Times*, 2 May 1963: RMAS, D56, Box 1, Cuttings Book 1961–4.
[108] RMAS, A12, Box 351, file 1, RMAS/297/G (SD), Commandant to all senior RMAS staff, 18 February 1966.
[109] Ibid., Box 372, file RMAS/1A Comdt., [Tillard] Review of Officer Cadet Training, Annex A, Summaries of Previous Relevant Report. DAT Working Party Report 1965 and the Howard-English Report.

who had presided over the development of the two-year Standard Military Course, was 'truly distressed by the thought that what we have accomplished recently may all be swept under the carpet'. The Commandant, General Philip Tower, urged the Assistant Commandant and the Academy's delegate on the Tillard Committee, J. H. Page, that he must not let himself 'be jostled into ill-considered haste & hasty decisions'. Page recognized that he was a 'lone voice crying out', but argued as 'vehemently as I could', emphasizing that creating '"instant officers" of limited outlook and intellectual development' would overturn recent success in overcoming the 'Blimpish' stereotype of the British officer and lead to a two-tier system dividing graduates and non-graduates.[110]

However, there was a lack of sympathy for Sandhurst elsewhere within the Army establishment. Some suspected this reflected the alternative perspective of those who had themselves come through the short-service route, but it also embodied persistent scepticism about the value of the education provided at the Academy.[111] 'The Sandhurst product', wrote one senior Army commander, 'is equipped with neither a practical military expertise nor a sound academic education of any worthwhile standard. The tempo ... is too slow, the course is too long, and the military instruction lacks a sense of purpose'.[112] How best to combine the academic and military components of the course had long been a problem. The academic staff complained that cadets were frequently too tired by physical exercise to study or placed a low priority on general education; for their part, the officers felt that military training was forgotten during the extended interludes devoted to academic work.[113] Periodic adjustments were made to alter the way in which the two elements were combined, but in 1980 the Director of Army Training complained that the two sides had been 'uneasy bedfellows' for thirty years.[114] Sandhurst's course also had a disjointed quality, reflecting dynamics not dissimilar to those that had determined the mixed economy of the university Devonshire courses for Colonial Service officers. 'You know, as I do', the Director of Army Training reminded Major-General Jackie Harman, Tower's successor, 'how artificially' the pre-1971 course was put together with 'a sort of auction for periods conducted by Heads of Department'.[115]

---

[110] Ibid., Box 369, file RMAS 299/4/Gword, G. S. Sale to Dr Vick, Vice-Chancellor, Queen's University, Belfast, copied to Commandant, 9 August 1971; P. T. Tower to J. H. Page, undated; J. H. Page to Brigadier Tillard, 15 June 1971; Page to Tower, 11 June 1971.

[111] Ibid., Box 372, file RMAS/1A/Comdt., R. C. Ford to Michael Howard, 24 April 1974. On weaknesses in Sandhurst training, see French, *Army*, pp. 62–4.

[112] Ibid., Box 351, file 4, comments by General R. C. McLeod, Gen. Officer CinC, HQ East co, n.d. but 1965.

[113] See, ibid., 'file 1, 'Academic Studies at RMAS, 1964', undated note by T. G. C. Ward, Department of Maths.

[114] Ibid., Box 371, file 'DAT Review – Offr Trg', vol. 5, comments on paper by Crawford, 17 February 1981.

[115] Ibid., Box 372, file RMAS/1A/Comdt., H. R. S. Pain to Major-General J. W. Harman, 8 October 1973.

In 1972, with the Academy's staff unable to muster sufficient external support, swingeing changes were imposed on Sandhurst. All cadets were initially to be admitted to a new 'Standard Military Course' (SMC), replacing the old Mons short-service commission programme. SMC cadets joined New College, briefly renamed Mons College, although at the insistence of a new Commandant, General Robert Ford, the Academy quickly reverted to the old name. Lasting only twenty-five weeks, the training comprised some weeks of professional academic education and a shorter period of military training. Successive cohorts graduated in record time, and several Sovereign's Parades were now held in one year.[116] After a period of additional specialist training appropriate to whatever branch of the service they were destined for, those graduating were given junior officer rank. Those of sufficient ability progressed to a Regular Career Commission (RCC) course, based at Old College, where, after a modification to the initial arrangements, they were given a 'Sandhurst commission' and the rank of '2nd lieutenant'. Those entering via the graduate entry courses based at Victory College were also given the rank of 2nd lieutenant or of lieutenant.[117] The MoD introduced a variety of other entry routes to try to encourage more applicants, including in 1976 a short service option into an existing university cadetship scheme with successful candidates awarded a bursary while at university in return for committing to serve in the British Army for at least three years on their graduation.[118] When in 1984 the Women's Royal Army Corps College at Camberley was also relocated to Sandhurst, the RMA became the only British centre for training army officers. Later, overseas women would also be included in the standard commissioning course. Both Harman, and his successor, General Ford, who arrived in December 1973, kept up a fight against the changes, successfully proposing an extension for the SMS to twenty-eight weeks and the RCC from 21 to 23; the difficulties experienced by the overseas cadets as well as by those who had come from Welbeck, were among the reasons cited in support.[119] Sandhurst training had become, Ford complained, 'far too much of an "Instant Platoon Commander-producing unit"'.[120] At stake was the issue of whether a Sandhurst training should now serve in effect as a foundation rather than a complete training in its own right.[121]

[116] *The Wish Stream*, XXVI, no. 2 (Autumn, 1972), intake lists; XXVII, no. 1 (Spring, 1973).
[117] RMAS, A12, Box 457, file RMAS 1600/G, papers on overseas students.
[118] Ibid., Box 448, file RMAS 1302/G, 'University Cadetship Scheme – SSC option'; 'RMAS 809/ DoS, 'Degree Training Policy', incl. 'Army Officers at University', February 1975.
[119] Ibid., Box 369, file RMAS 1714/G, 'Future training at RMA Sandhurst', paper by Ford, undated but 25 April 25; for Harman, see RMAS, A12, Box 372, file RMAS/1A/Comdt., Harman to Major-General F. R. S. Pain, 29 November 1973.
[120] Ibid., Box 372, file RMAS/1A/Comdt., RC Ford to Gen. Sir John Mogg, Deputy Supreme Commander, Supreme Head Quarter, Allied Powers Europe, 24 April 1974; RMAS/1714/G, 'Future Training at the RMAS' paper by Ford for Committee on Army Regular Office Training, April 1974.
[121] *The Wish Stream*, XXIX, no. 2 (Autumn, 1975), 'foreword'.

The Academy had 'changed out of all recognition' reported the Academy's journal *The Wish Stream*, introducing a short guide to the new courses and college arrangements.[122] It now offered a multiplicity of different courses, but none of the duration and scale of the old two-year training programme. Within the confines of the new courses it was harder to instil 'leadership', just as the wider social intake appeared to make this more necessary: state school entrants were often judged 'narrow in outlook' and arrived 'with less leadership experience'.[123] As the decade came to a close some of the old concerns persisted and there were new problems. Among a British officer class there were worries about pay and career prospects and difficulties reconciling home commitments with an officer's lifestyle organized around the mess. The loss of Britain's Empire, economic decline and social change, had all taken their toll. 'A cause and a great leader were wanted', it was reported as part of a review into 'the way ahead' in 1978.[124] A major review into 'Sandhurst in the 80s' inaugurated by the Director of Army Training led to a variety of proposals for fresh reform, including for an extension to the course. However, the following year, Sandhurst, like the universities, was hit by cuts in government spending. Although they 'were getting on with it', 'life' was no longer 'quite so much fun', the Commandant reported in 1981.[125]

An Instrument of Soft Power: Overseas Students at Sandhurst from the 1960s

Even as the British authorities struggled to maintain recruitment, and morale at the Academy plummeted, Sandhurst's reputation was apparently riding high overseas, with foreign and Commonwealth demand for admission to the Academy buoyant. As Table 6.2 shows, Sandhurst trained cadets from *all* new Commonwealth African states, and Figure 6.3 shows that the new post-war academy also admitted cadets from most other former British colonies, the only exceptions being the smaller island states and India.[126] Many cadets hailed too from Britain's erstwhile informal empire and Middle Eastern allies. In addition to Jordan, these included cadets from Saudi Arabia and the Gulf states. Sandhurst also took cadets from the former Belgian Congo, from 1964 renamed the Democratic Republic of the Congo, and, from 1971, Zaire.

---

[122] *The Wish Stream*, XXVIII, no. 1 (Spring, 1974).
[123] RMAS, A12, Box 372, file 'The new course at Sandhurst', 'Report on the Validation study of the standard of Military Course, the Regular Career Course, The Direct Entry Course and the Post-University Cadetship course at the RMAS', December 1978; Major-General P. MacLellan, RCB, to DAT, 19 April 1979.
[124] RMAS, A12, Box 351, file 3, 'The Way Ahead', 1978.
[125] RMAS, D56. Box 87, file 'RMAS Defence Cuts 1981', Lt. Col. B. J. Lockhard for Commandant to HQSE District, 1 October 1981.
[126] The evidence in the following paragraphs is drawn from data supplied by RMAS, and supplemented by further information from the intake lists in the Academy's journal, *The Wish Stream*.

Table 6.2. *Entrants to Sandhurst from Anglophone African colonies/states by country and year, 1951–89*[a]

Country	1951	1952	1953	1954	1955	1956	1957	1958	1959	1960
Gambia								1		
Ghana			1	1	1	6	2	13	8	10
Nigeria	2	3	1	2	7	3	4	6	13	9
Sierra Leone			1	1		3				2
East Africa[b]								1	4	2
Kenya										2
Tanzania								1	2	
Uganda										1
Somaliland								2	2	2
Malawi										
Zambia										
Rhod/Zimbabwe				5	9	7	10	2	5	5
Botswana										
Lesotho										
Swaziland										
Total	2	3	3	9	17	19	16	26	34	33

Country	1961	1962	1963	1964	1965	1966	1967	1968	1969	1970
Gambia										
Ghana	8	8	4	4	4	9	6	5	2	3
Nigeria	9	8	10	5				3	2	3
Sierra Leone	1	3								
East Africa	3									
Kenya		1	9	7	8	6	7	6		
Tanzania	1	3	5	7	6	8	6	2	1	
Uganda	2	1		3	2	5	4	4	3	3
Somaliland	2		2							
Malawi				2	2					
Zambia				6	6	6	4	4	3	4
Rhod/Zimbabwe	10	4	7	3	4					
Botswana										
Lesotho										
Swaziland										
Sudan										
Total	36	28	37	37	32	34	27	24	11	13

Table 6.2. (cont.)

Country	1971	1972	1973	1974	1975	1976	1977	1978	1979	1980
Gambia							1			
Ghana	2	1	2	3	3	5	2	5	4	2
Nigeria	6	9	7	5	5	7	8	4	2	
Sierra Leone		3	3	3	2	2	4	2	2	1
East Africa										
Kenya	1	2	2	2	2	2	4	5	4	4
Tanzania										
Uganda	2	6								
Somaliland										
Malawi		2	7	8	4	2	2	3	4	4
Zambia	3		2							
Rhod/Zimbabwe										1
Botswana		1					1	2	3	4
Lesotho									2	1
Swaziland										3
Sudan			1							2
Total	14	24	23	21	16	18	22	21	21	20

Country	1981	1982	1983	1984	1985	1986	1987	1988	1989	Total
Gambia	2			3	3	3			1	12
Ghana		2	2	2	1	2	1	1	1	138
Nigeria									2	145
Sierra Leone	1	1			2			3		40
East Africa										10
Kenya	5	3								82
Tanzania						2	1	2	1	48
Uganda								2	2	40
Somaliland								2	2	14
Malawi	3	1		2	2	2	2	2	1	55
Zambia									1	39
Rhod/Zimbabwe	1	3	3	3	2	2	2	3	1	92
Botswana	3	2	1	1	3	2	2	2	2	29
Lesotho					2		1	1		7
Swaziland	2	1	1	2	1		1	2	1	14
Sudan	2							1	2	8
Total	17	13	7	13	16	13	10	20	14	764

[a]Compiled from data supplied by the RMAS. The figures include all those admitted to the Academy, and may include some who subsequently withdrew.
[b]Some cadets from East Africa were listed as simply 'East African'.

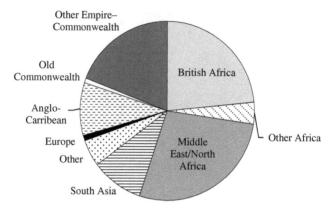

Figure 6.3. Overseas cadets admitted to Sandhurst between 1947 and the end of 2009 categorized by region or connection to Britain

*Notes

'British Africa' (total: 990): Botswana (62), Gambia (24), Ghana (158), Kenya (104), Lesotho (11), Malawi (83), Nigeria (168), Sierra Leone (42), Somaliland (14), Sudan (14), Swaziland (24), Tanzania (68), Uganda (56), Zambia (43), Rhodesia (71), Zimbabwe (39) plus another 10 categorized only as 'East African'.

'Other Africa' (total: 152): excl. 'British Africa', South Africa, and North Africa, but comprising, Burundi, Djibouti, Ethiopia, Ivory Coast, Mauritania, Mozambique, Namibia, Rwanda, Senegal, Zaire.

'Old Commonwealth' (total: 35): New Zealand (23) and South Africa (12).

South Asia (total: 418): Bangladesh (12) Bhutan (2), Burma (64), India (1), Maldives (11), Nepal (143, inc. 21 Nepalese commissioned into British Brigade of Gurkhas), Pakistan (50), Sri Lanka (135).

Middle East and North Africa (total: 1,148): Algeria (2), Bahrain (100), Egypt (16), Iran (19), Iraq (114), Jordan (146), Kuwait (81), Lebanon (1), Libya (5), Morocco (1), Oman and Muscat (194), Palestine (2), Qatar (101), Saudi Arabia (110), Syria (10), Tunisia (4), UAE (216), Yemen (26).

Caribbean (total: 399): Antigua (1), Barbados (15), Belize (92), Guyana (34), Jamaica (202), Trinidad and Tobago (42) plus another 13 categorized only as 'West Indian'.

Other British Empire and Commonwealth (total: 759): countries not included in categories above, and incl. Brunei (149), Fiji (42), Gibraltar (9), Malaya (188), Malaysia (131), Malta (103), Mauritius (28), Seychelles (2), Singapore (105), Tonga (2).

The first of these arrived in 1964 towards the end of the five-year crisis in the Congo that had followed the country's independence in 1960; between then and 1989 Sandhurst admitted some sixty in total from Zaire. The country's leader, President Joseph-Désiré Mobutu, who had seized power in the Congo, and who enjoyed western backing, was among many visiting ministers and dignitaries who also made their way to the Academy. Other visitors included, in March 1961, Kwame Nkrumah, who arrived to inspect Ghanaian cadets, followed later in the year by the Prime Minister of Northern Nigeria, Sir Ahmadu Bello, the Sarduna of Sokoto.[127] The transition of the East and Central African colonies to independence was felt in the next couple of years, with visits from the British Commander appointed to the head of the Tanganyikan Army in 1963 and the commander designate appointed as his successor, as well as the British commander designate of the new Malawi Army in 1965.[128] Later visitors included Samora Machel (Mozambique), General Yakubu Gowon (Nigeria) and Idi Amin and Yoweri Museveni (both Uganda).

Recruitment from Britain's former African colonies continued in the 1970s and 1980s, although the numbers fell, a reflection of the cuts to the British military assistance budget discussed in Chapter 2, as well as changing political circumstances in the sending countries and their greater use of other sources of training. Overseas needs also became less acute as new Commonwealth states began to build up their officer classes. As a result the geographical origin of cadets changed in the period: those from states that had progressed to independence first were prominent in the intakes of the 1950s and 1960s and those from states such as the high-commission territories and smaller Commonwealth countries that achieved independence later were more numerous in a later period. The last cadets from Rhodesia enrolled in 1965; the first from Zimbabwe in 1980.

Enrolment patterns also reflect the political and economic trajectories of postcolonial states and their shifting diplomatic and defence relations with Britain. For example, Britain initially responded to the military coup in Uganda that brought Idi Amin to power by offering military assistance, but from 1972 there ceased to be any Ugandans at the Academy as Amin increasingly turned to other countries for help; it was only in 1988 that Ugandans once again trained at Sandhurst. In contrast, Nigeria – unsurprisingly given its size, western political orientation and, from the 1970s, oil-rich economy – sent more than any other African country: 145 cadets. There was a hiatus in Nigerian recruitment from 1965, the year after the Nigerian Defence Academy opened. Since the early 1960s the Nigerian Government had also increasingly turned to other countries for military assistance.[129] However, the second Nigerian coup of July 1966 saw Yakubu Gowon, then a Lieutenant Colonel, and one of the first Nigerians to train at Sandhurst (1955–6 intake), become the new Nigerian head

[127] *The Wish Stream*, I–XIX (1947–1965); *The Sphere*, 18 March 1961, RMAS, D56, Box 1, RMAS, Cuttings Book, 1961–4.
[128] *The Wish Stream*, XXVII, no. 2 (Autumn, 1963); LXVIII, no. 1 (Spring, 1964).
[129] Amii Omara-Otunnu, *Politics and the Military in Uganda, 1890–1985* (Basingstoke, Palgrave Macmillan, 1987), pp. 108–25. Miners, *Nigerian Army*, pp. 102, 110.

of state. Nigerian cadets were once more admitted to the Academy in 1968.[130] Like Nigeria, Kenya, although officially non-aligned, was another African state friendly to the West.[131] As Table 6.2 shows, it sent eighty-two cadets in total, and possibly several more during the colonial period as in the 1950s the first cadets from East Africa were not identified by colony. Between 1963 and 1967 Kenya sent more than any other African state, although none arrived in 1969 and 1970.[132] The number of Ghanaians (138), however, is most striking. Indeed between 1953 when the first Ghanaian arrived and 1989 there was not a single year when the Academy did not admit at least one Ghanaian; the only African state for which this was the case.

As discussed shortly, because African (and other) countries did not secure all the places they sought, these figures are not solely a reflection of demand; rather they reflect also the priority accorded different states by the FCO, which had responsibility for allocating places. The data nevertheless show the enduring nature of connections forged as a result of the decolonization process. As Table 6.2 shows, by the end of 1989, 764 cadets from Anglophone Africa (including the former high-commission territories and Somaliland) had entered Sandhurst. The Academy also received a sprinkling of cadets from former French North Africa, as well as from Senegal (from 1980), and, following the extension of British military assistance from Zimbabwe to other front-line states bordering South Africa, Mozambique (12 between 1985 and 1989), and, from 1990, Namibia. In all between 1947, when it had reopened, and 2009 the Academy accepted over 4,500 overseas cadets from 103 countries. A declining proportion of these came from Commonwealth states, and, as Figure 6.3 shows, more cadets over 1,100 – came from North Africa and from the Middle East than anywhere else. But former British colonies and high-commission territories in Africa were the next most numerically significant, sending nearly 1,000 cadets to study at the Academy.[133] South Asian states accounted for over 400, with Sri Lanka and Nepal the most important of these sending nations. There were also nearly 400 from the Caribbean (of whom over half were from Jamaica alone), 35 from the 'old' Commonwealth, and more than 750 from the

---

[130] Gordon J. Idang, *Nigerian Internal Politics and Foreign Policy, 1960–66* (Ibadan University Press, Ibadan, 1973), pp. 139, 153–6.

[131] On Kenya's postcolonial foreign policies, see Daniel Branch, *Kenya: Between Hope and Despair, 1963–2011* (Yale University Press, New Haven, CT, 2011) and Percox, *Britain, Kenya and the Cold War.*

[132] This shift coincided with the onset of the Kenyan Asian crisis, when amidst the introduction of a policy of Kenyanization and British concerns about a possible flood of Kenyan Asians to Britain, new, more restrictive, British immigration legislation was introduced. The episode had the potential to complicate Anglo–Kenyan relations, but it is not clear whether the interruption to Kenyan attendance at Sandhurst should be connected to it.

[133] Data supplied to author by RMAS; see also Rouvez, *Disconsolate Empires*, p. 256, and Perraton, *History of Foreign Students*, pp. 136–7.

rest of the British Empire and Commonwealth, of whom over 300 were from Malaya and Malaysia, with a further 105 from Singapore.[134] The entry of so many overseas cadets was in many ways a success for Britain. Bringing cadets for training to the United Kingdom was a cornerstone of British foreign and Commonwealth policy, perceived as an important tool of defence collaboration, of gaining influence and for supporting arms sales. But delivering on this objective continued to strain British resources, sometimes to the extent that it threatened to undermine the very purpose British policy sought to achieve, while also continuing to generate significant and persistent resistance at Sandhurst.

This sustained demand from within the Empire and Commonwealth might seem surprising in view of a concurrent investment by overseas governments and the British Army in the development of local military training facilities. By the early 1960s several new states had opened new military academies modelled on Sandhurst. Like the Indian military academy, which maintained strong links with Sandhurst into the 1950s and also some conformity to it,[135] the Pakistan Military Academy drew on the Sandhurst model, offering a blend of military and academic instruction in English under the overall leadership of a British Director of Military Training.[136] A military college opened in Malaya in 1953,[137] and for the first ten years it was led by a member of Sandhurst's own staff. In January 1960 Ghana became the first of the former West African colonies to establish its own military academy, on the site of the Command Training School in Teshie. Like the military academies established in Asia, this also followed, and had strong connections to, the Academy. An eighteen- or twenty-four-month course was planned on the Sandhurst model, and members of Sandhurst's own academic staff, as well as British Army officers, were seconded to the new institution. W. W. Stallybrass from the Academy's Modern Languages Department was appointed as its first 'Director of Studies' and a British officer as Commandant, although in this instance these appointments proved of short duration, a consequence of political changes in Ghana and the expulsion of British personnel.[138] When a Nigerian Defence Academy opened in 1964, British officers were again seconded to fill teaching posts, although in this instance the institution was largely staffed and led by members of an Indian training mission. An East African Military Training School also followed.[139]

---

[134] There were small numbers from other states including in Europe but most of these were admitted in the 1990s and 2000s. The most significant exception in these categories was Thailand, which began sending cadets in 1950.

[135] Gutteridge, *Military Institutions and Power*, p. 97.

[136] *The Wish Stream*, IV–V (1950–1); IX, no. 1 (April 1955), 'Pakistan Military Academy – the Royal Military Academy Sandhurst', pp. 16–18.

[137] *The Wish Stream*, XVII, no. 2 (Autumn, 1963), p. 56.

[138] *The Wish Stream*, XV, no. 2 (1961), 'African Study Tour'; Gutteridge, *Military in African Politics*, p. 99.

[139] Clayton, 'Foreign Intervention in Africa', p. 224; Miners, *Nigerian Army*, p. 102.

The expansion of local military training facilities did not, however, necessarily lead to a cessation of demand for places at Sandhurst or at Mons, either in African states or in other Commonwealth countries.[140] Table 6.1 shows, for example, that there was a continuing stream of Ghanaians entering Sandhurst after the opening of the country's own military academy. Instead the new academies functioned as feeders, sending their best on to Sandhurst, and because they were modelled on Sandhurst itself this reinforced the connection to Britain and a preference for overseas training that corresponded to the practices and structures both of their own training facilities and of their armies. In some cases the leaders of new African states exploited the opportunities that British military technical assistance offered not just to aid the creation of a local officer class, but also because it served their own particular political agendas as they sought to reinforce their own authority. As indicated earlier, between 1963 and 1967 Kenya sent more cadets to Sandhurst than any other former African colony. Myles Osborne argues that this assisted Kenyatta as he sought to carry through not just a policy of Africanization, but also one of Kikuyization of Kenya's Army and officer class, reducing the influence of the Kamba, among whom British recruitment had focused.[141]

As a first cohort of those who had passed out from Sandhurst assumed senior positions in their national forces, they reproduced for a new generation professional connections to the Academy. When General Yakubu Gowon, by then commander in chief of the Nigerian Army as well as head of state, visited in 1973 (Figure 6.4), 'pomp and circumstance vied with informality and the air of a family reunion'. The General reportedly enjoyed 'visiting old haunts' and talking with Academy staff he remembered from the 1950s.[142] At a personal level a continuing link to Sandhurst validated the training of those who had been at Sandhurst.

Overseas cadets themselves felt that admission to Sandhurst marked them as high fliers among their peers and likely to receive rapid promotion; indeed their expectations on this front were probably encouraged by the experience of the first members of an African officer class who amidst an acute shortage of suitable candidates had enjoyed very rapid career advancement. Former Ghanaian officer cadet Godfried Twum-Acheampong recalls the 'hot competition' among the thirty or so junior officer cadets at the Ghanaian Military Academy for selection for RMAS, and his delight that he was one of two selected for entry in 1969. 'We all knew', he observes, 'that getting the opportunity to train at Sandhurst was not only an honour but it also meant getting

---

[140] 'Africans Seeking Pips on Their Shoulders', *The Times*, 31 January 1961, p. 11.
[141] Osborne, *Ethnicity and Empire*, pp. 237–8. Osborne argues that the Kamba had themselves sought to play up their loyalty and perceived role as a 'martial race' to secure benefits for themselves in the late colonial era.
[142] *The Wish Stream*, XXVII, no. 2 (Autumn, 1973), p. 91.

Figure 6.4. President Yakubu Gowon taking the Sovereign's Parade,
RMAS, 14 July 1973

a superior leadership training with huge prospects for accelerated career advancement'. Twum-Acheampong was one of many cadets who commented on how RMAS provided – as another put it – the 'best leadership training in the world'; Sandhurst's own emphasis on leadership as well as on inculcating loyalty and a sense of belonging among the cadets probably contributed to its own mythology. Sandhurst's British heritage and traditions were fundamental to its appeal. The site itself, with its historic and classically styled 'Old' and 'New' Colleges, amidst lawns, lake and parkland (Figure 6.5) was sure to impress. 'My first impression', wrote one cadet of his arrival at Sandhurst, 'was awe. The buildings and surroundings blew me away'.[143] Another Ghanaian, Afrifa declared that he 'was thrilled by Sandhurst' and that 'learning to be a soldier in a wonderful and mysterious institution with traditions going back to 1802' was the 'best part of my life'.[144]

For all this, for some Africans Sandhurst's appeal lay less in its long history (with which they may not have been familiar) than in their awareness

[143] RMAS, D56, Box 307, 'Sandhurst – a tradition of leadership': Papers and correspondence, Box 4, officer cadet responses to a questionnaire, c. 2005.
[144] Afrifa, *The Ghana Coup*, pp. 49–50.

Figure 6.5. View of Old College, RMAS, 1955

that senior local figures had been there. One Ghanaian cadet selected for the Academy in the mid-1970s remembers that he knew little about it before his arrival, but that senior cadets at the Ghanaian Military Academy 'described RMAS in very glorious terms'; learning that 'many senior serving and retired officers of the Ghana Armed Forces had also been to RMAS' was another source of 'motivation'. He found on his return that the Sandhurst course proved very useful because of the similarities in military traditions and that it opened fresh avenues for career advancement.[145]

As we have seen, the relocation of Mons to Sandhurst resulted in radical changes to training. In the wake of these Commandant Ford suggested that 'Maybe the time had come' to reconsider the advisability of admitting over-seas cadets for at least some of Sandhurst's courses. He had earlier counselled the Director of Army Training that he did not think the slimmed down post-1972 academic options, focusing as they did more on contemporary Britain (although there were also courses on communication skills and post-war inter-national affairs, including political change in Africa),[146] would be 'much use' to overseas cadets. To serve the latter he thought that perhaps a special stream would have to be introduced with bespoke area-studies pathways.[147] Whether Ford was using the issue of the overseas cadets to gain leverage in his attempts

---

[145] Written answers to author's question provided by Ghanaian Army officer, a cadet in the 1970s.
[146] RMAS, D52, Box 231, 'RMAS course notes – Dept Political and Social Science 1945–1994 and undated'.
[147] RMAS, A12. Box 372, file RMAS/1A/Comdt., R. C. Ford to Major-General H. R. S. Pain, 19 March 1974; Ford to DoS, 18 March 1974.

to modify the Tillard changes, or to exploit the opportunity afforded by the changes to try to reduce or remove the overseas element, or possibly simply to effect improvements in what those from overseas received, is not clear. Regardless, the transformation that occurred in the early 1970s did not reduce overseas interest and demand continued to outstrip capacity. Indeed it may even have increased demand: a Sandhurst training was now much shorter, and correspondingly less of a commitment in time and money for those students funded by their own governments.

Circumstances had now come full circle. Whereas the War Office worried in the 1950s that overseas recruits might soak up places needed by the British Army, in the 1970s the British Army had shrunk. However, rather than releasing capacity to accommodate all overseas demand, this had the effect of suppressing availability to overseas cadets since the Academy was unwilling to go beyond what had now been established as a ratio of one overseas student to every five British ones attending the new Standard Military Course. There was no cap on the number of overseas students who had proven themselves on the SMC progressing to the Regular Career Course, indicating that at this juncture the primary concern behind the dilution rate was about maintaining standards.[148]

Concerns about standards indeed persisted throughout the 1970s and beyond. Any candidate who did not meet the minimum requirement of proficiency in English had to attend a five-month language training course at the Army School for Languages in Beaconsfield, but in the 1980s the Academy complained that too many ill-qualified cadets were still being admitted to the Academy.[149] Much of the difference in attainment at Sandhurst reflected problems with English, written and spoken. Patterns were discerned in the performance of different nationalities – although the observation that among African students 'ability in English appears to be dependent on their intelligence and background' was hardly penetrating. Generally, those who came from former British colonies had better English, and performed correspondingly better than those who did not. Among African students those from Zaire did particularly badly, no doubt reflecting the differences of language in the former Belgian colony. There were also variations between cadets from different British African colonies, probably reflecting differences in wealth and educational provision. At least in some years Malawian students were to be found with the Zairians towards the bottom of the performance table. The fundamental orthographic differences between English and their native scripts caused Arab

---

[148] Ibid., Box 460, file 1800/G, Vol. 1, June 1971–December 1973, Lt. Col. A. R. Rees-Webbe (for Commandant), to MoD, 29 July 1973; no. 41, note by Capt. D. F. Harris for Commandant to MoD on overseas students to be nominated to attend the RMC.

[149] Ibid., Box 456, file RMAS 224/Pers, Major-General R. C. Kneightley, Commandant, to MoD, 9 December 1985.

cadets particular difficulties with written work. Caribbean cadets generally had a good basic knowledge, but were found often to 'lack accuracy', and while Malayans/Malaysians were among the most fluent in both written and spoken English, they had 'difficulty improving'.[150]

As, if not more problematic for RMAS, however, was the fact that although there were many among the overseas cadets who excelled and were valued within their companies,[151] some others were judged to show a lack of aptitude, vocation or physical fitness. These might have been 'back-termed' or despatched home had diplomatic considerations not applied. In the early 1980s the Academy complained that although all cadets were assessed at Beaconsfield on their attitude and physical fitness as well as attainment in the English language, decisions as to who could progress to the Academy were based entirely on the latter. Consequently on occasion cadets arrived wholly ill equipped for training. The Academy's request that a 'much firmer line' be taken and overseas cadets 'obviously unsuitable for entry' not be 'wished onto Sandhurst', however, met with a clear rebuff. 'Pathetic!' was one response within the Academy when reminded by the Director of Army Training that in some instances students would have to remain on the course lest their withdrawal lead to a diplomatic incident.[152]

In the 1970s Britain's inability to accept all those who sought places threatened the very objectives the British had hoped to secure via their admission to Sandhurst in the first instance. The Ministry of Defence worried that the constant 'rebuffs' to foreign states seeking places could lead to a loss of British influence. The FCO had the principal policy interest in UKMTAS following the merger of the FO and CRO in 1968 and was responsible for adjudicating between the claims of different states.[153] Each year it organized a conference to allocate places to bidding governments, but was regularly unable to meet all demand. For example, in April 1974 twelve countries were allocated fewer places than they desired and their candidates were placed on the waiting list for entry in 1975–6. Disappointed states included Ghana, Kenya, Sudan, Malaysia, Trinidad and Tobago, and the Maldives, as well as a number of Middle Eastern states.[154] Six years later 'bids' for places continued to exceed capacity. One hundred and fifty-one bids had been received in total for the three standard

---

[150] Ibid., file RMAS/224/AQ, M. H. Broadway (for Commandant) to MoD, 27 November 1981, responding to questions sent by MoD.
[151] Ibid., see discussions about the possible abolition of the ASL, and especially 'Standard of English Overseas' by Mrs J. D. Davies (RMAS), 7 January 1983.
[152] RMAS, A12, Box 454, file 1078/Coord & Trg, 'Overseas students at ASL Sandhurst', memo by M. H. Broadway, 15 October 1984; Lt Col. J. J. J. Phipps (for Commandant) to MoD, 22 October 1984; J. P. French for Director of Army Training to RMAS, 7 November 1984.
[153] See Chapter 2, p. 82.
[154] RMAS, A12, Box 460, file 1800/G, Vol. II, January 1974–April 1977, no. 4, Major J. F. Hibbert (for Director of Army Training), 'Vacancies at RMA Sandhurst for 1975', 8 April 1974.

military courses beginning in January, May and September 1980. It was agreed to offer ninety places in the expectation that some of those selected would not come. Ghana and Malawi each received four of the six places they had sought, Nigeria five out of twelve, and Zambia four out of twelve. Kenya, an important ally, received all four of the places it requested.[155] When, in 1979, overseas fees at British higher education establishments were sharply increased, some foreign and Commonwealth governments reportedly made 'threats of withdrawal' in protest at what they perceived as the high cost of attendance at British military training courses. But in 1980–1 most former British African colonies were still seeking places at Sandhurst including Ghana, Nigeria, Sierra Leone, Kenya, Zambia and Malawi, as well also as Lesotho and the former French and Belgian colonies of Senegal and Zaire.[156]

By then, Foreign and Commonwealth cadets were an established feature at Sandhurst, and procedures for dealing with them had been refined, entailing additional administrative and pastoral work.[157] In theory, embassies and high commissions had responsibility for greeting cadets newly arrived in Britain, and also handled some practical and administrative matters, but in practice the Academy found many issues on its own desk. As Academy staff complained to the Ministry of Defence, 'Too often these young men arrive at the airport with little understanding of English and no knowledge of what they are supposed to be doing and there is no one to meet them'. Some states were slow when it came to sending cadets on to Sandhurst. In 1972 the Academy reported the Nigerians as 'particularly bad' in this respect, and informed the Ministry that, if a new intake of Nigerian cadets did not arrive shortly, the Academy would refuse to take them.[158] The FCO was aware that Nigeria was a difficult customer with a poor track record; but, with the military in power in Nigeria, the chairman of the UK Joint Intelligence Committee viewed on-going UK military assistance to the country as important.[159] Some embassies and high commissions of cash-strapped developing countries were slow to pay allowances,[160] or to provide pay commensurate with that given to British cadets but generous in relation to

---

[155] Ibid., file RMAS/224/A/1, 1977-October 1980, RMAS SMC courses, 8 February 1979, annex to D/DAT/8/152/6, 'Overseas vacancies at Sandhurst 1980/81'.

[156] Ibid., On possible 'threats of withdrawal' see: A12, Box 460, file RMAS 224/AQ, note by Brigadier P. G. A. Prescott, Deputy D. A. T, 1 June 1979. On overseas fees, see Perraton, *History of Foreign Students*, p. 111.

[157] RMAS, A12, Box 456, file RMAS/224/AQ, M. H. Broadway (for Commandant) to MoD, 27 November 1981, responding to questions sent by MoD.

[158] Ibid., Box 460, file RMAS 1800/G, June 1971–73, unsigned letter addressed to Major-General A. G. Patterson, Director of Army Training, 5 May 1972.

[159] TNA, FCO 46/532, Sir E. Peck, chairman of the JIC, to F. Cooper, undated but c. 1970.

[160] See. e.g. discussion about Malayan and Nepalese officer cadets: RMAS, A12, Box 460, file 1800/G, June 1971–December 1973, no. 2, 'Pay and allowances of overseas cadets', Lieut.-Col. A. A. Dacre, GSO 1 Cord, 4 June 1971.

some overseas salaries. As a result some cadets were left in severely straitened circumstances, in receipt of allowances woefully small for living in Britain.[161] Fellow cadets clubbed together to buy a suit in Burtons for one such Afghan cadet admitted in 1978.[162] When in 1979 the Academy compiled a list of current cadets receiving what it regarded as inadequate money, they came from twelve different countries, including three African ones.[163] Recurrent problems were also experienced with chasing overseas students for the settlement of mess bills.

One particular preoccupation for Margaret Jones was finding hospitality for cadets in periods of leave when they were unable to return to their homes. In an ideal world these occasions could seem calculated to provide further opportunities for integration and influence. During weekends the Ministry of Defence hoped British cadets would mix socially with those from overseas, and 'entertain them privately as far as circumstances allow'. However, in practice, as the Ministry complained in 1972, at some training establishments British cadets 'usually disappear[ed] en masse', leaving their overseas colleagues 'to fend for themselves'. At Sandhurst, college commanders rejected this view, claiming that overseas cadets could take advantage of the various activities and training weekends on offer, a response that did not entirely address the particular objectives as set out by the Ministry of Defence.[164]

Longer recesses presented the greatest problem, although the introduction of the shorter course after 1972 reduced overall vacation time. One Ugandan enrolled on the pre-1972 course found his first holiday period in Britain 'rather boring and tiresome' until he was enlisted to assist with hosting some visiting underprivileged children, which proved more entertaining if taxing.[165] Embassies and high commissions were expected to help in finding the cadets 'worthwhile tasks', and while Academy staff admitted that the recesses had sometimes been problematic, they were inclined to blame the diplomats, or the cadets' own lack of initiative.[166] Nonetheless under Jones's direction efforts

[161] RMAS, A12, Box 460, file RMAS 1700/G, 1979–1982, 'Pay for Overseas Students at the RMAS', Major C. P. McMillen (for Commandant); see information sent to HC and embassies about an increase in British cadet pay.

[162] RMAS, D56, Box 305a, 'Sandhurst – a tradition of leadership': Papers and correspondence, box 2', memoirs/recollections submitted by former staff and cadets.

[163] RMAS, A12, Box 454, file RMAS 599/5/AQ, Col. J. N. Stansted, commander New College, 'Pay of overseas cadets', annex A, 31 May 1979.

[164] RMAS, A12, Box 460, file RMAS 1800/G, Vol. 1, June 1971–December 1973, no. 7, 'Administrative Instructions for Candidates sent from Overseas Countries to the United Kingdom for training for commissions' (October 1971) produced in MoD; no. 23, letter from Ministry of Defence, October 1972 and accompanying papers; no. 25, Capt. M. N. Roberts (for College Commander) to Adjutant, RMAS, 16 October 1972; no. 28, Major D. V. Fanshawe (for Commandant) to MoD, 20 October 1972.

[165] The Wish Stream, XXV, no. 2 (Autumn, 1971), 'A holiday with under-privileged children', p. 114.

[166] RMAS, A12, Box 460, file RMAS 1800/G, Vol. 1, June 1971–December 1973, no. 23, letter from Ministry of Defence, October 1972; no. 25, Capt. M. N. Roberts (for College

were made to solicit hospitality for the cadets; the offers received varied from invitations to a single meal to Christmas residential visits. Jones sought to match cadets and hosts, many of whom were from the military themselves or had connections to parts of the world from which the cadets came.[167] Scotland was a common destination, as the Academy was able to draw on the voluntary activities of the Victoria League in Scotland for Commonwealth Friendship. Two cadets from Kenya and Tanganyika were 'Christmas guests' in Stonehaven, Aberdeenshire, in December 1963, considered sufficiently newsworthy to be reported in the Scottish press.[168] One Ghanaian cadet despatched to Scotland after he cited his hobbies as camping, adventuring, reading and films, reportedly returned to the Academy 'a very happy man and with quite a new outlook on things British after all the kindness and hospitality which people had given him in their own homes',[169] indicating that such occasions were important to the broader British mission. For their British hosts, these occasions could also be rewarding. One host on a remote island in Argyll wrote how their Arab guests had enjoyed Arabian and Scottish dancing during their visit, as well as tree cutting; while for his own family the visit had 'revived many nostalgic moments' of their own 'happy times' in Middle Eastern countries 'with Arab friends'.[170] However, occasionally the visits ended less happily; some 'Sierra Leone guests' apparently behaved in 'a disgraceful way', ruining one colonel's home Christmas.[171]

Finding a sufficient number of British hosts willing to take in overseas cadets became increasingly difficult in the mid-1970s when the high cost of living and the decline in the number of households who could employ any kind of domestic help combined to make it harder for the Victoria League to recruit hosts.[172] Given its reliance on the League, the Academy also experienced most difficulties in placing cadets from outside the Commonwealth. For the large numbers of cadets from Arab countries, 'both rich and poor', it was 'rare to get invited by a British family', as Jones explained when writing to the Middle East Association to solicit their help.[173]

Commanders) to Adjutant, RMAS, 16 October 1972; no. 28, Major D. V. Fanshawe (for Commandant) to MoD, 20 October 1972.

[167] RMAS, A12, Box 460, file RMAS 224/AQ, 'Responsibilities towards Overseas Student Officers and Cadets', Lt. Col. K. J. Davey, GSO 1, 2 August 1978.

[168] Ibid., Box 460, file RMAS/224/AQ, 1977–October 1980, Annex A, 'Hospitality Overseas Students', 25 September 1979; *Scottish Daily Mail*, 25 December 1963: RMAS, D56, Box 1, Cuttings Book 1961–4.

[169] Ibid., Box 454, file RMAS 599/4/AQ, Lt. Col. Robin Crawford to Mrs Sunderland, Victoria League, 13 September 1977.

[170] Ibid., file RMAS 599/3/AQ, Alastair Livingstone to Robin Crawford, 18 April 1977.

[171] Ibid., General Philip Ward to Col. P. G. Warrington, 4 January 1978.

[172] Ibid., Miss Parker (VL in Scotland) to Gen. Ford, Commandant, 8 January 1976.

[173] Ibid., file RMAS 599/3/AQ, notes prepared by Miss Jones for writing thank you letters to hosts; Miss Jones to R. P. Owen, The Middle East Association, 25 July 1977.

Whereas in the 1950s and 1960s the Academy tended to rely on Jones to shoulder much of the additional pastoral work that came with overseas cadets, the early 1970s saw a tightening and enhancement of provision, perhaps following the sea change that occurred with the arrival of the Mons contingent and the greater numbers overall of overseas cadets now passing through the Academy on the shorter training courses. Amidst evidence of an 'increasing number of recent instances' that indicated staff at all levels were 'either unaware of or avoiding their responsibilities', the Assistant Commandant wrote in early 1974 advising college commanders of the procedures to be followed in relation to overseas cadets, warning that they should not shirk their own responsibilities by over reliance on Jones. This was bad 'man management', and since 'man management and good officer/soldier relationships is one of the traditional characteristics of the British Army' and one of those 'which overseas countries send their students to Sandhurst to learn about', they must, he urged, practise 'what we preach'.[174]

Arrangements were made to support Jones' pastoral work. A permanent member of the academic staff was appointed 'Senior Tutor (Pastoral) Overseas Officers and Cadets'.[175] Both Jones and the Senior Tutor were given an overseas cadet entertainment budget. Jones used some of hers to cover the costs of transporting overseas cadets to the lunch parties she hosted at her own home; other funds paid for regular 'get togethers'.[176] Cadets were encouraged to remain in touch with developments in their own countries through visits to their national high commissions, and for some of the period Sandhurst received national newspapers via the embassies and high commissions for deposit in the library.[177] The overseas cadets were also taken to visit sites of historic or military or naval interest, and on outings to places representing aspects of British society and culture. Anthony Clayton, who served as an unofficial tutor to overseas cadets, recalls outings to a dairy farm, the Houses of Parliament, HMS Victory, and to the Guinness Brewery – the latter 'very popular' if resulting in 'difficult return journeys'.[178] Despite being regarded as a good thing not just for individual students but from the 'point of view of international

---

[174] Ibid., Box 451, file with missing cover, no. 5. J. H. Page to college commanders, 7 February 1974.

[175] Ibid., Box 460, file RMAS 1700/G, 1979–1982, see no. 38, 'Responsibilities towards overseas student officers and cadets', Lt. Col. B. Aldridge, GSO 1, 20 January 1981.

[176] Ibid., Box 454, file 1078/Corod. & Trg., 'Expenses for entertainment and welfare of overseas cadets/amenity fund' (1983, when the funds available were increased to £720 per annum).

[177] Ibid., Box 457, unnumbered file (cover gone), no. 3, C. L. St H. Pelham-Burn for the Commandant to the Ministry of Defence, 21 September 1973.

[178] Written information provided by Tony Clayton to author.

goodwill', the outings were scaled back in 1980 when the Academy no longer felt able to afford to lay on the coaches required.[179] There was also greater effort to accommodate different traditions, cultures and beliefs. In 1972 concessions were introduced to facilitate fasting during Ramadan,[180] and Academy staff were asked to cease referring to the non-British cadets simply as 'overseas students' and wherever possible to refer to the student by their country of origin.[181] The following year it was decided to abandon dances and events specifically organized for overseas cadets 'which might be construed, no matter how slightly, as divisive'; college commanders were asked instead to make sure that overseas cadets joined in 'suitably partnered, College or Company social activities'.[182] 'Suitably' appears to have meant non-white because the following year at an 'international night', arrangements were made to bring in fifty-three female nurses from Commonwealth and other overseas countries working in local hospitals as potential company for overseas cadets.[183]

Behind this new attentiveness in the early 1970s was awareness that failure would undermine the Academy's public-relations function in relation to overseas cadets. 'RMA Sandhurst', wrote the General Staff Officer and Lieutenant-Colonel who had responsibility for the day-to-day running of the Academy, 'is held in a very special and high esteem by the countries that send their young men to us to be trained. The goodwill and influence that accrue to their country [sic] through these young men is incalculable. It is up to us to repay this trust by looking after these young men in the best possible manner'.[184] By the 1970s and 1980s Britain itself was a more racially and culturally diverse country than when the Academy had first begun admitting overseas cadets. Concerns nonetheless persisted about race relations between cadets as well as over tensions around weaker students within platoons.[185]

At Sandhurst the overseas cadets not only made for a visibly more diverse student body but also left a physical mark on the Academy in the form

[179] RMAS, A12, Box 457, file RMAS 806/7/DoS, 'Officer cadets and student officers – overseas entrants', no. 82, D. E. Lever, Deputy Director of Studies to D. A. H. Clayton, Dept of P & I S, 1 October 1980.
[180] Ibid., Box 460, file 1800/G, June 1971–3, no. 9, 'Muslim students at British army schools – Observation of Ramadan. Maintenance Charges', Major T. W. T. Hargreaves for Director of Army Training (MoD), 12 March 1972.
[181] Ibid., file RMAS 1800/G, Vol. 1, June 1971–December 1973, no. 39, 'Foreign and Commonwealth Students', memo by Major J. A. G. Moore for GSO Coord.
[182] RMAS, A12, Box 451, unnumbered file (cover gone), no. 10, Brigadier P. J. Bush to College commanders, 29 July 1974.
[183] Ibid., no. 45, 'International Night, 12 April 1975', March 1975.
[184] Ibid., Box 451, file with missing cover, no. 11, memo by Lt Col A. R. Rees-Webbe addressed to company commanders, 31 August 1974.
[185] Ibid., Box 456, file RMAS 124/OC, folio 140, 'minutes of a meeting to discuss arrangements for overseas cadets', 28 February 1991.

of buildings such as the Oman Hall opened in late 1978, following generous donations from Middle Eastern donors.[186] There were other less visual impacts. Several members of staff, including Clayton, developed academic careers studying the development of African armies and of African military history, producing between them some of the most significant literature at the time on these subjects. In the 1970s Clayton even compiled a collection of African soldiers' songs with the help of African cadets who came to his office to sing them.[187] Just as at Oxford and Cambridge, there was a dynamic relationship between the admission of overseas students and the development of the research interests of those who taught them.

Conclusion

The post-war history of the Royal Military Academy at Sandhurst might at first sight appear to run a directly contradictory path to British decolonization. As Britain's Empire shrank, and the British Army increasingly operated principally within Europe, the Academy itself had become an institution with a global intake and reputation. But if treated as a key element of the wider structure of the British Army, an institution that might be seen as representing a prime embodiment of 'hard' power, the post-war history of Sandhurst can in fact be seen as an outstanding example of how one institution's own fortunes mirrored the wider course of British decline. As the Army itself, and training for Britain's own officer class, was scaled back, Sandhurst became a significant instrument of 'soft' power in ways that exemplified the change in Britain's fortunes. Shorn of much of the economic and military muscle that had underpinned its world role, Britain was instead increasingly reliant on the exercise of influence.

Sandhurst also reflected the wider picture in that this transition was far from unproblematic. The admission of so many overseas cadets was frequently a source of friction between the Academy, the Army and Whitehall, and, in the 1950s and 1960s at least, it recreated on Sandhurst's lawns some of the tensions and dynamics of decolonization then playing out around the world. This chapter has thus showed the difficulties inherent for Britain, a power of diminished economic standing, in transitioning from imperial rule to a postcolonial 'role' via the exercise of influence. In the 1950s Sandhurst's overriding purpose was to fulfil Britain's own officer training requirements (at a point at which colonial counter-insurgencies had led the Empire to become a growing drain on British military resources), but the Colonial Office, and the Army,

---

[186] *The Wish Stream*, XXXIII, no. 1 (Spring, 1979).
[187] Published as *African Soldier Songs* (Ohio University Press); information provided by Anthony Clayton to author.

saw the Academy also as a tool of decolonization, while the CRO and the FO were fashioning a new role for Sandhurst as a vehicle of British foreign and Commonwealth policy.

While British military assistance was not given on the same scale as French aid, Britain nevertheless played a significant part in training the armies of successor states. A high proportion of the first African officers in new states had been at RMAS. For example, five years after Ghanaian independence forty-seven Ghanaian officers had been commissioned from RMAS, approximately one in six of the country's early officer class.[188] This first generation quickly attained high office, the consequence of the acute need for African officers. Malawian cadets selected for RMAS straight from school returned as full lieutenants.[189] In East Africa, less than a year after passing out from the Academy, Mrisho Sarakikya was promoted to Brigadier and placed in command of the new Tanganyikan Army formed after the old Tanganyikan Rifles was disbanded following the 1964 mutiny.[190] However, tensions arose in some national armies between those who had attended training in England and those who had been promoted through the ranks, notably in Uganda, where British-trained officers were among the earliest victims of Idi Amin's regime. Amin himself visited Sandhurst in 1971, but he was suspicious of those who had followed a different route to his own.[191] Witnessing this turn, and the direction of postcolonial African politics, with political neutrality interpreted as disloyalty in some one-party states, Clayton wondered retrospectively whether we 'were really doing African cadets a favour in teaching the British pattern'. 'Sandhurst training', he observes, 'could be a very mixed blessing'.[192]

The full significance of British training in shaping the character and practices of the overseas armies in which these Sandhurst alumni served lies beyond the scope of this chapter but was widely discussed in a contemporary literature precisely because in postcolonial Africa so many new armies seemed to develop along lines antithetical to the British ideal of political neutrality. In particular, the continent's record of military coups and regimes led scholars to debate the degree to which a propensity for military intervention in politics reflected the internal culture within armies (and by extension the attitudes of their officer classes) or the external political environment in which

---

[188] Gutteridge, *Military Institutions*, p. 103.
[189] Bodleian, Mss Afr. s. 1715, Box 15, file 225, ff. 7–8, Major W. H. Reeve (Malawi, 1964–6).
[190] Ibid., Box 6, file 132, p. 14; Emmanuel Akyeampong, 'Sarakikya, Mrisho', *Dictionary of African Biography*, Vol. 6, pp. 283–4.
[191] *The Wish Stream*, XXV, no. 2 (Autumn, 1971), p. 77; Bodleian, Mss Afr. s. 1715, Box 3, file 42, f. 65, Lt Col H. K. P. Chavasse; Box 3, file 55, ff. 28–9, Major Henry Crawford (Kenya 1959–62, Uganda, 1968–71).
[192] Written information provided by Anthony Clayton to the author.

they operated.[193] More specifically, several British scholars set out to evaluate a 'Sandhurst' effect. Writing in 1970 William Gutteridge argued that the rise of the British-trained military in the politics of some, but not all, new states pointed to the potentially greater significance of the different national environments and institutional cultures in the countries to which they returned in determining officer behaviour.[194] In his more rigorous, but less geographically wide ranging, study, focused on the role of the Nigerian military, Robin Luckham reaches similar conclusions. Luckham argues that despite the Army's intervention in the country's politics, Nigerian military institutions had a 'structure, pattern and vitality of their own'. He judges that institutions had in some respects been 'successfully transferred', and that Nigerians had 'learned' at the Academy, although he notes that conspiratorial groups had 'developed around the interstices of Sandhurst', as well as rank and career patterns. However, officer behaviour was shaped by the environment in which officers operated, since Africans took up commissions in an army whose social structure was distorted, with little generational difference between the most senior and junior officers, a consequence of the speed with which Nigerianization had been effected.[195]

From a wider British perspective it is difficult to evaluate the degree to which the admission of overseas cadets on such a large scale delivered on all policy fronts. These included the inculcation of British traditions and commercial objectives associated with arms sales. Nigeria, Ghana and Kenya, the three most significant states participating in British military training, were also Britain's most important African markets for arms in the 1960s.[196] Although other variables were also significant in determining the purchase of British arms, in 1985 the FCO described the Sandhurst course as 'very influential' in the promotion of sales.[197]

Above all, as the Academy's staff was bluntly reminded in 1991, overseas cadets were 'welcomed at RMAS' in the hope that they would form a 'very favourable opinion of Britain which, in due course of time, will be to our country's advantage when cadets assume positions of seniority and influence'.[198] Many did, and in postcolonial Africa they included Major General Murtala Muhammed (Nigeria) and Brigadier Andrew Juxon-Smith

[193] The different interpretations are associated with classic studies by, on the one hand, Samuel Huntingdon, *The Soldier and the State* (Harvard University Press, Cambridge, MA, 1967) and M. Janowitz, *The Military and the Political Development of New Nations* (University of Chicago Press, Chicago, 1964), and on the other S. E. Finer, *Man on Horseback* (Pall Mall Press, London, 1962).
[194] Gutteridge, 'A Commonwealth Military Culture?', p. 238.
[195] Luckham, *Nigerian Military*, pp. 4, 132.
[196] Andrew Pierre, *The Global Politics of Arms Sales* (Princeton University Press, Princeton, 1982), p. 263.
[197] RMAS, A12, Box 456, file RMAS 224/Pers, paper by Brigadier J. R. Templer for Commander in Chief HQ Landforces, 20 November 1985, 'Foreign and Commonwealth Training Study', annex B.
[198] RMAS, A12, Box 456, file RMAS 124/OC, folio 140, 'minutes of a meeting to discuss arrangements for overseas cadets', 28 February 1991.

(Sierra Leone) as well as Gowon, Afrifa, and Lieutenant General 'Fred' Akuffo (the latter seen with Afrifa in Figure 6.2), all of whom rose to political power because of the military's role in postcolonial African politics. Yet curiously a list of notable alumni compiled at Sandhurst fails to mention that the governments these officers led were *all* overthrown, in Gowon's case by Muhammed, who was himself killed during an attempted coup six months later. Akuffo and Afrifa, who had entered Sandhurst together as members of the same platoon in Normandy Company, were executed together in 1979, alongside other senior Ghanaian officers, including another former head of state, General Ignatius Acheampong.[199] If their accession to power represented at best a pyrrhic success for Britain, given its efforts to inculcate Britain's own model of political neutrality and a Westminster system, in other respects the rise of Sandhurst-trained officers (in some cases, however violently and briefly) only served to legitimate the British policy of assisting with postcolonial military training. As the FCO argued in relation to Nigeria, the advent of military regimes meant that the armies became more than ever the 'key to influence'.[200]

[199] Ibid., Box 459, file RMAS/224/G1, lists of distinguished alumni complied by T. A. Heathcote, curator, RMAS, 2 December 1988.
[200] TNA, FCO 46/532, Sir E. Peck (chairman of the Joint Intelligence Committee) to F. Cooper, undated but c. 1970.

Conclusion

This book has explored Britain in transition from colonial to ex-colonial power, in particular through analysis of the activities of domestic institutions that lay on the boundaries of the state, but which over time had become 'stakeholders' in the Empire. Following several centuries of involvement in Britain's Empire, such institutions had assumed responsibility for the delivery of services to the colonies or for other tasks within the British imperial system. This was partly a consequence of the distinctive nature of the British 'liberal' state, in which power was dispersed among institutions on its margins and beyond. Just as looking at *non*-state institutions 'on the ground' significantly reshapes accounts of British decolonization and its domestic impact, considering the bodies discussed here adds an important new dimension to our understanding. We find little evidence of imperial nostalgia during the winding up of Britain's Empire. Rather, individuals in the various sectors got on (albeit frequently reluctantly) with the business of preparing for, and adjusting to, colonial political change in ways that in no small part reflected contemporary investment in the idea of Commonwealth. The book has nevertheless illustrated the persistence in different locations within the British state and beyond – and long into the post-war era – of ideologies and perspectives associated with British imperialism at its height. In particular, for all Britain's weakened position, and the changed international environment, Britons working in different institutions continued to believe that they could, and should, shape developments overseas.

While these conclusions support a proposition that the Commonwealth ideal helped persuade many that – as Stuart Ward puts it – the 'Empire was not really in decline, but merely in a state of transition',[1] they may appear to sit uneasily with other narratives of the effects of decolonization in Britain.[2] As Ward also writes, European decolonization could be a source

---

[1] Ward, 'Introduction' in *British Culture*, p. 8.
[2] See Buettner, *Europe After Empire*, for the best general discussion of the themes discussed in this paragraph, esp. pp. 223–8; 254–70; 349–75; 417–90.

of dislocation, and even 'trauma'.[3] The end of Empire was accompanied by considerable Commonwealth immigration, generating tension and even violence, the focus of many existing accounts of the metropolitan dimensions of decolonization.[4]

Neither our institutions, nor the individuals associated with them, were immune from these wider currents and from racial conflicts. Indeed, bringing individuals from British colonies and Commonwealth countries very different in their politics and cultures to study not just in close proximity to Britons but to each other, created particular, and potentially quite explosive, scenarios. As we have seen, the different institutions were alert to the risks this entailed, especially at Sandhurst in the heated atmosphere of racial tension in Britain during the summer of 1958. Conversely, Britons seconded or posted overseas sometimes became the object of local hostility and suspicion, and for many associated with our institutions the end of Empire was personally and professionally disruptive. In the early 1960s British Army officers still serving overseas with African forces came to find their positions less comfortable, and in the course of the 1960s and 1970s, despite the Loan Service Personnel scheme, opportunities for overseas postings of this sort, hitherto frequently an important part of the career of British officers, steeply declined. With a British military retreat from East of Suez, a new generation of British Army officers now saw service principally in Europe. While it was business as usual at Oxford and Cambridge, as they shifted apparently almost seamlessly from teaching British recruits to the Colonial Service to focus exclusively on colonial and Commonwealth officials within overseas public services, the end of Empire saw many of the Britons they had previously taught suffer premature career loss, carried home on a wind of change. The Overseas Services Resettlement Bureau, which between 1958 and 1980 helped former Colonial Service personnel relocate and seek new employment, calculated in 1962 that up to 25,000 might need assistance with resettlement.[5] Some 10,000 had been successfully found new employment by the Bureau by the end of 1970.[6] As we have seen some 'stayed on', finding new employment within British and international technical assistance programmes,[7] and many others successfully embarked on new careers. But for many adaptation was difficult.[8] In the twenty-first century,

---

[3] Ward, 'Introduction' in *British Culture*, p. 11
[4] Among many see on race and immigration, Schofield, *Enoch Powell* and Brooke, 'Duncan Sandys'.
[5] TNA, LAB 8/2751, Memo by Director, OSRB, 'The Resettlement of HMOCS. The Future', 29 November 1962, tabled at 1st meeting of OSRB Advisory Council.
[6] TNA, LAB 8/2344, Minute by Barbara Green (MoL), 15 April 1966; LAB 8/2908, minutes of the 12th meeting of the OSRB Advisory Council, 2 July 1970.
[7] See p. 78.
[8] See e.g., TNA, LAB 8/2751, minutes of 1st meeting of OSRB, 18 December 1962, item 4, no. 34.

the Empire has cast a long shadow for some of these Britons, as they have become caught up or felt personally, if indirectly, implicated in the discussions about Britain's record at the end of Empire, ignited especially by the court case brought by Mau Mau veterans,[9] just one of a number of episodes that underscore the continuing potential of Britain's imperial past to disturb, many decades after the formal end of Empire.

Yet while for some of these Britons the end of Empire effectively resulted in a lost imperial future, and, at the very least, was a source of uncertainty, for the domestic British institutions considered here, it led to a new 'post-imperial' mission, as they reconfigured their established roles for a postcolonial age.[10] Britain's failure to carry through policies of institutional transfer, or development, or of Africanization of senior positions within institutions, meant that Britain's African colonies entered independence severely ill-prepared, lacking institutions necessary for independent statehood and reservoirs of suitably educated and experienced personnel to staff them. Independence was hence accompanied, or, more typically followed, by a process of state-building, and the advent of new British, as well as international, programmes of technical assistance. That various institutions had accumulated expertise relevant to a process of state-building below the level of parliamentary systems and crucial to the development of institutions on which the success of the British Westminster model depended, only served to reinforce expectations that they should play a key part in the delivery of this technical assistance. What is more, because the protracted nature of British decolonization produced a Janus-faced imperial state, in which parts focused on dealing with the still-functioning Empire while others adjusted to a new postcolonial world, British technical assistance had to cater both to the on-going colonial Empire *and* to newly independent states. In these circumstances, where the direction and likely pace of further constitutional change was not clear, it made sense to adapt existing British structures and activities to meet the needs of emergent states and existing colonies. The universities and Sandhurst secured a continuing role, training locals to take up positions in colonial services and forces alongside *postcolonial* locals. British approaches were thus important in shaping the experience of the postcolonial world, but were not developed exclusively *for* a postcolonial world.

Individuals within and beyond the British state shared an understanding of the role of the state that helped fashion British notions of what postcolonial

[9] David Anderson, 'Mau Mau in the High Court and the "Lost" British Empire Archives: Colonial Conspiracy or Bureaucratic Bungle?' *Journal of Imperial and Commonwealth History*, 39 (2011), pp. 699–716, and other articles in this issue on the case.
[10] The idea of 'lost futures' in the history of empires was explored at two workshops jointly organized by the departments of history at King's College London and the University of North Carolina at Chapel Hill in 2012 and 2014.

'state' aid might look like, and specifically that element of it concerning technical assistance as opposed to capital aid. Just as British imperialism had been 'a field of enterprise for the whole of British society',[11] the new Ministry of Overseas Development expected that individuals and institutions across civil society would become involved in the delivery of aid, with effective technical assistance 'a transfer of know-how from country to country, not simply from government to government'.[12] British officials also recognized that activities and initiatives associated with institutions such as Britain's universities, one step removed from the old imperial state, were less likely to provoke suspicions that the British were engaging in neo-colonialism in former colonies. Indeed, even though leaders of new states, such as Ghana's Kwame Nkrumah, were proactive in trying to diversify the sources from which they obtained technical assistance, only reluctantly accepting British personnel and training as a necessary means of advancing their own state-building projects, the reputation of British educational and military training institutions in former colonies remained relatively high. The institutions' established expertise contributed to their cultural capital, which also encompassed their long histories and reputations, enhanced by more 'ornamental' features: imposing, period architecture, and, in the case of the Mint and Sandhurst, the royal title. Furthermore, as a first generation trained in Britain or associated with British institutions attained positions of influence, some chose to continue associations to British institutions, not least because it ensured continuities in practice, as well as effectively validating their own professional credentials.

Sandhurst offers the most striking example of how in many ways the reputation of a British institution flourished among both the former colonized at the end of Empire and states that had once been part of a British informal empire. From the early 1950s the Academy began admitting African cadets who had been identified for promotion to an officer class within British colonial regiments. But the admission of overseas cadets, principally conceived as a means of facilitating a process of Africanization and of inculcating British values and models, became long-term practice.

Sandhurst had become a (sometimes reluctant) instrument of British foreign and Commonwealth policy. In contrast, at the other institutions individuals in, or associated with them, were proactive in carving out new roles in place of the old. For example, academics and administrators at the Universities of Oxford and Cambridge fought to preserve their role in delivering the Devonshire Colonial Administrative Service training courses, and their successive reincarnations, as British recruitment to the Service dwindled.

---

[11] As Magee and Thompson write, citing John Darwin and Alan Lester: *Empire and Globalisation*, p. 17.
[12] *Overseas Development*, para. 115.

In the early 1950s, when the intake to the Oxbridge courses was mostly new British cadets for the Service, this was because senior figures associated with the universities (but also with the Colonial Office) believed that the training was important for the future of the Service, and reflected the fact that Britain's oldest universities were crucial accessories to a project associated with the development of public administration. But as British recruitment ceased, the universities adapted the programmes so that they became training courses for public administrators overseas, part of Britain's package of technical assistance to new Commonwealth states. The Bank of England's 'stake' in the colonial Empire was quite different. After the Second World War Britain's remaining colonies were of enhanced importance to sterling and to the sterling area. Principally for this reason the Bank initially opposed colonial financial devolution and the creation of central banks in Britain's colonies. But once it became clear to senior Bank officials that they were unable to resist this development, they sought instead to exercise as much influence over the process as possible. In addition to advising on the creation of new banks, the Bank became involved in offering them two principal forms of technical assistance: personnel to help staff them, and training (mostly through the inauguration of a Commonwealth central banking course). These activities were planned and funded by senior Bank officials entirely independently of Whitehall. The creation of new national currencies in place of those issued by the colonial currency boards was a corollary to the establishment of new central banks. The Royal Mint, a parastatal body whose primary responsibility was the manufacture of coin for domestic circulation, had developed a significant imperial role in the course of the nineteenth and twentieth centuries, supplying both British and – as it came to be known – 'imperial coin' and specific local coinages to British colonies and some foreign states. Following African decolonization the Mint set out with singular determination to secure contracts for producing coin for new states. It also became involved in the provision of some technical assistance, specifically to a new Nigerian coin and security note manufacturing plant.

In these cases, policies and initiatives reflected a variety of self-interests, institutional and even individual. At Oxford and Cambridge, as Britain retreated from its Empire and there was no longer the same prestige associated with participation in training Britain's colonial or, increasingly Commonwealth, officials, academics still actively sought to preserve courses that paid for their posts and for associated structures within, but often marginal to, their universities. Within the Bank of England, at least initially, senior officials were principally motivated by a desire to secure the continued adherence of new states to sterling, the sterling area, the services of the City of London and the Bank's own model of central banking, while also seeking to nurture a new network of professional central bankers. The motivations of those at the Mint were primarily commercial, as they sought to protect an export business that had become crucial to its operations.

But alongside these specific and distinct motivations, individuals within institutions also acted from a common conviction in the value and relevance of British models, practice and expertise. With Britain economically enfeebled by the Second World War, and America indisputably the leading global power, W. R. Louis and Ronald Robinson argue that the British Empire became 'more than British and less than an imperium', transformed and internationalized 'as part of the Anglo-American coalition'.[13] Nevertheless, perhaps because those at their helm had risen through the ranks and acquired enduring mindsets in a period in which Britain had been more powerful, British institutions sought to promote their own models and practices over other, more generic, western ones, and had confidence in their ability to do so. Bank of England officials perceived American ideas as the antithesis of those they wished to promote, and not only because initially they hoped to sustain sterling alongside the dollar as an international currency. They held quite different views from those espoused by Americans concerning what constituted appropriate banking systems for developing states. The approach of individuals at the Bank, and in other sectors, embodied distinctively British ideas of a liberal state in which institutions could act independently of governments and be politically neutral, with perhaps surprisingly little reflection within the institutions about the suitability of their own models for African societies with their different structures, practices and conditions.

While the export of British practice suited institutional agendas and interests, the promotion of British models and connections also reflected a commitment to assisting new Commonwealth states, and, as indicated earlier, an investment in the Commonwealth ideal. Individuals within British institutions showed a perhaps surprising sense of 'mission', accepting responsibility to assist new institutions in emergent Commonwealth states, crafting them along lines that corresponded to their own notions of best practice. Similarly, as Chapter 2 argued, however much British technical assistance was designed to serve a variety of British interests and to deliver 'influence', it was also intended to advance a decolonizing process and assist with the construction of sound institutions, perceived as important to Commonwealth stability and unity. A commitment to the Commonwealth was most striking in the Bank's case, since it was sustained long after the sterling area had, first of all, ceased to matter, and then ceased to exist, and after the importance once invested by policymakers in the idea of the Commonwealth as a post-imperial association and vehicle for on-going British influence had withered. Institutions of quite different kinds

[13] W. R. Louis and Ronald Robinson, 'The Imperialism of Decolonization', *Journal of Imperial and Commonwealth History,* 22 (1994), pp. 462–511, quotation 462.

became involved in the development of institutions and services in emergent Commonwealth states, whether by seconding their own staff to fill senior posts within institutions in a transitional period, or through educational initiatives in Britain and overseas.

Through the provision of training, officials within the British state and beyond aimed to promote the development of a professional, African, middle class. Western-educated Africans, at the forefront of political campaigns to secure greater rights and equality of opportunity, had been regarded with suspicion and even hostility, not easily accommodated within systems of governance based on the incorporation of 'traditional' rather than 'new' elites (the term more commonly used in contemporary scholarship from the 1960s),[14] and a challenge to racial and social boundaries between the British and their colonial subjects.[15] But decolonization created a compelling need in states progressing to independence for Africans to take over senior positions in institutions from which they had previously been excluded. One result of this was that (although the size of what might be identified as an African middle class long remained small comparative to that of other world regions), processes of institutional development created greater and unique opportunities for rapid and remarkable individual career advancement in new states.[16] This might not be without consequence for both these individuals, and the institutions in which they were employed, as their rise sometimes led to tensions and to expectations among a wider cohort of comparably swift promotion.

The British perceived these African professionals as crucial to the success of liberal democracies on a western model, essential to ensuring the political neutrality of the public services, armies and financial institutions of new African states. Once 'the middle class becomes sufficiently distinct', as one Bank of England man seconded to Nigeria observed, it would be able 'to exercise an effect on public opinion and politics', implying that members of this middle class would also share a particular common ideological consciousness.[17]

---

[14] P. C. Lloyd ed. *New Elites of Tropical Africa* (Oxford University Press for the International African Institute, London, 1966).

[15] For one study of the formation of an African middle class and its political role, see Michael O. West, *The Rise of an African Middle Class. Colonial Zimbabwe, 1898–1965* (Indiana University Press, Bloomington & Indianapolis, 2002).

[16] The development of an African middle class is only now beginning to attract more attention alongside wider analysis of the rise of middle classes in the global South: see, e.g., Henning Melber ed., *The Rise of Africa's Middle Class. Myths, Realities and Critical Engagements* (Zed Books, London, 2016), esp. p. 8. Carola Lentz's chapter in this volume provides a useful review of the use of terms and of the changing ways in which this class has been conceptualized and described: 'African Middle Classes: Lessons from Transnational Studies and a Research Agenda', pp. 17–53.

[17] BoE, OV 68/7, no 183, personal reflections by P. B. Edgeley, 25 January 1961, addressed to Messrs Heasman, Watson and Parsons.

Networks of professionals based in successor institutions might also serve as potentially useful interlocutors for British institutions as they sought to negotiate a changing political landscape. As another senior figure at the Bank of England said, it was desirable that the Bank should have an 'old boy', a graduate of its own Commonwealth Central Banking Course, in the central banks of new Anglophone African states. At Sandhurst the British government admitted overseas cadets in a similar hope that they would attain positions of influence and be useful to Britain; in some British eyes this ambition was reinforced by political interventions in postcolonial states by African armies. Indeed, to the extent that the British were motivated by any high-minded commitment to the development of sound institutions, and best practice, as they perceived it, this was always accompanied, and perhaps increasingly so, by a more cynical desire to 'win' friends – an objective repeatedly articulated by officials administering both British civilian and military aid programmes and within our institutions.

Within each British institution particular individuals became especially prominent in the cultivation and management of these networks and connections. This was important because, as others observe, within African states there were developing neopatrimonial systems in which politics and business tended to be conducted along personal rather than institutional lines.[18] This personal diplomacy was reinforced by the extension of a variety of forms of hospitality by the institutions. This could help convey a sense of harmonious Commonwealth relations that belied the racial and cultural prejudices sometimes expressed in private, or which some from emergent states encountered in wider British society.

Considering several institutions across different sectors as we have done here serves to highlight such parallels and similarities between them. Moreover, exploring initiatives in relation to several sectors within the same frame of analysis is also important because they could be mutually reinforcing. For example, in Chapter 5 in particular we saw that legacy networks of British personnel and a diaspora of Bank of England officials played key roles in the Mint's success in securing orders from new states. Perhaps most importantly, a cross-sectoral account conveys the depth and breadth of postcolonial British engagement with its former colonies. What is more, the examples of technical assistance we have explored could be multiplied many times over. Many thousands of Britons served overseas in a great variety of roles in new Commonwealth countries, while equally huge numbers travelled to Britain to train in British universities, technical colleges or through attachments to different institutions. The wide range of forms of British technical cooperation

---

[18] See also Dimier, *Invention of a European Development*; Cullen, 'Kenya is No Doubt a Special Place', pp. 107–15.

included, as Simon Potter has shown, the BBC's assistance with the development of Commonwealth broadcasting services,[19] or, as Philip Murphy and Calder Walton demonstrate, MI5's help with developing intelligence services in new states.[20] Delivering technical assistance to new states and the pursuit of influence required significant mobilization of British resources and individuals and, as we have seen, often stretched Britain's resources, generating strains and necessitating compromises.

The institutional initiatives discussed in this book met with only mixed success. The Mint's record is easiest to evaluate, since this can be measured in straightforward commercial terms. Although the Mint was sometimes unable to control developments as it wished, it achieved the commercial success it sought, securing contracts to produce coins and other metallic products in all new Anglophone African states. As Chapter 5 argued, the Mint's successful negotiation of African decolonization helped underpin the Mint's transformation from an 'imperial' to a 'global' institution. Overseas demand for places at Sandhurst was also evidence of success of a kind, at least for the Foreign and Commonwealth Office. However, as argued in Chapter 6, Sandhurst's post-war history, and that of the British Army of which it was part, in many ways not only exemplifies a wider pattern of British decline, but also provides one illustration of how the exercise of soft power could produce tensions and problems. We saw in Chapters 3 and 4 that both those academics and personnel at the Universities of Oxford and Cambridge associated with the delivery of Colonial Administrative Service training and staff at the Bank of England also achieved some of their objectives when confronted with decolonization. Staff at the universities were proactive in ensuring that state funding previously awarded for training British entrants to the Colonial Service was now redirected towards training overseas public servants. But the universities also experienced chronic uncertainty over the future of the courses, eventually culminating in the closure of programmes that were the immediate descendants of the old Devonshire training regime. Turning to the Bank, we saw that through its central banking course especially, it forged connections with several generations of African bankers, many of whom already occupied, or were promoted to, senior posts within their own banks. Its efforts to exercise oversight over the creation of new African central banks and to ensure continued adherence to sterling and the sterling area met with more mixed results.

In both the short and longer term the British themselves often tended to judge 'success' by the crude measure of calculating how many of those brought to

---

[19] Potter, *Broadcasting Empire*, p. 151.
[20] Murphy, 'Creating a Commonwealth Intelligence Culture'; Walton, *Empire of Secrets*, esp. pp. 215–65. Britain's domestic intelligence service rather than Britain's foreign security service, the Secret Intelligence Service [MI6], had responsibility for Britain's Empire.

Britain for training attained positions of power. This reflects in part the intrinsic difficulties of measuring success in more meaningful ways, but also, as already indicated, the equally crude British ambition of winning friends among those likely to attain high office, whether in the public services, armies or banks of new states. As their enquiries showed, and as already indicated, there were significant numbers of Africans who had received some form of British training or who were in some other way associated with British institutions who did attain such office, especially in the early postcolonial era when accelerated promotion to senior posts was common. How far this resulted (as the British hoped) in a broader and more qualitative form of cultural transfer that saw the inculcation of other British values and models is yet harder to assess, and beyond the scope of this book. Although we have encountered some evidence to suggest that it did have some effect in this respect, the postcolonial direction of African politics represented a failure for liberal British visions of politically neutral institutions. For the Bank of England at least, the way African central banks evolved represented the failure of its ambitions to develop successor institutions along British lines.

Inevitably these outcomes varied from place to place in ways that reflected the specificities of local politics and the political orientation of new states, as well as regional dynamics associated with significant crises and conflicts such as Rhodesian UDI and the Nigerian Civil War. Everywhere, however, British technical assistance was negotiated by new elites in emergent states as a means of furthering their own state-building projects and political, as well as sometimes personal, objectives. British personnel often struggled to keep abreast of opaque and factionalized politics and of fast-changing, unpredictable situations. The British were just one of many potential sources of technical assistance on which new African states could draw, and their relations with African ministers and officials could be testy and fractious. Yet even where states, such as Ghana and Tanzania, sought to reduce their reliance on Britain and British personnel, there were still striking and on-going professional associations between their institutions and those in Britain. The central banks of both Ghana and Tanzania each matched Nigeria and Zambia's records of unbroken attendance at the Bank of England's Central Banking Course. Ghana was also alone among all former British African colonies in sending cadets to Sandhurst every single year, from the moment at which it attained independence until 1989. Conversely some states, notably Nigeria and Kenya, were clearly more important in strategic and economic terms to Britain than others and received correspondingly high allocations of aid.

The chronologically staggered nature of British decolonization was also important. This not only produced the Janus-faced late imperial state, but it also ensured that developments in the newly independent West African states, especially Ghana, had a dynamic impact upon those still transitioning to independence elsewhere. It was Ghanaian independence that first forced the British to confront the implications of African constitutional change, and led them to adopt initiatives at a point at which they still had confidence that they could direct developments in new states. Some of these initiatives provided opportunities that saw British institutions and individuals gain new experience that helped reinforce their credentials when they came to address politicians in other African states. That Ghanaians and Nigerians continued to make use of British training and services may also (within limits given the complex relations between African states) have helped influence other countries to do so. Less favourably for British institutions, Ghana's transition to become a one-party state, the rapid politicization of new institutions and the rejection of British personnel from some key positions within the new state occurred even as the British were still trying to develop British models elsewhere. In particular its experience in Ghana and Nigeria showed the Bank of England that neither exercising influence nor constructing institutions on British lines was any guarantee against change or rapid diversification away from sterling: the arrangements the Bank had put in place in West Africa were unravelling even before decolonization occurred in East and Central Africa. The West African states, especially Ghana, were also significant in encouraging international institutions like the IMF and World Bank to reform their own structures and provision of aid to accommodate African decolonization, as well as to themselves become a source of personnel and expertise, in ways that might complicate the British position elsewhere.

Yet for all the immediately disruptive effects of constitutional change, the evident difficulties British personnel faced as they struggled to keep on top of volatile local, and frequently factionalized, politics, and the potential of other external influences to undermine and supersede British influence, state-building took time. The new states' initial reliance on external assistance helped shelter British institutions from the full effects of the very real power that sovereignty bestows. This was most evident in the case of the Mint since it was only some years after African independence that many new central banks ceased to regard themselves as 'tied' customers of the Mint. Instead, the full impact of decolonization for the Mint and for our other British institutions was longer term, and was reinforced by other developments in Britain that were part of the broader changing landscape in which decolonization occurred. For the universities and Sandhurst this included the changing environment of British higher education. Most importantly, underlying British economic difficulties led to the devaluation of sterling in 1967, weakening the sterling area and requiring cuts in state expenditure on aid and defence. At Sandhurst these circumstances resulted in sweeping changes to the regular service commission course which some at

Sandhurst feared changed the Academy out of all recognition. State economies also led to the closure of the Oxford course on development in 1969, and in 1980 to the withdrawal of that at Cambridge. By then both courses had not only long since ceased to fulfil their original purposes, but as Africanization of the senior roles within overseas institutions progressed, and there were more alternative forms of training available, their newer function as adjuncts to a decolonization process, training overseas public administrators, had also ceased to have much logic to it.

Nevertheless, as we have seen, legacies of the Oxbridge courses and the Bank's association with new Commonwealth central banks survived into the twenty-first century, while Sandhurst and the Mint continue to cater to overseas clients, many of whom were first brought to them by the decolonization process. At some point these legacies of both Empire and the decolonization process evolved into structures and associations between Britain and its former colonies that were distinctively different, impossible to dismiss as 'imperial leftovers'. In exploring the effect of decolonization on British institutions we are not dealing simply with a one-off 'event', or even a series of them, or with legacies of Britain's involvement in Empire that were frozen in form at the moment of independence. Institutional activities and connections continued to evolve, and were shaped not least by the experiences of those returning to Britain after secondment overseas, or whose engagement in the processes of shaping decolonization also helped frame their understanding of it. This includes a generation of scholars who were observers and even participants in the processes they sought to analyse.

How do the stories of these institutions help us to achieve a better understanding of the impact of decolonization in Britain, or indeed the process of decolonization more generally? We have after all become increasingly accustomed to decolonization as something that society experiences and moves through, rather than simply a constitutional initiative by the state. The institutions discussed in this book, however, occupied a distinct position between the state narrowly defined – the focus of an established historiography of decolonization – and civil society, increasingly the subject of a new body of scholarship about the end of Empire. They were close to the state, and were affected by processes of constitutional change, but were not involved in making those decisions. These institutions were all symbolically important, perceived as embodying some of the key virtues and values regarded as representing the British imperial project and the cultural capital of Empire, and as such they might have been anticipated to experience significant damage during decolonization. They were on the radar of a political elite, and formed part of the 'establishment'. So, as we try to assess the overall British experience of decolonization, it may not be insignificant that some of these institutions found new roles that might have been psychologically self-reinforcing and perceived by them as morally constructive – roles that, crudely put, sometimes made them feel better about themselves, and that could have been seen as yielding new economic opportunities for them. Some of the energy that had gone into the imperial project was thus sustained and redirected to new ends at the British end of the British Empire.

Bibliography

Archival Sources

Bank of England Archive, London

Files in the following classes:
G 1
G 14
G 17
OV 7
OV 18/2: Eric Haslam, *Central banks in the making: The role of the Bank of England 1948–74* (unpublished ms). At the time of writing only the chapter on Ghana had been declassified.
OV 21
OV 67
OV 68
OV 69
OV 70
OV 71
OV 74
OV 75
OV 76
OV 138
4A73/1

Bank of Ghana (Corporate Records Management Office), Accra

TRG 20, 'Courses at Bank of England'

Bodleian Library, Oxford

Mss. Brit. Emp. s 415 (Furse Papers), boxes 4, 6, 7 and 10
Mss Afr. s. 1715 (King's African Rifles)

Mss Afr. s. 1734 (Royal West African Frontier Force)
Mss Perham (Perham Papers), boxes 244–5, 248–9 and 253.

Archives of the University of Oxford:
Files in the following classes:
UR 6: Col/2; Col/4 and 4/1; Col/6; Col/10; Col/16 and 16/1; Col/17; Col/22
CW 1/1–3; CW 3/1–4; CW 5/1–7; CW 6/1–2; CW 13; CW 14; CW 19; CW 21; CW 30; CW 31; CW 32; CW 33; CW 34; CW 39/1–4; CW 40; CW 44; CW 45; CW 46; CW 47; CW 58

Cambridge University Library, Cambridge

Archives of Cambridge University:
Archives of the Course on Development and earlier and later development studies programmes:
GBR/0265/CDEV 2/1–13; 22–3
GBR/0265/CDEV 4/17–18, 25
GBR/0265/CDEV 6/2–4, 6–9, 74–9, 82–4, 93, 101
GBR/0265/CDEV 7/27, 29, 31–2
GBR/0265/CDEV 11/1–4, 5, 16–17
GBR/0265/CDEV 12/1–2
GBR/0265/CDEV 13/1–3
Papers of the University General Board, GB 760/939

International Monetary Fund Archives, Washington DC

Central Banking Department Technical Assistance and Subject Files in: Boxes 6, 14, 18, 24, 33, 42 and 44.

King's College London Foyle Special Collections

FCO collection 4/520

King's College London, Liddell Hart Military Archive

Papers of Sir Basil Liddell Hart
Papers of Gen. Sir Hugh Stockwell

London School of Economics and Political Science Archive

Central Filing Registry:
Box 326
Box 327

The National Archives, Kew

Files from the following classes:
BW 2
CAB 129
CAB 148
CO 537
CO 847
CO 877
CO 968
CO 1025
DEFE 11
DO 35
FCO 41
FCO 46
FCO 296
LAB 8
MINT 20
OD 19
OV 19
T 296
WO 32
WO 163
WO 216

*Public Records and Archives Administration
Department of Ghana, Accra*

ADM 13/1
ADM 13/2
RG 2
RG 3
RG 6

Royal Bank of Scotland Archives, Edinburgh
GM/2074/2

Royal Military Academy Sandhurst

Archival material held at the RMAS is largely but not exclusively packed in files in numbered boxes in two rooms. As there appeared to be a different numerical sequence of boxes in each of the two rooms, citations include the details of the rooms in which the boxes consulted are located. It is possible that in the future the boxes may be relocated. Some boxes contained numbered or labelled files; others had loose material or unlabelled files and packages. Where further detailed descriptions exist I have given them in my footnotes.

Room A12: Boxes 13, 14, 251, 351, 352, 369, 370, 372, 373, 374, 381, 385, 388, 399, 401, 447, 448, 450, 451, 451, 452, 453, 454, 455, 456, 457,458, 459, 460

Room D56: Boxes 1, 2, 87, 88, 107, 108, 231, 256, 303a, 303b, 304a, 304b, 305a, 305b, 306, 307

Central Library, Royal Military Academy Sandhurst: post-expeditionary reports.

Royal Mint, Llantrisant

Material at the Royal Mint, Llantrisant, was consulted before the opening in spring 2016 of a new museum. The archival material consulted was packed principally in boxes labelled by country. More than one box exists for some countries but these are not labelled numerically nor to do they necessarily follow any chronological sequence. I have therefore chosen to refer to them as simply 'Nigeria Boxes' or 'Box' (where only one exists).

Boxes: French West Africa, Gambia, Ghana, Kenya, Liberia, Malawi, Nigeria, Sierra Leone, Tanzania Uganda, Zambia, Zimbabwe.

Minutes of the Royal Mint Advisory Committee, 1922–1982 (originally known as the Standing Committee on Coins, Medals and Decorations).

Senate House Library, London

Archives of the University of London
AC 1
ICS 85

Zambia National Archives, Lusaka

Cabinet Office:
CO 9/1/9
CO 17/1/6
CO 17/1/7
Ministry of Finance:
MF 1/3/41/225

Interviews

British officer, formerly at Sandhurst, 10 May 2016.
Written answers to author's questions provided by anonymous
Ghanaian army officer, a cadet in the 1970s.
Colin Newbury, 9 October 2015.
John Toye, 9 October 2015.
Graham Dyer, 20 January 2016.

Printed Primary Sources

Official Publications (United Kingdom)

Annual Reports of the Comptroller and Deputy Master of the Royal Mint
The Civil Service, Volume 1: Report of the Committee, 1966–68 (1968), PP. 1967–8,
    XVIII (Cmnd. 3638).
The Colonial Empire (1939–1947), PP 1946–7, X (Cmnd. 7167).
*Colonial Office. Report of the Public Services Conference Held in the Colonial Office,
    London 1st to 10th March 1960*, Col. No. 347 (HMSO, London, 1960).
*Colonial Office. Report of the West African Forces Conference, Lagos 20–24 April
    1953*, Col. No. 304 (HMSO, London, 1954).
*Colonial Office: Post-War Training for the Colonial Service: Report of a Committee
    Appointed by the Secretary of State for the Colonies*, Col. No. 198 (HMSO,
    London, 1946).
Colonial Office. Service with Overseas Governments (October 1960), PP 1959–60,
    XXVII (Cmnd. 1193).
Fifth Report from the Estimates Committee, 1967–8. The Royal Mint, PP 1967–8, IX
    (Cmnd. 364).
Guide to the Establishment and Operation of Trading Funds (HM Treasury, 2004).
H.M. Treasury. Aid to Developing Countries (September 1963) PP 1962–3, XXXI
    (Cmnd. 2147).
House of Commons Debates.
House of Lords Debates.
Ministry of Overseas Development/ODA, British Aid Statistics 1963–1972 (HMSO,
    1972).
*Ministry of Overseas Development. Overseas Development: the Work of the New
    Ministry (August 1965)*, PP 1964–5 (Cmnd. 2736).
*Ministry of Overseas Development. Public Service Overseas. The Future of the Overseas
    Service Aid Scheme and Other Supplementation Arrangements*, PP 1968–9, LIII
    (Cmnd. 3994).
Technical Assistance from the United Kingdom for Overseas Development, PP 1960–1,
    XXVII (Cmnd. 1308).

Official Publications of Other Governments

Central Bank of the Gambia. Annual Report (1971–2) (Central Bank of the Gambia, Banjul, 1973).

The First Ten Years. The Central Bank of Kenya (Central Bank of Kenya, Nairobi, 1976).

Report by Mr J.B. Loynes on the Establishment of a Nigerian Central Bank, the Introduction of a Nigerian Currency, and other Associated Matters (Lagos, 1957).

Report by J.B. Loynes on the Problem of the Future Currencies of Sierra Leone and the Gambia (Bathurst, 1961).

Report on the Establishment of a central bank in Malaya by Mr. G.M. Watson and Sir Sydney Caine (Kuala Lumpur, 1956).

Report on the desirability and practicability of establishing a central bank in Nigeria for promoting the economic development of the country (Lagos, 1953).

Reserve Bank of Malawi. Tenth Anniversary, 1965–75 (Reserve Bank of Malawi, Blantyre, 1975).

South Arabian Currency Authority, Report for the Year 1966; Southern Yemen Currency Authority, Report 1967–8.

Twenty Years of Central Banking in Nigeria: 1959–1979 (Research Department, central Bank of Nigeria, Lagos, 1979).

Publications of International Organizations

International Bank for Reconstruction and Development (the World Bank): The Economic Development of Nigeria (Johns Hopkins Press, Baltimore, MD, 1955).

The Reports of the Bank's General Survey Missions – A Synthesis (Central Economics staff series, EC 45, Washington, DC, 1956).

Tanganyika – Current Economic Position and Prospects (Africa Series, AF 13, Washington, DC, 1963).

The Economic Report: East African Community, Kenya, Tanzania, Uganda (Eastern Africa series AE 16, Washington, DC, 1971).

Newspapers and Serials

SOAS, *Bulletin*
The Times
The Wish Stream

Digital Sources

Oxford Dictionary of National Biography: www.oxforddnb.com/
The Royal Mint Museum: www.royalmintmuseum.org.uk/
The University of Oxford: www.ox.ac.uk/

Edited Collections of Primary Sources

Stephen R. Ashton and William Roger Louis eds., *East of Suez and the Commonwealth, 1964–1971* (British Documents on the End of Empire, Series A, Vol. 5, London, 2004).

Stephen R. Ashton and Sarah Stockwell eds., *Imperial Policy and Colonial Practice, 1925–1945* (British Documents on the End of Empire, Series A, Vol. 1, HMSO, 1996).
Ronald Hyam and William Roger Louis eds., *The Conservative Government and the End of Empire 1957–1964* (British Documents on the End of Empire, Series A, Vol. 4, HMSO, 2000).

PhD Theses

Brooke, Peter, 'Duncan Sandys and the Informal Politics of Decolonisation' (King's College London, PhD, 2016).
Feingold, Ellen, 'Decolonising Justice: A History of the High Court of Tanganyika, c. 1920–1971' (University of Oxford, D. Phil., 2011).
Gardiner, Nile, ' "Sentinels of Empire". The British Colonial Administrative Service, 1919–1954' (Yale University, PhD, 1998).
Crocker, Chester Arthur, 'The Military Transfer of Power in Africa: A Comparative Study of Change in the British and French Systems of Order' (Johns Hopkins University, PhD, 1969).
Cullen, Poppy, ' "Kenya Is No Doubt a Special Place": British Policy towards Kenya, 1960–1980' (University of Durham, PhD, 2015).
Mercau, Ezequiel, 'Empire Redux: The Falklands and the End of Greater Britain' (University of Copenhagen, PhD, 2016).
Sindab, Jean Nellie, 'The Impact of Expatriates on the Zambian Development Process' (Yale University, PhD, 1984).

Books and Articles

Adas, Michael, *Dominance by Design: Technological Imperatives and America's Civilizing Mission* (Harvard University Press, Cambridge, MA, 2006).
Adedze, Agbenyega, 'Commemorating the Chief: The Politics of Postage Stamps in West Africa', *African Arts* 37(2004), pp. 68–73.
Adi, Hakim, *Pan-Africanism and Communism: The Communist International, Africa and the Diaspora, 1919–1939* (Africa New World Press, Trenton, NJ, 2013).
Adu, A. L., *The Civil Service in Commonwealth Africa: Development and Transition* (George Allen and Unwin, London, 1969).
Afrifa, Akwasi A., *The Ghana Coup, 24th February 1966* (Frank Cass & Co. Ltd., Guildford and London, 1966).
Anderson, David, *Histories of the Hanged: Britain's Dirty War in Kenya and the End of Empire* (Weidenfeld and Nicolson, London, 2005).
'Mau Mau in the High Court and the "Lost" British Empire Archives: Colonial Conspiracy or Bureaucratic Bungle?', *Journal of Imperial and Commonwealth History* 39 (2011), pp. 699–716.
Anderson, David and David, Killingray eds., *Policing and Decolonisation: Politics, Nationalism and the Police, 1917–1965* (Manchester University Press, Manchester, 1992).

Anderson, Robert, *British Universities: Past and Present* (Hambledon, London, 2006).

Andrew, Christopher, *The Security Service, 1908–1945: The Official History* (Public Record Office, London, 1999).

Anglin, Douglas G. and Timothy M. Shaw, *Zambia's Foreign Policy: Studies in Diplomacy and Dependence* (Westview Press, Colorado, 1979).

Ashby, Eric, *Universities: British, Indian, African – A Study in the Ecology of Higher Education* (Harvard University Press, Cambridge, MA, 1966).

Ayensu, Edward S., *Bank of Ghana: Commemoration of the Golden Jubilee* (Bank of Ghana, Accra, 2007).

Bailkin, Jordanna, *The Afterlife of Empire* (University of California Press, Berkeley, CA, 2012).

Balogh, Thomas, 'The Apotheosis of the Dilettante: The Establishment of the Mandarins' in Thomas Balogh, Dudley Seers, Roger Opie, and Hugh Thomas eds., *Crisis in the Civil Service* (Anthony Blond, London, 1968), pp. 11–51.

Bamba, Abou B., 'Triangulating a Modernization Experiment: The United States, France, and The Making of the Kossou Project in Central Ivory Coast' special issue of *Journal of Modern European History*, 8 (2010), pp. 66–84.

Barber, Elino G., Philip G. Altbach, and Robert G. Myers eds., *Bridges to Knowledge. Foreign Students in Comparative Perspective* (University of Chicago Press, Chicago, IL, 1984).

Bareau, Paul, 'The Sterling Area' in Richard Sayers ed., *Banking in the British Commonwealth* (Clarendon Press, Oxford, 1952), pp. 460–85.

Barnet, Correlli, *The Collapse of British Power* (Methuen Publishing, London, 1972).

Barua, Pradeep P., *Gentleman of the Raj: The Indian Army Officer Corps, 1817–1949* (Praeger, Westport, CO, 2003).

Basu, Saroj K., *Central Banking in the Emerging Countries: A Study of African Experiments* (Asia Publishing House, London, 1967).

Bauer, Peter T., *Dissent on Development* (Weidenfeld and Nicolson, London, 1971).

Bayly, Christopher A., Vijayendra Rao, Simon Szreter, and Michael Woodcock eds., *History, Historians and Development Policy: A Necessary Dialogue* (Manchester University Press, Manchester, 2011).

Bennett, Brett M. and Joseph Hodge eds., *Science and Empire: Knowledge and Networks of Science across the British Empire, 1800–1970* (Palgrave Macmillan, Basingstoke, 2011).

Billig, Michael, *Banal Nationalism* (Sage Publications, London, 1995).

Black, Iain, 'Imperial Visions. Rebuilding the Bank of England, 1919–1939' in Felix Driver and David Gilbert eds., *Imperial Cities* (Manchester University Press, Manchester, 1999), pp. 96–113.

Boehmer, Elke, *Indian Arrivals, 1870–1915: Networks of British Empire* (Oxford University Press, Oxford, 2015).

Bond, Mick, 'Mporokoso' in Tony Schur ed., *From the Cam to the Zambesi: Colonial Service and the Path to the New Zambia* (I. B. Tauris, London, 2015), pp. 61–72.

Bond, Wendy, 'Mporokoso, Chinsali, Bancroft, Mongu, Lusaka, Kitwe' in Tony Schur ed., *From the Cam to the Zambezi: Colonial Service and the Path to the New Zambia* (I. B. Tauris, London, 2015), pp. 195–212.

Born, Arjen and Tom, Christensen, 'The Development of Public Institutions: Reconsidering the Role of Leadership', *Administration and Society*, 40 (2008), pp. 271–97.

Braibanti, Ralph et al., *Asian Bureaucratic Systems Emergent from the British Imperial Tradition* (Duke University Press, Durham, NC, 1966).

Branch, Daniel, *Kenya: Between Hope and Despair, 1963–2011* (Yale University Press, New Haven, CT, 2011).

Bridges, Sir Edward, 'Administration: What Is it? And How It Can Be Learnt' in A. Dunsire ed., *The Making of an Administrator* (Pub. on behalf of the Royal Institute of Public Administration, Manchester University Press, Manchester, 1956), pp. 1–36.

Brooke, Christopher, *A History of the University of Cambridge: Volume IV 1870–1990* (Cambridge University Press, Cambridge, 1993).

Buettner, Elizabeth, *Empire Families: Britons and Late Imperial India* (Oxford University Press, Oxford, 2004).

Europe after Empire: Decolonization, Society and Culture (Cambridge University Press, Cambridge, 2016).

Burnham, Jeremy, 'Mumbawa, Lundazi' in Tony Schur ed., *From the Cam to the Zambezi: Colonial Service and the Path to the New Zambia* (I. B. Tauris, London, 2015), pp. 2–41.

Burton, Antoinette, *Burdens of History: British Feminists, Indian Women, and Imperial Culture, 1865–1915* (University of North Carolina Press, Chapel Hill, NC, 1994).

Butler, Lawrence J., *Copper Empire: Mining and the Colonial State in Northern Rhodesia, 1930–1964* (Palgrave Macmillan, Basingstoke, 2007).

Butler, Lawrence J. and Sarah, Stockwell eds., *The Wind of Change: Harold Macmillan and British Decolonization* (Palgrave Macmillan, Basingstoke, 2013).

Cain, Peter J., 'Gentlemanly Imperialism at Work: The Bank of England, Canada, and the Sterling Area, 1932–1936', *The Economic History Review*, New Series, 49 (May, 1996), pp. 336–57.

Cain, Peter J. and Anthony G. Hopkins, *British Imperialism, 1688–1990* (Longman, Harlow, 1st pub., 1993; 3rd edn., 2016).

Cairncross, Alec, 'The Bank of England and the British Economy' in Richard Roberts and David Kynaston eds., *The Bank of England. Money Power and Influence, 1694–1994* (Clarendon Press, Oxford, 1995).

Capie, Forrest, *The Bank of England 1950s to 1979* (Cambridge University Press, Cambridge, 2010).

Chabal, Patrick and Jean-Pascal, Daloz, *Africa Works: Disorder as Political Instrument* (James Currey, Oxford, 1999).

Challis, Christopher E., ed., *A New History of the Royal Mint* (Cambridge University Press, Cambridge, 1992).

Chapman, Richard A., *Leadership in the British Civil Service: A Study of Sir Percival Waterfield and the Creation of the Civil Service Selection Board* (Croom Helm, London and Sydney, 1984).

Clarke, Ron, 'Institutions for Training Overseas Administrators: the University of Manchester's Contribution', *Public Administration and Development*, 19 (1999), pp. 521–33.

Clarke, Sabine, 'A Technocratic Imperial State? The Colonial Office and Scientific Research, 1940–1960', *Twentieth Century British History* 18 (2007), pp. 453–80.
'"The Chance to Send Their First Class Men Out to the Colonies": the Making of the Colonial Research Service' in Brett M. Bennett and Joseph Hodge eds., *Science and Empire. Knowledge and Networks of Science across the British Empire, 1800–1970* (Palgrave Macmillan, Basingstoke, 2011), pp. 187–208.

Clayton, Anthony, *The British Officer: Leading the Army from 1660 to the Present* (Pearson, Harlow, 2006).
'Foreign Intervention in Africa' in Simon Baynham ed., *Military Power and Politics in Black Africa* (Croom Helm, London, 1986), pp. 203–58.

Clayton, Anthony, 'The Military Relations between Great Britain and Commonwealth Countries, with particular reference to the African Commonwealth Nations' in W. H. Morris–Jones and Georges Fischer eds., *Decolonisation and After: The British and French Experience* (Routledge, London, 1980), pp. 193–223.

Clayton, Anthony and David Killigray, *Khaki and Blue: Military and Police in British Colonial Africa* (Ohio University Center for International Studies, Athens, OH, 1989).

Cohen, Stephen, *The Indian Army, Its Contribution to the Development of a Nation* (2nd edn., Oxford University Press, Oxford, 1990).

Collingham, Elizabeth M., *Imperial Bodies: The Physical Experience of the Raj* (Cambridge University Press, Cambridge, 2001).

Cooper, Frederick, *Citizenship between Empire and Nation: Remaking France and French Africa, 1945–1960* (Princeton University Press, Princeton, NJ, 2014).

Cormac, Rory, 'Organizing Intelligence: An Introduction to the 1955 Report on Colonial Security', *Intelligence and National Security* 25 (2010), pp. 800–22.

Cottrell, Philip L., 'The Bank in its International Setting' in Richard Roberts and David Kynaston eds., *The Bank of England. Money Power and Influence, 1694–1994* (Clarendon Press, Oxford, 1995), pp. 83–139.

Craggs, Ruth, 'Hospitality in Geopolitics and the Making of Commonwealth International Relations', *Geoforum*, 52 (2014), pp. 90–100.

Craggs, Ruth and Claire Wintle eds., *Cultures of Decolonisation* (Manchester University Press, Manchester, 2015).

Craig, Sir John, *The Mint: A History of the London Mint from AD 287 to 1948* (Cambridge University Press, Cambridge, 1953).

Darwin, John, *The Empire Project: The Rise and Fall of the British World System, 1830–1970* (Cambridge University Press, Cambridge, 2009).
'A World University' in Brian Harrison ed., *The History of the University of Oxford. Volume VIII: The Twentieth Century* (Clarendon Press, Oxford, 1994), pp. 607–38.

De Kock, Michiel H., *Central Banking* (3rd edn., Staples Printers, London, 1954).

DeRoche Andrew J., 'You Can't Fight Guns with Knives: National Security and Zambian Responses to UDI, 1965–1973' in Jan-Bart Gewald, Marja Hinfelaar, Giacoma Macola eds., *One Zambia, Many Histories* (Brill, Leiden, 2008), pp. 77–97.

Deslandes, Paul R, '"The Foreign Element": Newcomers and the Rhetoric of Race, Nation and Empire in "Oxbridge" Undergraduate Culture, 1850–1920', *Journal of British Studies*, 37 (1998), pp. 54–90.

Dilley, Andrew, *Finance, Politics and Imperialism: Australia, Canada and the City of London, 1896–1914* (Palgrave Macmillan, Basingstoke, 2012).

Dimier, Véronique, *Le gouvernement des colonies, regards croisés franco–britannique* (Presses Universitaire de Bruxelles, Brussels, 2004).

The Invention of a European Development Aid Bureaucracy. Recycling Empire (Palgrave Macmillan, Basingstoke, 2014).

'Three Universities and the British Elite: A Science of Colonial Administration in the UK' *Public Administration*, 84 (2006), pp. 337–66.

Dockrill, Saki, *Britain's Retreat from East of Suez: The Choice between Europe and the World, 1945–1968* (Palgrave Macmillan, Basingstoke, 2002).

Dorrance, G. S., 'The Bank of Canada', in Richard S. Sayers ed., *Banking in the British Commonwealth* (Clarendon Press, Oxford, 1952), pp. 121–49.

Dyer, Graham P. and Peter P. Gaspar, 'Reform, the New Technology and Tower Hill 1700–1966' in Christopher E. Challis ed., *A New History of the Royal Mint* (Cambridge University Press, Cambridge, 1992), pp. 398–606.

Eagleton, Catherine, 'Designing Change: Coins and the Creation of New National Identities', in Ruth Craggs and Claire Wintle eds., *Cultures of Decolonisation* (Manchester University Press, Manchester, 2015), pp. 222–44.

Eckert, Andreas, Stephen Malinowski and Corinna Ungereds., eds. *Modernizing Missions: Approaches to 'Developing' the Non-Western World after 1945, Special Issue of Journal of Modern European History* 8 (2010), no. 1.

Ekejiuba, Felicia, 'Currency Instability and Social Payments among the Igbo of Eastern Nigeria, 1890–1990', in Jane F. Guyer ed., *Money Matters: Instability, Values and Social Payments in the Modern History of West African Communities* (James Currey, London, 1985), pp. 133–61.

Elkins, Caroline, *Britain's Gulag: The Brutal End of Empire in Kenya* (Jonathan Cape, London, 2005).

Falola, Toyin, 'West Africa' in Judith M. Brown and William Roger Louis eds., *Oxford History of the British Empire. Volume 4. The Twentieth Century* (Oxford University Press, London, 1999), pp. 486–511.

Farwell, Bryon, *Armies of the Raj: From the Mutiny to Independence, 1858–1947* (Viking, London, 1989).

Faught, Brad, *Into Africa: The Imperial Life of Margery Perham* (I. B. Tauris, London, 2012).

Fforde, John, *Bank of England and Public Policy, 1941–1958* (Cambridge University Press, Cambridge, 1992).

Fieldhouse, David, 'Ronald Robinson and the Cambridge Development Conferences, 1963–70', *Journal of Imperial and Commonwealth History*, 16 (1988), pp. 173–99.

Finer, Samuel E., *Man on Horseback* (Pall Mall Press, London, 1962).

Frayling, Sir Christopher, 'Continuity through Change: The Royal Mint Advisory Committee' in Kevin Clancy ed., *Designing Change: The Art of Coin Design* (Royal Mint, Llantrisant, 2008), pp. 38–65.

French, David, *Army, Empire and Cold War: The British Army and Military Policy, 1945–1971* (Oxford University Press, Oxford, 2012).

The British Way in Warfare, 1688–2000 (Unwin Hyman, London, 1990).

Frey, Marc and Sönke, Kunkel, 'Writing the History of Development: A Review of the Recent Literature', *Contemporary European History*, 20 (2011), pp. 215–32.

Fry, Maxwell J., Charles A. E. Goodhart, and Alvaro Almeida, *Central Banking in Developing Countries: Objectives, Activities, and Independence* (Routledge, London, 1996).

Fuller, Harcourt, *Building the Ghanaian Nation State. Kwame Nkrumah's Symbolic Nationalism* (Palgrave Macmillan, Basingstoke, Palgrave, 2014).

Furse, Sir Ralph Furse, *Acuparius, Recollections of a Recruiting Officer* (Oxford University Press, Oxford, 1962).

Fyle, Magbaily C., *Historical Dictionary of Sierra Leone* (Scarecrow Press, Lanham, MD, 2006).

Gilbert, Emily and Eric Helleiner eds., *Nation States and Money. The Past, Present and Future of National Currencies* (Routledge, London, 1999).

Gilman, Nils, 'Modernization Theory. The Highest Stage of American Intellectual History' in David C. Engerman, Nils Gilman, Mark Haefele, and Michael E. Latham eds., *Staging Growth. Modernization, Development and the Global Cold War* (University of Massachusetts Press, Amherst, MA, 2003), pp. 47–80.

Grieveson, Lee and Colin MacCabe eds., *Film and the End of Empire* (Palgrave Macmillan with the British Film Institute, London, 2011).

Gunasekera, H. A., *From Dependent Currency to Central Banking in Ceylon: An Analysis of Monetary Experience, 1825–1957* (London School of Economic and Political Science, London, 1962).

Gupta, Partha S., 'The Debate on Indianization, 1918–1939', in Partha S. Gupta, and Anirudh Deshpande eds., *The British Raj and its Indian Armed Forces, 1857–1939* (Oxford University Press, Oxford, 2002), pp. 228–69.

Gutteridge, William, 'A Commonwealth Military Culture? Soldiers in the British Mould', *Round Table*, 60 (1970), pp. 327–37.

Military Institutions and Power in the New States (Pall Mall Press, London and Dunmow, 1964).

The Military in African Politics (Methuen and Co Ltd., London, 1969).

Guyer, Jane F., ed., *Money Matters. Instability, Values and Social Payments in the Modern History of West African Communities* (James Currey, London, 1985).

Haefele, Mark H., 'Walt Rostow's Stages of Economic Growth: Ideas and Actions' in David C. Enferman, Nils Gilman, Mark Haefele, and Michael E. Latham eds., *Staging Growth. Modernization, Development and the Global Cold War* (University of Massachusetts Press, Amherst, MA, 2003), pp. 81–103.

Hall, Catherine and Sonya Rose eds., *At Home with the Empire: Metropolitan Culture and the Imperial World* (Cambridge University Press, Cambridge, 2006).

Helleiner, Eric, 'The Southern Side of 'Embedded Liberalism'. America's Unorthodox Money Doctoring during the Early post-1945 Years' in Marc Flandreau ed., *Money Doctors: The Experience of International Financial Advising, 1850–2000* (Routledge, London, 2003), pp. 249–75.

The Making of National Money: Territorial Currencies in Historical Perspective (Cornell University Press, New York, 2003).

Hennessy, Elizabeth, 'The Governors, Directors, and Management' in David Kynaston and Andrew Roberts eds., *The Bank of England, Money, Power and Influence 1694–1994* (Oxford University Press, Oxford, 1995), pp. 185–216.

Hennessy, Peter, *Whitehall* (Secker and Warburg, London, 1989).

Heussler, Robert, *Yesterday's Rulers: The Making of the British Colonial Service* (Oxford University Press for Syracuse University Press, London, 1963).

Hewitt, Virginia, 'A Distant View: Imagery and Imagination in the Paper Currency of the British Empire 1800–1960' in Emily Gilbert and Eric Helleiner eds., *Nation States and Money. The Past, Present and Future of National Currencies* (Routledge, London, 1999), pp. 97–116.

Hodge, Joseph, 'British Colonial Expertise, Post–Colonial Careering and the Early History of International Development' in Andreas Eckert, Stephen Malinowski, and Corinna Unger eds., *Modernizing Missions. Approaches to 'Developing' the Non–Western World after 1945*, special issue of *Journal of Modern European History*, 8 (2010), no. 1, pp. 24–44.

Triumph of the Expert: Agrarian Doctrines of Development (Ohio University Press, Athens, OH, 2007).

Heffernan, Michael and Heike, Jöns, 'Degrees of Influence: The Politics of Honorary Degrees in the Universities of Oxford and Cambridge, 1900–2000', *Minerva*, 45 (2007), pp. 389–416.

Hogendorn, Jan S. and Henry A. Gemery, 'Continuity in West African Monetary History? An Outline of Monetary Development', *African Economic History*, 17 (1988), pp. 127–46.

Holtham, Gerald and Arthur Hazlewood, *Aid and Inequality in Kenya: British Development Assistance to Kenya* (Croom Helm, London, assoc. ODI, 1976).

Hopkins, Anthony G., 'Rethinking Decolonization', *Past and Present*, 200 (2008), pp. 211–47.

'The Creation of a Colonial Monetary System: The Origins of the West African Currency Board', *International Journal of African Historical Studies*, 3 (1970), pp. 101–32.

'The Currency Revolution in South–West Nigeria in the late Nineteenth Century', *Journal of the Historical Society of Nigeria*, 3 (1966), pp. 471–83.

Howe, Stephen, *Anti–colonialism in British Politics: The Left and the End of Empire 1918–1964* (Clarendon Press, Oxford, 1993).

'Internal Decolonization? British Politics since Thatcher as Post–Colonial Trauma', *Twentieth Century British History* 14 (2003), pp. 286–304.

'When if Ever Did Empire End? Internal Decolonization in British Culture since the 1950s' in Martin Lynn ed., *The British Empire in the 1950s. Retreat or Revival?* (Palgrave Macmillan, Basingstoke, 2006).

Hubbard, James P., *The United States and the End of British Colonial Rule in Africa, 1941–68* (McFarland and Co., Jefferson, NC, 2011).

Huntingdon, Samuel, *The Soldier and the State* (Harvard University Press, Cambridge, MA, 1967).

Hyam, Ronald, *Britain's Declining Empire: The Road to Decolonisation, 1918–1968* (Cambridge University Press, Cambridge, 2006).

'Imperial and Commonwealth History at Cambridge, 1881–1981: Founding Fathers and Pioneer Research Students', *Journal of Imperial and Commonwealth History*, 29 (2001), pp. 296–307.

Understanding the British Empire (Cambridge University Press, Cambridge, 2010).

Idang, Gordon J., *Nigerian Internal Politics and Foreign Policy, 1960–66* (Ibadan University Press, Ibadan, 1973).

Ittman, Karl, *A Problem of Great Importance: Population, Race, and Power in the British Empire, 1918–1973* (University of California Press Ltd., Berkeley and Los Angeles, CA, 2013).

Ireton, Barry, *Britain's International Development Policies: A History of DFID and Overseas Aid* (Palgrave Macmillan, Basingstoke, 2013).

Jackson, Ashley, 'British–African Defence and Security Connections', *Defence Studies*, 6 (2006), pp. 351–76.

'Empire and Beyond: The Pursuit of Overseas National Interests in the Late Twentieth Century', *English Historical Review* 122 (2007), pp. 1350–66.

'The Evolution and Use of British Imperial Military Formations' in Alan Jeffreys and Patrick Rose eds., *The Indian Army 1939–1947. Experience and Development* (Ashgate, Farnham, 2012), pp. 9–29.

Robert, Jackson, *Quasi-States. Sovereignty, International Relations and the Third World* (Cambridge University Press, Cambridge, 1990).

James, Harold, 'Who Owns "Ownership"? The IMF and Policy Advice' in Marc Flandreau ed., *Money Doctors. The Experience of International Financial Advising, 1850–2000* (Routledge, London, 2003), pp. 78–102.

James, Leslie and Elizabeth Leake, *Decolonization and the Cold War: Negotiating Independence* (Bloomsbury Academic, London, 2015).

Janowitz, Morris, *The Military and the Political Development of New Nations* (University of Chicago Press, Chicago, 1964).

Jeffreys, Alan, 'Training the Indian Army, 1939–1945' in Alan Jeffreys and Patrick Rose eds., *The Indian Army 1939–1947. Experience and Development* (Ashgate, Farnham, 2012), pp. 69–86.

Jeppesen, Chris, 'Sanders of the River: Still the Best Job for a British Boy: Recruitment to the Colonial Administrative Service at the End of Empire', *Historical Journal*, 59 (2016), pp. 469–508.

'A Worthwhile Career for a Man Who Is not Entirely Self-Seeking: Service, Duty and the Colonial Service during Decolonization' in Andrew W. M. Smith and Chris Jeppesen eds., *Britain, France and the Decolonization of Africa. Future Imperfect?* (University College London Press, London, 2017), pp. 134–55.

Johnson, Douglas, 'Political Intelligence, Colonial Ethnography, and Analytical Anthropology in the Sudan' in Helen Tilley and Robert J. Gordon eds., *Ordering Africa. Anthropology, European Imperialism, and the Politics of Knowledge* (Manchester University Press, Manchester, 2007), pp. 309–35.

Jöns, Heike, 'The University of Cambridge Academic Expertise and the British Empire, 1885–1962', *Environment and Planning* 48 (2016), pp. 94–114.

Joyce, Patrick, *The State of Freedom: A Social History of the British State since 1800* (Cambridge University Press, Cambridge, 2013).

Jucker-Fleetwood, Erin E., *Money and Finance in Africa. The Experience of Ghana, Morocco, Nigeria, the Rhodesias and Nyasaland, the Sudan and Tunisia from the Establishment of Their Central Banks until 1962* (George Allen & Unwin, London, 1964).

Kalinga, Owen J., *Historical Dictionary of Malawi* (4th edn., Scarecrow Press, Lanham, MD, 2012).

Katsakioris, Constantin, 'Soviet Lessons for Arab Modernization. Soviet Educational Aid towards Arab Countries after 1956' in Andreas Eckert, Stephen Malinowski, and Corinna Unger eds., *Modernizing Missions. Approaches to Developing the*

Non-Western World after 1945, special issue of *Journal of Modern European History* 8 (2010), no. 1, pp. 85–106.

Keegan, John, *World Armies* (Macmillan Press, London, 1979).

Killick, Tony, 'Policy Autonomy and the History of British Aid to Africa', *Development Policy Review*, 23 (2005), pp. 665–81.

Killingray, David, *The British Military Presence in West Africa* (Oxford Development Records Project, Report 3, 1983).

 Fighting for Britain. African Soldiers and the Second World War (James Currey, Woodbridge, 2010).

Kirk-Greene, Anthony H. M., 'Forging a Relationship with the Colonial Administrative Service, 1921–1939' in A. Smith and M. Bull eds., *Margery Perham and British Rule in Africa* (Frank Cass, London, 1991), pp. 62–82.

 On Crown Service: A History of H.M. Colonial and Overseas Civil Services, 1837–1997 (I. B. Tauris, London, 1999).

 'Public Administration and the Colonial Administration', *Public Administration and Development*, 19 (1999), pp. 507–519.

 Symbol of Authority: The British District Officer in Africa (I. B. Tauris, London, 2006).

 'The Thin White Line: The Size of the British Colonial Service in Africa', *African Affairs*, 79 (1980), pp. 25–44.

Kothari, Uma, 'From Colonial Administration to Development Studies: A Postcolonial Critique of the History of Development Studies', *A Radical History of Development Studies. Individuals, Institutions, and Ideologies* (Zed Books, London, 2005).

Krozewski, Gerold, *Money and the End of Empire: British International Economic Policy and the Colonies, 1947–1958* (Palgrave Macmillan, Basingstoke, 2001).

Kuklick, Henrika, *The Imperial Bureaucrat: The Colonial Administrative Service in the Gold Coast, 1920–1939* (Hoover University Press, Stanford, 1979).

Kumarasingham, Harshan, *A Political Legacy of the British Empire: Power and the Parliamentary System in Post-Colonial India and Sri Lanka* (I. B. Tauris, London, 2013).

Kuper, Adam, *Anthropology and Anthropologists: The British School in the Twentieth Century* (4th edn., Routledge, London, 2015; first published 1973).

Kynaston, David, 'The Bank and the Government', in David Kynaston and Richard Roberts, eds., *The Bank of England. Money Power and Influence, 1694–1994* (Clarendon Press, Oxford, 1995), pp. 19–55.

 Till Time's Last Sand: A History of the Bank of England 1694–2013 (Bloomsbury Publishing, London, 2017).

Lambert, David and Alan Lester eds., *Colonial Lives across the British Empire. Imperial Careering in the Nineteenth Century* (Cambridge University Press, Cambridge, 2006).

Lane, Anne, 'Foreign and Defence Policy' in Anthony Seldon and Kevin Hickson eds., *New Labour, Old Labour: the Wilson and Callaghan Governments, 1974–79* (Routledge, London and New York, 2004), pp. 154–69.

Larmer, Miles, 'Enemies Within? Opposition to the Zambian One-Party State, 1972–80' in Jan–Bart Gewald, Marja Hinfelaar and Giacoma Macola eds., *One Zambia, Many Histories* (Brill, Leiden, 2008), pp. 98–125.

ed., *The Musakanya Papers: The Autobiographical Writings of Valentine Musakanya* (Lembani Trust, Lusaka, 2010).

Le Breton, David ed., *I Remember it Well: Fifty Years of Colonial Service Personnel Reminiscences* (Published for the Overseas Service Pensioners' Association, Kinloss, 2010).

Lee, Michael, *African Armies and Civil Order* (Chatto and Windus, London, 1969).

Colonial Development and Good Government: A Study of the Ideas Expressed by the British Official Classes in Planning Decolonization 1939–1964 (Clarendon Press, Oxford, 1967).

'Commonwealth Students in the United Kingdom, 1940–1960; Student Welfare and World Status', *Minerva*, 44 (2006), pp. 1–24.

Lentz, Carla, 'African Middle Classes: Lessons from Transnational Studies and a Research Agenda' in Henning Melber ed., *The Rise of Africa's Middle Class. Myths, Realities and Critical Engagements* (Zed Books, London, 2016), pp. 17–53.

Livsey, Tim, 'Suitable Lodgings for Students: Modern Space, Colonial Development and Decolonization in Nigeria', *Urban History*, 41 (2014), pp. 1–22.

Lloyd, Peter C. ed., *New Elites of Tropical Africa* (Oxford University Press for the International African Institute, London, 1966).

Louis, William Roger and Ronald Robinson, 'The Imperialism of Decolonization', *Journal of Imperial and Commonwealth History*, 22 (1994), pp. 462–511.

Low, Donald A. and John Lonsdale, 'Towards the New Order, 1945–1963', in Donald A. Low and Alison Smith eds., *History of East Africa. Volume 3* (Oxford University Press, Oxford, 1976), pp. 1–63.

Loynes, John B. *The West African Currency Board, 1912–1962* (Eyre and Spottiswoode, London, 1962).

Luckham, Robin, *The Nigerian Military: A Sociological Analysis of Authority and Revolt 1960–1967* (Cambridge University Press, Cambridge, 1971).

Lynn, Martin, 'Nigerian Complications: The Colonial Office, the Colonial Service and the 1953 Crisis in Nigeria' in John Smith ed., *Administering Empire. The British Colonial Service in Retrospect* (University of London Press, London, 1999).

Mackenzie, John ed., *Imperialism and Popular Culture* (Manchester University Press, Manchester, 1986).

Madden, Frederick and David Fieldhouse eds., *Oxford and the Idea of Commonwealth. Essays Presented to Sir Edgar Williams* (Croon Helm, London, 1982).

Maekawa, Ichiro, 'Neo-colonialism Reconsidered: A Case Study of East Africa in the 1960s and 70s', *Journal of Imperial and Commonwealth History*, 43 (2015), pp. 317–41.

Magee, Gary and Andrew Thompson, *Empire and Globalisation: Networks of People, Goods and Capital in the British World, c. 1850–1914* (Cambridge University Press, Cambridge, 2012).

Mandler, Peter, *Return from the Natives: How Margaret Mead Won the Second World War and Lost the Cold War* (Yale University Press, New Haven, CT, 2013).

Marten, Lutz and Nancy Kula, 'Meanings of Money: National Identity and the Semantics of Currency in Zambia and Tanzania', *Journal of African Cultural Studies*, 20 (2008), pp. 183–98.

Masefield, Geoffrey B., *A History of the Colonial Agricultural Service* (Oxford University Press, Oxford, 1972).

Maxwell, Ian, *Universities in Partnership: The Inter-University Council and the Growth of Higher Education in Developing Countries, 1946–70* (Scottish Academic Press, Edinburgh, 1980).

McCann, Gerard, 'From Diaspora to Third Worldism and the UN: India and the Politics of Decolonising Africa', *Past and Present*, no. 218 (2013), Suppl. 8, pp. 258–80.

McClintock, Nicholas C., *Kingdoms in the Sand and Sun: An African Path to Independence* (Radcliffe Press, London, 1992).

McLoughlin, Philip, 'Crowned and Uncrowned Effigies: Developing a System of Portraits', *Coin News*, 51 (October 2014), pp. 47–50.

Melber, Henning ed., *The Rise of Africa's Middle Class: Myths, Realities and Critical Engagements* (Zed Books, London, 2016).

Mende, Tiber, *From Aid to Recolonization: Lessons of a Failure* (Pantheon Books, New York, 1973).

Miners, Norman J., *The Nigerian Army, 1956–1966* (Methuen, London, 1971).

Misra, Maria, *Business, Race and Politics in British India* (Clarendon Press, Oxford, 1999).

Morton, Kathryn, *Aid and Dependence: British Aid to Malawi* (Croom Helm, London, in assoc. with ODI, 1975).

Moyse-Bartlett, Hubert, *The King's African Rifles: A Study in the Military History of East and Central Africa, 1870–1945* (Gale and Polden Ltd, Aldershot, 1956).

Muehlenbeck, Philip E., *Betting on the Africans: John F. Kennedy's Courting of African Nationalist Leaders* (Oxford University Press, Oxford, 2012).

Murphy, Philip, 'Creating a Commonwealth Intelligence Culture: The View from Central Africa, 1945–1965', *Intelligence and National Security*, 17 (2002), pp. 131–62.

'"An Intricate and Distasteful Subject": British Planning for the Use of Force against the European Settlers of Central Africa, 1952–65', *English Historical Review*, 121(2006), pp. 746–77.

Monarchy and the End of Empire: The House of Windsor, the British Government and the Postwar Commonwealth (Oxford University Press, Oxford, 2013).

Party Politics and Decolonization: The Conservative Party and British Colonial Policy in Tropical Africa, 1951–1964 (Clarendon Press, Oxford, 1995).

Musakanya, Valentine, 'Chingola Elisabethville (Katanga), Lusaka' in Tony Schur ed., *From the Cam to the Zambezi: Colonial Service and the Path to the New Zambia* (I. B. Tauris, London, 2015), pp. 87–106.

Mwangi, Wambui, 'Of Coins and Conquest: The East African Currency Board, the Rupee Crisis, and the Problem of Colonialism in the East African Protectorate', *Comparative Studies in Society and History*, 43 (2001), pp. 763–87.

Myss, Marco, 'A Post-Imperial Cold War Paradox: The Anglo-Nigerian Defence Agreement 1958–1962', *Journal of Imperial and Commonwealth History*, 44 (2016), pp. 976–1000.

Newbury, Colin, 'The Origins of Linacre College', *Linacre Journal* (June 1997), pp. 5–27.

Newlyn, Walter T. *Money and Banking in British Colonial Africa. A Study of the Monetary and Banking Systems of Eight African Territories* (Clarendon Press, Oxford, 1954).

Nielsen, Jimmi and Stuart Ward, '"Cramped and Restricted at Home?" Scottish Separatism at Empire's End', *Transactions of the Royal Historical Society*, 25 (2015), pp. 159–85.

Nightingale, Bruce, *Seven Rivers to Cross: A Mostly British Council Life* (Radcliffe Press, London, 1996).

Nwaubani, Ebere, *The United States and Decolonization in West Africa, 1950–1960* (Rochester, New York, 2001).

Ofonagoro, Walter Ibekwe, 'From Traditional to British Currency in Southern Nigeria. Analysis of a currency revolution 1880–1948', *Journal of Economic History* 39 (1979), pp. 623–54.

Oliver, Roland, 'Prologue: The Two Miss Perhams' in Alison Smith and Mary Bull eds., *Margery Perham and British Rule in Africa* (Frank Cass, London, 1991).

Omara-Otunnu, Amii, *Politics and the Military in Uganda, 1890–1945* (Palgrave Macmillan, Basingstoke, 1987).

Omissi, David, *The Sepoy and the Raj: The Indian Army 1860–1940* (Palgrave Macmillan, Basingstoke, 1994), p. 240.

Onslow, Sue, 'Resistance to "Winds of Change": The Emergence of the "Unholy Alliance" between Southern Rhodesia, Portugal and South Africa, 1964–5' in Lawrence J. Butler and Sarah Stockwell eds., *The Wind of Change. Harold Macmillan and British Decolonization* (Palgrave Macmillan, Basingstoke, 2013), pp. 215–34.

Osborne, Myles, *Ethnicity and Empire in Kenya. Loyalty and Martial Race among the Kamba c. 1800 to the Present* (Cambridge University Press, Cambridge, 2014).

Ovendale, Ritchie ed., *British Defence Policy since 1945* (Manchester University Press, Manchester, 1994).

Owen, Nicholas J., *The British Left and India: Metropolitan Anti–Imperialism, 1885–1947* (Clarendon Press, Oxford, 2007).

Parsons, Timothy, *The African Rank-and-File: Social Implications of Colonial Military Service in the King's African Rifles, 1902–1964* (Heinemann, Portsmouth, NH, 1999).

The 1964 Army Mutinies and the Making of Modern East Africa (Praeger, Westport, CT, 2003).

Patterson, Steven, *The Cult of Imperial Honor in British India* (Palgrave Macmillan, New York, 2009).

Pearce, Robert D., 'Morale in the Colonial Service during the Second World War', *Journal of Imperial and Commonwealth History*, 11 (1983), pp. 175–96.

Pennybacker, Susan, *From Scottsboro to Munich: Race and Political Culture in 1930s Britain* (Princeton University Press, Princeton, NJ, 2009).

Percox, David, 'Internal Security and Decolonization in Kenya, 1956–1963', *Journal of Imperial and Commonwealth History*, 29 (2001), pp. 92–116.

Britain, Kenya and the Cold War: Imperial Defence, Colonial Security and Decolonisation (I. B. Tauris, London, 2004).

Perraton, Hilary, *A History of Foreign Students in Britain* (Palgrave Macmillan, Basingstoke, 2014).

Perry, Kennetta Hammond, *London is the Place for Me. Black Britons, Citizenship and the Politics of Race* (Oxford University Press, Oxford, 2015).

Phythian, Mark, *The Politics of British Arms Sales since 1964* (Manchester University Press, Manchester, 2000).

Pierre, Andrew, *The Global Politics of Arms Sales* (Princeton University Press, Princeton, 1982).

Pietsch, Tamson, *Empire of Scholars: Universities, Networks and the British Academic World 1850–1939* (Manchester University Press, Manchester, 2013).

Plumptre, A. F. W., *Central Banking in British Dominions* (University of Toronto Press, Toronto, 1940).

Porter, Bernard, *The Absent-Minded Imperialists: Empire, Society and Culture in Britain* (Oxford University Press, Oxford, 2004).

'Further Thoughts on Imperial Absent-Mindedness', *Journal of Imperial and Commonwealth History*, 36 (2008), pp. 101–17.

Potter, Simon, *Broadcasting Empire: The BBC and the British World, 1922–1970* (Oxford University Press, Oxford, 2012).

Prior, Christopher, *Exporting Empire: Africa, Colonial Officials and the Construction of the Imperial State, 1900–1939* (Manchester University Press, Manchester, 2013).

Pugh, Peter, *The Highest Perfection: A History of De La Rue* (Icon Books, London, 2011).

Pugsley, Christopher and Angela Holdsworth, *Sandhurst: A Tradition of Leadership* (Third Millennium Publishing, London, 2005).

Rathbone, Richard, 'The Colonial Service and the Transfer of Power in Ghana' in John Smith ed., *Administering Empire. The British Colonial Service in Retrospect* (University of London Press, London, 1999), pp. 149–66.

Redish, Angela, 'British Financial Imperialism after the First World War' in R. E. Dumett ed., *Gentlemanly Capitalism and British Imperialism. The New Debate on Empire* (Longman, London, 1999), pp. 127–40.

Reinfeld, Fred and Burton Hobson, *Catalogue of the World's Most Popular Coins* (10th edn., Sterling Publishing Company, New York, 1979).

Rimmer, Douglas, 'African Development in Economic Thought' in Douglas Rimmer and Anthony H. M. Kirk-Greene eds., *The British Intellectual Engagement with Africa in the Twentieth Century* (Palgrave Macmillan, Basingstoke, 2000), pp. 231–59.

Roberts, Andrew D., 'The British Empire in Tropical Africa' in Judith M. Brown and William Roger Louis eds., *Oxford History of the British Empire. Volume 4. Historiography* (Oxford University Press, Oxford, 1999), pp. 463–85.

Roberts, Richard and David Kynaston eds., *The Bank of England: Money Power and Influence, 1694–1994* (Clarendon Press, Oxford, 1995).

Rouvez, Alain, with Michael Coco, Jean-Paul Paddack, *Disconsolate Empires. French, British and Belgian Military Involvement in Post-Colonial Sub-Saharan Africa* (University Press of America Incorp., Maryland, MD, 1994).

Sayers, Richard S., ed., *Banking in the British Commonwealth* (Clarendon Press, Oxford, 1952).

Sayers, Richard S., *Central Banking after Bagehot* (Oxford University Press, Oxford, 1957).

Schenk, Catherine, *Britain and the Sterling Area: From Devaluation to Convertibility in the 1950s* (Routledge, London, 1994).

Hong Kong as an International Financial Centre. Emergence and Development, 1945–1965 (Routledge, London, 2001).

The Decline of Sterling: Managing the Retreat of an International Currency 1945–1992 (Cambridge University Press, Cambridge, 2010).

'The Origins of a Central Bank in Malaya and the Transition to Independence, 1954–1959', *Journal of Imperial and Commonwealth History*, 21 (1993), pp. 409–31.

Schmidt, Elizabeth, *Foreign Intervention in Africa: From the Cold War to the War on Terror* (Cambridge University Press, Cambridge, 2013).

Schofield, Camilla, *Enoch Powell and the Making of Postcolonial Britain* (Cambridge University Press, Cambridge, 2013).

Schur, Tony ed., *From the Cam to the Zambezi: Colonial Service and the Path to the New Zambia* (I. B. Tauris, London, 2015).

Schwarz, Bill, *The White Man's World* (Oxford University Press, Oxford, 2011).

Selgin, George, *Good Money: Birmingham Button Makers, the Royal Mint, and the Beginnings of Modern Coinage, 1775–1821* (University of Michigan Press, Ann Arbor, MI, 2008).

Sharples, John, 'Sovereigns of the Overseas Branches' in Graham P. and Dyer ed., *Royal Sovereign 1489–1989* (Royal Mint Publication, 1989), pp. 59–77.

Sheppard, Alan, *Sandhurst: The Royal Military Academy Sandhurst and Its Predecessors* (Country Life Books, London, 1980).

Simkin, C. G. F., 'Banking in New Zealand' in Richard S. Sayers ed., *Banking in the British Commonwealth* (Clarendon Press, Oxford, 1952), pp. 320–49.

Sinclair, Georgina, *At the End of the Line: Colonial Policing and the Imperial Endgame, 1945–1980* (Manchester University Press, Manchester, 2006).

Singleton, John, *Central Banking in the Twentieth Century* (Cambridge University Press, Cambridge, 2011).

Smith, John ed., *Administering Empire: The British Colonial Service in Retrospect* (University of London Press, London, 1999).

Smith, Alison and Mary Bull eds., *Margery Perham and British Rule in Africa* (Frank Cass, London, 1991).

Smith, Simon C., 'The Wind that Failed to Blow: British Policy and the End of Empire in the Gulf' in Lawrence J. Butler and Sarah Stockwell eds., *The Wind of Change. Harold Macmillan and British Decolonization* (Palgrave Macmillan, Basingstoke, 2013), pp. 235–51.

Smyth, Sir John, *Sandhurst: the History of the Royal Military Academy, Woolwich, the Royal Military College, Sandhurst, and the Royal Military Academy Sandhurst, 1741–1961* (Weidenfeld and Nicolson, London, 1961).

Soffer, Reba, *Discipline and Power: The University, History and the Making of an English Elite, 1870–1930* (Stanford University Press, Stanford, CA, 1994).

Sowelem, R. A., *Towards Financial Independence in a Developing Economy: An Analysis of the Monetary Experience of the Federation of Rhodesia and Nyasaland, 1952–1963* (George Allen and Unwin, London, 1967).

Spencer, Jonathan, 'Anti-Imperial London: The Pan-African Conference of 1900' in Felix Driver and David Gilbert eds., *Imperial Cities* (Manchester University Press, Manchester, 1999), pp. 254–67.

Stapleton, Tim, *African Police and Soldiers in Colonial Zimbabwe, 1923–1980* (University of Rochester Press, Rochester, NY, 2011).

Stockwell, Anthony J., 'Leaders, Dissidents and the Disappointed: Colonial Students in Britain as Empire Ended', *Journal of Imperial and Commonwealth History* (2008), pp. 487–507.

'Ends of Empire' in Sarah Stockwell ed., *The British Empire. Themes and Perspectives* (Wiley Blackwell, Oxford, 2008), pp. 269–93.

'Instilling the "Sterling Tradition": Decolonization and the Creation of a Central Bank in Ghana', *Journal of Imperial and Commonwealth History,* 26 (1998), pp. 100–119.

The Business of Decolonization: British Business Strategies in the Gold Coast (Clarendon Press, Oxford, 2000).

'Exporting Britishness: Decolonization in Africa, the British State and its Clients' in Miguel Banderia Jerónimo and António Costa Pinto eds., *The Ends of European Colonial Empires. Cases and Comparisons* (Palgrave Macmillan, Basingstoke, 2015), pp. 148–77.

'The Political Strategies of British Business during Decolonization: The Case of the Gold Coast/Ghana, 1945–1957', *Journal of Imperial and Commonwealth History,* 23 (1995), pp. 277–300.

'"Splendidly Leading the Way?" Archbishop Fisher and Decolonisation in British Colonial Africa' in Robert Holland and Sarah Stockwell eds., *Ambiguities of Empire: Essays in Honour of Andrew Porter* (Routledge, London, 2009), pp. 199–218.

'"Improper and Even Unconstitutional": The Involvement of the Church of England in the Politics of End of Empire in Cyprus' in S. Taylor ed., *From the Reformation to the Permissive Society. A Miscellany in Celebration of the 400th Anniversary of Lambeth Palace Library* (Boydell and Brewer, Woodbridge, 2010), pp. 583–655.

'Anglicanism in an Era of Decolonization' in Jeremy Morris ed., *The Oxford History of the Anglican Church. Volume 4: The Twentieth Century: Global Western Anglicanism c. 1910 to the Present* (Oxford University Press, Oxford, 2017), pp. 160–85.

Strachan, Huw, *The Politics of the British Army* (Clarendon Press, Oxford, 1997).

Symonds, Richard, *Oxford and Empire: The Long Lost Cause?* (Oxford University Press, Oxford, 1986).

The British and Their Successors: A Study of the Government Services in the New States (Faber, London, 1966).

Tajfel, Henri and John L. Dawson eds., *Disappointed Guests. Essays by African, Asian and West Indian Students* (Oxford University Press for the Institute of Race Relations, London, 1965).

Theakstone, John, 'Mumbwa, Broken Hill, Mkushi' in Tony Schur ed., *From the Cam to the Zambezi: Colonial Service and the Path to the New Zambia* (I. B. Tauris, London, 2015), pp. 221–30.

Thomas, Hugh, *The Story of Sandhurst* (Hutchinson, London, 1961).

Thompson, Andrew ed., *Britain's Experience of Empire in the Twentieth Century* (Oxford University Press, Oxford, 2011).

Thompson, W. Scott, *Ghana's Foreign Policy, 1957–1966* (Princeton University Press, Princeton, NJ, 1969).

Tickner, Frederick J., *Technical Cooperation* (Hutchinson and Co, London, 1965).

Tidrick, Kathryn, *Empire and the English Character* (I. B. Tauris, London, 1990).

Tignor, Robert L., *Capitalism and Nationalism at the End of Empire* (Princeton University Press, Princeton, NJ, 1998).

Tilley, Helen, *Africa as a Living Laboratory: Empire, Development and the Problem of Scientific Knowledge, 1870–1950* (University of Chicago Press, Chicago, IL, 2011).

Tilley, Helen and Robert J., Gordon eds., *Ordering Africa: Anthropology, European Imperialism, and the Politics of Knowledge* (Manchester University Press, Manchester, 2007).

Tinker, Hugh, 'Structure of the British Imperial Heritage' in Ralph Braibanti et al. eds., *Asian Bureaucratic Systems Emergent from the British Imperial Tradition* (Duke University Press, Durham, NC, 1966), pp. 23–86.

Torrent, Mélanie, 'A "New" Commonwealth for Britain? Negotiating Ghana's Pan-African and Asian Connections at the End of Empire (1951–8)', *International History Review*, 38 (2016), pp. 573–613.

Toye, John, 'Valpy Fitzgerald: Radical Macroeconomist of Development', *Oxford Development Studies*, 45 (2017), pp. 116–24.

Toye, Richard, 'Words of Change: the Rhetoric of Commonwealth, Common Market and Cold War, 1961–3' in Lawrence J. Butler and Sarah Stockwell eds., *The Wind of Change. Harold Macmillan and British Decolonization* (Palgrave Macmillan, Basingstoke, 2013), pp. 140–58.

Uche, Chibuike U., 'Bank of England vs the IBRD: Did the Nigerian Colony Deserve a Central Bank?', *Explorations in Economic History*, 34 (1997), pp. 220–41.

'From Currency Board to Central Banking: the Gold Coast Experience', *South African Journal of Economic History*, 10 (1995) pp. 80–94.

'From Currency Board to Central Banking: The Politics of Change in Sierra Leone', *African Economic History*, 24 (1996), pp. 147–58.

'J.B. Loynes and Central Banking Development in British West Africa', *South African Journal of Economic History*, 15 (2000), pp. 112–33.

Unger, Corinna, 'Industrialization vs. Agrarian Reform: West German Modernization Policies in India in the 1950s and 1960s' in Andreas Eckert, Stephen Malinowski, and Corinna Unger eds., *Modernizing Missions. Approaches to Developing the Non-Western World after 1945*, special issue of *Journal of Modern European History*, 8 (2010), no. 1, pp. 47–65.

Van Beusekom, Monica, *Negotiating Development: African Farmers and Colonial Experts at the Office du Niger, 1920–1960* (Heinemann, Portsmouth/NH, 2002).

Vinen, Richard, *National Service: A Generation in Uniform, 1945–1963* (London, Penguin, 2015).

Walton, Calder, *Empire of Secrets: British Intelligence, the Cold War and the Twilight of Empire* (William Collins, London, 2012).

Ward, Stuart ed., *British Culture and the End of Empire* (Manchester University Press, Manchester, 2001).

Watts, Carl, '"Killing Kith and Kin": the Viability of British Military Intervention in Rhodesia, 1964–5', *Twentieth Century British History*, 16 (2005), pp. 382–415.

Webster, Wendy, *Englishness and Empire 1939–1965* (Oxford University Press, Oxford, 2005).

'"There'll Always Be an England": Representations of Colonial Wars and Immigration, 1948–68', *Journal of British Studies*, 40 (October 2001), pp. 557–84.

West, Michael O., *The Rise of an African Middle Class: Colonial Zimbabwe, 1898–1965* (Indiana University Press, Bloomington & Indianapolis, 2002).

White, Nicholas J., *Business, Government and the End of Empire: Malaya, 1942–1957* (Clarendon Press, Oxford, 1996).

Williams, David, *International Development and Global Politics. History, Theory and Practice* (Routledge, London, 2012).

Wilson, Kathleen ed., *A New Imperial History: Culture, Identity, and Modernity in Britain and the Empire, 1660–1840* (Cambridge University Press, Cambridge, 2004).

The Sense of the People: Politics, Culture and Imperialism in England, 1715–1785 (Cambridge University Press, Cambridge, 1998).

Young, John W., *The Labour Governments, 1964–1970: Volume 2, International Policy* (Manchester University Press, Manchester, 2003).

Younger, Kenneth, *The Public Service in New States: A Study in Some Trained Manpower Problems* (Oxford University Press, London, 1960).

Zanier, Valeria and Robert Peruzzi, '1967 as Turning Point in Hong-Kong British PRC Economic Relations' in Priscilla Roberts and Odd Arne Westad eds., *China, Hong Kong and the Long 1970s: Global Perspectives* (Palgrave Macmillan, Basingstoke, 2017), pp. 233–56.

Index

Abai, Dr Abai Njoku, 185
Acheampong, General Ignatius, 285
Aden, 97, 152, 163, 193, 251
Admiralty, 77
Adomakoh, Adam, 172, 185, 188
Adu, A. L., 63, 65, 72, 106, 120, 140, 159
Afghanistan
  and Royal Military Academy
  Sandhurst, 255
Africa, 24, 42, 148, 150. *See also* country
  entries, East Africa, and the Central
  African Federation
African soldiers in the Second World War
  and post-war campaigns, 55–56
African students on the Devonshire and
  Overseas Service Courses, 98, 106–7,
  112–15, 119
and the Royal Mint, 45. *See also* Royal
  Mint
colonial currencies, 48–49, 51, 193
development of central banking in,
  151–90
development of middle class, 138, 146,
  187–88, 292
high-commission territories, 13. *See also*
  Botswana, Lesotho, and Swaziland
importance to sterling area, 44
numbers of African cadets at the Royal
  Military Academy Sandhurst, 270
share of British overseas aid, 89–91
share of UN technical assistance
  funding, 73
Africanization, 59–67, 72, 288
Afrifa, Brigadier Akwasi A., 253, 273, 285,
  284–85
Akuffo, Lieutenant General 'Fred', 284–85
Albania, 47
Amin, Idi, 72, 170, 269
  and the Royal Military Academy
  Sandhurst, 283
Amoaka-Atta, Kwesi, 171
Anderson, T. S. J., 236

anthropology, 27, 28, 116
Argentina, 41
Army Board, 236
Army Council, 8, 70, 236, 240, 244
Army School for Languages, Beaconsfield,
  275–76
Army, British, 3, 8, 16, 52–53, 259, 282
  after the Second World War, 238
  and colonial counter-insurgencies, 243
  and localization of colonial armed
  forces, 68
  and officer class, 250–51
  and Sandys Defence review, 258
  and the Royal Military Academy Sandhurst,
  235–37
  and withdrawal from east of Suez, 89,
  258–59
  officers seconded to serve with colonial
  forces, 173–76
  on the Rhine, 259
  Regular Commission Board, 64, 249
Asquith Commission on Higher Education in
  the Colonies, 30, 62
Association of African Central Banks, 188
Attlee, Clement, 24, 44
Australia, 3, 13, 23, 41, 46, 47, 50, 176,
  219, 269
  coinage, 223
  Commonwealth Development Bank of
  Australia, 167
  Reserve Bank of, 169
  sterling balances, 145

Bahrain
  and Royal Military Academy
  Sandhurst, 255
Bailkin, Jordanna, 15, 127
Balogh, Thomas, 109
Banda, Hastings, 197, 221
Banda, Rupiah, 138
Bangura, Yusuf, 146
Bank for International Settlements, 173

Bank of England, 3, 4, 6, 9, 13, 16, 18–19, 23–24, 38–45, 57, 91, 100, 142–90, 192, 195, 286–98
and the Commonwealth, 145–46, 291–92
and the development of African central banks, 67–70, 146–64
and the Nigerian Mint, 199–200
and the Royal Mint, 213–14
Central Banking Information Department, 143, 168
Centre for Central Banking Studies, 184, 189
Commonwealth Central Banking Course, 171–90, 290, 293, 295
Overseas Department (variously known as Overseas and Foreign Department, Exchange Control and Overseas Department), 143, 144, 151, 172
transfer of staff to African central banks, 171
Banque Centrale des États de l'Afrique de l'Ouest, 204
Baranski, Leon, 163
Barnes, R.K., 249
Bashford-Snell, Colonel John, 239, 252
Bates, Lt Col. P.G.T., 259
Bauer, Peter, 117
Begg, Admiral Sir Varyl, 259
Belgian Congo. See Zaire
Belgium, 181
Bello, Sir Ahmadu, 269
Beloff, Max, 129
Benians, Ernest, 35
Bennett, John, 77
Benson, Sir Arthur, 66
Betjeman, Sir John, 219
Biafra, 82
Birmingham mints. See the Mint, Birmingham Ltd and Imperial Metal Industries (Kynoch) Ltd
Black, Eugene, 167
Blair, Tony, 76
Blumenthal, Erwin, 161–62
Board of Trade, 230
Bolivia, 193
Bomani, Paul, 161
Borneo, 197
coinage, 211
Botswana
and the Royal Military Academy Sandhurst, 270
coinage, 232
Boulton, Matthew, 45
private mint, Soho, Birmingham, 45
Bowra, Sir Maurice, 101–2, 105
Bradbury Wilkinson and Co., 200
Bretton Woods, 43, 145, 146

Bridges Committee (on Training in Public Administration for Overseas Countries), 121–25
Bridges, Sir Edward (Lord), 109, 121, 123. See also Bridges Committee
British Broadcasting Corporation, 11, 107, 294
British Caribbean Currency Board, 204
British Columbia, 47
British Council, 79, 81, 112, 123, 134
British Expatriate Supplementation Scheme, 79
British state
character, 5–9, 13, 78, 137, 288, 291, 295
British World, the, 17, 41
Brunei, 197
coinage, 204
Buettner, Elizabeth, 15
Burma, 55, 57, 169, 170, 176
and the Royal Military Academy Sandhurst, 240, 244
currency, 51
Busia, K. A., 63

Cabinet Committee on Security in the Colonies, 68, 243–44
Cabinet Defence and Oversea Policy Committee, 76–77, 89
Cain, P. J., 18, 40, 182
and 'gentlemanly capitalism', 213
Cairncross, Alec, 174
Callaghan, James, 89
Cambridge Mission to Delhi, 35
Canada, 3, 13, 23, 39, 41, 42, 46, 168, 177, 223, 269
Bank of, 144, 176
coinage, 223
Cardwell army reforms, 52
Caribbean
and Oxford's Foreign Service Programme, 131
Carr-Saunders, Sir Alexander, 37–38
Casson, Sir Hugh, 219
Castle, Barbara, 76
Catto, Lord Thomas, 44
Central African Currency Board, 226
Central African Federation, 56, 79, 150, 164, 193, 223
and Africanization, 67
and the Royal Military Academy Sandhurst, 252
armed forces, 70
Bank of Rhodesia and Nyasaland, 69, 154, 169
dissolution of, 202
central banking. See also Bank of England
development of, 39–42
Ceylon. See Sri Lanka

Chabal, Patrick, 19
Challis, C. E., 209
Channon, H. J., 62, 65
China, 189
Church of England, 5
Churchill, Winston, 203
City, of London, 3, 6, 18, 38, 44, 143,
    145, 147, 173–76, 182, 184, 186,
    189, 290
civil service
    and the Fulton Committee on, 109
    and the 'generalist' tradition, 108–10
    and the Universities of Oxford and
        Cambridge, 108–10
Clark, Sir Kenneth, 219
Clayton, Anthony, 255, 280, 282, 283
Cobbold, Lord Cameron, 44, 142–43, 148,
    166–67
Cohen, Sir Andrew, 122
Coinage Act (1946), 194
Cold War, 74, 86, 248
Colombo Plan, 75
colonial currency boards, 3, 25, 42–43, 68,
    144, 147, 151, 174, 191
    winding up of, 165
colonial development, 76–80
Colonial Development and Welfare Act
    (1940), 24, 30, 34, 74
Colonial Development and Welfare Act
    (1945), 33, 62
Colonial Development and Welfare Act
    (1959), 75
Colonial Development Corporation, 75
    and the Nigerian Security Printing and
        Minting Company Ltd, 201
Colonial Office, 9, 11, 26, 29, 30, 31, 33–34,
    36, 37–38, 48, 81, 149–50, 157, 160, 165,
    195, 197
    and African central banking, 67
    and colonial higher education, 62
    and Colonial Service, 69
    and creation of the Department of Technical
        Co-operation, 76
    and Devonshire Courses, 96–100,
        104–6
    and Overseas Service Courses A and B,
        112–15, 118
    and Royal Military Academy Sandhurst,
        242, 282
    and University of Oxford, 125–26
Committee for Colonial Agricultural,
    Animal Health and Forestry Research, 30
Colonial Research Service, 30
Colonial Service, 1, 2, 17, 26–27, 62, 71,
    287–88. See also Overseas Civil Service,
    and the Devonshire and Overseas Service
    Courses

Administrative Service, 1, 3, 26–27,
    290
Administrative Service, Oxbridge interwar
    training course, 26, 28–29, 31–32
Agricultural Service, 29
    and Africanization, 63–64, 67
    expatriate recruitment to, 100–101
    Forestry Service, 29
    Report of the Public Services Conference
        (1960), 70, 119
Colonial Social Science Research Council,
    30
Commission for Technical Cooperation in
    Africa South of the Sahara, 76, 120
Commonwealth, 9, 10, 11, 13, 15, 17, 18,
    19, 20, 22, 24, 25, 35, 39, 41, 45, 47, 49,
    50, 55, 56, 57, 59, 68, 144, 145,
    147, 167, 168
    'Old' Commonwealth, 23
    and British monarch as head of, 222
    and Rhodesian UDI, 84
    and the Bank of England, 148, 171–90
    central banking co-operation, 145
    dominions, 13
    immigration to Britain, 287
    investment in the idea of, 286, 291–92
    London Declaration, 222
    Special Commonwealth African Assistance
        Plan, 75
    students in Britain, 80–81
    students on the Oxbridge development
        courses, 138
Commonwealth Development Act (1963),
    75
Commonwealth Development Corporation.
    See Colonial Development Corporation
Commonwealth Military Training Assistance
    Scheme, 81, 200–201, 247
Commonwealth Relations Office, 11, 199,
    230, 244
    and admission of Commonwealth cadets to
        the Royal Military Academy Sandhurst,
        242, 250, 283
    and creation of the Department of Technical
        Co-operation, 76
    and military assistance, 77
    merger with Foreign Office, 276
Commonwealth Scholarship and Fellowship
    Plan, 81
Commonwealth Trade and Economic
    Conference (1958), 75
Conference for the Organisation of African
    Unity (1965), 204
Congo. See Zaire
Congo crisis, 85
Congress of Universities of the British
    Empire, 29

Conservative governments
    (1970) foreign policy, 89
    (1979), 135
    and overseas aid, 76
Cooper, Frederick, 88
Cornes, Jerry, 98, 99, 112
Crabbe, V. C., 163
Craggs, Ruth, 15
Cromer, Lord, 143, 157
Crown Agents, 12, 26, 43, 69, 202, 213
Cullen, Poppy, 20
Cyprus, 101
    insurgency, 243
    new coinage, 204

Daloz, Jean-Pascal, 19
Darwin, John, 29
De Gaulle, General Charles, 204
De La Rue Company Ltd, 213, 230, 233
    and the Royal Mint, 214–18
    Nigerian Security Printing and Minting
        Company Ltd, 200–201
decolonization
    and state-building, 59, 88, 91, 291
    chronology of, 78, 137, 295
    historiography of, 15
    legacies of in Britain, 297–98
Democratic Republic of the Congo. See Zaire
Department for International Development, 76
Department of Technical Co-operation, 60, 94
    and the Devonshire Courses, 121–25
    establishment of, 76
Deslandes, Paul, 100
Deutsche Bundesbank, 160, 162
Devonshire Committee, 32, 34, 62, 101
Devonshire Courses, 3, 5, 26, 33, 31–38,
    91, 289
    1953 (Munster) conference, 98, 101–2,
        104–5, 106
    non-European recruitment to, 95–96,
        98, 106–7
    problems with, 96–98
    renamed courses 'A' and 'B', 104
Dimier, Véronique, 21, 31, 103, 108, 213
Djan, Ohene, 106
dominions, 22, 23, 39–40, 41, 49, 50, 55,
    219, 223. See also Australia, Canada,
    New Zealand and South Africa, and
    Commonwealth
Dowling, Alan, 205, 230–32

Eagleton, Catherine, 16, 220, 225
East Africa
    military training school, 86, 271
    mutinies, 86, 258, 283
    planned federation of, 158–62, 164, 202

East African Common Services
    Organization, 159
East African Community, 90
East African Currency Board, 42, 69, 151,
    158–60, 163, 193, 225
East African High Commission, 159
East African Land Forces Organization, 69
East India Company, 45, 46, 53
Eaton Hall, 64, 237
Edgeley, P. B., 188
Edward VII, 49
Edward VIII, 223
Eggleston, Alfred, 149, 153, 155, 166,
    170, 171
Egypt, 39, 47, 53, 248
Eire. See Ireland
El Salvador, 41
Elangot, John Robert, 185
Elizabeth II
    image on coin, 196, 220–3
Elliot Commission on Higher Education in
    West Africa, 62, 64
Engledow, Sir Frank, 30, 35, 125, 127
Equatorial Guinea
    and the Royal Mint, 232
Europe, 47, 146
    banking in, 39
European Commission, 21, 213
    Directorate General for Development and
        Cooperation, 21
European Economic Community, 89, 182,
    183
European Payments Union, 173

Falklands War, 259
Fenton, Roy, 143, 154, 155, 167–9, 171, 183,
    185, 199
Festing, Field Marshal Sir Francis, 87, 258
Fforde, John, 143
Fiji, 48, 50
    and the Royal Military Academy
        Sandhurst, 241
Finland, 82
First World War, 53, 54, 209
Fisher, John Lennox (Jack), 67, 144, 147, 148,
    149, 150, 151, 166
Fitzgerald, Edmund 'Valpy', 133
Ford Foundation, 94
Ford, General Robert, 262, 274
Foreign and Commonwealth Office, 203,
    235
    and military assistance, 77, 86, 89
    and the Commonwealth Military Training
        Assistance Scheme, 82
    and the Royal Military Academy Sandhurst,
        270, 276–77, 284

Overseas Development Administration, 76
Overseas Development Administration,
  and University of Cambridge Course on
  Development, 134–36
Foreign Office, 124
  and military assistance, 77
  and Royal Military Academy Sandhurst,
  242, 283
  and the creation of the Department of
  Technical Co-operation, 76
Fortes, Meyer, 116
Foster, Major General Norman, 72, 85
Foundation for Mutual Assistance in Africa
  South of the Sahara, 76
France, 90, 181
  African decolonization, 204
  and postcolonial Africa, 60
  CFA franc zone, 204
  French Community, 204
French West Africa
  and the Royal Mint, 204
French, David, 16, 237, 258
Frey, Marc, 21
Fuller, Harcourt, 218, 220, 225
Furse, Sir Ralph, 107
  and the Devonshire Committee, 31–38
  and the Devonshire Courses, 98–104

Gallagher, Jack, 118, 129
Gambia, 221
  Central Bank of the, 157–58, 170
  coinage of, 202, 223, 224
  Gambia Currency Board, 151, 158, 165
Gbedemah, Komlo, 149–50, 168, 195–97
George VI, 41, 226
George, Eddie, 189
Germany, 160
Ghana, 4, 58, 59–60, 87, 125, 140, 145, 146,
  148, 150, 152–57, 163, 166, 168, 171,
  178, 184, 188, 198, 202, 203, 216, 218,
  223, 295–96
  and Africanization, 63–65
  and Bank of Ghana, 67–69
  and British military assistance, 81–82,
  90, 295
  and British technical assistance, 79, 121
  and Devonshire and Overseas Service
  Courses, 106, 118
  and the Colonial Development Corporation,
  75
  and the Colonial Service, 71
  and the Royal Military Academy Sandhurst,
  240, 244–48, 257, 270, 271–74, 276–77,
  283, 295
  and the Royal Mint, 203, 232
  Army, 68–70, 85

Bank of Ghana, 4, 145, 150, 152–56,
  163, 170–71, 175, 181, 184, 185, 295
Bank of the Gold Coast, 149, 153, 171
  coinage, 195–97, 203, 210, 220, 222, 225
  colonial government and public administra-
  tion, 108
  Convention People's Party, 171
  Ghana Commercial Bank, 153, 155
  Military Academy, 271–74
  sterling reserves, 155–56
  students on Oxford's Foreign Service
  Programme, 131
  UK arms sales to, 284
Gillick, Mary, 223
Glyn, Mills and Co., 172
Gold Coast. See Ghana
gold standard, 39
Gondwe, Goodall, 185
Government Trading Funds Act (1973),
  208
Gowon, General Yakubu, 89, 269, 272,
  284–85
Guinea, 197
  Banque de la République de Guinée,
  205
  new coinage, 204, 205, 215, 221
Gulf War, 248
Gutteridge, William, 284
Guyana
  coinage, 204

Hall, Gordon E., 157, 169
Harlow, Margretta, 127
Harlow, Vincent, 127
Harman, Major General Jackie, 261
Haslam, Eric, 146
Heath, Sir Edward, 89
Helleiner, Eric, 147, 148
Her Majesty's Oversea Civil Service. See
  Overseas Civil Service
Hodge, Joseph, 21
Hong Kong, 47, 182, 216
Hong Kong and Shanghai Banking
  Corporation, 182
Hopkins, A. G., 18, 40, 182
  and 'gentlemanly capitalism', 213
Howard, Sir Michael, 260
Howe, Stephen, 14
Howell, Paul, 1, 113, 132–36
Hussein, King of Jordan, 256
Hutton, J. H., 35

IMF, 43, 74, 146, 156–57, 158, 161–63, 166,
  173, 185, 296
  Central Banking Institute, 184
  Central Banking Service, 156, 170

immigration, 14, 15
imperial and Commonwealth history, 116
  and area studies, 129
Imperial Chemical Industries, 210
Imperial College of Tropical Agriculture in
  Trinidad, 29
Imperial Metal Industries (Kynoch) Ltd, 210,
  228, 231
India, 9, 13, 22, 23, 30, 39, 41, 42, 46, 49, 53,
  54, 55, 56, 64, 139, 173, 176, 178, 196,
  220, 222, 244, 269, 271
  and the Commonwealth Military Training
    Assistance Scheme, 81–82
  and the Royal Military Academy Sandhurst,
    244
  Reserve Bank of India, 169
  sterling balances, 145
Indian Army, 3, 23, 53–55, 55, 56
Indian Civil Service, 26, 27, 31, 95, 108
Indian Military Academy, 54, 55, 271
Indonesia, 258
Ingham, Kenneth, 236, 255
Innes, John, 214
Institut des Hautes Etudes d'Outre-Mer,
  France, 122
Institute of Development Studies, University
  of Sussex, 122, 134, 135
International Bank for Reconstruction and
  Development. See World Bank
Inter-University Council for Higher Education
  in the Colonies, 31, 62
Iran
  and the Royal Military Academy Sandhurst,
    244
Iraq, 39, 169, 193
  and the Royal Military Academy Sandhurst,
    244
  revolution, 1958, 77, 248, 254
Ireland, 25, 47, 176
  Anglo-Irish Treaty 1921, 32
  coinage, 223
  Easter Rising, 204
Ireton, Barry, 76
Ironside, Christopher, 221, 223
Ivey, Captain Charles, 86

Jackson, Ashley, 258
Jackson, Robert, 9
Jamaica, 169
  and the Royal Military Academy Sandhurst,
    270
  Bank of, 183
  coinage, 230
James, Jack, 194, 197–200, 208–10, 215, 219
Japan, 47
Jawara, Sir Dawda Kairaba, 221
Jennings, Sir Ivor, 128

Jeppesen, Chris, 112
Johnson, Colonel Sir Robert, 47, 193, 208–9
Joint Intelligence Committee, 277
Joint Standing Committee on Colonial Service
  courses, 33
Jones, General Sir Charles, 259
Jones, Margaret, 255, 278–80
Jordan, 57, 258
  and the Royal Military Academy Sandhurst,
    240, 244, 255
Journal of Administration Overseas, 136
Journal of African Administration, 136
Jowett, Benjamin, 27
Joyce, Patrick, 5
Juxon-Smith, Brigadier Andrew, 284

Katsina, Hassan, 255
Katundu, M. J., 185
Kaunda, Kenneth, 221, 258
  and Rhodesian UDI, 84
Kaunda, Panji, 258
Kennedy, President John F., 74
Kent-Payne, Major, 85
Kenya, 20, 56, 86, 90, 101, 158, 216, 219,
  221, 222, 225, 295, 302, 304
  and Africanization, 63, 72
  and British military assistance, 82, 90, 295
  and the Royal Military Academy Sandhurst,
    270, 272, 276–77
  and the Royal Mint, 232
  Central Bank of, 161–63, 169, 232
  coinage, 202, 209, 226
  counter-insurgency, 242–43
  students at the University of Oxford, 129
  UK arms sales to, 284
Kenyatta, Jomo, 86, 221, 272
Kessels, Hubert, 155, 170
Khan, General Ayub, 247
King, General Sir Frank, 234
King's African Rifles, 53, 55–56, 64, 72, 243
  Africanization of the officer class, 64, 68,
    72
  and transformation into national armies,
    68–70
  establishment of military school, 66
Kirk-Greene, Anthony, 97, 113
Knox-Shaw, Thomas, 35
Kodwo Mercer, T. M., 196
Korean War, 56, 144
Kothari, Uma, 21
Krozewski, Gerold, 18
Kuklick, Henrika, 108
Kula, Nancy, 223, 227
Kumarasingham, Harshan, 11
Kunkel, Sönke, 21
Kuwait, 248, 258
Kuwani, Bitwell, 185

Labour governments
    1945, 44
    1964, 87
    and overseas aid, 76
    foreign policy, 89
Lane, Anne, 89
Latin America, 82, 144
    and the Royal Mint, 205
Latvia, 47
League of Nations
    financial conference (1920), 40
Lennox-Boyd, Sir Alan, 247
Lesotho
    and the Royal Military Academy Sandhurst,
        270
Lewis, Ian, 163, 170
Liberia, 221
Libya, 80, 86, 144, 169, 193
    currency, 51
Lithuania, 47
Loan Service Personnel Scheme, 80, 86, 287
London. *See also* City of London
    concern about colonial students in, 107
London School of Economics and Political
    Science, 28, 33, 37–38, 104–5, 110, 124,
        167, 176
Louis, W. R., 291
Loynes, John Barraclough (de), 151–67,
        167, 181–82, 187, 199, 217, 224, 255
    and the Royal Mint, 213–14
Loynes, Mrs., 154
Luckham, Robin, 284
Lund, Neil, 38

Macaulay, Thomas, 61
Machel, Samora, 269
Machin, Arnold, 222
Macleod, Iain, 76
Macmillan Commission on Banking and
    Currency (1933), 144
Macmillan, Harold, 2, 119, 135, 234
Magee, Gary, 4
Mai-Bornu, Alhaji Aliyu, 185
Mair, Lucy, 28
Malawi, 42, 197
    and Africanization, 64, 71
    and the Royal Military Academy Sandhurst,
        275, 277, 283
    coinage, 202, 204, 223, 225
    creation of national army, 70
    Malawian Congress Party, 225
    Reserve Bank of, 164–65, 169, 170,
        185
Malaya, 44, 56, 57, 99, 144, 145, 146,
        148, 151, 169, 197, 244
    and the Commonwealth Military Training
        Assistance Scheme, 81

    and the Royal Military Academy Sandhurst,
        240, 244, 271, 276
    coinage, 204, 211
    military college, 271
Malayan emergency, 239, 240, 242–43
Malaysia, 229
    and the Royal Military Academy Sandhurst,
        271, 276
    coinage, 204
Maldives
    and the Royal Military Academy Sandhurst,
        276
Mali, 204
Mallabar Committee, 208
Malta, 216
    and the Royal Military Academy
        Sandhurst, 244
Margai, Sir Milton, 221
Marshall Aid, 44
Marten, Lutz, 223, 227
Mau Mau, 243. *See also* Kenya
Maugham, Somerset, 1, 243
Mauritius, 48, 50
McCleery, Hugh, 113, 126
McClintock, N. C., 101
MI5, 110, 294
Middle East, 13, 47, 82, 183
    and the Royal Military Academy Sandhurst,
        270, 276
    and the Royal Mint, 205
Middle East Association, 279
military assistance, 16, 77–78, 295. *See also*
    the Commonwealth Military Training
    Assistance Scheme, the United Kingdom
    Military Training Assistance Scheme and
    the Loan Service Personnel scheme
    and arms sales, 87
    Britain, 80–87
Ministry of Defence, 86, 90
    and military assistance, 77
    and the Royal Military Academy Sandhurst,
        235–37, 262, 276–78
Ministry of Overseas Development, 2, 76, 79,
        91, 94, 289, 303
    and the University of Cambridge Course on
        Development, 134–36
    reform of the Oxbridge courses, 130–33
Mint, Birmingham Ltd, 210, 228, 231
Mládek, J. V., 161
Mobutu, Joseph-Désiré, 221, 268
Moi, Daniel Arap, 221
Mons Officer Cadet School, 64, 67, 235, 237,
        252, 272
    relocation to Royal Military Academy
        Sandhurst, 260–62, 274, 280
Montgomery, Field Marshal Lord Bernard,
        237

Mozambique
  and the Royal Military Academy Sandhurst,
    257, 270
  new coinage, 205
Mubiru, Joseph, 170
Muhammed, Major General Murtala, 284–85
Munster, Lord, 102
Murphy, Philip, 222, 294
Murray, H. P. W., 113
Musakanya, Valentine, 110, 113, 116, 141
Museveni, Yoweri, 269
Myint, Hla, 117
Mynors, Humphrey, 167, 173

Namibia
  and the Royal Military Academy Sandhurst,
    270
Napier, Alex, 200
Nasser, Colonel Gomal Abdel, 248
National Service, 235, 237, 258
NATO, 237
neocolonialism, 87, 289
neopatrimonialism, 293
Nepal, 80, 82
  and the Royal Military Academy Sandhurst,
    270
New Zealand, 13, 23, 41, 42, 48, 176, 198, 229
  coinage, 50, 223
  sterling balances, 145
Newbolt, A. F., 101, 105
Newfoundland, 39
Newlyn, W. T., 160
Nicaragua, 193
Nicholson, General Sir Cameron, 244
Nicol-Cole, Samuel B., 185
Niemeyer, Sir Otto, 144
Nigeria, 58, 60, 66, 85, 125, 142, 144, 145,
    146, 148, 150, 168, 171, 183, 192,
    221, 295
  and Africanization, 63, 65, 66–67
  and British military assistance, 295
  and the establishment of a central bank,
    67–69
  and the Royal Military Academy Sandhurst,
    240, 269–70, 272, 277
  and the University of Oxford Foreign
    Service Programme, 117, 131
  Army, 72, 85, 284
  British technical co-operation agreement
    with, 79
  Central Bank of Nigeria, 142, 148–49,
    152–56, 169, 171, 172, 185, 188, 199,
    201, 295
  coinage, 198, 210, 211, 219, 223, 224, 230
  Colonial Sevice Special List A and B, 71

defence agreement with Britain, 77–78, 82
  education in, 65
  establishment of a defence academy, 271
  independence medal, 203
  Nigerian Security Printing and Minting
    Company Ltd, 198–202, 205, 215, 216
  sterling reserves, 155–56
  students in Britain, 81
  UK arms sales to, 284
Nigerian Civil War, 83, 269, 295
Nightingale, Bruce, 100
Nkrumah, Kwame, 59, 154, 155, 169, 218,
    220, 221, 289
  and the Royal Military Academy Sandhurst,
    244–48, 269
  coup against, 1966, 253
  image on coinage, 197, 203, 212, 220, 225
Norman, Sir Montagu, 40–42, 43, 44,
    143, 147
Northcote-Trevelyan reforms, 7, 108
Northern Rhodesia. See Zambia
Notting Hill riots, 254
Nyasaland. See Malawi
Nyerere, Julius, 221

O'Brien, Sir Leslie, 144, 151, 172
Okotie-Eboh, Chief Festus, 155, 198, 200
Oliver, Lieutenant General Sir William, 244
Oliver, Roland, 104
Opie, Redvers, 174
Oppenheimer, Sir Ernest, 125
Orwell, George, 1
Osborne, Myles, 272
Overseas Aid Act (1961), 78
Overseas Civil Service, 2, 71, 76, 79
  expatriate recruitment to, 112
Overseas Development and Service Act
  (1965), 75
Overseas Food Corporation, 75
Overseas Service Aid Scheme, 78–80, 88–90
Overseas Service Courses A and B. See
  also University of Oxford, Course on
  Government and Development and
  University of Cambridge, Course on
  Development
  Course A curriculum, 110–18
  non-European recruitment to, 110–17, 119
  replacement with single course, 123
  uncertain future in the early 1960s, 118–25
Overseas Services Resettlement Bureau, 287

Page, Brigadier J. H., 239, 261
Paget, Humphrey, 220, 226
Pakistan, 9, 56, 57, 95, 139, 170, 173, 176,
    178, 196, 201, 244, 269, 271

and the Commonwealth Military Training
    Assistance Scheme, 81–82
and the Royal Military Academy Sandhurst,
    240
military academy, 247, 271
Mint, 198, 200
sterling balances, 145
Palestine, 24
    Currency Board, 43
Paley, Major General A.G.V., 87
Paraguay, 193
Payton, S. W., 163, 183
Perham, Margery, 28, 31, 28, 63, 67, 93, 98,
    99, 102–4, 117, 255
Pfleiderer, Otto, 160
Philip, Prince, Duke of Edinburgh, 219,
    222, 226
Philippines, the, 147
    coinage, 205
Pietsch, Tamson, 4, 29
Poland, 47
Portugal
    and African decolonization, 205
Potter, Simon, 11, 294
Prior, Christopher, 100, 117
Public Administration and Development, 136

Qatar
    and Royal Military Academy Sandhurst, 255

race relations, 14, 113–14, 126–27,
    252–4, 281, 287
Rhodes, Cecil, 137, 226
Rhodesia, 178, 202, 222
    UDI, 80, 84, 178, 222, 258, 295
Rhodesian African Rifles, 56
Ribadu, Muhammadu, 85
Richards, Audrey, 116
Rizzello, Michael, 221, 223
Robertson, Dennis, 174
Robinson, E. A. G., 127
Robinson, Kenneth, 115
Robinson, Ronald, 27, 30, 118, 122, 125, 128,
    130, 291
Romania, 47
Rowe, E. G., 113–14, 120, 140
Royal Botanic Gardens at Kew, 226
Royal Canadian Mint, 216, 229, 232. *See also*
    Royal Mint: Canadian branch
Royal Institute of Public Administration, 121
Royal Military Academy (formerly College)
    Sandhurst, 3, 7–8, 16–17, 19,
    23–25, 51, 53, 55, 51–58, 60,
    66, 67, 77, 81, 91, 236, 234–86,
    286–98

Academic Advisory Council, 260
academic curriculum and teaching,
    238–40, 274
admission of overseas cadets, 64, 242,
    263–75
and British arms sales, 284
and Muslim cadets, 281
and the Howard-English review, 1965, 260
and the Indian army, 53
Arab cadets at, 254, 275, 279
arrangements for overseas cadets, 254–55,
    276–81
co-location of Mons Officer Cadet School at
    Sandhurst and changes to officer training,
    260–63
companies at, 238
concerns about standards of overseas
    cadets, 249–50, 277
criticism of, 261
during the Second World War, 55
early history of, 52
expeditions, 239–40, 251–52
experience of overseas cadets at, 256–57,
    272–74
impact of defence cuts and social change in
    the 1960s and 70s, 259–63
military coups in post-colonial Africa and
    the 'Sandhurst effect', 283–84
New College, 52, 238, 262
Old College, 51, 52, 238, 262
Oman Hall, 282
opening, 1947, 240
race relations at, 252–54, 281
Regular Career Commission Course,
    262, 275
relationship to Army and Whitehall, 235–37
South Asian cadets at between the wars,
    53–55, 257
Standard Military Course, 262, 275
The Wish Stream, 243, 259, 263
Tillard Committee, 260–61, 275
Victory College, 52, 238
Royal Military Academy Woolwich, 7, 8, 51,
    52, 55, 236
Royal Mint, 3, 4, 6–7, 10, 16, 23–25,
    45–51, 92, 174, 191–233,
    286–98
and De La Rue Company Ltd, 214–18
and the Bank of England, 213–14
and the Nigerian Security Printing and
    Minting Company Ltd, 212
Australian branches, 47, 50, 229
becomes a trading fund, 208
Canadian branch, 47, 50
creation of the Royal Mint Ltd, 208

Royal Mint (*cont.*)
  Marketing and Sales Division established, 230
  move to Llantrisant, 194
  move to Tower Hill, 45
  profits, 208
  Queen's Award for Industry for Export Achievement, 191, 205, 230
  South African branch, 47, 50
Royal Mint Advisory Committee on the Design of Coins, Medals, Seals and Decorations, 50, 195–97, 227–28
Royal Mint Services Ltd, 217
Royal Ordnance Factories, 208
Royal West African Frontier Force, 53, 55–56, 234, 242–43
  and Africanization of the officer class, 66
  establishment of a military school, 66
  transformation into national armed forces, 68–70
Royal Zoological Society, 226

Sale, Geoffrey S., 261
Sam, A. K., 249
Sanders of the River, 1, 94, 112
Sandys, Duncan
  defence review, 258
Sarakikya, Mrisho, 256, 283
Sarawak, 198
Saudi Arabia, 183, 251
  and the Royal Military Academy Sandhurst, 244, 263
Saunders, J. T., 35
Sayers, R. S., 68, 174, 175
Scarborough Report on Oriental, Eastern European, Slavonic and African Studies, 36
Schenk, Catherine, 18, 145, 146
School of Oriental and African Studies, University of London, 33, 36, 37, 38, 104–5, 304
Schwarz, Bill, 15
Scotland, 172, 279
Scott, L. J., 170
Scott, Mike, 243
Second World War, 24, 25, 42, 43, 50, 54, 55
  and the Royal Mint, 204
Selwyn Lloyd, John, 155
Sempa, Amos Kalule, 159
Senegal
  and the Royal Military Academy Sandhurst, 270, 277
Shapcott, Brian, 216

Sierra Leone, 61, 169, 217, 221
  and the Royal Military Academy Sandhurst, 277
  British technical co-operation agreement with, 79
  Central Bank of, 157–58, 169, 185
  commemorative coin, 203
  independence medal, 203
  new coinage, 202, 224, 227
Sillman, Norman, 221, 226–27
Singapore, 151, 216
  and the Royal Military Academy Sandhurst, 271
  coinage, 204
Singleton, John, 44
Smith, Alison, 127
Smith, Ian, 80
Sobhuza II, King, 221
social sciences, the, 28
Solomon Islands
  new coinage, 227
Somalia, 193
  coinage, 204
South Africa, 3, 13, 23, 41, 47, 48, 80, 91, 151, 173, 176, 202, 240
  sterling balances, 145
South African War, 52
South America, 41, 47, 147, 173, 181
  and De La Rue Company Ltd, 214
  and the Royal Mint, 205
South Arabia, Federation of, 151, 166
  coinage, 204
  Front for the Liberation of Occupied South Yemen, 251
  National Liberation Front, 251
South Arabian Monetary Authority, 158, 163, 165, 217
South Asia, 24, 145, 176
South Korea, 147
South Yemen, 165. *See* Aden and South Arabia, Federation of
Southern Rhodesia, 150. *See also* Rhodesia
Southern Rhodesian Currency Board, 42
Soviet Union, the, 12, 47, 203
Sri Lanka, 57, 147, 148, 173, 176, 216, 219, 244
  and the Commonwealth Military Training Assistance Scheme, 81
  and the Royal Military Academy Sandhurst, 240, 244, 270
  Bank of Ceylon, 148, 151, 169
  sterling balances, 145
St Cyr Military Academy, 256
Staff College, Camberley, 81, 237
Stallybrass, W. W., 271

Standing Committee on Coins, Medals and
    Decorations. *See* Royal Mint Advisory
    Committee on the Design of Coins,
    Medals, Seals and Decorations
Stanley, Oliver, 62
Statute of Westminster (1931), 49
sterling, 3, 38–40, 186, 294
    Basle Agreements,1968, 164
    convertibility crisis, 1947, 144–45
    devaluation, 1949, 44, 144
    devaluation, 1967, 89, 164, 228, 296
    restoration of convertibility, 1958,
        44, 146
    suspension of convertibility of, 1947, 44
sterling area, 3, 24–25, 39, 44–45, 86, 145–46,
        151, 152, 166, 173–75, 177, 184, 186,
        294, 296
    sterling balances, 39, 43, 44, 144–45
Stockwell, Major General Sir Hugh, 234
Stone, Douglas, 155, 167, 168, 170–71, 188
Streeten, P. P., 129
Stride, Harry, 195–96, 209, 215, 219
Sudan, 39, 80
    and the Royal Military Academy Sandhurst,
        276
Sudan Political Service, 26, 132
Suez Canal, 56
Suez Crisis, 77, 248
Swaziland, 221
    and military assistance, 90
    and the Royal Military Academy Sandhurst,
        270
Symonds, Richard, 19, 61, 126

Tanganyika. *See* Tanzania
Tanzania, 165, 178, 219, 221, 225, 295
    and Africanization, 63, 72
    Bank of, 159–63, 170, 295
    becomes a republic, 222
    new coinage, 202, 223, 224, 227
    students on Oxford's Foreign Service
        Programme, 131
Taylor & Challen Ltd, 200
technical assistance, 2, 9, 12, 20, 59–60,
        73–80, 112, 129, 130, 141, 148, 151, 156,
        166, 170, 186, 187, 192, 200, 201, 235,
        272, 289, 291
    British, 144–45, 76–80, 87–90, 288–89,
        293–94, 295
    British training for overseas public adminis-
        trators, 95, 110, 138
Templer, General Sir Gerald, 87, 243–44,
        251–52, 258
    Cabinet Committee on Security in the
        Colonies, 68

Thatcher, Margaret, 91
Thomas, Cecil, 227
Thompson, Andrew, 4
Thompson, Sir Lionel, 195–97, 208–9
Tillard, Brigadier F. B., 260
    and Tillard Committee, 260–61
Tolbert Junior, W. R., 221
Touré, Sekou, 197, 221
Tower, General Philip, 261
Toye, John, 133
Toye, Richard, 10
Treasury, 6–7, 9, 39, 40, 43, 46, 48, 89, 144,
        146, 172, 194, 195, 199–200, 207
    and the Royal Mint, 209, 215, 230
Trenchard, Lord Hugh, 31
Trinidad and Tobago
    and the Royal Military Academy Sandhurst,
        276
    coinage, 204
Tunisia
    and the Royal Mint, 232
Turkey, 82
Turner, Ralph, 38
Tuvalu
    new coinage, 227
Twum-Acheampong, Godfried, 272

Uche, Chibuike, 18, 67, 146
Uganda, 86, 159, 160, 170, 203, 217, 283
    and Africanization, 63, 72
    and the Royal Military Academy Sandhurst,
        269
    Bank of, 161–63, 168, 170, 185, 188
    coinage, 202, 222, 225, 229
United Kingdom Military Training Assistance
        Scheme, 82, 276
United Nations, 43, 84, 119
    and technical assistance, 73, 94, 120
    Expanded Programme of Technical
        Assistance, 59, 73
United States of America, 12, 29, 47, 146, 269
    Agency for International Development, 94
    and development of central banking, 147, 152
    and overseas aid, 59, 74
    and post-war economy, 44
    Anglo-American loan, 1946, 43, 44
    Federal Reserve Bank, 39, 68, 147, 169
United States Mint, 50, 205, 209, 230
Universities' Mission to Central Africa, 35
University Grants Committee, 7, 123
University of Cambridge, 1, 3, 5, 7, 9, 17,
        21, 23–38, 57, 93–141, 286–98. *See
        also* Devonshire Courses and Overseas
        Service Courses A and B
    and British intelligence, 110

University of Cambridge (*cont.*)
  and the British Empire and Commonwealth, 27–31
  and the civil service, 107–10
  and the Devonshire Courses, 32–38
  colonial agricultural probationers' course, 29
  colonial students at, 102
  Colonial/Overseas Service Club, 113, 127
  Colonial/Overseas Studies Committee, 36, 105, 112, 118, 123, 128, 130, 135
  Course on Development, 1, 128, 126–36
  curriculum and teaching, 127–29, 134
  Department of Land Economy, 29, 136
  development conferences, 130
  imperial and Commonwealth history at 27
  M.Phil in Development Studies, 136
  Queens' College, 35
  School of Agriculture, 29
  summer school in African administration, 125–26
  Wolfson College, 127
University of East Anglia, School of Development Studies, 135
University of London, 26
  and the Devonshire Courses, 31, 32–38, 96, 104–5
  Institute of Commonwealth Studies, 36, 37
  Institute of Education, 36, 105
University of Manchester, 121, 135
University of Oxford, 3, 5, 7, 9, 17, 20, 21, 26, 23–38, 57, 93–141, 286–98. *See also* Devonshire Courses and Overseas Service Courses A and B
  and British intelligence, 110
  and the British Empire and Commonwealth, 27–31
  and the civil service, 107–10
  and the Devonshire Courses, 32–38
  Balliol College, 27, 103
  colonial students at, 102
  colonial studies at, 29, 102
  Colonial/Commonwealth Services Club, 113, 127, 130
  Committee for Colonial/Commonwealth Studies, 34, 99, 101, 103, 105, 123, 129, 130
  Course on Government and Development, 128, 126–30
  curriculum, 127–29
  Foreign Service Programme, 131, 135, 139
  Franks Commission, 127
  imperial and Commonwealth history at, 27
  Imperial Forestry Institute, 29

Indian Institute, 27
Institute of Colonial/Commonwealth Studies, 35, 102, 118, 126, 129, 130
Linacre College, 127
Nuffield College, 28, 102
Queen Elizabeth House, 125–26, 129, 130–31, 136
Rhodes scholarships, 29
Wolfson College, 127
Uruguay, 193

Vasey, Ernest, 160
Veale, Sir Douglas, 31–32, 108, 109, 118, 126
  and the Devonshire Courses, 98–104
Venn, J. A., 35, 105
Victoria League in Scotland for Commonwealth Friendship, 279
Vincze, Paul, 197, 221, 223, 226

Walker, Eric, 35
Walt Rostow
  The Stages of Economic Growth, 74
Walton, Calder, 110, 294
War Office, 7, 55–56, 56, 57, 80, 237
  and military assistance, 77
  and the King's African Rifles, 69
  and the Royal Military Academy Sandhurst, 235–37, 240–42, 244–48, 253, 275
Ward, Stuart, 14, 15, 286
Watson, Guy, 144, 172, 173, 176
Webster, Wendy, 14
Welbeck School, 238
West African Currency Board, 42–43, 153, 157, 202
West, H. W., 113, 133
Western Samoa
  coinage, 204
Whistler, Sir Lashmer (Bolo), 247
Wilson, Harold, 84, 89, 258
Wina, Arthur, 67
Wintle, Claire, 15
Women's Royal Army Corps College, 262
World Bank, 43, 68, 144, 146, 156–57, 163, 167, 173, 296
  Development Advisory Service, 73
  Economic Development Institute, 73
  mission to Nigeria, 69, 148–49, 153
  mission to Uganda, 160

Yes, Minister, 107
Younger, Kenneth, 65
Yugoslavia, 47

Zaire, 82, 221
  and the Royal Military Academy Sandhurst,
    263, 275, 277
Zambia, 42, 64, 90, 140, 221
  and Africanization, 67, 72
  and the Loan Service Personnel scheme,
    83–85
  and the Royal Military Academy
    Sandhurst, 277
  and Universities of Oxford and
    Cambridge, 120

  Bank of, 164–65, 185, 211, 295
  creation of a national army, 70
  education in, 65
  new coinage, 202, 226–27
  United National Independence Party,
    140
Zanzibar, 86, 162
Zimbabwe, 91, 178
  and the Royal Military Academy
    Sandhurst, 269
  new coinage, 202